Dane

Commentary on 1 and 2 Corinthians

By

James Burton Coffman
Minister of the Gospel
Houston, Texas 77098

Vol. VII

A·C·U PRESS
Abilene, Texas

ISBN 0-915547-02-3

DEDICATION

This volume on the Corinthian letters is lovingly dedicated to my wife:

THELMA BRADFORD COFFMAN

She is known to many as "Sissy"; and her newsletter, "Sissy's Sendout," is widely read throughout the United States and several foreign countries. It is through her patient and skillful efforts that we have been enabled to keep in touch with loved ones and friends throughout a long ministry with its inevitable moving about from city to city. It is in the "Sendout" that many have read of these commentaries and ordered them. Also, she has greatly aided the motivation necessary for the continuation of such a long and arduous task as writing a commentary on the NT. In the reading of manuscripts and proof, in the performance of many duties in order to free this writer's time for research and typing, and in countless other ways, her contribution to this series of commentaries continues to be invaluable. Both of us are grateful to Almighty God for that measure of health and strength required for the pursuit of our long established goal of completing this series, and which the Father's grace has abundantly given thus far.

JAMES BURTON COFFMAN

CONTENTS

PREFACE

Substantially more than three-fourths of the Firm Foundation Series of Commentaries on the New Testament have been completed; and it is appropriate that our appreciation should be expressed for the enthusiastic reception and commendation which have marked their publication. Several of the largest congregations, such as Camelback in Phoenix, Broadway in Lubbock, Madison in Tennessee, MacArthur Boulevard in Irving, as well as others in Garden City, Kansas, and Plainview, Texas, and with many others where plans are not yet final, are aiding in making the series available to serious students of the word of God.

As an example of such activity, the Broadway congregation in Lubbock, through its elders, purchased 23 sets for use by missionaries supported by that congregation in twenty foreign nations. They also conducted a three-day Bible Emphasis Program attended by more than three thousand people, resulting in the distribution of hundreds of the commentaries.

Joe G. Barnett, minister at Broadway, wrote: "I think more churches need to publicize this significant work. It is deserving of encouragement and publicity. These commentaries are excellent and a very significant contribution to the literature of the Restoration."

THE PUBLISHERS

1 Corinthians

INTRODUCTION

The Grecian peninsula is almost severed by a great curved arm of the sea which lacks only about four miles of separating the entire Peloponnesus from the continent of Europe. Upon that tiny isthmus, and southwestward, lay the ancient city of Corinth, the citadel of which, called the Acro-Corinthus, towered to an altitude of 1,886′, some 1,500′ above the streets of the city, and dominated all of the land routes to Europe from the Peloponnesos.[1] Hardly any ancient city was as favorably situated for both commerce and defense as was Corinth. The Gulf of Corinth and the Gulf of Patrai formed the western passage to the Mediterranean Sea, and the Saronic Gulf opened upon the east to Asia Minor and Israel. The ancient city of Corinth was served by a port at each end of the isthmus, Lechaeum on the west and Cenchrea on the east.

History: Before the dawn of history, Corinth was a builder of ships, as attested by the mythology which names it as the place Jason's ship was constructed and sailed away in search of the Golden Fleece. Medea, Sisyphus and Bellerophon lived there; and later the city became prosperous and powerful in the seventh century B.C., being noted for pottery, bronze metal work and decorative handicraft. Corinthian glory perished in 146 B.C. when the city was utterly destroyed by the Romans who even carted off all of the art treasures and demolished it so completely that it remained nothing but a heap of rubbish for a hundred years.

In 46 B.C., exactly a hundred years later, however, Julius Caesar rebuilt the city and populated it with his discharged veterans. It flourished greatly and soon regained and surpassed the size and opulence of its earlier history. The carnality and wickedness returned in a greater degree than ever, making the city a stronghold of paganism. Apollo, Poseidon, Aphrodite and other deities were worshiped there,

---

[1] *Encyclopaedia Britannica* (Chicago: William Benton, Publisher, 1961), Vol. 6, pp. 441ff.

the temple of Aphrodite Pandemos occupying the top of Acro-Corinthus, and being served by a thousand religious prostitutes.

Corinth was 105 years old when the apostle Paul entered it about the middle of the first century. The triumph of Christianity in such a culture as that of Corinth is one of the great miracles of faith.

The possibility of a canal that would cut the isthmus and save over 200 miles sailing around the Peloponnesus was a dream of the ancient king of Macedon (300 B.C.), and later of both Julius Caesar and Nero who actually started work on it; but it was a dream unrealized until 1893. Great earthquakes destroyed the city in 1858 and again in 1928. All that remains is "a poor village, mostly Albanian, with a population in 1951 of 17,728."[2] See more on Corinth in CA, p. 350.

Founding of the church: The record of Paul's founding the church in Corinth is given by Luke in Acts 18:1-18. In the eighteen months after Paul sailed from Athens, many converts for Christ were won at Corinth; and not even the Jewish opposition which culminated before the judgment seat of Gallio prevented the wide success of the gospel. It was here that Paul met Aquila and Priscilla who became his true friends and sailed with him when he left. Crispus and Sosthenes were among the more able converts; but many of those who obeyed the gospel were from among the lower classes in the pagan culture (1 Cor. 6:9-11). The problems which inevitably arose in the conflict between Christianity and paganism resulted in the writing of both of the epistles to the Corinthians.

Authorship and authenticity: Romans, 1 and 2 Corinthians and Galatians are usually distinguished as the "four great" epistles of Paul; and it is true of all of them that their genuineness and accuracy "preserve to the church an impregnable defense of historical Christianity."[3] The hypothesis of fiction regarding any of these is "an absurdity."[4] "It is unnecessary to discuss the authenticity of this letter. It has

---

[2]*Ibid.*
[3]*ISBE.*
[4]*Ibid.*

been denied only by fanciful scholars who have looked upon all the Pauline correspondence as falsifications."[5] Both external and internal witnesses to the truth and authenticity of 1 Corinthians are so overwhelming and convincing that those who deny it succeed only in proving "their own incompetence as critics."[6] Any good Bible encyclopaedia will give the following:

A. External evidence: Both Corinthians were mentioned by Clement of Rome (95 A.D.), who himself wrote a letter to Corinth in which he made a direct quotation from 1 Corinthians, saying: "Take up the letter of Paul the blessed apostle; what did he write you first in the beginning of the gospel? Verily, he gave you spiritual direction regarding himself, Cephas and Apollos, for even then you were dividing yourselves into parties."[7] Of course, there are many other testimonies, but this is the most important.

B. Internal evidence: Only one who has lost touch with reality can read the impassioned words of 1 and 2 Corinthians and imagine them to have been forged. They are in tone, teaching, vocabulary and style, absolutely Pauline. Such things as the mention of 500 people still living who had seen Christ after his resurrection, along with the scores of coincidences with Acts and with other Pauline letters are "beyond chance or invention."[8] Even F. C. Baur and Renan admit that these letters of Paul "are incontestable, and uncontested."[9]

Date: Craig favored a date of 55 A.D.; ISBE made it the same year; Metz set it at "the mid-fifties"; Hillyer dated it in "the spring of 54 A.D.": "The outside dates of the two canonical Epistles (1 and 2 Corinthians) are 51 and 57 A.D."[10] Pauline chronology is an extensive field of study in its own right; and there is little to be gained by disputing whether 54 or 55 is the true date.

---

[5]Clarence Tucker Craig, *Interpreter's Bible* (New York: Abingdon Press, 1953), Vol. X, p. 13.

[6]Donald S. Metz *Beacon Bible Commentary* (Kansas City: Beacon Hill Press, 1968), p. 295.

[7]*ISBE*, p. 711.

[8]Norman Hillyer, *The New Bible Commentary, Revised* (Grand Rapids: Wm. B. Eerdmans Publishing Co., 1967), p. 1051.

[9]*ISBE*, p. 712.

[10]Norman Hillyer, *op. cit.*, p. 1051.

How many letters? It is certain that Paul wrote to the Corinthians other communications than those contained in the two NT letters; and despite the fact that nearly any sequence of events that may be compiled may be challenged, the following is a practical approximation of the order of events which led to Paul's writing both 1 and 2 Corinthians:

1. Paul founded the Corinthian church (Acts 18:1-18).
2. Paul wrote a letter to them which was lost (5:9).
3. The Corinthians wrote Paul a letter requesting information; and about the same time, Paul received disturbing news from "the household of Chloe."
4. Paul replied in the letter of 1 Corinthians.
5. Paul made an unrecorded visit to Corinth.
6. Paul's anxiety for the church was so great that he could not wait in Troas for Titus, but hurried on to Macedonia.
7. In Macedonia, Paul met Titus and learned from him that the Corinthians had responded to his first epistle. All was well in Corinth. In response to the good news, Paul wrote 2 Corinthians.

The occasion of 1 Corinthians: Having received a letter from the Corinthians asking questions which betrayed their spiritual blindness in many instances, and also having received first-hand reports from members of Chloe's household (1:11), and also from Stephanas, Fortunatus and Achaicus, the conditions at Corinth were revealed to Paul as most deplorable. He at once wrote 1 Corinthians with a view to correcting disorders and giving much needed instructions to the young church struggling for its existence in the very eye of ancient paganism. Some think that Stephanas, Fortunatus and Achaicus were the same as "the members of Chloe's household"; but this is not certain.

Outline: Any classical outline is nearly impossible; because, as Bruce Barton said, "The sentences tumble over each other like hot boulders out of a volcano." It is possible to contrive an outline thus: (1) Paul discussed topics brought up in the letter the Corinthians had sent to him. There are four main topics in this division: (a) marriage, (b) meat offered to idols, (c) spiritual gifts, and (d) the collection, the last of these being deferred in Paul's discussion till the last chapter (16:1). (2) Paul discussed topics concerning which he had received information independently of the Corinthians themselves. These were (a) the factions, (b) the case of incest, (c) the lawsuits, (d) free customs of the women, (e) abuses of the Lord's Supper, and (f) denial of the resurrection. The study of this epistle is best achieved by following the sequence of the epistle itself.

ABBREVIATIONS

AV = Authorized Version
RV = Revised Version
RSV = Revised Standard Version
NE = New English Bible
NT = New Testament
OT = Old Testament
LXX = Septuagint Translation
EE = Eldred Echols (see bibliography) and Al Horn
*CM = Commentary on Matthew
*CMK = Commentary on Mark
*CL = Commentary on Luke
*CJ = Commentary on John
*CA = Commentary on Acts
*CR = Commentary on Romans
*CH = Commentary on Hebrews
*CD = The Ten Commandments
†GG = The Gospel in Gotham
ISBE = The International Standard Bible Encyclopaedia
*CMR = The Mystery of Redemption
H.S. = The Holy Spirit

*Books by James Burton Coffman (Abilene: ACU Press)
†Book by the same author (Shreveport, La.: Gussie Lambert, Publisher, 1960).

CHAPTER 1

Paul began, as always, with a salutation (1-3), and thanksgiving (4-9), moving immediately to the principal objective of the epistle, which was that of correcting rampant disorders in the Corinthian church. He first took up the problem of disunity (10-17), expounded on the glory and power of the cross of Christ (18-25), and brought forward the character of the Corinthian congregation itself as proof of the wisdom of God in Christ (26-31).

Verse 1, *Paul, called to be an apostle of Jesus Christ through the will of God, and Sosthenes our brother.*

The words *to be*, added by the translators, are unnecessary and even cloud the meaning. Paul was stating what he was, not what he intended to be. As in most of his writings, Paul stressed his divine commission as an apostle, thus invoking the authority needed for dealing with the errors prevalent in Corinth.

"Sosthenes . . ." Many identify this brother with the one mentioned in Acts 18:17, but it is not certain. Apparently he was the amanuensis by whose hand the letter was written, Paul himself inscribing only the salutation and lovingly including his helper. The emphatic first person singular pronoun in verse 4 denies that Sosthenes had anything to do with the content of the epistle.

Verse 2, *Unto the church of God which is at Corinth, even them that are sanctified in Christ Jesus, called to be saints, with all that call upon the name of our Lord Jesus Christ in every place, their Lord and ours.*

"The church of God . . ." The church did not belong to the Corinthians but to God, unto whom they were set apart (sanctified) to serve God by reason of the fact that they were "in Christ."

"In Christ . . ." denotes the status of all Christians, a relationship brought about through an obedient faith when they were baptized "into" him (Gal. 3:27, 1 Cor. 12:13 and

Rom. 6:3). The epic importance of this phrase appears in the fact that it is used no less than 169 times in Paul's epistles.[1]

"Called to be saints . . ." Again, *to be* is an unnecessary additive to the text. The Corinthian Christians were not merely candidates for sainthood but were in fact already entitled to this designation by virtue of their being in the spiritual body of Christ, "in him," and therefore possessing a complete identity with the Saviour.

"With all that call upon the name . . ." makes this epistle applicable to the saints of all ages in every place and circumstance.

"Lord Jesus Christ . . ." This use of the compound name *Jesus Christ* by Paul, and by the whole church, barely a quarter of a century after the crucifixion of Christ in A.D. 30 declares the historical accuracy of John's gospel, which recorded the first usage of it by the Saviour himself in the great prayer of John 17, making it certain that "in Christ Jesus" is equivalent to "in thy name" of John 17:3, 11 and 26.

"Lord . . ." Likewise, this title of Jesus was not a development in the last first-century church but was firmly established by the time of Paul's writing here, having been used by Paul in his very first encounter with Jesus (Acts 9:5).

Verse 3, *Grace to you and peace from God our Father and the Lord Jesus Christ.*

"Grace and peace . . ." This double salutation combined the common greetings of both Greeks and Hebrews, but with a remarkable extension of the meaning of both. *Chairein* was the Greek word for "greeting"; but Paul's word *charis* means "grace," calling attention to God's unspeakable gift to humanity. The Hebrew salutation, *shalom*, meaning "peace," was united with an affirmation of its coming through Jesus Christ alone.[2]

In Paul's style of mentioning himself first, then the addressee, and next a formal greeting, he followed the format

---

[1]John Mackay, *God's Order* (New York: Macmillan Company, 1953), p.67
[2]Leon Morris, *Tyndale Commentary* (Grand Rapids: Wm. B. Eerdmans Publishing Company, 1958), 1 Cor., p. 35.

employed by all educated persons of that era. "When Paul wrote letters he wrote them on the pattern which everybody used."[3] However, Paul always extended the form somewhat in order to adorn it with the distinctive sentiments and teachings of Christianity. In these three verses, it is plain that "The distinguishing feature is its stress upon the sanctity of the church."[4]

The Thanksgiving

Verse 4, *I thank my God always concerning you, for the grace of God which was given you in Christ Jesus.*

"I thank my God . . ." This is one of the most amazing words in the NT. How incredible it appears on the surface that a church troubled by so many errors and outright sins, as in the case of the Corinthians, should have been the occasion of fervent thanksgiving by an apostle! The explanation lies in the key words *in Christ Jesus.* In the Lord, the Corinthians were credited with the holy righteousness of Christ himself, even as the Christians of all ages; and the blood of Christ, operative in his spiritual body, was cleansing them from all sins *continually* (1 John 1:7).

Verse 5, *That in everything ye were enriched in him, in all utterance and all knowledge.*

Grosheide explained the last phrase of this verse as meaning that "Their richness in Christ consists especially in the ability to speak well about the revelation of God."[5]

"In everything . . ." has the meaning of "in everything that really matters." The Corinthians were of the same status as all of them "that know the truth" (2 John 1). Although every Christian is required to study and learn continually, there is a certain corpus of truth that he must know before he can become a Christian; and that body of teaching having been acquired, and the believer having acted upon it by being

---

[3]William Barclay, *The Letters to the Corinthians* (Philadelphia: The Westminster Press, 1954), p. xvi.

[4]F. W. Grosheide, *The New International Commentary on the NT* (Grand Rapids: Wm. B. Eerdmans Publishing Company, 1953), 1 Cor., p. 25.

[5]*Ibid.*, p. 28.

baptized into Christ, he is at that point "enriched in everything." This was the enrichment enjoyed by the Christians at Corinth. "All things" therefore has in view elementary knowledge and not in the superlative sense of knowing absolutely everything they needed to know, else there would have been no need for Paul to write to them. That Paul intended this verse as a compliment to the Corinthians upon their ability to speak in tongues is evidently a false interpretation.

Verses 6-7, *Even as the testimony of Christ was confirmed in you: so that ye come behind in no gift; waiting for the revelation of our Lord Jesus Christ.*

"Testimony of Christ was confirmed in you . . ." is Paul's way of declaring that the Corinthians had believed and obeyed the gospel of Christ as it had been preached to them. This was the source of all the riches of grace which they had received through their being united with Christ and "in him."

"Ye come behind in no gift . . ." The reference here is to the entire galaxy of gifts, in the general sense, which attended establishment of churches of Christ under the apostolical preaching. As Grosheide said:

> In early Christian times people must have seen all the gifts of the Holy Spirit, the special as well as the permanent, as a unity. They were not differentiated, neither had the church as yet experienced that the special gifts were not going to remain.[6]

"Waiting for the revelation of our Lord Jesus Christ . . ." This is a reference to the Second Advent of Christ, indicating that the final redemption of men will take place then, and that the time of probation is essentially a period of waiting and expecting. There is no hint here that Paul or the Corinthians believed that the last Advent would come immediately, or in their lifetime.

Verse 8, *Who shall also confirm you unto the end, that ye be unreprovable in the day of our Lord Jesus Christ.*

"Who shall also confirm you unto the end . . ." Some scholars refer back to God as the antecedent of "who" in this

---

[6]*Ibid.*, p. 29.

place; but Guthrie seems correct in seeing here an exhortation for the Corinthians not to trust in spiritual gifts which they had received, but that they should look to Christ who would be their strength even to the end.

"To the end . . ." is "a gentle reminder that the Corinthians had not yet 'arrived' at perfection, despite their many gifts."[7] Full redemption for all men must await *that day* when the Lord shall come in his glory and all his holy angels with him (2 Tim. 4:8).

Verse 9, *God is faithful, through whom ye were called into the fellowship of his Son Jesus Christ our Lord.*

Here is the ninth reference in as many verses to Jesus Christ.

"God is faithful . . ." The thought is that God, having begun a good work in the Corinthians, would not change his purpose of leading them into eternal life. Bad as conditions were with the church at Corinth, God's purpose would continue operative on their behalf.

"Ye were called . . ." "Called, that is, called to be a Christian, is in the NT always *a call obeyed.*"[8]

On the Problem of Disunity

Verse 10, *Now I beseech you, brethren, through the name of our Lord Jesus Christ, that ye all speak the same thing, and that there be no divisions among you; but that ye be perfected together in the same mind and in the same judgment.*

"I beseech you . . ." Paul's tone in this is one of tender and affectionate appeal, delivered in the all-powerful name of Christ.

"No divisions . . ." All divisions are contrary to the will of Christ; and by reference to the perfect unity which is the ideal of Christian relationships, Paul highlighted the broken fellowship which had marred the body of Christ in Corinth.

---

[7]Donald Guthrie, *The New Bible Commentary* (Grand Rapids: Wm. B. Eerdmans Publishing Company, 1970), p. 1053.

[8]*Ibid.*

"Be perfected together . . ." This comes from a versatile Greek word, meaning "to adjust the parts of an instrument, the setting of bones by a physician, or the mending of nets."[9] The general meaning would appear to be "put the broken unity back together"; and thus by the use of such an expression Paul states by implication the disunity of the church in Corinth. Paul at once stated the source of his information concerning such a disaster.

Verse 11, *For it hath been signified unto me concerning you, my brethren, by them that are of the household of Chloe, that there are contentions among you.*

"The household of Chloe . . ." It is generally assumed by commentators that Chloe was a respected member of the church, and Metz expressed confidence that she was "a woman of character and good standing";[10] but it should be noted that it was not Chloe who gave Paul the information regarding Corinth, but her "household," a term usually applied in the NT to the *familia*, or household slaves, as in the case of "the household of Aristobulus" (Rom. 16:10). Guthrie pointed out that

> Chloe was the popular name of the goddess Demeter, who had 56 temples in Greece, including one at Corinth; and *Chloe's people* appear as disinterested critics outside the church parties mentioned.[11]

This is the only mention of Chloe in the NT, making it impossible to solve the question of who she might have been. The principal point, perhaps, is this: Paul named the source of the evil report he had received, not relying at all upon mere gossip or rumor.

Verse 12, *Now this I mean, that each of you saith. I am of Paul; and I of Apollos; and I of Cephas; and I of Christ.*

Are there three sinful parties in view in this passage, or four? Despite the numerous opinions to the effect that "I of Christ" denotes a sinful division no less than the other slogans,

---

[9]S. Lewis Johnson, Jr., *Wycliffe Bible Commentary* (Chicago: Moody Press, 1971), p.591.

[10]Donald S. Metz, *Beacon Bible Commentary* (Kansas City: Beacon Hill Press, 1968), Vol. VIII, p. 314.

[11]Donald Guthrie, *op. cit.*, p. 1053.

this student cannot agree that there was ever anything wrong with a follower of the Lord claiming to be "of Christ." The glib assertions of many to the effect that the Christ party was a self-righteous little group insisting that they alone had the truth are as ridiculous as they are unsupported by any solid evidence whatever. Paul himself declared that he was "of Christ" (2 Cor. 10:7); and, indeed, the evidence is strong enough that he made such a declaration in this verse, the final "AND I OF CHRIST" being the words not of a faction at Corinth but of the blessed apostle himself. Guthrie admitted that "I belong to Christ could be Paul's own corrective comment."[12] William Barclay punctuated the verse thus: "I am of Paul; I am of Apollos; I am of Cephas—but *I belong to Christ.*"[13] As Adam Clarke expressed it, "It is not likely in any sense of the word that Christ could be said to be the head of a sect or party in his own church."[14] Macknight, commenting on "and I of Christ," said, "Chrysostom thought this was said by Paul himself to show the Corinthians that all ought to consider themselves the disciples of Christ."[15] Any other interpretation of this passage cannot be made to fit.

What was wrong with the first three of these slogans? Those who were using them were glorying in men; but then it follows as a certainty that those who were saying "and I of Christ" were glorying in the Lord. Thus the uniform construction of the four slogans which is made the basis of construing them all as sinful becomes the positive reason for denying it. It is impossible to make glorying in Christ a parallel sin with glorying in men, the latter being condemned by Paul and the glorying in Christ being commanded. It should be remembered that all of the speculative descriptions of these various groups are unsupported by a single line in the NT. Shore's comment that "a faction dared to arrogate to themselves the name of Christ,"[16] on the basis of having seen and heard Christ preach

---

[12]*Ibid.* p. 1054.
[13]William Barclay, *op. cit.*, p. 17.
[14]Adam Clarke, *Commentary* (New York: Carlton & Porter, 1831), NT, Vol. II, p. 192.
[15]James Macknight, *Apostolical Epistle, with Commentary and Notes* (Grand Rapids: Baker Book House, 1969), Vol. II, p. 22.
[16]T. Teignmouth Shore, *Ellicott's Commentary on the Whole Bible* (Grand Rapids: Zondervan Publishing House, 1959), Vol. XII, p. 290.

personally, is an example of unscholarly guessing, apparently engaged in for the purpose of imputing blame to those who were doing exactly what they should have done in affirming that they were indeed "of Christ." Would to God that all men, even as Paul, were "of Christ."

The three schismatic groups which were glorying in the names of men have had their counterparts in all ages. Such conduct then, as it still is, was sinful. Paul moved at once to show how ridiculous is the device of glorying in human teachers.

Verse 13, *Is Christ divided? was Paul crucified for you? or were ye baptized into the name of Paul?*

In Paul's dealing with the parties, it should be discerned that this triple question was designed to expose and correct the sin of the three groups glorying in men, but they do not cast the slightest reflection upon those who were "of Christ," who could have given the proper response to Paul's question. The other three groups, however, would have been forced to confess that neither Paul, Apollos, or Peter had been crucified for them, and that they had not been baptized into any of those three names. As McGarvey observed, "We should note how inseparably connected in Paul's thought were the sacrifice of the cross and the baptism which makes us partakers of its benefits."[17]

Verses 14-15, *I thank God that I baptized none of you, save Crispus and Gaius; lest any should say that ye were baptized into my name.*

It was Paul's custom to entrust the physical act of baptizing converts to an assistant such as John Mark, Silas or Timothy. There were occasions, however, when he found it necessary to do the actual baptizing with his own hands, as in the cases here cited. He, in this passage, viewed it as providential that he had baptized so few of them, thus denying them any excuse for connecting his name with a party. Both Gaius and Crispus were prominent Christians, Crispus having been the ruler of a synagogue.

---

[17]J. W. McGarvey, *Commentary on First Corinthians* (Cincinnati: Standard Publishing Company, 1916), p. 54.

Verse 16, *And I baptized also the household of Stephanas: besides, I know not whether I baptized any other.*

"Stephanas . . ." was of "the firstfruits of Achaia" (16:15), evidently having been baptized by Paul before the beginning of his great work in Corinth (Acts 18:5ff).

Verse 17, *For Christ sent me not to baptize, but to preach the gospel: not in wisdom of words, lest the cross of Christ should be made void.*

"Christ sent me not to baptize . . ." Some have been diligent to make this passage an excuse for denying the necessity of the believer's baptism into Christ, as for example, Metz, who said, "The gospel of grace and faith that he proclaimed was as free from outer ritual and ceremony as it was devoid of legal observances."[18] If such a view is tenable, how can Paul's baptism of Stephanas, Gaius, and Crispus be explained? Of course, what Paul referred to here was the *administration of the rite of baptism*, there being nothing here to the effect that Paul preached salvation without baptism. He like all the apostles had been commanded to "make disciples of all nations, baptizing them" (Matt. 28:19).

"Not in wisdom of words . . ." The great apostle renounced the pretentious rhetorical flourishes so dear to the Greek intellectuals, deliberately rejecting the complicated elocutionary devices which were the stock in trade of the philosophers. The Greek word *sophist* (wise man) had fallen from its glory, and in Paul's day had come to denote a nimble tongue and an empty brain. Dio Chrysostom described the Greek wise men thus:

> They croak like frogs in a marsh; they are the most wretched of men, because, though ignorant, they think themselves wise; they are like peacocks, showing off their reputation and the number of their pupils as peacocks do their tails.[19]

It is clear, then, that Paul used the word "wisdom" in a sarcastic sense in this phrase having the meaning of "gobbledegook" as now used. See more on this under 2 Corinthians 11:5.

---

[18]Donald S. Metz, *op. cit.*, p. 316.
[19]William Barclay, quotation from *Chrysostom, op. cit.*, p. 22.

So-called intellectuals of our own times are by no means exempt from the conceited shallowness of the Greek philosophers. Even a sermon may be well organized, rhetorically excellent, stylishly delivered, "beautiful" and worthless.

"Lest the cross of Christ should be made void . . ." Digressions are frequent in Paul's works; and this word "cross," mentioned as the antithesis of the philosophers' so-called wisdom, was made the subject of a characteristic Pauline digression.

The Glory of the Cross

Verses 18-19, *For the word of the cross is to them that perish foolishness; but unto us who are saved it is the power of God. For it is written,*

> *I will destroy the wisdom of the wise,*
> *And the discernment of the discerning will I bring to naught.*

All of the value judgments of men were nailed to the cross of Christ. Men glorify the arrogant, proud, mighty and successful, but Christ was patient, meek, humble and submissive. A crucified Saviour was simply beyond the boundaries of human imagination.

"It is the power of God . . ." There are two reactions to the mystery of the cross on the part of two classes of people who behold it. The two classes are those who are perishing and those who are being saved (RV margin). To the former, the cross is foolishness, but to the latter it is the power of God. As an illustration of God's power contrasted with human wisdom, Paul cited Isaiah 29:14 where, according to Marsh,

> The prophet, referring to the failure of worldly statesmanship in Judah in the face of the Assyrian invasion, states a principle that the wisdom of man is no match for the power of God.[20]

Verse 20, *Where is the wise? where is the scribe? where is the disputer of this world? hath not God made foolish the wisdom of the world?*

---

[20]Paul W. Marsh, *A New Testament Commentary* (Grand Rapids: Zondervan Publishing House, 1969), p. 377.

"The wise . . ." refers to the worldly wise such as the Greek sophists. "The scribe . . ." denotes the expert in Jewish religion. "The disputer of this world . . ." includes both the others as well as all others who rely upon their own intelligence and do not trust in God.

"Hath not God made foolish the wisdom of the world? . . ." Although Paul doubtless had in mind that phase of wisdom relating to the eternal things of the spirit, there is also an undeniable application to *all* phases of human wisdom. History is one long dramatic denial of the world's wisdom. The pyramids of Egypt, upon which generations of men worked for centuries, are merely colossal monuments to human stupidity. The textbooks of a generation ago are worthless today. Permanence has never yet come to any human government. Every mystery ever solved unlocks a hundred others and raises infinitely more questions than are answered, leading to conviction that the ultimate wisdom on the part of men can never be attained by new formulas and gadgets, that the infinite wisdom is a person, Almighty God, and that men may know him only through Jesus Christ our Lord.

Verse 21, *For seeing that in the wisdom of God the world through its wisdom knew not God, it was God's good pleasure through the foolishness of preaching to save them that believe.*

"Knew not God . . ." The ineffectiveness and frustration of human wisdom are nowhere more dramatically evident than in the long pre-Christian history of the Gentiles, who, turning away from God and walking in the light (!) of their own intelligence, drowned the whole earth in shameful debaucheries. Paul developed this thought extensively in the first chapters of Romans, and there is a brief mention of the same thing here. Who can believe that modern man, now in the act of turning away from God, will be any more successful in finding the good life apart from his Creator than were his ancient progenitors?

"The foolishness of the preaching . . ." has reference to the foolishness of the thing preached (RV margin), that is, foolishness from the human viewpoint.

"To save them that believe . . ." "Believe" is here a synecdoche for turning to God through obedience of the gospel, and it includes such things as repentance and baptism.

Verses 22-23, *Seeing that Jews ask for signs, and Greeks seek after wisdom: but we preach Christ crucified, unto Jews a stumbling block, and unto Greeks foolishness.*

Dummelow paraphrased this thus, "The Jews will not believe unless a miracle is wrought before their eyes; the Greeks will accept no truth that is not commended by philosophical speculation."[21]

Of course, the Jews had witnessed many miracles, not only by the Lord of life, but also by the holy apostles; but what they demanded was the performance, at their bidding, of some spectacular wonder of their own choosing, which, even if it had been wrought, would have had no moral value and would have proved just as ineffective as the true miracles they had already seen (Matt. 16:1).

"We preach Christ crucified . . ." The cross is central to the Christian religion; no person may be a true follower of the Lord who is unwilling to take up his cross and follow the Master (Matt. 16:24).

Despite the Jewish law which declared, "He that is hanged on a tree is accursed of God" (Deut. 21:23), and the hierarchy of Israel having accomplished such a death for the Lord of glory, the cross was the instrument of Jesus' atonement for the sins of the whole world. It was the place where God, having entered our earthly life as a man, paid the penalty of human transgression, bruised the head of Satan, and purchased the church with his own precious blood. The glory of the cross is seen in what it denied, what it declared, what it accomplished, whom it defeated, and whom it saved. All the human wisdom of all the ages is powerless to achieve the most infinitesimal fraction of the redemption that was achieved to the uttermost on Calvary.

Verse 24, *But unto them that are called, both Jews and Greeks, Christ the power of God, and the wisdom of God.*

"Called . . ." This should not be understood in the narrow and restricted sense, for God has called all men to receive

---

[21]J. R. Dummelow, *Commentary on the Holy Bible* (New York: The Macmillan Company, 1937), p. 895.

eternal life in Christ, the usage here having reference to men who heed and obey the call.

"Both Jews and Greeks . . ." This has the meaning of "all men" of whatever race or nation, time or circumstance.

Verse 25, *Because the foolishness of God is wiser than men; and the weakness of God is stronger than men.*

Christ on the cross appeared to be weakness in the eyes of men; but that "weakness of God was stronger than men and everything that men could produce."[22] The sign-seeking Jews could not comprehend the mighty "sign of the prophet Jonah," enacted before their very eyes; and the wisdom-seeking Greeks could not discern the most profound wisdom in all history, not even after it had been preached to them! Despite this, however, the rolling centuries have vindicated the truth which Paul here proclaimed.

The Glory of the Shame

We have borrowed this subtitle from Barclay, for it accurately summarizes the argument Paul was about to make. He would use the character of the Corinthian church itself as a demonstration of God's foolishness being wiser than men.

Verse 26, *For behold your calling, brethren, that not many wise after the flesh, not many mighty, not many noble, are called.*

Many of the earliest Christians were slaves, a majority were poor, most were uneducated; and few of them had any claim to distinction in the wretched world of their day; but they were the roots from which all that is holy and beautiful has blossomed in succeeding centuries. In their achievements through faith in Christ one reads the pattern of many wonderful things which have happened in America. As Emma Lazarus' poem on the Statue of Liberty reads:

Your wretched refuse of all lands—your poor,
    Your huddled masses yearning to breathe free,
    Homeless and rejected, send them to me.
I lift my lamp beside the Golden Door!

---

[22]Leon Morris, *op. cit.*, p. 47.

How those rejected ones have blessed the world! but this is only a feeble parable of what Christianity did on a cosmic scale. As Barclay put it, "Christianity was and still is literally the most uplifting thing in the whole universe."[23]

Look at that congregation in Corinth, rescued from the dens of vice and debauchery, gleaned from the dregs of a cruel and heartless society, recruited from the hopeless ranks of slaves, delivered from the treadmills of commerce and industry; but Christ redeemed them, named upon them the eternal name, announced from heaven the plenary discharge of their sins, and made them partakers of the inheritance of the saints in light. Thank God for the church at Corinth and everywhere.

However, it should be kept in mind that Christianity was not denied to the noble, the mighty, and the wise; for Paul did not say that "none" of what might be called the higher echelons of society were called. Indeed, the truly wise, the really noble, also received the Lord, despite the tragedy of many failing to do so.

The treasurer of Queen Candace became a Christian (Acts 8:27).
The proconsul of Crete, Sergius Paulus, accepted the gospel (Acts 13:6-12).
Dionysius the Areopagite, a mighty judge at Athens, believed (Acts 17:34).
Crispus and Sosthenes were both rulers of a synagogue when they obeyed the gospel (Acts 18:8, 17).
Erastus, Chamberlain of the City of Corinth, became a Christian (Rom. 16:23).
Many women of the nobility in Thessalonica and Beroea accepted the truth (Acts 17:4,12).

Such examples as these, however, were the exception, the vast majority of the Christians, at first, coming from the ranks of earth's unfortunate and poor.

Verse 27, *But God chose the foolish things of the world, that he might put to shame them that are wise; and God chose the weak things of the world, that he might put to shame the things that are strong.*

---

[23]William Barclay, *op. cit.*, p. 24.

Those "foolish" Christians of Corinth triumphed over all the vaunted learning of the philosophers; those "weak" followers of Christ spread the truth over the world while Corinth and Athens crumbled. To go with Christ is to go with the future!

Verse 28, *And the base things of the world, and the things that are despised, did God choose, yea and the things that are not, that he might bring to naught the things that are.*

This verse taken in conjunction with verse 27 gives five designations to Christians (as they were esteemed by the world of that period). The foolish, the weak, the base, the despised, the things that "are not" (in other words, the "nobodies"); but the great apostle's words on behalf of those who were despised by the world are to the effect that the triumph, the success, the honor, and the glory belong to them. In the last three designations, as in this verse, the Jewish attitude of despising all Gentiles and actually speaking of them as "dogs" appears to be in Paul's thinking (see Matt. 15:26).

Verse 29, *That no flesh should glory before God.*

How incredible it is that a man, a creature of flesh and blood, created of the dust and to the dust certain to return, whose glory at its zenith is only for a moment, whose days are spent in frustration, whose tears flow incessantly, whose very righteousness is filthy rags—how unbelievable is it that such a creature as man should glory before God! Such is the wretched state of Adam's race that only God can give salvation and even God could do so only at the extravagant cost of the blood shed on Calvary. God desires that man should recognize and confess his sin and unworthiness, and, like those poor mortals of Corinth, turn to the heavenly Father through Jesus Christ the Lord. If the first converts to Christianity had been the wealthy rulers of earth, there would inevitably have prevailed an impression that such persons had earned eternal life. However, no man, but no man, was ever capable of earning one second of eternal life; and Paul's thought here stresses the wisdom of God in saving the outcasts of Corinth in order that no flesh should glory before God. Those former debauchees of unspeakable Corinth deserved salvation as much as the wisest and greatest of earth, which is not at all; and fortunate is every man who comprehends this basic truth of salvation in Christ.

Verses 30-31, *But of him are ye in Christ Jesus who is made unto us wisdom from God, and righteousness and sanctification, and redemption: that, according as it is written, He that glorieth, let him glory in the Lord.*

"In Christ Jesus . . ." In Christ alone is there salvation; and in Christ the saved possess all things. Behold here the only true ground of justification in the eyes of God. Jesus is perfect, holy, undefiled, righteous in the superlative degree. In Christ and as Christ and as fully identified with him, it is true also that Christians are holy, righteous, etc. It is not their righteousness, of course, in the sense that they achieved it; but it is theirs in the sense that Christ achieved it and they "are Christ," being members of his spiritual body. Satan, death and hell have no claim on the one who is "in Christ." Why? Because what is true of the head is true of the entire body; and our head, which is Christ, having paid the penalty of death for sin, the whole spiritual body (the church) has likewise paid it in the person of Christ. That is what is meant by being dead to sin by the body of Christ (Rom. 6:11).

There are four things mentioned by Paul in this passage which belong to the Christian by virtue of his being "in Christ."

Wisdom of God. In Christ are hidden all the treasures of wisdom and knowledge (Col. 2:3). The person "in Christ," by reason of having believed and having been baptized "into Christ" is thus identified with Christ, being a part of his spiritual body; and thus, *as Christ* he has become the possessor of the wisdom of God.

Righteousness. All that has been said of wisdom in the above paragraph pertains with equal force to righteousness, which may be acquired by the believer in no other way except through being baptized into Christ. The notion that "this righteousness is forensic,"[24] that is, an imputed righteousness, bestowed on the grounds of faith alone, is incorrect. It is not an imputed, forensic, bestowed righteousness in any sense whatever. It is a pure, perfect, genuine, and *actual* righteousness performed and achieved by Jesus Christ our Lord; and when

---

[24]S. Lewis Johnson, Jr., *op. cit.*, p. 593.

the believer becomes a part of the Lord's spiritual body, that true righteousness belongs to him as being "in Christ," "of Christ," and in fact part of the spiritual body which "is Christ." And when does one become a part of that spiritual body which is Christ? "In one Spirit were we all baptized into one body" (1 Cor. 12:13), as Paul declared a little later in this same epistle.

Sanctification. The person who is "in Christ" is sanctified, set apart for spiritual service, and through spiritual growth endowed with whatever may be needed for development in the Christian life.

Redemption. Significantly, the salvation of the soul is a reality only for those "in Christ." Although Paul gave only an abbreviated list of four blessings in this verse, as resulting from the believer's being "in Christ," it must be construed as merely a token list, despite the all-importance of the four. In his letter to the Ephesians, Paul stated that "every spiritual blessing in the heavenly places" is "in Christ" (Eph. 1:3). It is not fair to leave this brief discussion of the salvation (inclusive of all spiritual blessings) which is "in Christ," without pointing out for those who truly desire to know the truth that in all the holy scriptures there is no other way revealed by which a believer might acquire the status of being "in Christ," except through being baptized "into him" (Rom. 6:3; Gal. 3:27; 1 Cor. 12:13). Could there be any wonder, therefore, that Jesus himself said, "He that believeth and is baptized shall be saved" (Mark 16:16).

"He that glorieth, let him glory in the Lord . . ." In this concluding sentence in the paragraph, Paul quoted Jeremiah 9:23, where the meaning is that men should glory in God; and, by his application of this text to Jesus Christ, he testified to the deity and godhead of our Lord Jesus Christ. As Morris said, "No higher view could be taken of the Person of Christ."[25]

---

[25]Leon Morris, *op. cit.*, p. 51.

CHAPTER 2

One of the problems in Corinth was related to the pretentious, empty philosophy of the Greeks who so highly regarded the eloquent speeches of the popular leaders of such sophistry; and Paul gave his reasons for not following the popular methods of oratory in his preaching of the word of Christ (1-5). However, fully mature Christians could look forward to an understanding of the true wisdom of God (as contrasted with the current sophistry); and the mystery of God, far more wonderful than the so-called mysteries of the Greeks, could be participated in by those of genuine spirituality (6-16). Throughout this chapter, Paul made it clear that the glory of the Christian faith is resident in the content of the gospel and not in the manner of its presentation.

Verse 1, *And I, brethren, when I came unto you, came not with excellency of speech or of wisdom, proclaiming to you the testimony of God.*

Paul had been educated at Tarsus which Strabo preferred as a school of learning above either Alexandria or Athens, and also had been schooled "at the feet of Gamaliel" (Acts 22:3), the famed scholar in Jerusalem. "Paul was a university man, the outstanding scholar of his generation."[1] Nevertheless, he despised the pedantry, superficiality and narrow conceit of those who were received as intellectuals. Paul rejected their methods because he was above them, not because he was inferior to them. Paul had a wide acquaintance with all the learning of his generation. He quoted Aratus (Acts 17:28), Epimenides (Titus 1:12), and Menander (1 Cor. 15:33);[2] but he counted all such polite learning as mere dross, as compared with the gospel of Christ (Phil. 3:8).

Therefore, the meaning of this verse is that when Paul went to Corinth he renounced all of the tricks and devices of oratory,

---

[1]Henry H. Halley, *Bible Handbook* (Grand Rapids: Zondervan Publishing House, 1927), p. 545.

[2]J. W. McGarvey, *Commentary on 1 Corinthians* (Cincinnati: Standard Publishing Company, 1916), p. 58.

refused to accommodate the gospel to the style of the Greek philosophers, and did not try to adorn the truth with pagan wisdom. That Paul had the ability to do such things may not be doubted for a moment; but he wanted their faith to be in the power of God, not in the ability of men (v. 5).

"Excellency of speech . . ." "When the preaching itself is stressed to the degree that it obscures its own content, there is a case of excellency of speech."[3]

"Testimony of God . . ." This means that the gospel is founded upon the word and the authority of God himself; and, by this word, as Macknight said,

> The apostle insinuated that the credibility of the gospel depended neither on its conformity to the philosophy of the Greeks, nor on the eloquence of its preachers, but on the attestation of God, who confirmed it by miracles.[4]

Verse 2, *For I determined not to know anything among you, save Jesus Christ, and him crucified.*

It is the style among certain commentators to construe Paul's method in view here as a reversal of what he allegedly did in Athens. They say Paul tried to preach philosophically in Athens, sustained a miserable failure, learned his lesson and announced his return to a more simple advocacy of the gospel in these verses. Despite the popularity of such a view, however, there is nothing, either in the word of God or in history, to give the slightest credibility to it.

There is no hint whatever, either in this passage or in Acts 17, that Paul preached "Christ crucified" at Corinth because of a sense of failure of the philosophical approach in Athens. As a matter of fact, "His sermon at Athens was not basically philosophical."[5] He preached the resurrection of the dead, and when did that get to be philosophical? Furthermore, his preaching in Athens was in no sense whatever a failure.

---

[3]F. W. Grosheide, *The New International Commentary* (Grand Rapids: Wm. B. Eerdmans Publishing Company, 1953), p. 58.

[4]James Macknight, *Apostolical Epistles and Commentary* (Grand Rapids: Baker Book House, 1959), p. 32.

[5]S. Lewis Johnson, *Wycliffe Bible Commentary* (Chicago: Moody Press, 1971), p. 594.

Dionysius the Areopagite, Damaris, certain men, and others with them were converted (Acts 17:34). An exceedingly large number of people in Athens became Christians. "The church in Athens was one of the strongest congregations in the empire in the second and third centuries,"[6] and Lange pointed out that "A Christian congregation in Athens flourished in an eminent degree."[7] The "others with them" of Acts 17:34 may not be construed as "a mere handful," except arbitrarily and with no logic to support it. It is also most probable that Sosthenes and his household were converted in Paul's work in Athens (see CA, under 17:34).

In the light of the above, we feel that comments to the effect that "There (in Athens) Paul had one of his very few failures";[8] "He feared a failure similar to that in Athens";[9] "Athens was a sad memory for Paul. He never mentions her name in an epistle. He sends no word of greeting to any of her children";[10] etc.—that all such notions are absolutely untenable. For example, how can it be known that Paul never wrote to the saints in Athens, there being at least one letter to the Corinthians which was lost?

Grosheide's views on this question are undoubtedly correct. He declared that:

> The answer to the question of whether Paul had ever preached anything but Jesus Christ must of course be negative. The meaning is not that the apostle did not resolve to preach Christ till he came to Corinth . . . but that he had to go on preaching Christ.[11]

"Determined not to know anything . . ." has the meaning that Paul would rely upon no earthly wisdom for power in his preaching.

---

[6]Don De Welt, *Acts Made Actual* (Joplin, Mo.: College Press, 1958), p. 243.
[7]John Peter Lange, *Commentary on Acts* (Grand Rapids: Zondervan Publishing House, 1866), p. 331.
[8]William Barclay, *The Letters to the Corinthians* (Philadelphia: The Westminster Press, 1954), p. 26.
[9]David Lipscomb, *First Corinthians* (Nashville: The Gospel Advocate Company, 1935), p. 39.
[10]T. Teignmouth Shore, *Ellicott's Commentary on the Whole Bible* (Grand Rapids: Zondervan Publishing House, 1959), p. 283.
[11]F. W. Grosheide, *op. cit.*, p. 59.

"Save Jesus Christ and him crucified . . ." This cannot mean that Paul would henceforth leave off preaching the resurrection, the final judgment, the brotherhood of humanity, the unity of God, the sin of idolatry, etc.; but, as John Wesley said, that here, "a part is put for the whole,"[12] thus indicating that this is another NT example of the figure of speech called synecdoche in which a group of related things is denoted by the mention of one or two of them. What a shame it is that Wesley failed to see the same figure in "saved by faith."

Verse 3, *And I was with you in weakness, and in fear, and in much trembling.*

Such was Paul's dauntless courage that it may not be supposed that this has reference to any fear of physical danger; but it suggests Paul's recognition of human weakness and his realization that the salvation of so many persons was dependent upon so feeble an instrument as himself. Dummelow paraphrased this verse thus: "It was with much anxiety and self-distrust that I preached the gospel to you."[13]

Verse 4, *And my speech and my preaching were not in persuasive words of wisdom, but in demonstration of the Spirit and of power.*

Macknight's paraphrase of this is:

> Paul's discourses were neither composed nor pronounced according to the rules of Greek rhetoric, yet they were accompanied with the powerful demonstration of the Spirit, who enabled him to prove the things he preached by miracles.[14]

Of course, there was a reason for Paul's renunciation of the methods of the rabble-rousers; and that reason he at once emphatically stated.

Verse 5, *That your faith should not stand in the wisdom of men, but in the power of God.*

---

[12]John Wesley, *One Volume NT Commentary* (Grand Rapids: Baker Book House, 1972), in loco.

[13]J. R. Dummelow, *Commentary on the Holy Bible* (New York: The Macmillan Company, 1937), p. 895.

[14]James Macknight, *op. cit.*, p. 32.

"What depends upon a clever argument is at the mercy of a clever argument";[15] and Paul desired that the faith of the Corinthians should be grounded in the facts and certainties of the Christian gospel, not in the showy eloquence of polished oratory. There can hardly be any doubt that this paragraph condemns much of the preaching of our own times.

Up to this point Paul was stressing the truth that the gospel of Christ owes nothing to human wisdom, and that his renunciation of the popular methods of advocating it had resulted in its being despised by those who considered themselves sophisticated; but, beginning in the next verse, Paul effectively refuted the notion that "Christianity is contemptible, and proceeded to show something of its profundity and dignity."[16] He showed that it is not wisdom which he rejected but false wisdom; he preached God's wisdom, which is higher than man's wisdom, and the only true wisdom.

Verse 6, *We speak wisdom, however, among them that ore full-grown: yet a wisdom not of this world, nor among the rulers of this world, who are coming to naught.*

"Among them that are full-grown . . ." All Christians begin as "babes in Christ" (3:1); but through prayerful study and growth they may attain unto the "stature of the fullness of Christ" (Eph. 4:13). To all who are thus full-grown is revealed a measure of the knowledge of God's wisdom. The rational and intellectual dimensions of the Christian religion infinitely surpass all of the achievements of mortal intelligence; and Paul's blunt reference to this truth states that it forcefully applies even to "the rulers of this world." Not even they ever attained to any wisdom whatever in any manner comparable to the wisdom of God, the proof of it being that they themselves "are coming to naught."

"Are coming to naught . . ." The subject of this clause is "the rulers of this world"; but the meaning is not restricted to such persons as governors and emperors. "Paul had in mind all of those who set the pattern of this world, including the rulers

---

[15]S. Lewis Johnson, Jr., *Wycliffe Bible Commentary* (Chicago: Moody Press, 1971), p. 594.

[16]Leon Morris, *Tyndale Commentary* (Grand Rapids: Wm. B. Eerdmans Publishing Company, 1958), p. 53.

in the sphere of science and art."[17] The proof of what Paul said here came within a few years when the Jewish state, Jerusalem and the temple were utterly destroyed in 70 A.D. Nor was it any less true of Rome, where the period of the phantom emperors soon came; and the mighty empire itself eventually sank under the ravages of the invading hordes of vandals and barbarians. But it is also true of all history. If human wisdom had any genuine merit, the depredations of war, famine and pestilence might be controlled; but every generation has fulfilled its destiny of proving that "It is not in man that walketh to direct his steps" (Jer. 10:23). Therefore, human wisdom stands condemned in the very areas where it might be supposed to be effective. And beyond that, "Man's knowledge cannot bring about the redemption of the race."[18]

"We speak wisdom . . ." "The plural we implies that Paul did not stand alone among the apostles in his method of teaching."[19] None of the apostolical preachers of Christ taught in any other manner than that of Paul.

Verse 7, *But we speak God's wisdom in a mystery, even the wisdom that hath been hidden, which God foreordained before the worlds unto our glory.*

"Mystery . . ." The mystery of the Christian religion far surpasses anything affected in the mysteries of the Greeks, and notably in the fact of its having been foreordained in God's purpose even before the creation of the world. The usual definition of mystery, to the effect of its being something once unknown now revealed, while true enough, is inadequate. Some elements of the mystery of God will not even be finished until "the days of the voice of the seventh angel" (Rev. 10:7). Russell said that:

> The mystery in the scriptures denotes (a) something above the ordinary human understanding (Mark 4: 11); (b) something formerly hidden in the counsel of God, but afterward revealed as a plan understood by its own

---

[17]F. W. Grosheide, *op. cit.*, p. 63.
[18]Donald S. Metz, *Beacon Bible Commentary* (Kansas City: Beacon Hill Press, 1968), p. 324.
[19]T. Teignmouth Shore, *op. cit.*, p. 293.

fulfillment; and (c) as something always accompanied by vastness depth and power.[20]

The Mystery

The NT refers to many mysteries: of Christ and his church (Eph. 5:32), of lawlessness (2 Thess. 2:7), of seven stars and seven candlesticks (Rev. 1:20), of the resurrection (1 Cor. 15:51) of the blindness of Israel (Rom. 11:25), of the harlot church (Rev. 17:7), and of the kingdom of heaven (Matt. 13:11).

However, it is not to any of these, specifically, that reference is made here. There is a greater and more comprehensive mystery containing all of these and exceeding them. This greater mystery is often mentioned in the NT scriptures where it is called *great* (1 Tim. 3:16), the mystery (Rom. 16:25), the mystery of God's will (Eph. 1:9), the mystery of Christ (Eph. 3:4), the mystery of the gospel (Eph. 6:1), the mystery of God (Col. 2:3), the mystery of the faith (1 Tim. 3:9), and the mystery of godliness (1 Tim. 3:16)—it is to *that* mystery that Paul refers here.

It is this mystery which dominates the sixty-six books of the Bible. God announced the mystery in Eden; Satan's part in it was revealed; the mystery deepened in the death of Abel; the mystery was progressively unfolded verbally in the OT prophecies, systematically prefigured in the types and shadows of the Mosaic dispensation, explicitly heralded in the lives of great typical men of the old covenant, and came to crisis on the cross of Christ, where in its great essentials, it was fully unveiled. There are many corollaries of the central mystery; and the ultimate goals of it are projected into the future. A six-line summary of this "great mystery" is in 1 Timothy 3:16. Running throughout the entire Bible is the record of the "mystery of lawlessness" which is antagonistic to the true mystery, but which is to be resolved finally in the overthrow of Satan and the purging of wickedness out of God's universe.[21]

---

[20]John William Russell, *Compact Commentary on the NT* (Grand Rapids: Baker Book House, 1964), p. 406.

[21]*The Mystery of Redemption* is more elaborately discussed in a book of that title authored by the writer of this series of commentaries. James Burton Coffman, *The Mystery of Redemption* (Austin: Firm Foundation Publishing House, 1976).

"Unto our glory . . ." highlights the benevolent purpose of God in the amazing and overwhelmingly comprehensive work of the Father looking to human redemption.

Verse 8, *Which none of the rulers of this world hath known: for had they known it, they would not have crucified the Lord of Glory.*

One great essential element in the mystery is that of the incarnation of God in Christ, this being the precise element of the mystery unknown to the rulers of this world. Christ made it clear that the Jewish religious hierarchy did indeed know who Christ was, in the sense of knowing that he was the lawful heir of the temple, the promised Messiah, a holy and righteous prophet of God, and also the undisputed heir to the throne of David. What they did not know was that the "fullness of the Godhead" dwelt in him bodily (Col. 2:9). In Matthew 21:38, the Jewish leaders, under the figure of wicked husbandmen, said, "This is the heir; come, let us kill him, and take his inheritance." Had the human wisdom of the world's leaders been capable of recognizing God in Christ, they would not have crucified him.

"The Lord of glory . . ." Wesley declared that "The giving Christ this august title, peculiar to the great Jehovah, plainly shows him to be the supreme God."[22] Thus "the Lord of glory," "the Father of glory" (Eph. 1:17), and "the Spirit of glory" (1 Peter 4:14), indicate that the three members of the Godhead alike receive this title. Psalm 29:3 and Acts 7:2 mention "the God of glory."

"Crucified the Lord of glory . . ." "These words brought into juxtaposition the lowest ignominy, and the most splendid exaltation."[23]

Verse 9, *But as it is written,*

Things which eye saw not, and ear heard not,
And which entered not into the heart of man,
Whatsoever things God prepared for them that love him.

---

[22]John Wesley, *op. cit.*, in loco.
[23]F. W. Farrar, *Pulpit Commentary* (Grand Rapids: Wm. B. Eerdmans Publishing Company, 1950), Vol. 19, p. 60.

These words are usually thought of as suggesting heaven and the glories of the future world; but Paul did not hesitate to apply them here to what God has already done for his children. "They certainly belong to the present state, and express the wondrous light, life and liberty which the gospel communicates."[24] "While it is true that heaven will be so wonderful that we cannot comprehend it, Paul was talking about here, the present dispensation."[25]

Learned men have conjectured that these lines are from an early Christian hymn, which had been formed by combining certain OT expressions; but, despite this, as Grosheide said:

> The view that Paul quotes the OT, using passages like Isaiah 64:4, LXX (64:3 in the Hebrew) for the first and last part of the quotation, and Isaiah 65:17 for the middle, remains the most plausible.[26]

Verse 10, *But unto us God revealed them through the Spirit: for the Spirit searcheth all things, yea, the deep things of God.*

"Unto us . . ." The things which eye had not seen, etc., were revealed through God's Spirit to the apostles. It is a mistake to construe "us" in this passage as indicative of all Christians, except to the extent of their having received God's revelation through the holy apostles.

"The Spirit searcheth all things . . ." This is true, "not in the sense of 'needing information,' but in the sense of penetrating all things."[27] Ellicott and Wesley also concurred in the restriction of the emphatic "us" in this verse to "Christ's apostles and (inspired) teachers."[28]

"The deep things of God . . ." have reference not to some abstract inscrutability of God but to the concrete work of salvation."[29] The mystery already mentioned is of the deep things of God.

---

[24]Adam Clarke, *Commentary on the Whole Bible* (New York: Carlton & Porter, 1831), Vol. VI, p. 199.

[25]George W. DeHoff, *Sermons on First Corinthians* (Murfreesboro, Tenn.: The Christian Press, 1947), p. 30.

[26]F W. Grosheide, *op. cit.*, p. 66.

[27]Donald Guthrie, *The New Bible Commentary* (Grand Rapids: Wm. B. Eerdmans Publishing Company, 1970), p. 1055.

[28]John Wesley, *op. cit.*, in loco.

[29]F. W. Grosheide, *op. cit.* p. 8.

Verse 11, *For who among men knoweth the things of a man, save the spirit of the man, which is in him? even as the things of God none knoweth, save the Spirit of God.*

The only way to know God is through the revelation of God through the Holy Spirit to the apostles. Greek wisdom, apart from the inspiration of God's Spirit, found the mind of God impenetrable, in the same manner of its being impossible to read another man's thoughts.

"The things of God none knoweth . . ." is not to be understood as saying that men know nothing of God, for this would deny revelation. Again from Farrar, "All that is meant is that our knowledge of God must always be relative, not absolute. It is not possible to measure the arm of God with the finger of man."[30]

Verse 12, *But we received, not the spirit of the world, but the Spirit which is from God; that we might know the things that were freely given to us of God.*

"Not the spirit of the world . . ." By this, Paul did not mean that such a spirit of the world, comparable in a sense to the Holy Spirit and opposed to him, actually exists. Nor can we agree with Marsh that "It may mean Satan."[31] What Paul had in view here was the secular, materialistic thinking of unregenerated men. The Germans had a word for it, the *Zeitgeist*, which means "the spirit of the times," or "the intellectual and moral tendencies of an age or epoch."

"The Spirit which is from God . . ." "What is meant here is not the perpetual indwelling of the Spirit in the congregation, but the historical fact of his coming."[32] The reference here is to Pentecost and the coming of the Holy Spirit to guide the apostles into all truth.

Verse 13, *Which things also we speak, not in words which man's wisdom teacheth, but which the Spirit teacheth; combining spiritual things with spiritual words.*

---

[30]F. W. Farrar, *op. cit.*, p. 60.
[31]Paul W. Marsh, *A New Commentary* (Grand Rapids: Zondervan Publishing House, 1969), p. 379.
[32]F. W. Grosheide, *op. cit.*, p.70.

This writer agrees with James Macknight that the declaration here refers to the Holy Spirit's giving "words" of wisdom to the apostles, not leaving them free to clothe ideas and impressions in their own words merely, but in words which "the Spirit teacheth."[33] Some deny that anything of this kind is meant; but when they deny it, they are left with no explanation whatever of what Paul meant.

"Combining spiritual things with spiritual words . . ." is a disputed rendition. Grosheide translated it, "comparing spiritual things with spiritual";[34] Macknight rendered it, "explaining spiritual things with spiritual words,"[35] holding that Paul had in view here what Paul called "the form of sound words" (2 Tim. 1:13). The theory that God gave men the ideas without imposing any vocabulary upon them breaks down when it is asked, "How may any idea be conveyed without the use of words?" Clearly, the "combining" in this verse pertains to what the Spirit of God did, not to what Paul did; and the fact of the Spirit's combining spiritual things (ideas) with spiritual words would leave the choice of words to the Spirit, not to men. How otherwise can the writings of the NT be understood?

Verse 14, *Now the natural man receiveth not the things of the Spirit of God: for they are foolishness unto him; and he cannot know them, because they are spiritually judged.*

"The natural man . . ." is rendered from the Greek "physical man," and has the meaning indicated by Macknight, being that of "an animal man."[36] It is an abuse of this passage to make it mean that unregenerated men cannot understand spiritual things until God, in some independent action, opens their hearts, or regenerates them. The receiving of the truth by the unconverted is not in view here at all. De Hoff gave this exegesis:

> Paul means that ordinary man cannot receive or give a revelation from God, because God has not selected him and filled him with the Holy Spirit. Only the apostles and

---

[33]James Macknight, *op. cit.*, p. 41.
[34]F. W. Grosheide *op. cit.*, p. 72.
[35]James Macknight, *op. cit.*, p. 41.
[36]*Ibid.*

> certain other writers of the NT were so selected and guided.[37]

The application of this in its primary context is that none of the brilliant orators of Greece had the slightest knowledge of the wisdom of God, such wisdom appearing to the sophists as foolishness.

Verse 15, *But he that is spiritual judgeth all things, and he himself is judged of no man.*

This applies to the company of inspired apostles and evangelists who delivered the great corpus of Christian doctrine. Such men, "endowed with the Holy Spirit could discern and discriminate what is of God, and teach all things God revealed."[38]

"He that is spiritual judgeth . . . himself is judged of no man . . ." In context, this applied to Paul himself, especially, as an affirmation of the authority he was about to exercise in correcting the disorders in Corinth. In the wider application, it means that only the inspired men of Paul's generation were to be credited with any capability whatever, as regards what is, or is not, the truth of God. The inspired company of apostles and evangelists were "judged of no man." As Lipscomb emphatically stated it, "This applies to the original revelations."[39] However, he went on to point out that Christians are instructed to "Believe not every spirit, but prove the spirits, whether they are of God; because many false prophets are gone out into the world" (1 John 4:1), adding that "Men now test all teaching by the truths delivered by the inspired men."[40] This, however, is a secondary application of Paul's affirmation in this verse. That secondary application, nevertheless, is valid, as outlined by Metz:

> The Christian has a spiritual capacity to sift, to investigate, to examine, and to discern all things within the framework of the divine revelation of redemption. On the other hand, the natural man does not have the ability to subject the Christian way of life to examination and

---

[37]George W. DeHoff, *op. cit.*, p. 32.
[38]David Lipscomb, *op. cit.*, p. 43.
[39]*Ibid.*, p. 44.
[40]*Ibid.*

judgment, for he is completely unacquainted with the meaning of spiritual life.[41]

Verse 16, *For who hath known the mind of the Lord, that he should instruct him? But we have the mind of Christ.*

David Lipscomb and Adam Clarke concurred in rendering this verse, "Who hath known the mind of the Lord that he should teach it (that is, teach the truth)?"[42] This would appear to be preferable, because the thought of any mortal "instructing God" is evidently not in the passage at all.

The thought is that 'none of you uninspired men have any notion whatever of what the truth of God may be.'

"But we have the mind of Christ . . ." "We" indicates that Paul did not claim this status for himself only, but for all of the inspired apostles and evangelists of the NT dispensation.

Isaiah 40:13 speaks of Jehovah in words like those Paul here used of Christ. "This is another passage significant for Paul's view of Christ. The passage in Isaiah refers to the *mind of Jehovah*, but Paul moved easily to the *mind of Christ*."[43] By this Paul made the mind of Christ to be equivalent to the mind of Jehovah, thus attesting the deity of our Lord.

The Mind of Christ

Precisely what is it to have the mind of Christ? There are a number of expressions in the NT which clearly have reference to the same condition: Being "in God," God's being "in us," our being "in Christ," Christ's being "in us," the Holy Spirit's being "in us," our being "in the Holy Spirit," or our having the word of Christ dwell "in us," and our having the mind of Christ "in us," as here and in Philippians 2:5, are all references to the saved condition, not to eight different conditions.

There is a distinction, however, between the Christians of all ages having the mind of Christ and the fact of Paul and the other inspired teachers of the NT era having the mind of Christ as affirmed in this verse. It is a matter of degree; and they had plenary power to preach God's word to mankind.

---

[41]Donald S. Metz, *op. cit.*, p. 328.
[42]David Lipscomb, *op. cit.*, p. 62.
[43]Leon Morris, *op. cit.*, p. 62.

"The whole trend and meaning of the chapter is that none could know or teach the word of God by human wisdom."[44] Today, all men are dependent for a knowledge of the will of God upon the revelation made by God's Spirit through the apostles and inspired teachers of that era. "No man ever had any greater right than Paul to say, 'We have the mind of Christ.' "[45]

---

[44]David Lipscomb, *op. cit.*, p. 45.
[45]John Wesley, *op. cit.*, in loco.

CHAPTER 3

This chapter falls logically into two divisions having reference to fellow-laborers in God's field (1-9a), and to fellow-workers in God's building (9b-17), with a short summary and recapitulation of the apostle's argument in the epistle to this point (18-23).

THE FIELD

The unspiritual, worldly conduct of the Corinthians, glorying in various parties, was the occasion for Paul's introduction of the metaphor of farm workers, such a comparison no doubt coming to the recipients of this letter as somewhat of a shock.

Verse 1, *And I, brethren, could not speak unto you as spiritual, but as unto carnal, as unto babes in Christ.*

"Brethren . . ." Tempering the stern things he was about to say, Paul began with this word of loving affection.

"Spiritual . . . carnal. " There is little profit in seeking out the technical denotation of the Greek words from which these terms are translated, because Paul himself explained exactly what he meant. The *spiritual* were those who, after conversion, had continued to grow in the grace and knowledge of the Lord, no longer continuing as "babes in Christ." The *carnal* were those who were continuing to live like the unconverted, full of envy, jealousy and strife.

The background of Paul's words here was probably the allegation of false apostles (2 Cor. 11:12-15), or teachers, who had made the simplicity of Paul's teaching (when the Corinthians were converted) an excuse to "criticize him as a shallow teacher,"[1] insinuating that Paul was deficient, as compared with themselves. This verse is thus a refutation of the false teachers. Paul flatly told the Corinthians that their immature

---

[1]J. W. McGarvey, *Commentary on First Corinthians* (Cincinnati: Standard Publishing Company, 1916), p. 62.

spiritual condition rendered them incapable of receiving any more advanced instruction than he had provided.

It appears that some of the Corinthians had been impressed by the pretentious claims of false teachers; but Paul in this chapter affirmed that "Their philosophical pretense was a sign of their spiritual infancy, produced faction, tended to destroy the church (17), and resulted in no permanent value (12-15)."[2] Speaking of such a false teacher, Macknight said, "He had represented Paul as either ignorant or unfaithful, and boasted concerning himself that he had given them complete instruction."[3]

"Babes in Christ . . ." It is evident from the next verse that Paul did not blame them for being immature at the time of their conversion; nevertheless this expression, as used by Paul, "was deprecatory."[4] See Hebrews 5:11ff and 6:1,1.

Verse 2, *I fed you with milk, not with meat; for ye were not able to bear it: nay, not even now are ye able.*

"Milk . . . meat . . ." Hebrews 5:11-14 and 1 Peter 2:2 employ this metaphor and explain it. The milk is the first principles (Heb. 6:1, 2); meat is more advanced learning. "It is the symbol of preaching in which it is possible to unfold the full richness and magnificence of the gospel."[5]

"Not even now are ye able . . ." is written as censure. "This describes a condition wholly inexcusable; by now they should have grown up."[6] It is expected of young Christians that they should be weak "as babes," this having been true of the Twelve themselves, of whom Jesus said, "I have yet many things to say unto you, but ye cannot bear them now" (John 16:12).

Verse 3, *For ye are yet carnal: for whereas there is among you, jealousy and strife, are ye not carnal, and do ye not walk after the manner of men?*

---

[2]Henry H. Halley, *Bible Handbook* (Grand Rapids: Zondervan Publishing Company, 1927), p. 545.

[3]James Macknight, *Apostolical Epistles and Commentary* (Grand Rapids: Baker Book House, 1969), p. 44.

[4]T. Teignmouth Shore, *Ellicott's Commentary on the Whole Bible* (Grand Rapids: Zondervan Publishing House, 1959), p.295.

[5]F. W. Grosheide, *The New International Commentary* (Grand Rapids: Wm. B. Eerdmans Publishing Company, 1953), p. 71.

[6]Paul W. Marsh, *A New Commentary* (Grand Rapids: Zondervan Publishing Company, 1969), p. 380.

"Carnal . . ." Paul by this word did not deny that the Corinthians were Christians; they were still "brethren"; but their lives were marred by serious failures. Russell declared that Paul used this word,

> Not in the modern meaning of "sensual," but as meaning earthly secular, worldly, having the worldly spirit of partisan strife, like (some) politicians rather than Christian disciples.[7]

"Jealousy and strife . . ." These call to mind Paul's list of the works of the flesh (Gal. 5:19-21); and "Where these exist, the flesh rules. Had they been spiritual, they would have looked to Christ and would not have been partisans of men."[8]

"After the manner of men . . ." means "like ordinary, unconverted men."

Verses 4-5, *For when one saith, I am of Paul; and another, I am of Apollos; are ye not men? What then is Apollos? and what is Paul? Ministers through whom ye believed; and each as the Lord gave to him.*

"I am of Paul . . ." It is incorrect to suppose that either Paul or Apollos encouraged or approved any such divisions, nor is there the slightest hint that any rivalry existed between them. "Paul always spoke of Apollos with the highest esteem and affection."[9]

"What then is Apollos . . . Paul . . ." Certainly, such persons even as Paul and Apollos are nothing worthy of receiving any adoration and glory from men who have been redeemed by the blood of Christ. Significantly, it appears here that Paul and Apollos were instruments only, and not, in any sense, the source of divine grace. The second word is not that the Corinthians believed "in" Paul and Apollos, but "through" them.

"Ministers . . ." Although Paul was the grandest apostle of the New Covenant, he nevertheless refers to himself here with

---

[7]John William Russell, *Compact Commentary on the NT* (Grand Rapids: Baker Book House, 1964), p. 407.

[8]David Lipscomb, *Commentary on First Corinthians* (Nashville: The Gospel Advocate Company, 1935), p. 47.

[9]*Ibid.*

a title which, as variously translated in the NT, means "servant," "minister," or "deacon." Paul would countenance no party, not even one that proposed to honor him as a man.

"And each as the Lord gave to him . . ." Any benefit that had come to the Christians at Corinth originated not with the instruments through whom it was conveyed, but with the Lord of glory.

Following up on the humility that should pertain to all mortal servants of God, Paul climaxed his argument with an analogy in which he and Apollos were represented merely as laborers working on a farm belonging to another.

Verses 6-8, *I planted, Apollos watered; but God gave the increase. So then neither is he that planteth anything, neither he that watereth; but God that giveth the increase. Now he that planteth and he that watereth are one: but each shall receive his own reward, according to his own labor.*

The location depicted here is fully identified later as "God's field" (9). The thought is that Paul planted the crop; Apollos cultivated and watered it. There is no reference to baptism in "watered."

"Are one . . ." They were one in mutual love and respect for each other, one in purpose, one in status as God's servants, and one in their reliance upon the Lord who would reward both.

"According to his own labor . . ." reveals that the gospel preacher's reward will be measured according to his work, and not according to his success. The injunction of God is not that men shall go and "convert" all nations, but that they shall "preach the gospel to the whole creation."

Verse 9, *For we are God's fellow workers: ye are God's husbandry, God's building.*

"God's fellow-workers . . ." is ambiguous, and may refer either to men who cooperate with God, or to men who cooperate with each other in God's service."[10] Despite the fact of there being a sense in which Christians are God's partners at the present time, and that this partnership shall be expanded at

---

[10]F. W. Grosheide, *op. cit.*, p. 82.

the judgment (Matt. 25:23), it is hard to believe that Paul was stressing such a thought here. Marsh said that the Greek text favors the idea of partnership with God, and that the context indicates the other meaning.[11] Since the oneness of Paul and Apollos had just been mentioned, it is natural to assume that the meaning here is "fellow-servants" under God. It would not have suited Paul's purpose to announce himself as "God's partner." However, the higher meaning of this expression, "occurring only here in the NT,"[12] may not be denied. The Greek text has: "God's fellow-workers; God's husbandry; God's building."

"Ye are God's husbandry . . ." In the analogy, the Corinthian congregation was the vineyard, or field, where Apollos and Paul had been fellow-workers. Shore thought that this word "husbandry," which is translated from a Greek word *Georgion*, "might have been the cause of the Christian name 'George' becoming so popular in the church."[13]

Paul dramatically shifted to another metaphor in the same line, that of God's building, house, or temple.

"God's building . . ." Practically all of the next eight verses have reference to the church as the temple of God. For extended remarks on the church as the true temple, see under Acts 7:47-50 in this series of commentaries (CA, pp. 142-144). See also under verse 16, below.

Verse 10, *According to the grace of God which was given unto me, as a wise masterbuilder I laid a foundation; and another buildeth thereon. But let each man take heed how he buildeth thereon.*

"A foundation . . ." The foundation which Paul laid at Corinth is Jesus Christ (v. 11), and this was done through the faithful proclamation of the whole gospel of our Lord.

"Another buildeth thereon . . ." Although Farrar believed that "the allusion here may be to Apollos,"[14] it may be that

---

[11]Paul W. Marsh, *op. cit.*, p. 381.
[12]*Ibid*
[13]T. Teignmouth Shore, *op. cit.*, p. 296.
[14]F. W. Farrar, *Pulpit Commentary* (Grand Rapids: Wm. B. Eerdmans Publishing Company, 1950), p. 94.

Paul, in this new metaphor, considered that both Apollos and himself had laid the foundation in the preaching of Christ, a work which had also been shared by all of the apostles and inspired teachers. The entire apostolical community could do little more than lay the foundation (of Christ); and Christians themselves were expected to continue the building of God's true temple, the church. As Grosheide said:

> They leave the work of building to the congregation itself. The Corinthians were actually engaged in building, but in a way the apostle felt obliged to condemn. Paul was not content with what the Corinthians had done themselves.[15]

The words *another* and *each man* are too indefinite to apply to Apollos, having rather an application to all who labor in God's building.

Verse 11, *For other foundation can no man lay than that which is laid, which is Jesus Christ.*

In Matthew 16:15, Jesus declared that his church would be built upon the rock, and here is revealed what the rock is; it is Christ. "Paul said that Christ is the only foundation that can be laid."[16] No man may begin anywhere else. "This is still worthy of emphasis in a day when so many build their 'Christianity' without Christ, on a foundation of good works, humanism or science."[17] Of course, this is not the only metaphor of Christ's preeminence in his kingdom. He is also called the door of the sheepfold (John 10:7), the chief corner stone (Eph. 2:20), the head of the body (Eph. 1:22, 23), etc.

Verse 12, *But if any man buildeth on the foundation gold, silver, costly stones, wood, hay, stubble.*

Two widely held misconceptions are grounded on this verse, which is understood (1) as "applicable primarily, if not exclusively to teachers,"[18] and (2) as applying to *doctrines* of two classes, (a) gold, etc., and (b) wood, etc. It is evident, of

---

[15]F. W. Grosheide, *op. cit.*, p. 74.
[16]David Lipscomb, *op. cit.*, p. 51.
[17]Leon Morris, *Tyndale Commentary* (Grand Rapids: Wm. B. Eerdmans Publishing Company, 1958), p. 67.
[18]John Wesley, *One Volume NT Commentary* (Grand Rapids:. Baker Book House, 1972), in loco.

course, that the six kinds of building materials are of two classes: (1) the valuable and permanent and (2) the cheap and destructible; but the conviction of this writer is that the two kinds of people built into God's temple, the church, constitute the reality indicated here.

If these words had been directed primarily to Christian teachers, it seems inconceivable that Paul would have used the words "each man" and "any man" no less than six times in verses 10-15. Ministers as a class of persons different from the rank and file of Christians were not a feature of the churches of that era, every Christian being a builder in God's temple; and such is indicated by these words.

Regarding the view that the six classes of materials are various doctrines used in building God's temple, a view advocated by an unbelievably large number of scholars, was nevertheless refuted by Macknight thus:

> As the apostle is speaking of the Christian church, consisting of the believers of all nations, of which church Christ is the foundation, it is evident that the materials built on this foundation (gold, silver, etc.) cannot represent the doctrines, but the disciples of Christ . . . In no passage of scripture is the temple or church of God said to consist of doctrines, but of the disciples of Christ, who are called living stones built up of a spiritual house or temple (1 Peter 2:5,6).[19]

In addition to the views of Macknight cited here, there is also the consideration that all of the true doctrine of Christianity is comprehensively included in Christ himself, that the totality of his doctrine *is* the foundation, and that there remain no more doctrines of gold, silver, hay or stubble that are to be built into God's church by men. The two classes of materials must refer, therefore, to the two kinds of people built into God's temple (the church) by the advocates of Christianity, whether by ministers and teachers, or by the so-called laity. As for seeing only two classes in these six kinds of materials, McGarvey observed that:

---

[19]James Macknight, *Apostolical Epistles and Commentary* (Grand Rapids: Baker Book House, 1969), p. 52.

> The first three kinds were found in their fireproof temples, materials worthy of sacred structures; and the latter three were used in their frail, combustible huts, but which were in no way dedicated to divinity.[20]

McGarvey made the application of this verse as follows:

> The church should be built of true Christians, the proper material; and not of worldly-minded hypocrites, or of those who estimate the oracles of God as on a par with the philosophies of men. The day of judgment will reveal the true character of all who are in the church.[21]

Verse 13, *Each man's work shall be made manifest: for the day shall declare it, because it is revealed in fire; and the fire itself shall prove each man's work of what sort it is.*

"The day . . ." according to McGarvey, and many others, is a reference to the judgment day when Jesus shall be revealed from heaven "in flaming fire" (2 Thess. 1:7); but some have understood it as a day of terrible persecutions such as the "fiery trial" (1 Peter 4:12) prophetically mentioned by both Paul and Peter. Despite the fact of there being an element of testing in times of great persecution, agreement is felt with Morris who declared: "*The day* is clearly the day when Christ returns, the day of judgment."[22]

Only the judgment day will reveal what is and what is not a part of the true temple of God; and, according to Christ himself, it will be a time of many surprises (Matt. 7:15-23; 25:34-46).

Verses 14-15, *If any man's work shall abide which he built thereon, he shall receive a reward. If any man's work shall be burned, he shall suffer loss: but he himself shall be saved, yet so as through fire.*

The fact that men do not fully understand this passage is implicit in the truth that some have built up the theory of purgatory, based partly on what is stated here. The whole concept of purgatory is foreign to the word of God, but the advocates of it are still deriving immense revenues through the preaching of it. Again from Macknight:

---

[20]J W McGarvey, *op. cit.*, p. 64.
[21]*Ibid.*
[22]Leon Morris, *op. cit.*, p. 68.

> The Romish clergy, seeing that this doctrine properly managed, might be made an inexhaustible source of wealth to their order, have represented this fire of purgatory as lighted up from the very beginning of the world, and have kept it burning ever since, and have assumed to themselves the power of detaining souls in that fire, and of releasing them from it; whereby they have drawn great sums of money from the ignorant and superstitious.[23]

This writer is grieved to know that even now there are some, who were once baptized into Christ and served as elders of God's church, whose children are paying to get them prayed out of purgatory!

What this verse actually means is that the persons led to Christ through the efforts of any Christian may defect from the faith, proving themselves wood, hay or stubble, and that the loss of such souls will not affect the salvation of a Christian teacher, whose reward would in some manner unknown to us have been far greater if they had not defected, and whose salvation "so as through fire" is understood by such language to be only by the narrowest margin, "by the skin of his teeth" (Job 19:20).

"Yet so as through fire . . . has the meaning of "something resembling" an escape from fire, as in "snatching them out of the fire" (Jude 23); and it is certain that this phrase has absolutely nothing in it of actual fire. It is a figure of speech, prompted possibly by Paul's reference to the judgment and the fire of that day, but not to be identified as the same thing.

The doctrine of purgatory is not merely unscriptural and anti-scriptural, there being not one word in the entire scriptures to support such a monstrous thesis; but it is effectively refuted in a single question: "If any church believes in such a thing, and in their own power, through prayer, to deliver men from it; why do they not pray all men out of it immediately for sweet charity's sake?"

Verse 16, *Know ye not that ye are a temple of God, and that the Spirit of God dwelleth in you?*

---

[23]James Macknight, *op. cit.*, p. 53.

The words of this text are sometimes applied to individuals; but, as Morris said, "The reference here is to the church."[24] There is no article before *temple* in the Greek; and it would be more accurately translated, "Ye are the temple of God."[25] "The building of which the apostle speaks is the Christian church, called in this verse The Temple of God."[26]

THE CHURCH THE TEMPLE OF GOD

Of all the beautiful metaphors of God's church such as the bride of Christ, the vineyard of the Lord, the household of God, the pillar and ground of the truth, the spiritual body of Christ, and the flock of Christ, none is more beautiful or intriguing than "The Temple of God."

The first suggestion ever made regarding a temple for the one true God was made by David, whose conscience was stricken with the thought of his own house of cedar compared with the humble tent-shrine which housed the ark of the covenant. Nathan the prophet, however, explained to David that God had never once expressed any desire to have such a house (temple), stating emphatically that after David's death, David's son would build God a house, that his kingdom would be established for ever in the person of that "seed" (which was Christ, of course). See 2 Samuel 7:1-13. Concerning the Greater Son of David, who is Christ, it was prophesied that he would build a house (temple) for God's name and that his throne would be established for ever. From the remarkable teachings in this passage from Samuel it is absolutely clear that God never intended that a physical temple would be constructed in Jerusalem. The departure of Israel from God's word in 2 Samuel 7 is exactly parallel to their departure from God's word in 1 Samuel 8.

How did David react to the prophet's forbidding him in God's name to build a temple, and promising that "the Son of David" would build God's temple (a prophecy of the church)? He said, in effect, "Well, that has to be Bathsheba's boy!

---

[24]Leon Morris, *op. cit.*, p. 69.
[25]*Ibid.*
[26]James Macknight, *op. cit.*, p. 46.

Solomon will build the temple!" To be sure he did so, but there is no evidence whatever that the building of a material temple in Jerusalem was any different in the sight of God than the setting up of the earthly monarchy in the days of Samuel. God permitted both. He used both. He accommodated to the hardness of the people's heart; but that extravagant earthly temple of the Jews was only a second outcropping of the fleshly desire of Israel to be like the nations around them, which had their richly ornamented temples erected to pagan deities.

It is known that God would not permit David to build the temple because of his wickedness. He was a man of blood. But was Solomon any less wicked and bloody? His notorious debaucheries were the scandal of forty generations.

Moreover, the temple proved to be as big a stumbling block to the Jews as the secular kingdom was. Christ's first announcement to his generation included the fact that "One greater than the temple is here!" (Matt. 12:6). While Christ was on earth, the true temple was "his body" (John 2:21); and after Pentecost, the true temple has been nothing other than the spiritual body of Christ. This was the element of Stephen's speech that so infuriated the religious partisans in Jerusalem that they mobbed him. See under verse 9, above.

Therefore, Paul's designation of the body of Christ in this passage as the temple of God is of the utmost significance. Paul himself had, with difficulty, come to understand this. As soon as he was converted, he went straight to that old secular temple; and God told him to get out of the place, even out of the city (Acts 22:17-21); and Paul, even after that, returned to the temple where he was mobbed; and in the behavior of the temple partisans (including the high priest), Paul finally read the will of God as it had been declared by Jesus that the temple was nothing but a "den of thieves and robbers" (Mark 11:17), that it was not God's house at all, but the house of the Jews, and that it was left unto them "desolate" (Matt. 23:38).

The above reflections are not denied by the fact of God's using the temple after the Jews constructed it against his will; he did the same thing with the secular kingdom.

The true temple of God, therefore, has never been anything else except the church of Jesus Christ our Lord. In it alone, not in some man-made shrine, men are called to worship and serve the Lord of glory. Meeting houses are not, in any sense, "true" sanctuaries.

The fact of God's Spirit dwelling in the spiritual body of Christ which is the church does not deny the residence of the Spirit of promise in the hearts of individual Christians (Acts 2:38ff; Eph. 1:13).

Verse 17, *If any man destroyeth the temple of God, him shall God destroy; fur the temple of God is holy, and such are ye.*

The conduct of the Corinthians was such that the Spirit of God would be grieved and denied of any place in their hearts, thus destroying God's true temple; and just as any defilement of the ancient tabernacle had been punishable by death, there would be fearful retribution against all who defile the church. In context, this was a terrible warning to the Corinthians, but it applies to all who ever became a part of God's church. As Grosheide declared: "It is clear that the judgment of God is meant; it may refer to suffering loss (verse 15), but also to eternal life."[27]

Summary of Preceding Admonitions

Verse 18, *Let no man deceive himself. If any man thinketh that he is wise among you in this world, let him become a fool, that he may become wise.*

Here begins the summary of what Paul had written up to here. This through verse 23 gives the highlights of what Paul had written up to this point.

Dummelow's paraphrase of this is:

> Do not deceive yourselves; but if there be any of you priding himself on his worldly wisdom, let him quickly unlearn it, that he may learn the true wisdom.[28]

Macknight gave another interesting paraphrase of the same verse:

---

[27]F. W. Grosheide, *op. cit.*, p. 89.
[28]J. R. Dummelow, *Commentary on the Holy Bible* (New York: The Macmillan Company, 1937), p. 898.

> Let no teacher deceive himself with false notions of prudence. If any teacher among you thinketh to be wise, in this age of spreading the gospel, by misrepresenting its doctrines for the purpose of making it acceptable to bad men, let him become a fool in his own eyes, by preaching the gospel sincerely, that he may be really wise.[29]

This verse is a short summary of much Paul had written in Corinthians thus far; and it has the effect of condemning intellectual pride, one of the most hurtful of human vanities. In this vivid phrase Paul urged the man who would be wise to become a fool. "This is a simple way of urging a man to be humble enough to learn."[30]

Verse 19, *For the wisdom of this world is foolishness with God. For it is written, He that taketh the wise in their craftiness.*

As Shore observed:

> With the exception of the reference in James 5:11 to the "proverbial patience" of Job, this is the only allusion to Job, or to the book of Job in the NT.[31]

Paul's quotation is from Job 5:13, where Eliphaz the Temanite was speaking against Job, declaring that "God frustrates the devices of the crafty . . . and taketh the wise in their own craftiness." Eliphaz was wrong in his application of these words to Job, but the words themselves are true. Adam Clarke gave an example of God's doing just that type of thing when:

> The pagans raised up persecution against the Church of Christ in order to destroy it; but this became the very means of quickly spreading it over the earth, and of destroying the whole pagan system. Thus the wise were taken in their own craftiness.[32]

Of course, history affords countless examples of the same thing.

Verse 20, *And again, The Lord knoweth the reasonings of the wise, that they are vain.*

---

[29]James Macknight, *op. cit.*, p. 55.

[30]William Barclay, *The Letters to the Corinthians* (Philadelphia: The Westminster Press, 1954), p. 39.

[31]T. Teignmouth Shore, *op. cit.*, p. 297.

[32]Adam Clark, *Commentary on the Whole Bible* (New York: Carlton & Porter, 1831), Vol. VI, p. 206.

This quotation is from Psalm 94:11. The teaching is not merely that "Human thought is fruitless in the sense of not producing anything of spiritual value that redeems man from sin,"[33] but that it is likewise ineffectual in devising any worthwhile solutions of the secular, political, economic and social problems which plague the entire world.

Verse 21, *Wherefore, let no one glory in men. For all things are yours.*

The brief summary concludes with the first clause here, except for the beautiful doxology. As Grosheide said, "Paul is here recapitulating all he has said before. The Corinthians named themselves after men; and those who do that love the wisdom of the world."[34]

Therefore, this verse makes it crystal clear what Paul condemned in 1:12. It was the sin of their calling themselves after the names of men; and, as the name Christ is not that of a man in the sense of the words use here, there cannot be the slightest condemnation upon those who said they were "of Christ." This same truth is evident in the next verse also.

Verse 22, *For all things are yours; whether Paul, Apollos, or Cephas, or the world, or life, or death, or things present, or things to come; all are yours.*

This precious doxology reminds one of the famous passage in Romans 5:31-37; but this has a positive implication not in evidence there. "Things present, things to come, etc.," are there viewed as opposing the Christian but failing to thwart him; here the Christian is viewed as the possessor of everything in Christ.

This means that Christians are not to choose certain things, such as certain teachers; for all things are theirs. A Christian is in fact a member of no sect or party, because he has entered "into the possession of a fellowship and love which are as wide as the universe."[35]

---

[33]Donald S. Metz, *Beacon Bible Commentary* (Kansas City: Beacon Hill Press, 1968), p. 337.
[34]F. W. Grosheide, *op. cit.*, p. 93.
[35]William Barclay, *op. cit.*, p. 40.

"Paul, Apollos, or Cephas . . ." Conspicuous by its absence is the so-called "Christ party" in this list, proving that the words "And I am of Christ," spoken in 1:12, are the words of the apostle Paul himself, and not the slogan of any kind of a sect at Corinth.

Verse 23, *And ye are Christ's; and Christ is God's.*

Of course, the Christian's possession of all things in Jesus Christ derives absolutely from the fact of who Jesus Christ is; he is God incarnate in human flesh, the eternal Word, one with the Father, who is and was and will be before all time and now and for ever.

That Christ is God's, as here stated, "in no way detracts from his deity."[36] His essential oneness and equality with God are not under discussion in this verse, "but his subordination for the sake of human redemption."[37]

---

[36]Paul W. Marsh, *op. cit.*, p. 382.
[37]*Ibid.*

CHAPTER 4

Paul had stressed the inspiration of the apostles in the previous chapter; but in the first paragraph here he pointed out that even apostolical authority was not absolute and that even he himself and Apollos were but stewards of Christ, their first concern being to please the Lord, and not to accommodate their teaching to win favor with false teachers. He stated that the lower courts of conscience and public opinion were inferior to the judgment of the Lord (1-5). We agree with Adam Clarke that a more logical division of the chapters would have been to extend chapter 3 through the fifth verse here.[1]

In verse 6, Paul pointed out that his use of his own name and that of Apollos was not to be construed as an admission that he and Apollos had actually headed any divisive parties in Corinth, but that he had used these names figuratively for the purpose of teaching against all divisions.

Most of the remainder of the chapter deals with the false teacher, without naming him, ending with a dramatic promise that he would return to Corinth, the Lord willing, and that the Lord would enable him to vanquish the false teacher and set the Corinthians once more in the right way of humility and service. He severely condemned their vain-glorious boasting, egotism and conceit (7-21).

Verse 1, *Let a man so account of us, as of ministers of Christ, and stewards of the mysteries of God.*

This refers to both Paul and Apollos, and the word "minister" here is not the same as in 3:5. "It is *hyperetes*, and originally meant an under-rower in a trireme."[2] This is very similar to a word Luke used of ministers. "The word Luke used

---

[1]Adam Clarke, *Commentary on the Whole Bible* (New York: Carlton & Porter, 1831), Vol. VI. p. 207.

[2]Paul W. Marsh, *A New Commentary* (Grand Rapids: Zondervan Publishing House, 1969), p. 382.

(1:2, 4:20) is *huperetai*, used in medical terminology to refer to doctors who served under a principal physician."[3]

"Stewards of the mysteries of God . . ." There are two extremes to be avoided in the Christian's attitude toward teachers. "We should love and respect them; but we ought not, however, to worship them or seek to form a party about them."[4] Stewards in ancient times were very important people.

> The steward was the *major domo*, in charge of the whole administration of the house or estate. He controlled the staff, issued supplies and rations and ran the whole household; but he himself was still a slave where the master was concerned.[5]

However, as will appear in the next verse, it was not so much the importance of a steward that Paul stressed; it was his faithfulness.

Verse 2, *Here, moreover, it is required in stewards, that a man be found faithful.*

Trustworthiness was the outstanding characteristic of a good steward, and it was that which Paul brought into view here. Furthermore, the proper person to pass on such a question was not to be found among the people who knew the steward or did business with him, but he was the steward's lord. The next three verses would deal with that thought.

In the NT, the term "steward" was applied to all Christians, "as good stewards of the manifold grace of God" (1 Peter 4:10), to elders of the church; "A bishop then must be blameless as God's steward" (Titus 1:7), and to apostles and preachers of the gospel in this verse. "It is important that those entrusted with the truth of God as stewards should be faithful and honest."[6] A failure to teach men God's truth leaves the blood of the lost on the hands of unfaithful stewards who neglected or refused to teach it.

---

[3]Herschel H. Hobbs, *An Exposition of the Gospel of Luke* (Grand Rapids: Baker Book House, 1966), p. 19.

[4]George W. DeHoff, *Sermons on First Corinthians* (Murfreesboro, Tenn.: The Christian Press, 1947), p. 41.

[5]William Barclay, *The Letters to the Corinthians* (Philadelphia:. The Westminster Press, 1954), p. 41.

[6]David Lipscomb, *Commentary on First Corinthians* (Nashville: The Gospel Advocate Company, 1935), p. 59.

Verses 3-4, *But with me it is a very small thing that I should be judged of you, or of man's judgment; yea, I judge not mine own self. For I know nothing against myself; yet am I hereby not justified: but he that judgeth me is the Lord.*

In this and the following verse, Paul considers the three tribunals of judgment, these being (1) conscience, (2) the court of public opinion, and (3) the Lord the righteous judge of all men. The supremacy of that court of last resort is dramatically affirmed.

The implication of Paul's words here as directed toward the false teacher is as follows:

> If I do not regard my own opinion of myself as of high value, 1 cannot be suspected of undervaluing you when I say that I do not much regard your opinion. If I do not estimate highly my own opinion of myself, then it is not to be expected that I should set a high value on the opinions of others.[7]

Farrar's paraphrase of the thought is:

> The verdict of my own conscience acquits me of all unfaithfulness; but this is insufficient, because God sees with clearer eyes than ours. Who can understand his errors? (Ps. 19:12).[8]

Regarding the lower and higher courts which come into view in this passage, the following is submitted:

LOWER AND HIGHER COURTS

I. The court of public opinion. Later on in this epistle, Paul indicated that, despite its inferiority, the court of public opinion is of some importance and not to be ignored by Christians. These Corinthians were bringing the whole Christian movement into disgrace by their ecstatic tongue-speaking; and Paul wrote: "If therefore the whole church be come together in one place, and all speak with tongues . . . will they not say that ye are mad?" (14:23). Timothy was instructed to

---

[7]Albert Barnes, *Notes on the NT* (Grand Rapids: Baker Book House, 1949), 1 Cor., p. 69.

[8]F. W. Farrar, *Pulpit Commentary* (Grand Rapids: Wm. B. Eerdmans Publishing Company, 1950), Vol. 19, p. 132.

have regard to this court through the requirement that any man appointed as a bishop should have a good report from "them that are without" (1 Tim. 3:7). The sacred evangelist Luke stressed that Jesus himself advanced in favor with men (Luke 2:52), and that the believers in Jerusalem had "favor with all the people" (Acts 2:47).

Nevertheless, desirable as a favorable public opinion undoubtedly is, it should always be courted within the strictest limits of absolute fidelity to the Lord Jesus Christ. Public opinion is a lower court, not a higher one.

Paul said, "I for my part care very little about being examined by you or by any human court." All men should have this attitude where any question of faithfulness to the Lord is involved; and what a pity it is that there are some like the wretched parents of the man born blind (John 9) who would not even acknowledge the Lord of glory out of deference to the wicked Pharisees.

Vox populi vox Dei (The voice of the people is the voice of God) is a suitable motto in politics, but not in holy religion. The voice of the people is frequently the voice of Satan, as when the people cried, "Make us gods to go before us" (Acts 7:40), or when the people prepared to offer sacrifice to Paul and Barnabas (Acts 14:11). God pity the poor soul which pauses on the threshold of any clear duty and asks, "Will this be popular?"

II. The voice of conscience. This is a higher court than that of public opinion, but not the highest court. It is exceedingly important that men respect it, for "If our heart condemn us, God is greater than our hearts" (1 John 3:20). Paul always respected and honored the court of conscience (Acts 23:1; 24:16), being far more attentive to it than to the court of public opinion. And yet we are indebted to Paul for the information that, regardless of its value, this court is still not the final tribunal. He said, While my conscience does not trouble me at all, that does not prove that I am innocent."[9]

---

[9]Edgar J. Goodspeed, *The New Testament, An American Translation* (Chicago: The University of Illinois Press, 1923), p. 318.

The great difficulty with conscience is that it is much like a watch, the value of which (as a timepiece) is determined by the accuracy of its synchronization with the correct time, determined not by the watch, but by the movement of the sun over a certain meridian. Just so, a man's conscience must be monitored and adjusted to be in perfect harmony with the will of God before it can be of much value.

Like a watch, conscience can have many things wrong with it. It can be evil (Heb. 10:22), seared (1 Tim. 4:2), defiled (Titus 1:15), ignorant (1 Tim. 1:13), choked with dead works (Heb. 9:14), etc. Is there any wonder then, that it was a proverb millenniums ago that said "He that trusteth in his own heart is a fool" (Prov. 28:6)?

III. The highest court of all. This is the great assize at the Last Advent of Jesus Christ, when the dead, small and great, as well as all who are then alive, shall be summoned before the Great White Throne for the final judgment. None shall escape the judgment and sentence of this court (2 Cor. 5:10); it shall be presided over by Jesus Christ our Lord (Acts 10:42). Then shall be exposed the secrets of men's hearts (Rom. 2:16). The court crier, an angel of light, shall stand with one foot on the land and one on the sea, and blow the trumpet that shall herald the gathering of the myriads of earth to the final judgment before the King of kings and Lord of lords. How infinitely blessed shall be those who are able to stand before that tribunal of righteousness and truth!

"I judge not mine own self . . ." In 11:31, Paul said, "If we judged ourselves truly, we should not be judged"; but "two different words are used. There the apostle is emphasizing the necessity of self-examination";[10] but in this statement, he is saying:

> "I myself am not competent to assess the quality of my apostolic service and pronounce a verdict on it; only One can do that; and I shall submit myself to his decision: "It is the Lord who judges me."[11]

---

[10]F. F. Bruce, *Answers to Questions* (Grand Rapids: Zondervan Publishing House, 1972), p. 90.

[11]*Ibid.*

Verse 5, *Wherefore judge nothing before the time, until the Lord come, who will bring to light the hidden things of darkness, and make manifest the counsels of the hearts; and then shall each man have his praise from God.*

It is a mistake to read into such passages as this and in 15:51 that "Paul evidently expected the Advent of Christ within the lifetime of himself and his converts."[12] Since the time of the Second Advent was unknown by all of the apostolical preachers, and not even known by the Lord himself as a man (Matt. 24:36), it was altogether proper that the certainty of that event (whenever it was to come) was a legitimate basis of appeal and motivation for Christians of *every* generation, including the first. It is a positive certainty that both Christ and his apostles taught that the Second Coming was an event to be expected at a very remote time in the future, although not impossible at *any time*. See CL, pp. 456-457. Paul's great prophecy of the apostasy (2 Thess. 2:1, 2) makes it certain that he did not expect the coming of Christ in his own lifetime; and the apostle John devoted the last chapter of his gospel to shooting down the proposition that Jesus had promised to come in John's lifetime (21:23).

The import of this verse, according to Morris, is "Stop judging!"[13] This injunction is necessary because (1) the only judgment that matters will be announced by the Lord at the final judgment and, besides that, (2) men do not have sufficient information or competence to judge one another, not even themselves.

"Each man shall have his praise from God . . ." Shore's perceptive comment on this is: "God, unlike man who selects only some one for praise, will give to every worker his own share of approval."[14] Moreover, it must not be supposed that no blame will be assigned in the judgment, for "The word rendered *praise* denotes in this place reward,"[15] indicating that

---

[12]J. R. Dummelow, *Commentary on the Holy Bible* (New York: The Macmillan Company, 1937), p. 898.

[13]Leon Morris, *Tyndale Commentary* (Grand Rapids: Wm. B. Eerdmans Publishing Company, 1958), p. 76.

[14]T. Teignmouth Shore, *Ellicott's Commentary on the Whole Bible* (Grand Rapids: Zondervan Publishing House), p. 298.

[15]Albert Barnes, *op.cit.*, p. 71.

God will reward every man according to his works "whether good or bad" (2 Cor. 5:10). Some misunderstand this place as teaching universal salvation, as Johnson for example, "Wonder of wonders—every man (believer) shall have some praise from God!"[16] Regarding Paul's probable reason for stressing praise rather than blame in this verse, Farrar noted that:

> He was thinking of faithful teachers like Cephas, Apollos and himself, who were depreciated by rival factions; and like all the apostles, he had an invariable tendency to allude to the bright side, rather than the dark side of judgment.[17]

"The hidden things . . ." and "counsels, of the hearts . . ." show "how much that is needful for a correct estimate of men's conduct lies now under an impenetrable veil."[18]

The background of Paul's teaching in these profound lines was a sordid condition among the community of Corinthian believers.

> There must have been a very considerable group of church leaders, Paul's own converts, who, in Paul's absence, had become influential and self-important, and were trying to run away with the church. They had become haughty, overbearing, and boastful in their attitude toward Paul.[19]

Verse 6, *Now these things, brethren, I have in a figure transferred to myself and Apollos for your sakes; that in us ye might learn not to go beyond the things which were written; that no one of you be puffed up for the one against the other.*

The first clause here was spoken by way of anticipating and refuting any notion that Paul had conceded (in his use of the names of himself and Apollos) any approval of factions, the allegation here being that Paul had used these names as a figure of what was going on, the real culprits being, not himself or Apollos, but the factious leaders in Corinth.

---

[16]S. Lewis Johnson, Jr., *Wycliffe Bible Commentary* (Chicago: Moody Press, 1971), p.599.

[17]F. W. Farrar, *op. cit.*, p. 133.

[18]John Wesley, *One Volume NT Commentary* (Grand Rapids: Baker Book House, 1972, in loco.

[19]Henry H. Halley, *Bible Handbook* (Grand Rapids: Zondervan Publishing House, 1927), P. 545.

"That ye might learn not to go beyond the things which are written . . ." The traditional use of this clause as a commandment that Christians should order their lives and their service of God by the holy scriptures, and that it is prohibited that they should go beyond the word of God is without any doubt whatever the true interpretation. Farrar said that "This text, like so many others, has only a very remote connection with the sense in which it is usually quoted";[20] but like all such denials, it is unsupported by any logical evidence. There is no other valid meaning of this passage except that traditionally assigned to it.

"Not to go beyond what is written . . ." is in the Greek literally, "Not beyond what is written."[21] "These words must be a sort of quotation, or in any case a standing expression,"[22] associated with the preaching of Paul and all the apostles. It has the effect of a universal proverb among Christians, "well known to the Corinthians, so that Paul could assume the words to be clear."[23] Russell declared the meaning to be: "The things which are written . . . no special text, but the teaching of the Scriptures as a whole, which no leader, however gifted, may supersede."[24] "This was a catch-cry familiar to Paul and his readers directing attention to the need for conformity to scripture."[25] There is no need to multiply scholarly support of the usual view of this place; no other explanation is tenable.

And, of course, it was precisely in this matter of going beyond the word of God that the factions in Corinth had developed. They were evaluating the word and authority of men upon a parity with the holy scriptures, thinking of men more highly than they should, and spurning the meekness and humility taught throughout the Bible. Thus, as Grosheide said, "The whole question of factions was raised to a higher level,"[26] namely that of violating the scriptural rule of faith for

---

[20]F W. Farrar, *op. cit.*, p. 134.
[21]Paul W. Marsh, *op. cit.*, p. 382.
[22]F. W. Grosheide, *The New International Commentary* (Grand Rapids: Wm. B. Eerdmans Publishing Company, 1953), p. 103.
[23]*Ibid.*
[24]John William Russell, *Compact Commentary on the NT* (Grand Rapids: Baker Book House, 1964), p. 408.
[25]Leon Morris, *op. cit.*, p. 78.
[26]F W. Grosheide, *op. cit.*, p. 103.

the believer. "It is not his own words that Paul insists that the Corinthians must not go beyond; it is the word of God."[27]

"Puffed up for the one against the other . . ." An interesting phase of this rebuke is that instead of puffing up their favorite teachers, it was themselves which had become puffed up! This is a sure result of "blowing up" any man.

Verse 7, *For who maketh thee to differ? and what hast thou that thou didst not receive? but if thou didst receive it, why dost thou glory as if thou hadst not received it?*

It is God who gives to every man life, talent, ability, opportunity, health, personality, strength—everything that he is or has; and what kind of conceit blinds the eyes of men who behave as if this were not so?

Verse 8, *Already are ye filled, already ye are become rich, ye have come to reign without us: yea, and I would that ye did reign, that we also might reign with you.*

The first three clauses are directed against the false teachers, who had promoted themselves in the eyes of their admirers, were receiving honors and emoluments from them, and affecting all the airs of "big men," not merely in the church, but in the whole city. The three pungent clauses are spoken in irony and disapproval, the true state of such imposters being far different from what they imagined.

"I would that ye did reign . . ." has the equivalent meaning of "Oh, if it were only true, what you think of yourselves because if it were true, together we could go on building up the temple of God."

Verse 9, *For, I think, God hath set forth us apostles last of all, as men doomed to death: for we are made a spectacle unto the world, both to angels and men.*

Beginning with verse 7, the remainder of this chapter is devoted to the rebuke of the false teachers and exposure of their sins of worldliness, vanity, conceit, vain glory and division. At the very moment of their sporting all those prideful airs of popularity and success, Paul in this verse

---

[27]William Barclay, *op. cit.*, p. 43.

reminds them how it is with the *genuine* teachers of the true faith, the holy apostles.

The imagery here is that of the Roman Coliseum. "Paul pictures himself and fellow apostles as 'the last and most worthless band' brought forth to die in the great arena, where the whole world, including men and angels, view the spectacle."[28]

We are not informed in scripture of the exact manner in which angels are concerned with earth life; but the fact is plainly stated. See CH, p. 35. There is a similar scene suggested by Hebrews 12:1.

Verse 10, *We are fools for Christ's sake, but ye are wise in Christ; we are weak, but ye are strong; ye have glory, but we have dishonor.*

The power of these words derives from the truth that Paul was himself the founder of the church in Corinth. He had rescued them from the temples of vice and debauchery, preached to them the unsearchable riches of Christ, nurtured them in their weakness and immaturity as Christians, and suffered and toiled among them, even working in order to eat bread; and now, at the first visible signs of material prosperity among them, they openly despised their teacher, heaped unto themselves popular, shallow leaders after their own lusts, and were indulging the most amazing boastfulness and conceit. It was truly a disgusting development; and Paul's words here exposed the moral ugliness of their behavior.

"Fools . . ." means "fools in the eyes of the world."

"We . . . yet, etc . . ." contrasts Paul with the Corinthians in terms of their own egotistical reversal of the true values. Forsaking the true values and methods as taught by the apostles, those at Corinth had discovered a way of preaching "so as to procure a name of wisdom, reputation and profundity."[29] To discover such a way and then to walk in it has been a temptation to every preacher of the word of God who ever lived.

---

[28]T. Teignmouth Shore, *op. cit.*, p. 299.
[29]David Lipscomb, *op. cit.*, p. 65.

Verse 11, *Even unto this present hour we both hunger, and thirst, and are naked, and are buffeted, and have no certain dwelling place.*

All of these terms refer to genuine, bitter hardships, involving insufficient food and clothing, beatings and chastisements by enemies of the truth, and that lonely itinerancy which was the invariable mark of apostolic preachers. The false teachers in Corinth suffered none of these injuries or discomforts.

Verse 12, *And we toil, working with our own hands: being reviled, we bless; being persecuted, we endure.*

"And we toil . . ." "The Greeks despised all manual labor, regarding it as the duty of slaves or people mentally unfit for anything else."[30] Paul was a tent-maker by trade and frequently worked in order to support himself.

"Reviled . . . persecuted . . ." Instead of retaliating in kind, Paul returned good for evil, blessing for reviling, and patient endurance for persecution.

Verse 13, *Being defamed, we entreat: we are made as the filth of the world, the offscouring of all things, even until now.*

The imagery here is still that of the Coliseum, where, after the bloody games were over, the grounds-keepers cleaned the theater by the removal of the bloody corpses, the offal and the debris. Paul, in this remarkably blunt, shocking paragraph, merely stated the true facts with a view to bringing the giddy and irresponsible Corinthians to their senses.

Verse 14, *I write not these things to shame you, but to admonish you as my dear children.*

What a wealth of abused and suffering love lies in such a tender appeal as this! Not a word of blame, in the sense of recrimination not a trace of bitterness, just the appeal of a loving father for his wayward children. The great thrust of this whole argument was accurately seen by Morris "as an emphasis on the contradiction between the values of true

---

[30]Donald S. Metz, *Beacon Bible Commentary* (Kansas City: Beacon Hill Press, 1968), p. 343.

Christians, and those of the worldly-wise Greeks."[31] The Corinthians had simply become mixed up regarding what were true values and what were not. The word from which "admonish" is translated in this place is the root of the cognate noun "admonition" (Eph. 4:4), where "It is used of the duty of a father to his children."[32] Thus the metaphor of his being the father of the Corinthians was already in Paul's mind.

Verse 15, *For though ye have ten thousand tutors in Christ, yet have ye not many fathers; for in Christ Jesus I begat you through the gospel.*

"Ten thousand tutors . . ." An element of humor is in this, for certainly that many tutors is too many; and if the word is rendered "guides," as by some, it would still be far too many. Just how many guides could one follow, anyway? As McGarvey said, "The large number rebukes their itch for teachers."[33] The meaning both of "tutor" and of "guide" derives from the Greek word here, *paidagogos*, "who was a slave who escorted his master's child to school."[34] Of course, such an attendant might form a strong attachment for a child, but his love would never approach that of a father.

"I begat you through the gospel . . ." This is used loosely in a metaphorical sense; because in the highest sense, men are begotten only by the gospel. As Farrar put it: "We are begotten only by the will of God, by that word of truth (James 1:18), to which Paul alludes here in the words 'through the gospel.'"[35]

Verse 16, *I beseech you therefore, be ye imitators of me.*

Paul never meant this in any absolute sense but in the sense of "Be ye imitators of me, even as I also am of Christ" (11:1). See also Ephesians 5:1, Philippians 3:17, 2 Thessalonians 3:9 and 1 Thessalonians 1:6.

Verse 17, *"For this cause have I sent unto you Timothy, who is my beloved and faithful child in the Lord, who shall put you*

---

[31]Leon Morris, *op. cit.*, p. 82.
[32]*Ibid.*, p. 83.
[33]J. W. McGarvey, *Commentary on First Corinthians* (Cincinnati: Standard Publishing Company, 1916), p. 70.
[34]Donald Guthrie, *The New Bible Commentary* (Grand Rapids: Wm. B. Eerdmans Publishing House, 1970), p. 1057.
[35]F. W. Farrar, *op. cit.*, p. 136.

in remembrance of my ways which are in Christ, even as I teach everywhere in every church.

From this, it is clear what Paul meant regarding imitation of himself, namely, that they should imitate his ways "in Christ," meaning as Paul was truly in the Lord and fully identified with Christ, ways of which Timothy would shortly remind them.

> Paul had sent Timothy and Erastus to Macedonia, probably with instructions to go to Corinth if convenient; since it is not certain that Timothy will arrive there (16:10). This was probably while Paul was at Ephesus (Acts 19:22).[36]

Verse 18, *Now some are puffed up, as though I were not coming to you.*

Some considerable time had elapsed following Paul's dispatch of Timothy to Corinth; and, when the word came of Timothy's intended arrival, some of the factionists said, "Ah, Paul is afraid to show his face here and is sending Timothy instead of coming himself." However, Paul would explode that misconception with the stern warning written a moment later.

Verses 19-21, *But I will come to you shortly, if the Lord will; and I will know, not the word of them that are puffed up, but the power. For the kingdom of God is not in word, but in power. What will ye? shall I come unto you with a rod, or in love and a spirit of gentleness?*

"If the Lord will . . ." Paul's purpose of going to Corinth to set things in order was dependent only upon the divine pleasure. These words have the effect of "unless providentially hindered."

"Not the word . . . but the power . . . not in word, but in power . . ." Paul was conscious of his own apostolic power. Elymas had been stricken blind for opposing Paul's teaching at Paphos (Acts 13:11), and many other notable miracles had been wrought by him; and there can be no doubt that Paul counted fully upon the confirmation of the word of God which he

---

[36]Albert Barnes, *op. cit.*, p. 78.

proclaimed at Corinth by just such signs and wonders and mighty deeds as God had enabled previously.

"What will ye? . . ." has the effect of "All right, do you really want to put me to the test? If so, I am ready." Paul concludes this particular admonition with a suggestion that it would be far better if they amended their behavior to enable Paul to come to them in loving affection, rather than for the purpose of punishing their wickedness.

CHAPTER 5

This entire chapter is devoted to the case of the incestuous member of the church in Corinth, the woman involved having apparently no connection with the church; as no rebuke or teaching of any kind concerning her is recorded.

Verse 1, *It is actually reported that there is fornication among you, and such fornication as is not even among the Gentiles, that one of you hath his father's wife.*

"Paul was vitally concerned about a new morality!"[1] The old morality of the Corinthians had already been discredited, exposed and revealed in the degradations and shameful debaucheries which invariably resulted from it. The new morality had come to Corinth in the preaching of Jesus Christ. Chastity, sobriety, honesty, truthfulness and kindness were among the features of the new ethic which came to mankind through Jesus Christ, that ethic being the only "new morality" ever heard of on earth.

"Paul was also relevant in his preaching!"[2] He pointed the finger of divine condemnation squarely at the offender, also making the whole congregation to blame for the complacency with which they had looked upon so brazen a resurgence of the old morality.

"Fornication . . ." is here used as a general term for all sexual vice, incest being the specific sin here. For further elaboration of this subject, see CH, p. 325. "Shocked as Paul was at this sin, he was even more shocked by the attitude of the Corinthian church,"[3] which condoned it and went on being puffed up with pride. Johnson thought that they might have been "even proud of their liberty";[4] and Guthrie also believed

---

[1]Donald S. Metz, *Beacon Bible Commentary* (Kansas City: Beacon Hill Press, 1968), p. 346.

[2]*Ibid.*, p. 347.

[3]William Barclay, *The Letters to the Corinthians* (Philadelphia: The Westminster Press, 1954), p. 49.

[4]S. Lewis Johnson, Jr., *Wycliffe Bible Commentary* (Chicago: Moody Press, 1971), p. 601.

that their leaving such a glaring sin uncondemned was "Presumably on the ground of their 'liberty' in Christ."[5]

"Not even among the Gentiles . . ." does not mean that incest was not practiced by the Gentiles, but that such vice was unacceptable among them. The feelings, even of pagans, were shocked by it; and Cicero spoke of such a crime (near Corinth), saying, "Oh, incredible wickedness, and, except in this woman's case, unheard of in all experience."[6]

"Hath his father's wife . . ." "Hath refers not to just one trespass, but to a life of sin."[7] Speculations on the circumstances attending this sin, as to the question of whether the father was alive, or divorced, or the question of whether the incestuous couple were married or not, are all fruitless. The relationship itself was sinful, no matter what the circumstances; and if it had been profitable to know more of the details of this sordid incident, it is safe to conclude that Paul would have provided them. Some have identified the man who "suffered the wrong" (2 Cor. 7:12) as the father in this case; and; if correct, this would prove that the father was alive. Farrar was of this opinion.[8] Lipscomb expressed the opinion of McGarver and many others that, "From the complete silence as to the crime of the woman, it is inferred that she was a heathen."[9]

Verse 2, *And ye are puffed up, and did not rather mourn, that he that had done this thing might be taken away from among you.*

"Puffed up . . ." Barnes understood this thus: "They were not puffed up on account of this wickedness, but they were filled with pride notwithstanding it, or in spite of it."[10]

---

[5]Donald Guthrie, *The New Bible Commentary* (Grand Rapids: Wm. B. Eerdmans Publishing Company, 1970), p. 1058.

[6]F. W. Farrar, *Pulpit Commentary* (Grand Rapids: Wm. B. Eerdmans Publishing Company, 1950), Vol. 19, p. 165.

[7]F. W. Grosheide, *The New International Commentary* (Grand Rapids: Wm. B. Eerdmans Publishing Company, 1953), p. 120.

[8]F. W. Farrar, *op. cit.*, p. 166.

[9]David Lipscomb, *Commentary on First Corinthians* (Nashville: The Gospel Advocate Company, 1935), p. 72.

[10]Albert Barnes, *Notes on the NT* (Grand Rapids: Baker Book House, 1949), p. 83.

"Mourn . . ." "This is the word that is used in mourning for the dead";[11] and when such a sinful contradiction of truth and righteousness as this case of incest exists in a congregation of believers, it should be an occasion of the most intense sorrow. What an incongruous thing was that prideful boasting of the Corinthians contrasted with this wretched immorality tolerated among them!

Verses 3-4, *For I verily, being absent in body but present in spirit, have already as though I were present judged him that hath so wrought this thing, in the name of our Lord Jesus Christ, ye being gathered together, and my spirit, with the power of the Lord Jesus.*

The question of Paul's coming to Corinth had just been mentioned (4:21); but by the first clause here, Paul said, "I do not have to be present in Corinth to judge such a shameful sin as this. My spirit is already with you in the general assembly which I now order you to convene for the purpose of throwing the offender out."

"In the name of the Lord Jesus Christ . . ." may be applied to a number of things in this passage; but the principal thrust of the words is to invoke the authority of Christ himself (through the apostle) for casting out the offender. They must not seek to separate from him privately, or in any hushed-up manner; the whole church was commanded to pronounce the apostolic judgment on the sinful member.

Verse 5, *To deliver such a one unto Satan for the destruction of the flesh, that the spirit may be saved in the day of the Lord Jesus.*

"Deliver . . . to Satan . . ." This was the apostolic sentence; but the full meaning of it is not fully clear, there being a great many things that men simply do not know concerning what is here revealed.

Some things are crystal clear. Paul denounced this sin in the strongest language found in the NT; and such a judgment could have been pronounced and executed only by an apostle of Christ. There is a hint that Paul expected that the man would

---

[11]William Barclay, *op. cit.*, p. 49.

die upon the announcement of his judgment, in the same manner as Ananias and Sapphira had died in Jerusalem. The salvation held out as a hope for the condemned was not envisioned as following his return to the congregation, but as something he would receive "in the day of the Lord Jesus," a certain reference to the final judgment. If these implications should be allowed, this exceedingly severe judgment "might have been an act of mercy, as well."[12] See CA, under 5:5.

The opinion that this offender repented and came back into the congregation is founded upon 2 Corinthians 7:12; but there is little certainty that this application is correct. If that is what happened, then what became of "the destruction of the flesh" enunciated in this judgment?

The frequent opinion that "The sinful man (was) delivered to Satan, to suffer physical affliction, to bring him to repentance and turn out for the good of his soul,"[13] is another example of what the passage is thought to teach.

Another thing that is certain, with reference to this, was pointed out by Adam Clarke:

> No such power as this remains in the Church of God; none such should be assumed; and the pretensions to it are as wicked as they are vain. It was the same power by which Ananias and Sapphira were struck dead, and Elymas the sorcerer struck blind. Apostles alone were intrusted with it.[14]

Even an apostle like Paul exercised such power and authority only upon rare occasions, another instance being that of Hymenaeus and Alexander (1 Tim. 1:20).

Verse 6, *Your glorying is not good. know ye not that a little leaven leaveneth the whole lump?*

"Your glorying . . ." Their glorying failed to take any note at all of the cancer of immorality in their very midst.

---

[12]F. F. Bruce, *The Book of Acts* (Grand Rapids: Wm. B. Eerdman Publishing Company, 1954), p. 114.

[13]F. F. Bruce, *Answers to Questions* (Grand Rapids: Zondervan Publishing House, 1972), p. 91.

[14]Adam Clarke, *Commentary on the Whole Bible* (New York: Carlton & Porter, 1831), Vol. VI, p. 213.

"A little leaven . . ." Although there are exceptions, leaven in the NT usually refers to some evil principle, in this case unrebuked immorality, which was fully capable of destroying the whole church. This would account for the severity of the judgment imposed.

Verse 7, *Purge out the old leaven, that ye may be a new lump, even as ye are unleavened. For our passover also hath been sacrificed, even Christ.*

"Ye are unleavened . . ." This is a figure for "you are not contaminated with sin." Despite the sinful lapses visible in the church, the action of their being cleansed in the blood of Christ was constant and effectual. Serious sins would be punished and purged from the Lord's church;, and the essential purity of it was affirmed even in this moment of her shameful deficiency. This purity was not of themselves, but of Christ "in whom" they continued to be.

Christ Our Passover

In the above verse, Paul affirmed that Christ is our passover; but, as in most analogies, there are points of likeness and unlikeness.

I. Points of likeness:

A. In both the Jewish passover and the passover of Christians (who is Christ), there is the death of a sinless, blameless victim (John 14:30; S:46; Heb. 4:15).

B. In both, there is the design of deliverance from the wrath of God; in the Jewish passover, it was from the destruction of the death angel, and for Christians it is from God's eternal wrath (Rom. 1:18).

C. In both, deliverance came through the vicarious death, in their case, that of the lamb, in our case, that of Christ who died for us (Rom. 3:25; 5:6; Matt. 20:28; 1 Peter 3:18).

D. In both, the slain victim became the food of the redeemed. The Jews actually ate the passover lamb; and Christians partake of Christ who is their spiritual food (John 6:53).

E. In both, a personal participation on the part of the redeemed was an absolute requirement. The lamb had to be slain for every family; each member had to eat; the blood was sprinkled on every door. Every man must be "in Christ" to be saved (1 Cor. 12:13).

F. In both, the line of demarcation between the saved and lost is clear and emphatic. Egyptians did not partake of the passover. The evil men of the world do not partake of Christ.

G. In both, there is a pledge of fellowship. Eating together is one of the oldest bonds of fellowship; and, in both dispensations, God made use of this instrument to cement the bonds of fellowship among his people.

II. Points of unlikeness:

A. There is a contrast in the redemptions procured, one being temporal and earthly, the other being heavenly and eternal.

B. There is a contrast in the victims provided. Is not a man of more value than a sheep?

C. There is a contrast in the efficacy of the blood offered, that of animals being unable to take away sin (Heb. 10:4), but the blood of Christ providing remission of sins (Heb. 9:14).

D. There is a contrast in that which was purged out, in the case of the Jews being the old leaven of actual bread, but in the case of Christians the purging of sin from the hearts of those saved.

III. The entire institution of the Passover was typical of the entire institution of Christianity:

A. The passover lamb, sacrificed the first day, was fulfilled by the crucifixion of Christ at the very hours the lambs were slain.

B. The lamb was a type of the person of Christ in that it was innocent, died vicariously, was a male of the flock, and without blemish, and in that not a bone of it was broken (Ps. 34:20).

C. Just as the passover was slain and eaten in Jerusalem so Christ suffered, died, and rose again in the same city.

D. The passover was typical of the Lord's supper in some ways, though not in others. Both were divinely instituted, both were commemorative, both were continuative, moving for millenniums through history; both began a new kingdom, the passover that of the Jews; the Lord's Supper distinguished the kingdom of Christ; and in both cases the actual beginning of the kingdom was a little later than the institution of the rite. Who but God could have so designed the religious economy of Israel that all of it would have served to typify and identify the Christ who should come into the world?

Verse 8, *Wherefore let us keep the feast, not with old leaven, neither with the leaven of malice and wickedness, but with the unleavened bread of sincerity and truth.*

"Keep the feast . . ." It seems incredible to this student that anyone would apply this to keeping the Jewish passover. "We are obliged to keep the feast, i.e., the feast of unleavened bread."[15] This whole paragraph is absolutely metaphorical; for, when Paul commanded the Corinthians to "purge out thy old leaven," he referred to purging out sin. Therefore "feast" in this place has the meaning of Christian life and fellowship. Farrar read it "Keep the feast of Christ's resurrection in the spirit of holiness."[16] Barnes interpreted it as "Let us engage in the service of God by putting away evil."[17] "Keeping the feast suggests the continuous life of the Christian, a day-by-day walking in holiness, strength and joy."[18] There is not a reference here to the Lord's Supper specifically; but of course it is included in the larger sphere of the entire Christian pilgrimage.

"Not with old leaven . . ." This is a reference to the old morality of the Corinthians, under the figure of the Jews' actions at passover. All sexual vice, as well as malice and other forms of wickedness, are specific examples of what Paul meant by "leaven."

"Unleavened bread . . ." refers to the new life in Christ from which the old works of the flesh have been purged and replaced by "sincerity and truth."

Verses 9-10, *I wrote unto you in my epistle to have no company with fornicators; not at all meaning with the fornica-*

---

[15]F. W. Grosheide, *op. cit.*, p. 126.
[16]F. W. Farrar, *op. cit.*, p. 168.
[17]Albert Barnes, *op. cit.*, p. 88.
[18]Donald S. Metz, *op. cit.*, p. 355.

tors of this world, or with covetous and extortioners, or with idolators; for then must ye needs go out of the world.

"In my epistle . . ." This most probably refers to another epistle Paul had written to the Corinthians, but which was lost; and, since they misunderstood it, perhaps it was lost providentially. Skilled efforts to make this a reference to previous passages in this same epistle are unconvincing.

The crux of Paul's teaching here is that when he had commanded the Corinthians not to keep company with fornicators (in that lost letter), the congregation had taken it to mean that they were not to associate with *anybody* guilty of that sin, whether in the church or out of the church. Paul here stated that he did not mean that "at all"; and, if he had meant that, they could have obeyed him only by leaving the present world! What a commentary this is upon the depraved condition of Corinth and the whole world of that era.

"Fornicators . . . covetous . . . extortioners . . . idolators . . ." Significantly, Paul here extended the prohibition to include association with any grossly wicked people, specifically the four classes mentioned, who might be called "brethren."

Furthermore, despite the fact of its being allowable for Christians to associate with the wicked in the necessary business and commerce of the world, such persons having no connection with Christianity, this is definitely not meant to encourage such associations. Every time a child of God is in the company of the wicked, even in cases where it is necessary and allowable, he runs a certain risk; and there is no way that he should be satisfied and comfortable in such associations. Wall, as quoted by Macknight, said:

> It is an everlasting rule that a conscientious Christian should choose, as far as he can, the company, intercourse, and familiarity of good men, and such as fear God; and avoid, as far as his necessary affairs will permit, the conversation and fellowship of such as Paul here describes.[19]

---

[19]James Macknight, *Apostolical Epistles and Commentary* (Grand Rapids. Baker Book House, 1969), p. 79.

Verse 11, *But as it is, I wrote unto you not to keep company, if any man that is named a brother be a fornicator, or covetous, or an idolator, or a reviler or a drunkard, or an extortioner; with such a one no, not to eat.*

"But as it is . . ." or "Now I write . . ." as in the RV margin.

"I wrote unto you . . ." carries the meaning of "what I meant when I wrote to you."

The blanket rule laid down here requiring the Christian to forego any association with unfaithful Christians was stated thus by Russell:

> Have no familiar intercourse with one that is named a brother but is false to his profession; withdraw from all associations indicating brotherhood. He does not mean that Christians should go out of the world; monastic seclusion is not for a moment contemplated.[20]

Verses 12-13, *For what have I to do with judging them that are without? Do not ye judge them that are within? But them that are without God judgeth. Put away the wicked man from among yourselves.*

Despite what was said under verse 5 of the unique authority involved in delivering the sinner "to Satan," it may not be supposed that putting away evil men out of the Christian fellowship has no relevance now. However it is to be done, it must be done. Morris said, "Paul's main point is that the church must not tolerate the presence of evil in its midst, and this is clearly of permanent relevance."[21]

Paul also guarded against any thought that the wicked "without" shall escape judgment; God will judge them. Regarding the last verse here, Macknight wrote:

> The apostle wrote this and the preceding verse to show the Corinthians the reason why, after commanding them to pass so severe a sentence on the man, he said nothing to them of the woman who was guilty with him. The

---

[20]John William Russell, *Compact Commentary on the NT* (Grand Rapids: Baker Book House, 1964), p. 410.

[21]Leon Morris, *Tyndale Commentary* (Grand Rapids: Wm. B. Eerdmans Publishing Company, 1953), p. 93.

discipline of the church was not to be exercised on persons out of it. Hence it appears that this woman was a heathen.[22]

[22]James Macknight, *op. cit.*, p. 80.

CHAPTER 6

Just as chapter 5 was devoted to the subject of the incestuous man and related thoughts, so this is devoted to another serious problem at Corinth, that of Christians going to law with one another before the pagan judges (1-11), and a special paragraph on sexual vice (12-20), the entire subject matter in both chapters being discussed in the light of the conceited glorying which characterized the Christian community in Corinth.

On Going to Law

Verse 1, *Dare any of you having a matter against his neighbor, go to law before the unrighteous, and not before the saints?*

"Against his neighbor . . ." means "against a Christian neighbor," because it would be impossible to force a pagan into a Christian tribunal unrecognized by the law of the land.

"Before the unrighteous . . ." This is not a charge that all the pagan judges were unrighteous, but distinguishes between those within the church and those without, all of the latter being unrighteous in the sense of not being Christians.

"Not before the saints . . ." Christ himself had laid down the rules for any follower of the Lord having a matter against his brother; and this rule involved (1) a personal confrontation between wronged and wrongdoer, (2) another attempt at reconciliation if the first failed, with witnesses present, and (3) a general examination before the whole church. See Matthew 18:15-17. Also for extended discussion of this subject, see CM, pp. 279-281. McGarvey stated that "By going to law before the pagan tribunals, they were not only disobeying the Lord but committing treason against their own brotherhood."[1] As De Hoff noted. however, "It is sometimes necessary for Christians

---

[1]J. W. McGarvey, *Commentary on First Corinthians* (Cincinnati: The Standard Publishing Company, 1916), p. 74.

to appear in courts for justice; Paul himself appealed to Caesar."[2] "The Rabbis taught the Jews never to take a case before the Gentiles";[3] and there were reasons excellent enough why the Christians should have likewise stayed out of pagan courts, except through the utmost necessity. Not only were the Christians more competent in an ethical sense, but the use of pagan courts would involve oath-taking in the names of pagan deities and other practices abhorrent to Christians.

Verse 2, *Or know ye not that the saints shall judge the world and if the world is judged by you, are ye unworthy to judge the smallest matters?*

"Or know ye not . . ." These words are the key to understanding this difficult passage. Macknight said:

> Because this question is repeated six times in this chapter, Locke thinks it was intended as a reproof to the Corinthians, who boasted of the knowledge they received from the false teacher, (but) were extremely ignorant in religious matters.[4]

Dummelow unhesitatingly interpreted this and the two following verses as sarcasm on Paul's part:

> They appeal to the "knowledge" of the Corinthians, who were puffed up with spiritual pride; and in their conceit had spoken of their hope to judge men and angels. If this be their expectation surely they can judge in matters of daily life.[5]

This interpretation makes sense and is supported by many circumstances. First, the matter of human beings judging men and angels is just such a thing as would have been advocated by the conceited false teachers in Corinth; but there are many other reasons:

(1) The greatest importance attaches to the words "know ye not," which occur ten times in the letters of Paul to the

---

[2]George W. De Hoff, *Sermons on First Corinthians* (Murfreesboro, Tenn., 1947), p. 56.

[3]Donald Guthrie, *The New Bible Commentary* (Grand Rapids: Wm. T. Eerdmans Publishing Company, 1970), p. 1058.

[4]James Macknight, *Apostolical Epistles and Commentary* (Grand Rapids: Baker Book House, 1969), p. 84.

[5]J. R. Dummelow, *Commentary on the Holy Bible* (New York: The Macmillan Company, 1937), p. 901.

Corinthians, and only twice in all the rest.[6] Farrar says that "(these words) are a fitting rebuke for those who took for knowledge their obvious ignorance."[7] Furthermore, this expression occurs six times in this chapter in verses 2, 3, 9, 15, 16 and 19; therefore some very special significance attaches to it. This student believes that the words are a sarcastic reference by Paul to conceited arrogance of the Corinthians who professed to "know" so much.

(2) All other interpretations involve vast difficulties. Jesus never promised that even apostles would judge angels. The passage in Matthew 19:28 speaks of their "judging the twelve tribes of Israel"; and, as Morris noted, "There is no record of Christ having said that all believers would share in that."[8]

(3) The notion that men will judge angels, except in the most poetic sense, as in the thought of their doing so through preaching the gospel, or through their godly living, etc.; such a notion raises impossible questions. What angels shall men judge? Does it mean the devil's angels? They have already been judged and cast down and reserved in chains of darkness, etc. (2 Peter 2:4). True, Peter said, "reserved unto judgment," but this means "until the judgment day," their sentence only being reserved and their judgment already determined.

(4) Without going into all the fanciful interpretations heaped upon these words, this writer confesses full agreement with Adam Clarke who said:

> This place is generally understood to imply that the redeemed of the Lord shall be, on the great day, assessors with him in judgment; and shall give their award in the determinations of his justice. On reviewing this subject, I am fully of the opinion that this cannot be the meaning of these words; and that the interpretation is clogged with a multitude of absurdities.[9]

---

[6]F. W. Farrar, *Pulpit Commentary* (Grand Rapids: Wm. B. Eerdmans Publishing Company, 1950), Vol. 19, p. 192.

[7]*Ibid*

[8]Leon Morris, *Tyndale Commentary* (Grand Rapids: Wm. B. Eerdmans Publishing Company, 1953), p.94.

[9]Adam Clarke, *Commentary on the Whole Bible* (New York: Carlton & Porter, 1831), Vol. VI, p. 216.

Thus it is believed that the matter of Christians judging men and angels is no valid Christian doctrine at all, but the speculative nonsense of the vainglorious experts in Greek philosophy at Corinth.

(5) Christians themselves will be judged at the last day; and in 4:4, Paul had just declared that the one who judges "is the Lord." Although it is said of saints that they shall "reign" with Christ, it is nowhere said that they shall judge with him. Despite many learned opinions to the contrary, therefore, this writer strongly inclines to the views expressed above.

Verses 3-4, *Know ye not that we shall judge angels? how much more things that pertain to this life? If then ye have to judge things pertaining to this life, do ye set them to judge who are of no account in the church?*

Paraphrase: You who know all about judging angels in the last day, how about judging some of these petty disputes you are disgracefully airing in the courts of the pagans? And in your practice of resolving these little earthly matters, how is it that you set the pagan judges over such trivialities, such judges being of no account at all in the church, as they are not members of it.

If the sarcastic vein is denied here, the rendering of the words "do ye set" would be imperative, that is, a command that they should choose some humble member of the congregation to be a judge of disputes. In such an interpretation, which is by no means unreasonable, the admonition would stress the rejection of value-judgments of the world, letting the humble decide, instead of the mighty.

Taking the words "do ye not know" as meaning "of course, it is a fact, requires some kind of thesis on just "how" the saints are going to judge the earth. Thus Johnson explained such judging metaphorically: "The saints shall judge the world, because of their union with the Messiah, to whom all judgment is committed."[10] Shore likewise took the judging to be figurative, "arising out of the apostle's intense realization

---

[10]S. Lewis Johnson, Jr., *Wycliffe Bible Commentary* (Chicago: Moody Press, 1971), p. 604.

of the unity of Christ and his Church Triumphant."[11] McGarvey wrote,"The saints will only participate as mystically united with Christ the judge."[12]

Before leaving this subject, a word with regard to Daniel 7:22 is appropriate: The passage reads:

> Until the Ancient of Days came, and judgment was given to the saints of the Most High; and the time came that the saints possessed the kingdom.

The judge in this place is mentioned in the first clause, being the Ancient of Days; and it was his judgment which was given to the saints, the same being a judgment upon their behalf, and not a judgment made by them. The great passage in Matthew 25:31-46 is in complete harmony with this interpretation of Daniel 7:22. In all probability, the false teachers at Corinth had indulged in some very wild speculations.

Verse 5, *I say this to move you to shame. What, cannot there be found among you one wise man who shall be able to decide between his brethren?*

"To move you to shame . . ." The sharpness of Paul's biting sarcasm in the previous three verses was no doubt keenly felt in Corinth; and by this expression Paul means, "I meant for it to hurt." However unusual the explanation offered here with regard to those Corinthian saints "judging angels" may seem to Christians today, there was probably no one in Corinth who could have failed to know what Paul meant.

"Wise man . . . to decide . . ." In this clause, Paul dropped the sarcasm for a moment, asking, "Why don't you appoint one of the wiser members to settle such disputes?" Thus it appears that Paul could not have meant in verse 4 that church members who were of "no account" should be entrusted with such an assignment. The apostles themselves when appointing brethren for such a purpose demanded that the ones appointed should be men "full of the Spirit and wisdom" (Acts 6:3). Thus,

---

[11]T. Teignmouth Shore, *Ellicott's Commentary on the Whole Bible* (Grand Rapids: Zondervan Publishing House, 1959), p. 303.

[12]J. W. McGarvey, *op cit.*, p. 75.

here is another strong reason for accepting the thesis that Paul's words in verses 2-4 were spoken in irony.

Verse 6, *But brother goeth to law with brother, and that before unbelievers.*

Ellicott's paraphrase of this is: "Your dragging these disputes before the tribunals of the heathen would imply that it is not possible to find a Christian friend to settle these trivial disputes."[13]

Verse 7, *Nay, already it is altogether a fault with you, that ye have lawsuits one with another. Why not rather take wrong? why not rather be defrauded?*

Passing beyond the question of "where" their lawsuits should be settled, Paul in this rebuked them for *having* any "lawsuits with one another." The Christian is of a different temperament from the man who is always screaming about his "rights," it being a far better way of life to "go the second mile . . . give the cloak also . . . and turn the other cheek" (Matt. 5:38-42).

Verse 8, *Nay, but ye yourselves do wrong, and defraud, and that your brethren.*

There were some in the Corinthian congregation who made a habit of defrauding their brethren, using sinful devices, procuring advantage by the instrumentality of the pagan system of justice. Such persons would have been those who were skilled in such lawsuits, or those who through some circumstance might have enjoyed preferment in such courts. In any case, some of the Christians were being defrauded by other members of the church.

Verses 9-10, *Or know ye not that the unrighteous shall not inherit the kingdom of God? Be not deceived: neither fornicators, nor idolators, nor adulterers, nor effeminate, nor abusers of themselves with men, nor thieves, nor covetous, nor drunkards, nor revilers, nor extortioners, shall inherit the kingdom of God.*

---

[13]Ellicott, as quoted in *One Volume NT Commentary* (Grand Rapids: Baker Book House, 1972), in loco.

A vast proportion of the whole Corinthian population participated in such sins as are catalogued here; and the prevalence of such wickedness throughout the ancient empire resulted in its total destruction, after these debaucheries had run their course; but it was not the destruction of an empire that Paul had in view here; it was the loss of souls. The various actions mentioned in this paragraph are designated as unrighteousness. The people who continue in such wickedness "shall not inherit the kingdom of God."

"Fornicators . . ." is a general term for several kinds of sexual vice. It is here made the head of a shameful list of sins; and, in verse 12, Paul returned to a fuller discussion of it.

"Idolators . . ." In context, this referred to the patrons of the temple of Aphrodite atop the Acro Corinthus which dominated the Corinthian scene. As Halley said, "A thousand public prostitutes, kept at public expense, were always ready (in the temple) for immoral indulgence as worship to their goddess!"[14] In such an atmosphere, some of the Corinthians were finding it difficult to adjust to the strict code of Christian morality.

"Adulterers . . ." has special reference to persons not faithful to the marriage vows.

"Effeminate . . ." Macknight wrote that this word is translated from a Greek word meaning "catamite,"[15] the technical word for "a boy used in pederasty."[16] "Those wretches who suffered this abuse were likewise called *pathics*, and affected the dress and behavior of women."[17] Catamites were the passive partners in sodomy.

"Abusers of themselves with men . . ." were the sodomites. Regarding the passive and active homosexuals referred to in these words, it should be remembered that an apostle of Jesus Christ condemned such persons in the judgment that they shall not inherit the kingdom of God. What is to be thought of churches which not only condone this sin, but in widely

---

[14]Henry H. Halley, *Bible Handbook* (Grand Rapids: Zondervan Publishing House,1927), p. 546.

[15]James Macknight, *op. cit.*, p. 88.

[16]*Britannica World Language Dictionary* (New York: Funk & Wagnalls Company, 1959.

[17]James Macknight, *op. cit.*, p. 83.

publicized cases have actually ordained homosexuals to the ministry? It is the judgment of this writer that churches exhibiting such a total disregard of the NT have, in so doing, forfeited all identity with Christianity.

William Barclay's masterful discussion of homosexuality should be read by every Christian. This was the cancer in Greek life that invaded Rome, and brought the vaunted empire to destruction. Fourteen of the first fifteen Roman emperors practiced this vice; others guilty of it were Socrates and Plato. Nero castrated and married a boy called Sporus, which he held as his wife, and at the same time married Pythagoras and called him his husband! Barclay's conclusion may not be denied that:.

> In this particular vice in the time of the early church, the world was lost to shame; and there can be little doubt that that was one of the main causes of its degeneracy and the final collapse of its civilization.[18]

"Thieves . . . covetous . . . drunkards . . . revilers . . . extortioners . . ." Significantly, Paul classed thieves and extortioners as equally criminal, the latter referring to organized, "white-collar" crime, and thievery to common pilferage.

"Covetousness" is the inordinate desire, or love, of money, the same being a ruling passion, not only with the unregenerated, but also with many Christians themselves, who despite their prosperity give little or nothing to the church or philanthropy. This vice is rated with idolatry, sodomy, extortion, etc., being essentially a denial of God in human life.

"Drunkards . . ." Who is a drunkard? The "wisdom" of this age recognizes no such character, the same having been elevated in the popular mind to the status of "an alcoholic"! As such he is not blameworthy in any degree, but merely suffering from "a disease," the same required to be treated, tolerated, and even appreciated by the community. This is merely a part of the blindness of worldly wisdom. No man can become an alcoholic except by his own repeated violations of the Christian law of sobriety. While it may be true, of course, but only in a

---

[18]William Barclay, *The Letters to the Corinthians* (Philadelphia: The Westminster Press, 1954), p. 60.

sense, that drink No. 5,689 is a disease, drink No. 1 is a moral problem. The burning liquors on sale today are not fit for human consumption; and the use of any of them, even socially, is reprehensible. This writer does not expect social drinkers to approve of this viewpoint; but there is actually no intelligent denial of it. If one is really concerned with living the Christian life, far the best thing for him to do is to deny beverage alcohol any place whatever in his life. The whole Moslem world has known for centuries the true nature of the curse of alcohol, making abstinence from it a cardinal rule of their faith.

Verse 11, *And such were some of you: but ye were washed, but ye were sanctified, but ye were justified in the name of the Lord Jesus Christ, and in the Spirit of our God.*

"Such were some of you . . ." This was intended by Paul to call attention to the conditions from which they had been rescued by Christ.

"But ye are washed . . . sanctified . . . justified . . ." This refers to the conversion of the Corinthians. "By 'sanctified' is meant, not the progressive course of sanctification, but the consecration to God by baptism."[19] As always, however, the scholars who deny baptism's necessity in any true conversion strive to soften the impact of these words, as in: "Nothing in the context identifies this with baptism."[20] "(They) submitted to baptism as *the sign of the washing* away of sin."[21] Etc.

Two considerations require the understanding of this place as a reference to Christian baptism, along with the sanctification and justification accomplished in the ceremony itself, when performed scripturally upon a believing penitent. (1) There is the use of "the middle voice for *washed*, as in Acts 22:16, carrying the meaning of 'you had yourselves washed.' "[22] (2) There is the appearance in the verse itself of the trinitarian formula for the administration of baptism. As Guthrie noted:

---

[19]F. W. Farrar, *op. cit.*, p. 193.

[20]Paul W. Marsh, *A New Commentary* (Grand Rapids: Zondervan Publishing House, 1969), p. 386.

[21]J. R. Dummelow, *op. cit.*, p. 901.

[22]Paul W. Marsh, *op. cit.*, p. 386.

> "In the name of . . . Christ . . . Spirit . . . God . . ." Note the unconscious Trinitarianism. The words may recall the actual formula used in baptism and the complementary baptism of the Spirit . . . There is a reference here to the external and internal essential of baptism.[23]

Justification has reference to the status of the believer "in Christ" who by virtue of his identity with the Saviour does not deserve any punishment whatever; it is a total and complete justification bestowed upon the believer when he is baptized "into Christ."

CONCERNING FORNICATION

Verse 12, *All things are lawful for me; but not all things are expedient. All things are lawful for me; but I will not be brought under the power of any.*

Paul here used a catch phrase which evidently had wide acceptance among the Corinthians. The liberty in Christ which made "all things lawful" was a relative, not an absolute principle; and any notion that the existence of appetites justified their gratification was not true then, or ever. "Some of them were evidently quoting this to justify their promiscuous sexual behavior; but Paul positively stated that it did not so apply."[24]

Verse 13, *Meats for the belly, and the belly for meats: but God shall bring to naught both it and them. But the body is not for fornication, but for the Lord; and the Lord for the body.*

"Meats for the belly . . ." This was probably another current proverb among the Corinthians with the meaning suggested by Marsh.

> As one indulges an appetite for food, that being the function of the stomach, so should the physical urge for sexual indulgence be gratified. Paul refutes the argument, stomach and food being temporal; but not so the body.[25]

---

[23]Donald Guthrie, *op. cit.*, p. 1059.
[24]Henry H. Halley, *op. cit.*, p. 546.
[25]Paul W. Marsh, *op. cit.*, p. 386.

"But for the Lord . . ." The purpose of the body is not the gratification of its appetites; but it is for the Lord, a reference to the indwelling of the Spirit mentioned in v. 19. Sensuality is neither the highest nor the most satisfying use of the body. "Body" as used here has reference to the whole person including the physical body; and the highest happiness of the person is impossible of attainment through gratification, such happiness deriving only from the proper union between man and his Creator.

Verse 14, *And God both raised the Lord, and will raise up us through his power.*

The resurrection of Christians is promised here, the proof of it already having been demonstrated in the resurrection of Christ. As the resurrection of Christ was bodily, so shall be that of Christians; and, in this light, an eternal purpose with reference to the body itself is indicated, the same being a telling argument against wasting the physical body through lust and sensuality.

Verse 15, *Know ye not that your bodies are members of Christ? and shall I then take away the members of Christ, and make them members of a harlot? God forbid.*

"Know ye not . . ." is still being used sarcastically in this passage, not in the sense of denying that Christians' bodies are members of Christ, but as protesting the incongruity of debasing such members in immorality. Paul's use of "body" in this passage makes it certain that the physical body is meant.

Verse 16, *Or know ye not that he that is joined to a harlot is one body? for, The twain, saith he, shall become one flesh.*

"Or know ye not . . ." carries the thought of "With all of your conceited knowledge, has it never occurred to you that participation with a harlot makes the participant and the harlot one flesh?" Paul proved it by the reference to Genesis 2:24. As Dummelow said, however,

> The words spoken by God (in the reference cited) were first spoken of marriage, and are here applied to an unholy union. Paul does not place the two on the same

plane but only points out that in this one respect they are similar.[26]

Verse 17, *But he that is joined unto the Lord is one spirit.*

"One spirit . . ." The true Christian, having been joined to the Lord through his conversion from sin, is one in spirit with the Lord, seeking in all things to conform his thoughts, words and deeds to such actions as are approved by the Lord and in harmony with the Holy Spirit.

Verse 18, *Flee fornication. Every sin that a man doeth is without the body; but he that committeth fornication sinneth against his own body.*

"Flee fornication . . ." For further remarks on this, see in CH, p. 325. The sin of fornication is against: (a) God (Gen. 39:9), (b) one's body (as here), (c) the church, (d) the marriage institution, (e) the life of the nation, and (f) the very soul itself (Prov. 6:32).

"Against his own body . . ." Although Paul doubtless had specifically in mind the impact of sin against the physical body, his words are true in the widest possible application. No matter how "body" is understood, whether the physical body, the body of the family, the body of the Lord, the body of the social order, or even any corporate body— fornication is "against" any and all of these, many a corporation having been wrecked through fornication.

Verse 19, *Or know ye not that your body is a temple of the Holy Spirit which is in you, which ye have from God? and ye are not your own.*

What Paul had affirmed earlier with reference to the church's being the temple of the Holy Spirit is here declared to be true of individual members of the church. God's temple belongs to God, and therefore the individual who partakes of the nature of God's temple belongs not to himself but to God; and thus he is not free to indulge his lusts and appetites but is obligated to conform his activities to those things which will honor and glorify the Lord whose property the Christian is. For

---

[26]J. R. Dummelow, *op. cit.*, p. 901.

extended comments on "The Indwelling Spirit," see CR, p. 291, and on "The Witness of the Spirit," see CR, p. 298.

Verse 20, *For ye were bought with a price: glorify God therefore in your body.*

"Ye were bought with a price . . ." has reference to the blood of the Lord Jesus Christ which is the purchase price of the church (Acts 20:28).

"Glorify God in your body . . ." identifies the body as an instrument to be used by the Christian in the service of God and for his glory. The honor of the physical body is also implicit in such a view. In true Christianity, there is no hatred of the body, no torturing of the flesh, and no asceticism.

Guthrie pointed out that Paul's language here "reflects a contemporary custom"[27] prevalent in Corinth. Resort to a temple prostitute meant resort to a strange god; and the participants in temple immorality became the property of the god of that temple, the pagan society holding such persons to be free or "liberated"! "Our redemption by Christ from the enslavement of sin was no such fiction."[28]

---

[27]Donald Guthrie, *op. cit.*, p. 1059.
[28]*Ibid.*

CHAPTER 7

This is one of the most interesting chapters in the NT, due to the nature of its being Paul's apostolical answers to no less than six questions propounded in a letter from the church at Corinth, that letter being lost, of course, and thus leaving the communications in this chapter to be understood very much in the same manner as listening to one end of a telephone conversation.

Significantly, Paul had sternly reprimanded the Corinthians for the various sins already noted in the first six chapters, before getting down to the problem of their questions. Therefore, the second major division of the epistle begins at this point, from whence through the next nine chapters he would deal with questions raised in the lost letter.

The six questions treated in this chapter are:

(1) Should married couples continue normal sexual relations after becoming Christians? Answer: Yes, it is their duty to do this (vv. 1-7).

(2) Should single persons get married? Answer: Yes, in all normal situations; but for the gifted, such as Paul, celibacy was advantageous, especially in unsettled times (vv. 8-9).

(3) Is divorce permitted for Christians? Answer: No (vv. 10-11).

(4) When one partner of a pagan couple becomes a Christian, the other refusing to do so, is such a marriage binding? Answer: Yes, except when the unbeliever deserts the Christian partner (vv. 12-16).

A brief digression. At this point Paul, having given an exception in the matter of mixed marriages, allowing liberty in certain cases, interjected a comment on the general rule that becoming a Christian does not free any man from obligations already binding upon him. Evidently there was at Corinth, even at this early date, some impression that becoming a Christian wiped out all prior debts, contracts, even marriages and all other obligations existing prior to conversion. It will be recalled that this very error was the principal motivation for vast numbers of knights and princes who participated in the Crusades at a much later time (vv. 17-24).

(5) Should Christian fathers (or guardians) give their daughters in marriage? Answer: The fathers and guardians were given authority to solve their individual problems, there being no sin involved, however the decision went; but certain guidelines were suggested (vv. 25-38).

(6) May a Christian widow remarry? Answer: Yes, provided only that she marry "in the Lord" (vv. 39-40).

Like many other chapters which are sometimes labeled "difficult," this one contains some of the most instructive teaching in the NT, and affords glimpses of the apostolical method which add greatly to one's faith in the integrity of the apostles.

Verse 1, *Now concerning the things whereof ye wrote: It is good for a man not to touch a woman.*

The development of this paragraph a little later indicates that the question regards the conduct of Christian couples toward each other, a question no doubt related to the broader question of celibacy as a way of life, this being a deduction from the terminology "not to touch a woman." "Epictetus used this word to denote one's *marrying*."[1] Morris also agreed that "In this context *touch* refers to marriage."[2]

"It is good not to touch a woman . . ." Paul first addressed himself to the prior question of celibacy, admitting here that, in a sense, it was "good." The word "good" in this place "does not mean morally good, but that it is for man's best interests in some circumstances to remain single."[3] "He is teaching that because of the persecution of Christians, it is better not to get married and bring children into the world to be killed and

---

[1]James Macknight, *Apostolical Epistles and Commentary* (Grand Rapids: Baker Book House, 1969), p. 98.
[2]Leon Morris, *Tyndale Commentary* (Grand Rapids: Wm. B. Eerdmans Publishing Company, 1958), p. 105.
[3]Donald S. Metz, *Beacon Bible Commentary* (Kansas City: Beacon Hill Press, 1968), p. 872.

suffer persecution.[4] It should be carefully observed, however, that Paul in no sense advocated celibacy, except in certain situations and circumstances, and that even in those cases it was merely "allowable," and not commanded. There is no disparagement of marriage here, Paul's writings in Ephesians 5:22, 23, etc., making it abundantly clear that he held the institution of marriage in the very highest esteem. As Marsh said, "He is not writing a treatise on marriage, but answering their questions within the context of current attitudes and circumstances."[5] Marsh translated this place, "It is *well* for a man not to touch a woman . . . meaning *commendable*, but not morally or intrinsically better."[6] It is true now, even as it was in the beginning, that "It is not good for man to be alone" (Gen. 2:18). As Lipscomb noted, "Paul's teaching here regards the persecution then raging against the Christians; and, on account of these, if a man could restrain his lusts, it was better not to marry."[7]

The background of this paragraph included widespread agitation of the question of the desirability of marriage. Many of the Greek philosophers, such as Menander, held marriage to be "an evil, but a necessary evil";[8] but the Jews, on the other hand, "absolutely required that every man should marry, and reputed those as murderers who did not."[9]

Verse 2, *But because of fornications, let each man have his own wife, and let each woman have her own husband.*

Christianity is opposed to polygamy, concubinage, divorce and all related evils. Also, there is implicit in this verse a practical condemnation of celibacy. Celibacy being an absolutely unattainable state for the vast majority of mankind, marriage is required as the only practical alternative.

---

[4]George W. DeHoff, *Sermons on First Corinthians* (Murfreesboro, Tenn., 1947), p. 63.

[5]Paul W. Marsh, *A New Commentary* (Grand Rapids: Zondervan Publishing House, 1969), p. 387.

[6]*Ibid.*

[7]David Lipscomb, *Commentary on First Corinthians* (Nashville: The Gospel Advocate Company, 1935), p. 95.

[8]Adam Clarke, *Commentary on the Whole Bible* (New York: Carlton & Porter, 1881), Vol. V1, p. 220.

[9]*Ibid.*

"But because of fornications . . ." By these words and the command following, Paul refuted absolutely the false argument of Jerome who said, "If it is good for a man not to touch a woman, it must be bad to do so; and therefore celibacy is a holier state than marriage."[10] Far from being a holier state than marriage, celibacy, enforced upon the clergy of the historic church contrary to nature, became the worst of evils. As Barnes said:

> How much evil, how much deep pollution, how many abominable crimes would have been avoided, which have grown out of the monastic system, and the celibacy of the clergy . . . if Paul's advice had been followed by all professed Christians![11]

"Let every man have . . ." This was an apostolical order, "a rule, and not a mere permission";[12] and Paul applied it equally to women as to men. Such a commandment does not allow any exception for persons who, early in life, take vows of perpetual chastity; because, as Macknight observed, "No person in early life can foresee what his future state of mind may be . . . therefore vows of celibacy and virginity taken in early life, must in both sexes be sinful."[13]

Verse 3, *Let the husband render unto the wife her due: and likewise also the wife unto her husband.*

> In marriage, the sensuous impulse, by being controlled and placed under religious sanctions is refined and purified . . . Instead of being any longer the source of untold curses to mankind, it becomes a condition of their continuance and an element in their peace, because it is then placed under the blessing of God and of his church.[14]

"Unto the wife her due . . . also unto the husband . . ." The sexual relationship in married couples, far from being wrong, is a lawful and necessary function of Christian marriage. This verse establishes the idea that "Among some of the Corinthians there existed an exaggerated spiritualistic tendency

---

[10]F. W. Farrar, *Pulpit Commentary* (Grand Rapids: Wm. B. Eerdmans Publishing Company, 1950), Vol. 19, p. 228.
[11]Albert Barnes, *Notes on the NT* (Grand Rapids: Baker Book House, 1949).
[12]F. W. Farrar, *op. cit.*, p. 224.
[13]James Macknight, *op. cit.*, p. 98.
[14]F. W. Farrar, *op. cit.*, p. 224.

which threatened to injure conjugal relations."[15] There existed a view among ascetics that sex relations were in and of themselves wicked, or evil; and the blight of this monastic error has fallen upon all succeeding generation.

Verse 4, *The wife hath not power over her own body, but the husband: and likewise also the husband hath not power over his own body, but the wife.*

It may be assumed that Paul delivered such teachings as here, not through any love of the subject, but because all kinds of unnatural and immoral propositions were being advocated by ascetics and "super-spirituals" among the Corinthians. The equality of husband and wife in the marriage partnership is in the foreground here. Neither partner in marriage was to subscribe to any form of "sexless" behavior, because there was a positive duty that each owed the other in marriage.

Verse 5, *Defraud ye not one another, except it be by consent for a season, that ye may give yourselves unto prayer, and may be together again, that Satan tempt you not because of your incontinency.*

"Except it be for a season . . ." In such an apostolical directive as this, there disappears totally the notion that sexual relations between Christian marriage partners were allowable only for procreation. On the other hand, the refusal of one of the partners to cohabit is designated as fraud.

"May give yourselves unto prayer . . ." Abstinence from the normal marital relations was allowable only upon the consent of both partners, and even then only for purposes of prayer (in some special sense), and only "for a season."

"Fasting . . ." in this verse (AV) was an interpolation, being not found in any of the primary manuscripts; but despite this, the requirement that married couples live apart during Lent was grounded on this interpolation.[16]

Verse 6, *But this I say by way of concession, not of commandment.*

---

[15]Donald S. Metz, *op. cit.*, p. 878.
[16]F. W. Farrar, *op. cit.*, p. 224.

This verse has been grossly misunderstood as a denial of his inspiration on Paul's part, as if he had said that he was in some manner unsure of the advice he gave. This is not true at all; but it indicates that such behavior as celibacy and married couples refraining from cohabitation for "a season" were allowable, but not required, a concession not a commandment. There is no restriction whatever upon Paul's inspiration visible in this verse.

Verse 7, *Yet I would that all men were even as I myself. Howbeit each man hath his own gift from God, one after this manner, and another after that.*

"Would that all men . . ." Paul could not have meant that he wished that all men were unmarried, like himself, but rather that all men had the gift of continence, which is clearly "his own gift from God."

"Even as I myself . . ." The question of whether or not Paul was ever married always surfaces here, there being many dogmatic opinions supporting either view. One thing is certain, Paul was at this time not married. Halley gave his opinion that "This chapter seems to have been written by one who knew something of the intimacies of the married life,"[17] and combined this with the fact of Paul's voting in the Sanhedrin (Acts 26:10), for which, it was said, marriage was a prerequisite, making these the two reasons for supposing that Paul had been married. Shore, however, declared that "The almost universal tradition of the early church was that Paul was never married."[18] However, that tradition appears to be weak. Farrar stated that it "has no certain support of tradition";[19] and the testimony of both Tertullian and Jerome (in favor of the "unmarried" view) he wrote off as inadmissible, because both of them "were biased witnesses."[20] It is not a matter of great import either way, but this student inclines to the belief that Paul was a widower, his wife having deserted him at the time of his conversion. Moreover the tradition of

---

[17]Henry H. Halley, *Bible Handbook* (Grand Rapids: Zondervan Publishing House, 1927), p. 546.

[18]T. Teignmouth Shore, *Ellicott's Commentary on the Whole Bible* (Grand Rapids: Zondervan Publishing House, 1959), p. 807.

[19]F. W. Farrar, *op. cit.*, p. 225.

[20]*Ibid.*

Paul's never having been married was most likely fostered by the historic church as a support of their unscriptural doctrine of celibacy for the clergy.

Verse 8, *But I say to the unmarried and to widows, It is good for them if they abide even as I.*

Paul here began his answer to the question of whether unmarried persons (widows, naturally included) should marry or not.

"It is good for them if they abide even as I . . ." This was the permission of the apostle, and even his approval, that for those who were able to live chastely without marriage, it would be better for them not to marry due to "the distress that is upon us" (v. 26). A savage persecution against the church was then raging, and it was an inopportune time for marrying; but, even so, Paul did not forbid it.

Verse 9, *But if they have no continency, let them marry: for it better to marry than to burn.*

McGarvey's analysis of Paul's answer has this: "He advises the unmarried who have the gift of self-control to remain unmarried, but those lacking it should avoid unlawful lusts by marriage"[21]

"Better to marry than to burn . . ." has reference to being on fire with passion.

Verse 10, *But unto the married I give charge, yet not I, but the Lord, That the wife depart not from her husband.*

"Not I but the Lord . . ." The third question from Corinth had asked if divorce was permitted; and Paul here answered in the negative. The words "not I but the Lord" have been construed by some as an admission on Paul's part that some of his advice in this chapter was not inspired, but no such meaning is logically derived from what is said here. What Paul declared here is that it was unnecessary for him to give any inspired utterance on such a subject, because the Lord himself had given specific commandment on this very thing (Matt. 5:32; 19:9; Mark 10:9; Luke 16:18). "Paul here distinguished

[21]J. W. McGarvey, *Commentary on First Corinthians* (Cincinnati: Standard Publishing Company, 1916), p. 80.

between Jesus' command during his ministry and his own apostolic rulings, for which inspiration is claimed."[22]

Verse 11, *(But should she depart, let her remain unmarried, or else be reconciled to her husband); and that the husband leave not his wife.*

Paul left out of view in this verse the exception Jesus gave in Matthew 19:9, "except it be for fornication"; but this may not be construed as a denial of it. Paul's failure to mention the exception was likely due to the fact that it did not apply in the case propounded by the letter from Corinth. As De Hoff said, "Paul told her either to remain unmarried or else be reconciled to her husband. Divorce never solves a problem; it only creates more problems." Of course, exactly the same rule applied to husbands who left their wives.

Verse 12, *But to the rest say I, not the Lord: If any brother hath an unbelieving wife, and she is content to dwell with him, let him not leave her.*

"Say I, not the Lord . . ." The meaning here is not that Paul's injunction here had any less inspiration and authority behind it, but that its authority derived from his own apostolical commission, and not from any direct commandment uttered by Jesus during his ministry, such as that he had just cited. There is not the slightest disclaimer here of full and absolute authority for what Paul commanded in the Spirit of God. As Marsh expressed it, "In this instance Paul cannot refer to any direct command of Christ, as he could for the previous case; but his words carry the full weight of inspiration and authority."[23] One must deplore the blindness of many commentators on this exceedingly important point.

Jesus' teaching on marriage was directed to the Jews who were all in covenant relationship with God; and his words had no application at all to mixed marriages which Paul dealt with here; hence the necessity for Paul to issue the command himself in the fullness of his apostolical authority. How easy it would have been for him to attribute some saying to Jesus on

---

[22]Donald Guthrie, *The New Bible Commentary* (Grand Rapids: Wm. B. Eerdmans Publishing Company, 1970), p. 1059.

[23]Paul W. Marsh, *op. cit.*, p. 888.

this, instead of assuming full responsibility for it himself; but, in the light of his example, we may be sure that no apostle ever did such a thing. How vain, therefore, are the speculations of a certain school of critics who accuse the apostles of attributing to Jesus words which were, in fact, their own deductions and not the words of the Lord. Paul's distinguishing such things in this verse is an overwhelmingly powerful testimony to the truth of the entire NT.

This verse through verse 16 deals with the problem of divorce in mixed marriages, that is, marriages between Christians and pagans, a situation which arose, not from Christians marrying pagans, but from the conversion of one out of a pagan couple. Paul's command here is that the marriage stands, unless the unbeliever is unwilling and will not allow it to stand.

Verse 13, *And the woman that hath an unbelieving husband, and he is content to dwell with her, let her not leave her husband.*

The teaching here is the same as in the previous verse, except it applies to the Christian woman, just as verse 12 applied to the Christian man, with an unbelieving marriage partner. See under above verse.

Verse 14, *For the unbelieving husband is sanctified in the wife, and the unbelieving wife is sanctified in the brother: else were your children unclean; but now are they holy.*

"Sanctified . . ." "This verb cannot mean 'holy in Christ before God,' because that kind of holiness cannot be predicated of an unbeliever."[24] Paul here uses such a term in a ceremonial sense, rather than in a sense suggesting the salvation either of the unbelieving partner or of the children. As Johnson said:

> Paul simply means that the OT principle of the communication of uncleanness does not hold. The union is lawful and confers privileges on the members, such as the protection of God and the opportunity of being in close contact with one in God's family.[25]

---

[24]Donald S. Metz, *op. cit.*, p. 878.
[25]S. Lewis Johnson, Jr., *Wycliffe Bible Commentary* (Chicago: Moody Press, 1971), p. 608.

Those who seek to find here any authority for infant church membership are frustrated by the fact that nothing of the kind is even intimated. "There is not one word about baptism here, not one allusion to it; nor does the argument in the remotest degree bear upon it."[26] Furthermore, as Morris pointed out, the "holiness" here ascribed to children applies only "until the child is old enough to take responsibility upon himself."[27]

Verse 15, *Yet if the unbelieving departeth, let him depart: the brother or the sister is not under bondage in such cases: but God hath called us in peace.*

"The brother or sister is not under bondage . . ." Some question whether or not such a brother or sister might remarry; but the view here is that, if not, then the brother or sister would still be in bondage. [This is another exception, distinguished from the "adultery" mentioned by the Lord (Matt. 19:9), but the desertion of a Christian partner by an unbeliever is thought by some to be presumptive proof of adultery also.] Besides that, Paul was dealing with mixed marriages, which were not in the purview of Jesus' teaching at all. Many have disputed this interpretation. De Hoff declared that "This does not mean that he (the forsaken one) is free to marry again."[28] David Lipscomb also believed that, "In such cases, remarriage is not approved";[29] but he went on to add that if the departing unbeliever should marry again, the wife or husband forsaken would be at liberty to remarry. It seems to this student, however, that Macknight's view of this place is correct. He said:

> Here he declares that the party who was willing to continue the marriage, but who was deserted notwithstanding a reconciliation had been attempted, was at liberty to marry. And his decision is just, because there is no reason why the innocent party, through the fault of the guilty party, should be exposed to the danger of committing adultery.[30]

See note at end of chapter 7.

---

[26]Albert Barnes, *op. cit.*, p. 117.
[27]Leon Morris, *op. cit.*, p. 110.
[28]George W. De Hoff, *op. cit.*, p. 66.
[29]David Lipscomb, *op. cit.*, p. 102.
[30]James Macknight, *op. cit.*, p. 107.

Metz was doubtless correct in the comment that "Paul's directive does not grant permission for a Christian to marry an unbeliever."[31] The guidelines apply to situations in which one of a pagan couple accepts Christianity, and the other does not. Even then, the marriage is binding unless the unbeliever deserts the faithful partner.

Verse 16, *For how knowest thou, O wife, whether thou shalt save thy husband? or how knowest thou, O husband, whether thou shalt save thy wife?*

Bruce believed that "A mixed marriage of the kind Paul had in mind is fraught with missionary possibility,"[32] indicating that Paul's meaning here is that perhaps the faithful partner might be able to convert the unbeliever. There is another possible meaning of this somewhat ambiguous verse. It could mean, "God's aim for us is peace, which will best be secured by separation; the possibility of saving the heathen partner is, after all, quite uncertain."[33] Morris preferred the latter view, adding that "Marriage is not to be regarded simply as an instrument of evangelism."[34] Despite this, it seems that the first view, advocated by Bruce, is preferable. The principal deterrent to this is the reference to God's having called us to peace (at the end of verse 15). It is a known fact that many a marriage with unbelievers has proved to be the means of converting the unbeliever; but Paul certainly did not advocate marriage with such an end in view. This verse concludes Paul's teaching on mixed marriages; and, as always, there is evident in it the most devout and sincere desire for the salvation of men's souls. Everything else is secondary.

Verse 17, *Only, as the Lord hath distributed to each man, as God hath called each, so let him walk. And so ordain I in all churches.*

The problem of the innocent party in a mixed marriage disposed of, Paul here made a digression to legislate in the

---

[31]Donald R. Metz, *op. cit.*, p. 879.
[32]F. F. Bruce, *Answers to Questions* (Grand Rapids. Zondervan Publishing House, 1972), p. 92.
[33]J. R. Dummelow, *Commentary on the Holy Bible* (New York: The Macmillan Company, 1937), p. 908.
[34]Leon Morris, *op. cit.*, p. 111.

power of the Holy Spirit on the larger question behind it, that greater question deriving from an error being advocated at Corinth by certain false teachers. "The Judaizers taught that, by embracing the true religion, all former obligations under which the convert lay were dissolved."[35] Any widespread acceptance of such an error would have resulted in social chaos and precipitated even more savage and relentless persecutions against the church; therefore, for both practical and ethical reasons the error had to be struck down.

"As the Lord hath distributed to each man . . ." refers to the status of each man in the fabric of the social order, some being wealthy, others poor, some free, others slaves, etc.

"As God hath called each, so let him walk . . ." Accepting the gospel did not change prior conditions and obligations of the convert in any legal sense, despite the fact that the holy principles of Christianity were inherently charged with power to destroy many shameful institutions in the pagan society. "The gospel, instead of weakening any moral or just political obligation, strengthened them all."[36]

Verses 18-19, *Was any man called being circumcised? let him not become uncircumcised. Hath any been called in uncircumcision? let him not be circumcised. Circumcision is nothing, and uncircumcision is nothing; but keeping the commandments of God.*

"Let him not become uncircumcised . . ." Through surgery, it was possible to do this; and Macknight related how "Apostate Jews (by such action) fancied that they freed themselves from their obligation to obey the law of Moses."[37]

"Circumcision is nothing . . . etc." Three times Paul made this statement, each time concluding with a powerful statement of that which *is everything*; here it is "keeping the commandments of God." In Galatians 5:6, it is "faith working through love"; and in Galatians 6:15, it is "a new creation." Any reconciliation of these epic pronouncements with the Protestant heresy of salvation "by faith alone" is impossible.

---

[35]James Macknight, *op. cit.*, p. 108.
[36]*Ibid.*
[37]*Ibid.*

As the apostle John said, "And hereby we know that we know him, if we keep his commandments" (1 John 2:3).

"Let him not be circumcised . . ." is an order applicable to all of every class who become Christians; and it may not be allowed that the practice of this rite, which is essentially racial and religious, could be acceptable under any circumstances in the church for any persons whomsoever. Paul's circumcision of Timothy has no bearing whatever on this.

Verses 20-21, *Let each man abide in that calling wherein he was called. Wast thou called being a bondservant? care not for it: nay, even if thou canst become free, use it rather.*

There is nothing in this passage which forbids any man to strive for betterment of conditions in his life; but what is forbidden is any thought that such "better conditions" could denote any higher spiritual condition. A slave could be just as noble and successful a Christian as anyone else. Furthermore, many Christians have destroyed their spiritual lives, or greatly damaged them, by inordinate desire to improve their economic or social status. There is something of what Paul wrote to Timothy in this admonition here: "Godliness with contentment is great gain . . . having food and covering we shall be therewith content" (1 Tim. 6:6-8).

"Even if thou canst become free, use it rather . . ." There is an amazing uncertainty among the wisest scholars as to what Paul meant by this, and this is reflected in the various versions.

> RSV: If you can gain your freedom, avail yourself of the opportunity. (Footnote on last clause: make use of your present condition instead.)
> NEB: If a chance of liberty should come, take it. (Footnote: But even if a chance of liberty should come, choose rather to make good use of your servitude.)

Practically all scholars agree with Shore that the interpretation given in the footnotes "is most in accordance with the construction of the sentence in the original Greek."[38] Furthermore, that view is in perfect harmony with the whole thrust of

---

[38]T. Teignmouth Shore, *op. cit.*, p. 810.

Paul's paragraph here, as well as with his teaching elsewhere and his invariable practice.

Perhaps, if the circumstances of the slaves at Corinth to whom these words were originally addressed could be known, more light on the true meaning would be available. For example, was Paul addressing the slaves of pagans, or of Christians? If it should be allowed here that Paul advised continuation in servitude, even for one who might have procured his liberty, it would not necessarily follow that such was intended as the will of God for all ages to come. McGarvey believed that Paul meant that "If freedom can be obtained, it is to be preferred";[39] and if master and slave are both Christians, it should be bestowed, as Paul clearly suggested to Philemon. Thus, there can be no doubt of the repugnance in which the apostle held the whole institution of slavery; but he held that conviction in the caution of a very wise restraint. Although the word *emancipation* seemed to be always trembling upon Paul's lips, he never uttered it. Why?

If one single word could have been quoted in Rome as tending to excite slaves to revolt, it would have quadrupled the intensity and savagery of the imperial government's hatred and persecution of Christians at a time when persecution was already under way; and that fact could have resulted in Paul's recommendation here. Furthermore, Lipscomb gave this further analysis:

> Nor would the danger of preaching the abolition of slavery be confined to that arising from external violence of Rome against the church; it would have been pregnant with danger to the purity of the church itself. Many would have been led to join a communion which would have aided them in securing their freedom. In these considerations, we find ample reasons for the position of non-interference with slavery which Paul maintained.[40]

In keeping with such circumstances, Paul only hinted that Philemon should free Onesimus; and here he advised that slaves continue to serve God in their condition of servitude. Lipscomb preferred the rendition of Paul's words as, "If the

[39]J. W. McGarvey, *op. cit.*, p. 82.
[40]David Lipscomb, *op. cit.*, p. 107.

Christian slave could be free, he should prefer his condition as a converted slave."[41]

Before leaving this, it should be noted that the apostolical commandment regarding what was preferable under those peculiar and exceptional circumstances may not be understood as binding at the present time and in far different circumstances.

Verse 22, *For he that was called in the Lord being a bondservant, is the Lord's freedman: likewise he that was called being free, is Christ's bondservant.*

"The man who is a slave is free in Christ, and the man who is free is the servant of Christ."[42] Thus there is the fulfillment of the principle, "Let the brother of low degree glory in his high estate: and the rich, in that he is made low" (James 1:9, 10).

Verse 23, *Ye were bought with a price; become not bondservants of men.*

Bruce favored the preferred renditions of RSV and NEB in verse 21, because, he said, "This interpretation is more in line with the principle of verse 23."[43] However, it is the conviction here that Paul used the word "bondservants" in a different sense here, it being extremely unlikely that anyone would voluntarily have become a bondservant of another. What is meant is that "Christians should not be dragooned by others in the way they should live.[44] In context (which we do not certainly know), Paul could have meant, "Do not allow yourselves to be made bondservants of those who are agitating the slavery question. You do not belong to *them*; you belong to Christ, having been purchased by his precious blood."

Verse 24, *Brethren, let each man, wherein he was called, therein abide with God.*

This is a pointed recapitulation of the whole paragraph (vv. 17-24).

---

[41]*Ibid.*
[42]Donald R. Metz, *op. cit.*, p. 882.
[43]F. F. Bruce, *op. cit.*, p. 92.
[44]Donald Guthrie, *op. cit.*, p. 1061.

Verse 25, *Now concerning virgins I have no commandment of the Lord: but I give my judgment, as one that hath obtained mercy of the Lord to be trustworthy.*

This is the fifth question answered in this chapter; and, "Apparently, the church at Corinth had asked Paul's opinion regarding unmarried daughters and the responsibilities of parents in such instances."[45] This comment is correct as far as it goes; but the duties of guardians as well as those of parents must be included; and sons as well as daughters were also included by the term "virgins" as used here.

"Virgins . . ." Wesley said this means "of either sex."[46] Barclay's objection that "It is hard to see why Paul used the word *virgin* if he meant *daughter*"[47] is refuted by the fact that Paul did not mean daughter, but unmarried young people of both sexes. As Adam Clarke noted, "The word in this place means young unmarried persons of either sex, as is plain from verses 26, 27, 32-34, and from Revelation 14:4."[48] The fact that the word *virgin* has a different meaning in our day does not alter its evident meaning in this place.

"I have no commandment of the Lord . . ." is not a disclaimer of inspiration on Paul's part at all; it is a statement that the Lord during his ministry did not make a specific pronouncement upon this subject. The meaning is like that in verse 12, above; Paul made a distinction between words that Jesus delivered during his ministry and his own inspired teachings, doing so, no doubt, out of respect to the Lord, but with no sense of diminishing the authority of his own inspired teachings. As Morris said:

> Moffatt points out that Paul's careful discrimination between a saying of the Lord and his own injunction tells strongly against those who maintain that the early church was in the habit of producing the sayings it needed and then ascribing them to Christ.[49]

---

[45]Donald R. Metz, *op. cit.*, p. 888.
[46]John Wesley, *One Volume NT Commentary* (Grand Rapids: Baker Book House, 1972), in loco.
[47]William Barclay, *The Letters to the Corinthians* (Philadelphia: The Westminster Press, 1954), p. 74.
[48]Adam Clarke, *op. cit.*, p. 225.
[49]Leon Morris, *op. cit.*, p. 109.

"As one that hath obtained mercy of the Lord to be trustworthy . . ." In context, this is a full affirmation of Paul's apostolical power and authority, added to prevent any misunderstanding of the fact that the Lord had not *personally* legislated on this question.

Verse 26, *I think therefore that this is good by reason of the distress that is upon us, namely, that it is good for a man to be as he is.*

That the meaning of "virgins" in verse 25 includes both sexes is implicit in the specific mention of "men" here. As Macknight said,"Paul declared, beginning with the case of the male virgin, that it was good in the present distress to remain unmarried."[50] Here again, as in verse 1, "good" denotes not what was commanded but what was advisable.

Verse 27, *Art thou bound to a wife? seek not to be loosed. Art thou loosed from a wife? seek not a wife.*

"The present distress . . ." mentioned in the previous verse looms ominously in the background of these remarks. History has not revealed the nature of the awful persecution inflicted upon the Christians at this particular point, but it should be remembered that both Jewish and Gentile enemies of the faith would have seized any opportunity to exterminate, if possible, the Christian religion. The situation at Corinth was probably a local outburst of the persecutions which became more general at a later date. In any case, it may not be denied that some terrible onslaught against the faith of Christ was under way in Corinth at this very time. It was simply no favorable time for any man to be seeking to alter his marital status.

Verse 28, *But shouldest thou marry, thou hast not sinned; and if a virgin marry, she hath not sinned. Yet such shall have tribulation in the flesh: and I would spare you.*

Regardless of the practical wisdom against it, Paul still allowed that marriage was honorable and that those entering such a state did not sin.

"If a virgin marry . . ." This refers to virgin daughters, making it clear that *both* sexes are in view here, men having been mentioned in verse 26.

---

[50]James Macknight, *op. cit.*, p. 97.

"Tribulation in the flesh . . ." is a reference to the sufferings and deprivations invariably associated with persecutions in the first century. Such tribulations would be far more severe upon the married than upon the unmarried.

Verses 29-30, *But this I say, brethren, the time is shortened, that henceforth both those that have wives may be as though they had none; and those that weep, as though they wept not; and those that rejoice as though they rejoiced not; and those that buy as though they possessed not.*

This affectionate warning was given in the light of the transience of life, man's span upon the earth being indeed "shortened" as compared with the longevity of the patriarchs. All earthly pursuits should be made and all obligations and conditions considered in the light of the tragic fact that "Upon my day of life the night is falling!"

"Let us not for one moment think that this principle was evolved by Paul from a mistaken belief that the Second Advent was close at hand."[51] There is not the slightest hint in this passage of Christ's second coming, except in the general sense of its being always proper for Christians to live as expecting it and being prepared for it. The time of Christ's return was one point upon which Jesus declared that the apostles *could not* be informed; and it was the only point upon which they *were not* informed. It is a weariness to read the carpings of the exegetes always prating about how the apostles and the early church were *mistaken* about this. All of them with even elementary knowledge of what Jesus taught *knew* that the time of the Second Coming had not been revealed, not even to the Son of God (Matt. 24:36); and the various apostolical exhortations with respect to "expecting" it were given in the light of that knowledge. Instead of a conceited glorying in their so-called "mistake" on such exhortations, it would be far better for Christians today to take the same attitude as the apostles and pray, "Even so, come quickly, Lord Jesus" (Rev. 21:20), such words having exactly the same meaning for us as they had for the apostles who uttered them, and in neither case being any kind of "mistake"!

---

[51]T. Teignmouth Shore, *op. cit.*, p. 812.

Verse 31, *And those that use the world, as not using it to the full: for the fashion of this world passeth away.*

This really belongs with the two previous verses, being a part of the same exhortation to prudence in view of the transcience of earthly existence and the swift changes that accompany our mortality.

Verse 32, *But I would have you to be free from cares. He that is unmarried is careful for the things of the Lord, how he may please the Lord.*

This was the basis of Paul's recommendation of the single status for those whose self-restraint made it possible, the unencumbered being able more wholeheartedly to serve the interests of true religion than those pressed down with cares and obligations.

Verse 33, *But he that is married is careful for the things of the world, how he may please his wife, and is divided.*

Paul did not condemn man's efforts in the secular sphere, but was pointing out the preemption of time and efforts required in the support of a wife and family, such a division of the Christian's energies being inherent in such a thing as marriage. All of this was said as persuasion to induce any who *could* to avoid marriage during that "present distress."

Verse 34, *So also the woman that is unmarried and the virgin is careful for the things of the Lord, that he may be holy both in body and in spirit: but she that is married is careful for the things of the world, how she may please her husband.*

This verse properly begins with "is divided," which was included with verse 33 above. The teaching here is the same as there, except that it would appear that Paul, in the word"unmarried," included widows along with virgin daughters as subjects of the same advice. However, Macknight very probably has the true meaning in his rendition of this verse thus:

> There is difference also between a wife and a virgin: the unmarried woman careth for the things of the Lord, that she may be holy both in body and spirit: but she that

> is married careth for things of the world, how she may please her husband.[52]

Also, note that the antecedent of the masculine pronoun here is "virgin."

Verse 35, *And this I say for your own profit; not that I may cast a snare upon you, but for that which is seemly, and that ye may attend upon the Lord without distraction.*

Paul's personal preference for celibacy on the part of persons who were capable of it, and in certain circumstances, for more complete dedication, has always appealed to some in every age; and it is not right to depreciate such behavior. Shore pointed out that England's Queen Elizabeth I was one who made exactly the choice Paul recommended in these verses, although for a different purpose, and yet a high purpose.

> Elizabeth I declared that England was her husband and all Englishmen her children, and that she desired no higher character or fairer remembrance of her to be transmitted to posterity than this inscription engraved upon her tombstone: "Here lies Elizabeth, who lived and died a maiden queen."[53]

Verse 36, *But if any man thinketh that he behaveth himself unseemly toward his virgin daughter, if she be past the flower of her age, and if need so requireth, let him do what he will; he sinneth not; let them marry.*

The RSV has butchered this text in the most deplorable and high-handed mistranslation of it that could possibly be imagined.

"If any man . . ." was used by Paul here for the purpose of including guardians of young women of marriageable age as well as parents; and to make "any man" in this passage refer to any man shacked up in some kind of platonic partnership with a member of the opposite sex is nothing but a shameful rape of this passage. As Foy E. Wallace noted, "They made the virgin daughter in this place the girl-friend of another man to whom the virgin was betrothed, advising him to be free in his

---

[52]James Macknight, *op. cit.*, p. 114.
[53]T. Teignmouth Shore, *op. cit.*, p. 818.

behavior!"[54] Wallace caught the spirit of the RSV exactly in his words: "The passage is perverted to allow sexual satisfaction 'if his passions are strong,' and 'to do what he will,' and 'he does not sin' in such pre-marital relations."[55]

Dummelow affirmed unequivocally that "any man" in the above passage means "any parent or guardian."[56] There is no way to understand this passage except in the light of the customs of the day, "And the father (or guardian) had control of the arrangements for his daughter's marriage."[57] The kind of situation assumed to have been the object of Paul's remarks (as in the RSV and NEB) was absolutely impossible in the first century. No father or guardian would have allowed such an arrangement (as that supposed) under any threat or circumstance whatever. Therefore, with the utmost confidence, the perversion of this place by some of the new translations and even by the RSV is condemned as being sinful, incorrect, and even blasphemous. It was not some passionate suitor Paul had in mind, but the daughter's father; because, as F. F. Bruce said,"The word rendered *giveth in marriage* twice in verse 38 (RV) is normally used of a father's giving his daughter in marriage."[58] "The then universal custom of Jews, Greeks and Romans (was) that the father or guardian disposed of the daughter's hand (in marriage)."[59]

"If she be past the flower of her age ... and need so requireth ..." Any denial of marriage to an aging daughter would indeed seem unseemly to a loving parent, who should feel no sense of sin in giving his daughter's hand in marriage.

"Let them marry ..." This was the injunction to parents and guardians, and it has no reference at all to some passionate suitor shacked up with his girl-friend.

"Let him do what he will ... he sinneth not ..." This means allow the parents or guardians in such cases to do what they

---

[54]Foy E. Wallace, Jr., *A Review of the New Versions* (Fort Worth: The Foy E. Wallace, Jr., Publications, 1978), p. 488.
[55]*Ibid.*
[56]J. R. Dummelow, *op. cit.*, p. 904.
[57]S. Lewis Johnson, *op. cit.*, p. 610.
[58]F. F. Bruce, *op. cit.*, p. 98.
[59]John William Russell, *Compact Commentary on the NT* (Grand Rapids: Baker Book House, 1964), p. 415.

believe is best; no sin is involved in contracting marriages, despite all that Paul had said about celibacy.

Verse 37, *But he that standeth stedfast in his heart, having no necessity, but hath power as touching his own will, and hath determined this in his own heart, to keep his own virgin daughter, shall do well.*

"To keep his own virgin daughter . . ." here is the opposite of "giveth his own virgin daughter in marriage" in the next verse, absolutely requiring the sense in verse 37 to be that of *not* giving her in marriage, making it absolutely certain that the problem of whether or not to give daughters in marriage was the problem Paul was discussing in this passage. The sense of this verse is that a Christian parent or guardian fully determined to withhold his daughter's hand in marriage might do so without sin, and might even be commended for it.

Verse 38, *So then both he that giveth his own virgin daughter in marriage does well; and he that giveth her not in marriage shall do better.*

Either solution of the problem on the part of parents and guardians was acceptable; but, as throughout this chapter, due to the present distress, Paul still recommended (although he did not command) not to give the daughter's hand in marriage.

Verses 39-40, *A wife is bound for so long a time as her husband liveth; but if the husband be dead, she is free to be married to whom she will; only in the Lord. But she is happier if she abide as she is, after my judgment: and I think that I have the Spirit of God.*

This was the sixth question Paul answered in this chapter; and the answer to this one was easy. Yes, widows might indeed marry again, but "only in the Lord." It was never intended that Christians marry unbelievers, as Paul spelled out more fully in 2 Corinthians 6:14ff. It is a rare and exceptional thing indeed that mixed marriages between Christians and unbelievers can produce anything but sorrow. As Barclay said:

> One thing it must be, Paul laid down here; it must be a marriage in the Lord . . . Long, long ago, Plutarch, the wise old Greek, laid it down that "marriage cannot be

> happy unless husband and wife are of the same religion."[60]

"I think that I have the Spirit of God . . ." This is not the expression of any uncertainty but the polite insistence of Paul that his words in this chapter and throughout his writings were inspired by God's Spirit. The judgment of the church through the ages concurs in this. As Wesley said:

> Whoever would conclude from this that Paul was not certain he had the Holy Spirit neither understands the true import of the words, nor considers how expressly he lays claim to the Spirit, both in this epistle (2:16; 14:37) and the other (13:3).[61]

Wesley also thought that the words "I think," as used by Paul here and elsewhere, "*always* imply the fullest and strongest assurance."[62] Leon Morris, one of the *more* able scholars, also believed this. He wrote:

> There is nothing tentative about the authority with which Paul speaks. He has throughout this discussion made it clear when he is quoting Christ and when he is not. Now he gives his firm opinion that in what he says he has the Spirit of God. He is conscious of the divine enablement. What he says is more than the opinion merely of a private individual.[63]

Note on v. 15:

The view that desertion of a Christian partner by an unbeliever is also presumptive proof of adultery is actually irrelevant to the meaning of this passage. The exception granted by the apostle Paul is grounded upon the fact, not of adultery, but of *desertion* by an unbelieving partner. The authority of this lies in the plenary authority of the blessed apostle, inspired and guided by the Holy Spirit, making this therefore to be an additional exception given by Christ himself *through* the apostle Paul. Any other view of the apostolical writings is absolutely untenable. It is our view that God, through the Holy Spirit, is the author of *all the NT*.

---

[60]William Barclay, *op. cit.*, p. 79.
[61]John Wesley, *op. cit.*, in loco.
[62]*Ibid.*
[63]Leon Morris, *op. cit.*, p. 123.

Furthermore, we do not believe that any man or any group of men is endowed with authority to set aside or countermand any declaration in the sacred text upon the basis of their interpretations of related passages. What Paul said, *stands.* Let men keep their hands off of it!

Also, there is no conflict between Paul's word here and Matthew 19:9. There is a covenant relationship there which is *not* in this situation. Paul and Jesus were speaking of two utterly different situations.

CHAPTER 8

Beginning here and through 11:1, this epistle discusses food (especially meat) sacrificed to idols; and in the culture and society of the people who first received it the problems here dealt with were paramount and practically universal. The total meat supply, in any practical sense, came from the sacrifices to the idol gods of the Gentiles, a portion of each sacrifice being the perquisite of the pagan priest, and the rest of it consumed in the temple area itself, carried to the homes of the worshipers, or sold, either by them or the priests, in the common meat markets.

It might be inquired, what relevance is the apostolical teaching, with regard to Christians partaking of such meats, to the peoples of this present age; to which it must be replied that they are of the most commanding relevance and importance. This is true because the apostle Paul established four timeless principles of Christian behavior in the course of his writing on this subject, these being (1) that what is permissible behavior for one man may, in certain circumstances, be dangerous and sinful in another, (2) that no Christian conduct should be evaluated solely from the standpoint of knowledge, but in the light of the love of brethren, with regard to its possible influence upon others, and in the light of what others may think of it, (3) that no Christian has a right to practice anything, however innocent it may be to him, if in so doing he shall damage the faith of another, and (4) that whatever is done, even to the weakest member of the body of Christ, is also done to Christ himself, and that weakening or destroying the faith of even the least and weakest of Christ's members is a sin of the greatest magnitude against Christ himself. "A pleasure or an indulgence which may be the ruin of someone else is not a pleasure but a sin."[1]

---

[1]William Barclay, *The Letters to the Corinthians* (Philadelphia: The Westminster Press, 1954), p. 85.

Verse 1, *Now concerning things sacrificed to idols: We know that we all have knowledge. Knowledge puffeth up, but love edifieth.*

"Now concerning . . ." These words indicate that "the Corinthians had asked Paul questions in regard to these matters,"[2] a fact also indicated by the use of quotation marks to set off portions of this verse and in verses 4 and 5 in the RSV.

"We all have knowledge . . ." This was the conceited declaration of the questioners from Corinth who evidently indulged themselves in the pagan temples without regard to weak brethren; and the first thing Paul did was to nail down the fact that "knowledge" without love was the grossest ignorance.

"Knowledge puffeth up, but love buildeth up . . ." is the way this stands in the Greek (RV margin); and it is a shame that our translators changed it. Knowledge without love only puffs up the one who fancies he is wise and does nothing for others, whereas love builds up both its possessor and others.

The evident concern of Paul's questioners did not refer to themselves (they already knew everything), but "they wanted to know how to deal with the people who refused to eat meat sacrificed to idols."[3] Despite this conceit, some of them were actually "sitting at meat in an idol's temple"! (v. 10). As some would say today, they were bringing their "culture" into the church!

The problem regarded several possibilities: (1) Should a Christian partake of the feasts in the idol temples? (2) Was it permissible for him to buy food in the public markets, where most if not all of it had been procured from the sacrifices? (3) Might he, when invited to a friend's house, eat flesh which had been sacrificed to idols?

Verse 2, *If any man thinketh that he knoweth anything, he knoweth not yet as he ought to know.*

"Thinketh that he knoweth . . ." All earthly knowledge is partial and fragmentary. "Knowledge is proud that it has

---

[2]David Lipscomb, *Commentary on First Corinthians* (Nashville: The Gospel Advocate Company, 1935), p. 117.
[3]F. W. Grosheide, *The New International Commentary* (Grand Rapids: Wm. B. Eerdmans Publishing Company, 1953), p. 189.

learned so much. Wisdom is humble that it knows no more."[4] In thinking that they knew everything and at the same time despising the brethren they denominated as ignorant, the Corinthians indeed knew nothing as they should have known.

Verse 3, *But if any man loveth God, the same is known by him.*

This verse ends surprisingly with "the same is known by him," instead of "the same knows him," as might have been expected; and Farrar was probably correct in the observation that:

> Paul did not wish to use any terms which would foster the already overgrown conceit of knowledge which was inflating the minds of his Corinthian converts. Furthermore he felt that "God knoweth them that are his" (2 Tim. 3:19).[5]

Also, as Morris said, "The really important thing is not that we know God, but that he knows us!"[6]

Verse 4, *Concerning therefore the eating of things sacrificed to idols, we know that no idol is anything in the world, and that there is no God but one.*

The sophisticated arguments of the "knowledge" party in Corinth are apparent in this. Since idols had no existence in fact, they felt safe in ignoring the popular superstitions regarding them; and Paul allowed the argument to stand, for the moment, it certainly being true that there is no God but one, and that an idol actually had no existence in reality.

However, although Paul did not recognize idols "as having any real existence, even as false deities,"[7] he was "certain that evil spirits and demons exist, and that in reality these were behind the idols and were using them to seduce men from the worship of the true God."[8] (See 10:20.)

---

[4]Attributed to Kay by Leon Morris, *Tyndale Commentary* (Grand Rapids: Wm. B. Eerdmans Publishing Company, 1958), p. 125.

[5]F. W. Farrar, *Pulpit Commentary* (Grand Rapids: Wm. B. Eerdmans Publishing Company, 1950), p. 264.

[6]Leon Morris, *op. cit.*, p. 125.

[7]John William Russell, *Compact Commentary on the NT* (Grand Rapids: Baker Book House, 1964), p. 416.

[8]William Barclay, *op. cit.*, p. 83.

"No idol is anything in the world . . ." Of course, the world was full of idols; but, as Wesley said:

> *Idol* here does not mean a mere image; but, by an inevitable transition of thought, the deity worshiped in the image. By this, Paul says that Zeus, Apollo, etc., have no existence; they are not to be found in the world.[9]

Furthermore, Paul does not by such a statement (that they are not in the world) leave room for the thought that they may be anywhere else. The "world" as used here refers to the whole universe.

"There is no God but one . . ." He is the God of Abraham, Isaac and Jacob, the God of the OT and of the Christian scriptures. He only is God in the true sense. He alone may rightfully be worshiped, and that through his Son Jesus Christ our Lord.

Verses 5-6, *For though there be that are called gods whether in heaven or on earth; as there are gods many, and lords many; yet to us there is one God, the Father, of whom are all things, and we unto him; and one Lord, Jesus Christ, through whom are all things, and we through him.*

The multiple names of pagan mythology illustrate the truth Paul mentioned regarding gods many and lords many; but the very fact of their being thought of as operating in heaven or on earth proved that none of them controlled "all things," hence the fragmented nature of deity as misunderstood in paganism.

"One God, the Father, of whom are all things . . ." There is no limitation with God, who cannot be localized like the false gods of the pagans. He is the Creator and sustainer of all things in heaven or upon earth.

"To us there is one God . . ." There is a difference in Christianity and false religions. "The Christian is not a syncretist, who attempts to harmonize the teachings of all religions."[10]

---

[9]John Wesley, *One Volume NT Commentary* (Grand Rapids: Baker Book House, 1972), in loco.

[10]Donald S. Metz, *Beacon Bible Commentary* (Kansas City: Beacon Hill Press, 1968), p. 392.

"Gods many and lords many.." Grosheide distinguished between the so-called deities of the pagans and their "heroes or demigods";[11] but the terms are here considered to be synonymous.

> *Lord* was the usual way of referring to deity in the various cults of the time, which makes Paul's frequent application of it to Jesus Christ significant. Paul simply made it clear that the heathen world worshiped a multitude of deities, putting no difference between them.[12]

"One Lord Jesus Christ . . ." There is affirmed here the oneness of God and Christ. God is honored as the Creator of all things and Christ his Son as the Creator of the New Creation. Jesus Christ is called "God" no less than ten times in the Greek NT. See CH, p. 31.

"We through him . . ." means "for whom we exist."[13]

"Through whom are all things . . ." in this clause "must be co-extensive with the 'all things' in the preceding verse, that is, the universe."[14]

Verse 7, *Howbeit there is not in all men that knowledge: but some, being used until now to the idol, eat as of a thing sacrificed to an idol; and their conscience being weak is defiled.*

"There is not in all men that knowledge . . ." Some facts are of a different quality from the ordinary; and, whereas the existence of an idol is no fact at all, there is the psychological fact of its existence in the *minds of men*; and Paul here drew attention to that fact, so totally passed over by the "knowledge" crowd at Corinth.

> The great mass of the heathen world *did* regard the dumb idols as the proper objects of worship, and supposed that they were inhabited by invisible spirits.[15]

Barnes declared that "Although the more intelligent heathen

---

[11]F. W. Grosheide, *op. cit.*, p. 192.
[12]Leon Morris, *op. cit.*, p. 126.
[13]F. W. Grosheide, *op. cit.*, p. 192.
[14]David Lipscomb, *op. cit.*, p. 120.
[15]Donald S. Metz, *op. cit.*, p. 391

put no confidence in them, yet the effect of the great masses was the same as if they had had a real existence."[16]

Regarding the rationalization by which intelligent men may worship images, and the specious logic by which the historical church itself consecrated and adored them, see full discussion in CR, pp. 44-45.

"Their conscience being weak is defiled . . ." For fuller comment on the subject of "conscience," see in CR, p. 469, and in CH, pp. 198-200.

When a man violates his conscience, he assaults the central monitor of his spiritual life; and regardless of whether or not the conscience is properly instructed, the violation of it is a spiritual disaster. This is why a person who thinks a certain action is a sin may not safely take such action.

"Defiled . . ." means polluted, sullied and damaged; and when the conscience is defiled, any true spiritual life becomes impossible.

Verse 8, *But food will not commend us to God: neither if we eat not, are we the worse; nor, if we eat, are we the better.*

In a sense, it was absolutely immaterial where the meat came from, whether sacrificed to idols or not; because salvation is simply not a matter of diet at all. Christ took away all prohibitions, "making all meats clean" (Mark 7:19); and Paul himself wrote that "every creature of God is good, and nothing is to be rejected, etc." (1 Tim. 4:4); but for a Christian who had not learned such vital truth, and who considered it sinful to eat certain things, it was definitely a sin for him to do so. In the situation at Corinth, therefore, it was not a question of determining what was right or wrong, merely in the abstract sense.

Verse 9, *But take heed lest by any means this liberty of yours become a stumblingblock to the weak.*

Many of the Corinthian Christians, so recently won over from paganism, still had lingering impressions of the reality of idol gods; and, besides those, there were many of Jewish

---

[16]Albert Barnes, *Notes on the NT* (Grand Rapids: Baker Book House, 1949), p. 141.

background whose entire lives and training were absolutely incompatible with any kind of indulgence regarding meat offered to idols. For both classes, it was against their conscience to eat such things.

"This liberty of yours . . ." If through the example of those who boasted "knowledge" to eat such meat, the weak brethren were induced to follow their example, irreparable damage to their souls would result. Paul here prohibited such heartless indifference toward the weak brethren. He said in effect: "Let your motto be forbearance, not privilege, and your watchword charity, not knowledge."[17]

It is considered significant that Paul here made no reference whatever to that so-called Council in Jerusalem which had directed all Christians to "abstain from things sacrificed to idols" (Acts 15:29); and, as more particularly advocated in CA, pp. 292ff, Paul's own authority was amply sufficient to teach God's will on such a subject, his authority and understanding of God's true will having been, in fact, the means of correcting the Council itself. Dummelow thought that Paul believed "The Corinthians would be more infiuenced by argument than by an appeal to authority, seeing they prided themselves on their wisdom";[18] but the conviction expressed here is that Paul did not feel that any word from the Council could have added anything whatever to his own authority. However, as Dummelow said, "Paul said nothing inconsistent"[19] with the judgment of the Council.

Verse 10, *For if a man see thee who hast knowledge sitting at meat in an idol's temple, will not his conscience, if he is weak, be emboldened to eat things sacrificed to idols?*

"See thee who hast knowledge . . ." There positively has to be a vein of sarcasm in this. What kind of "knowledge" did any Corinthian have that could justify sitting down in the degrading festival carried on in an idol's temple? "Many of these functions were often accompanied by shameful licentious-

---

[17]F. W. Farrar, *op. cit.*, p. 265.
[18]J. R. Dummelow, *Commentary on the Holy Bible* (New York: The Macmillan Company, 1937), p. 904.
[19]*Ibid.*

ness."[20] Paul did not digress here to point out that spiritual damage was almost certain to be sustained even by those who professed to have "knowledge" in such a participation as sitting down to a banquet in the temple of an idol, especially in a place like Corinth. Paul's great concern was damage to the weak brother and the wound thus inflicted upon the body of Christ which is the church. As Macknight said, "Paul could not have meant that they had a right to eat of the sacrifices in the idol's temple."[21] Although he passed over it here, Paul returned in 10:15-21 "to treat the other side of the question, that concerning the danger to which the strong believer exposed himself."[22] "To recline at a banquet in the temple of Poseidon or Aphrodite, especially in such a place as Corinth, was certainly an extravagant assertion of their right to Christian liberty."[23]

Verse 11, *For through thy knowledge he that is weak perisheth, the brother for whose sake Christ died!*

This was a hand grenade detonated in the faces of the "knowledge" group in Corinth. The word "knowledge" throughout this chapter belongs in quotations; because certainly it was not knowledge but the most incompetent ignorance that would approve of behavior capable of murdering an immortal soul.

That school of interpreters holding to the impossibility of apostasy on the part of believers strive to soften the impact of "perisheth." Thus Barnes saluted this verse with "No one who has been truly converted will apostatize and be destroyed."[24] Johnson declared this refers "to bodily perishing, not eternal perishing";[25] but he did not explain how eating meat against one's conscience could kill him! As Wesley put it, regarding "he that is weak perisheth":

---

[20]Henry H. Halley, *Bible Handbook* (Grand Rapids: Zondervan Publishing House, 1927), p. 517.

[21]James Macknight, *Apostolical Epistles and Commentary* (Grand Rapids: Baker Book House, 1969), p. 126.

[22]Attributed to Godet by John Wesley, *op. cit., in loco.*

[23]F. W. Farrar, *op. cit.*, p. 265.

[24]Albert Barnes, *op. cit.*, p. 146.

[25]S. Lewis Johnson, Jr., *Wycliffe Bible Commentary* (Chicago: Moody Press, 1971), p. 613.

> He is from that moment in the way of perdition... if this state continues and becomes aggravated, as is inevitable in such cases, eternal perdition is the end of it.[26]

Leon Morirs' words regarding the last clause of this verse are beautiful. He wrote:

> The last clause could hardly be more forcible in its appeal; every word tells; "the brother," not a mere stranger; "for the sake of whom" precisely to rescue him from destruction; "Christ," no less than he; "died," no less than that![27]

Verse 12, *And thus, sinning against the brethren, and wounding their conscience when it is weak, ye sin against Christ!*

Exclamation points have been used in this and the preceding verse to indicate the epic nature of these pronouncements.

"Sinning against the brethren . . . ye sin against Christ . . ." Whatever is done to the church, even in the person of its weakest and most insignificant members (as men count insignificance), is done to Christ. Paul learned this on the Damascus road, and he never forgot it. Was it right to override the scruples of young and weak Christians by indulgence of the appetite for meat? A million times NO! To do so was an unmitigated sin against the Redeemer himself. Paul did not require the support of any opinions from Jerusalem to add any weight to such a decree. This principle is eternally binding, forever true, and as wide in its application as the world itself.

Despite such an apostolical order, however, Paul diligently strove to evoke a feeling of tenderness in the conceited boasters of their "knowledge." The two words repeatedly stressed in the passage are weak (5 times) and *brother* (4 times). "These should have evoked tenderness and love, but received only the callous disregard of a misguided knowledge."[28]

Verse 13, *Wherefore, if meat causeth my brother to stumble, I will eat no flesh for evermore, that I cause not my brother to stumble.*

---

[26]John Wesley, *op. cit., in loco.*
[27]Leon Morris, *op. cit.*, p. 129.
[28]Paul W. Marsh, *A New Commentary* (Grand Rapids: Zondervan Publishing House, 1969). p. 391.

Paul did not lay down rules for others which he was unwilling to honor himself, being of a different sort altogether from the wicked Pharisees (Matt. 23:4).

Despite his firmness, however, Paul's pledge here is conditional. "If meat causeth my brother to stumble," is the qualifying clause; and this has the meaning of "stumble, so as to fall and be lost." Gutherie noted that: "Paul's decision is conditional, not absolute: He does not say he will henceforth always be a total abstainer, but only *if* and *when* such eating may cause a brother to fall."[29] De Hoff also has a fine paragraph on this. He wrote:

> On the other hand, there is such a thing as a brother who is not nearly so weak as he thinks, but who has been in the kingdom for years and is a crank and a fanatic. He has a tender conscience, he claims; and he tries to use it to control everybody else. His favorite passage is what Paul said about meats, which he applies to anything he wants to keep other people from doing. Of course, we shall just have to get along with this fellow as best we can![30]

This whole chapter exposed the shallowness and conceit of that "knowledge" which had no loving concern for weak and immature Christians, and bound upon all true Christians their responsibility for setting the correct example, regarding the scruples of others and for establishing a pattern of behavior which will build up others in the holy faith of Jesus Christ.

---

[29]Donald Guthrie, *The New Bible Commentary* (Grand Rapids: Wm. B. Eerdmans Publishing Company, 1970), p. 1062.

[30]George W. De Hoff, *Sermons on First Corinthians* (Murfreesboro, Tenn., 1947), p. 71.

CHAPTER 9

This whole chapter is devoted to the discussion of the rights of an apostle, and by extension, the rights of ministers of the gospel to support by their congregations, seven distinct and convincing arguments being given (vv. 1-14), with the remaining part of the chapter being taken up by Paul's explanation of why, in his own case, he did not compel the honoring of such right by the Corinthians. It begins with a pointed proof of his being a genuine apostle (vv. 1-3).

Verses 1-3, *Am I not free? am I not an apostle? have I not seen Jesus our Lord? are not ye my work in the Lord? If to others I am not an apostle, yet at least I am to you; for the seal of my apostleship are ye in the Lord. My defence to them that examine me is this.*

By the last sentence here Paul took knowledge of the slander then current in Corinth to the effect that he was not a true apostle, the alleged proof of it being that Paul had supported himself instead of claiming the emoluments of an apostle as the other apostles were doing. As De Hoff noted, "It is a common occurrence for some minister to preach on an evil and have the evil-doer condemn the preacher instead of repenting of the evil."[1]

Paul refuted the charge that he was not a genuine apostle with two indubitable proofs: (1) he had seen the Lord Jesus, and (2) God had marvelously blessed his apostleship, the Corinthian church itself being the stark proof of it, "the seal," as Paul called it, of his apostleship.

It is important to see in this short paragraph the impossibility of any man's being a true apostle unless he had seen Jesus Christ after our Lord's resurrection, thus being an eyewitness of the resurrection.

---

[1]George W. De Hoff, *Sermons on First Corinthians* (Murfreesboro, Tenn.: The Christian Press, 1947), p. 73.

First Argument

Verses 4-6, *Have we no right to eat and drink? Have we no right to lead about a wife that is a believer, even as the rest of the apostles, and the brethren of the Lord, and Cephas? Or I only and Barnabas, have we not a right to forbear working?*

"Have we no right . . .?" is a Hebrew idiom for "We certainly do have the right."

"To eat and drink . . ." means "entitled to be fed by the church."[2] It is incorrect to refer this to eating and drinking in an idol's temple.

"Wife that is a believer . . ." In view here, as Morris noted, is not the rights of apostles to marry; nobody in the first century would have raised any such question; rather, the thing in view is "the right to lead about a wife,"[3] maintaining her (along with her husband) at the church's expense.

"The rest of the apostles.. and Cephas . . ." This means that all of the other apostles, and Cephas (Peter) in particular, carried their wives with them on their missionary journeys; and Paul as a true apostle had the same right to do so. Significantly, Peter appears in this passage not as a celibate, but as a family man. It will be recalled that his mother-in-law was healed by Jesus (Matt. 8:14). Thus, it is certain that Peter did not forsake the married state to discharge his apostolical office.

"Brethren of the Lord . . ." These were James, and Joseph, and Simon and Judas (Matt. 13:55); and there is nothing in the NT that requires these to be understood in any other way than as the half-brothers of Jesus, the natural children of Joseph and the Virgin Mary, her virginity following the birth of Jesus being nothing but a superstition. For more on Mary's so-called perpetual virginity, see in CM, pp. 9-11.

"Or I only and Barnabas.." It appears that Barnabas also gave up his right to be supported by the churches. While

---

[2]J. W. McGarvey, *Commentary on First Corinthians* (Cincinnati: Standard Publishing Company, 1916), p. 89.

[3]Leon Morris, *Tyndale Commentary* (Grand Rapids: Wm. B. Eerdmans Publishing Company, 1958), p. 133.

commendable in the highest degree, this renunciation of the right of support on the part of Paul and Barnabas resulted in their being looked down upon by some who were steeped in the culture of the Greeks. "The philosophers regarded the men who performed menial tasks as inferior."[4] Working with one's hands for his own support was detested by them.

As Metz considered it, so do we, that the "wife" to be carried about as mentioned here could have any possible reference to some woman who was not the wife of the missionary, but a mere female companion or woman assistant, is "morally preposterous."[5] It is a fact, however, that the historic church did so pervert the meaning of this place; and of such perversion Farrar said:

> It was the cause of such shameful abuses and misrepresentations that at last the practice of traveling about with unmarried women, who went under the name of "sisters," "beloved," or "companions," was distinctly forbidden by the third canon of the Council of Nice.[6]

Paul's argument is simply that he was as fully entitled to be supported by the churches as were any of the other apostles, a right proved by the general acceptance of it throughout the brotherhood of that day.

Second Argument

Verse 7, *What soldier ever serveth at his own charges? who planteth a vineyard, and eateth not the fruit therof? or who feedeth a flock and eateth not the milk of the flock?*

This argument derives from the inherent right of soldiers to be supported by their goverment, the right of the owner of a vineyard to eat the crop, and the right of a shepherd to drink of the milk of the flock. Such rights have been universally recognized and accepted in all ages. These examples are pointedly appropriate in their application to ministers of the gospel. "The Christian minister fights evil (as a soldier), plants

---

[4]Donald S. Metz, *Beacon Bible Commentary* (Kansas City: Beacon Hill Press, 1968), p. 397.

[5]*Ibid.*, p. 396.

[6]F. W. Farrar, *Pulpit Commentary* (Grand Rapids: Wm. B. Eerdmans Publishing Company, 1950), Vol. 19, p. 287.

churches (like the planter of a vineyard), and shepherds congregations."[7]

Third Argument

Verses 8-10, *Do I speak these things after the manner of men? or saith not the law the same? For it is written in the law of Moses, Thou shalt not muzzle the ox when he treadeth out the corn. Is it for the oxen that God careth, or saith he assuredly for our sake? Yea, for our sake it was written: because he that ploweth ought to plow in hope, and he that thresheth, to thresh in hope of partaking.*

Paul's argument here is founded on the quotation from Deuteronomy 25:4, which Paul affirmed to be applicable to the support of ministers of the word of God. However, when Paul said that "God does not care for oxen" (the meaning of the interrogative), it is not a denial that God commanded righteous men to regard even their beasts. In the sense that God sought to protect even a beast from abuse, God did indeed care for oxen; Paul's point here is, he would care infinitely more for the proper care and support of his ministers.

The scene in view is that of an ancient threshing floor, the like of which may still be seen in some places. The wheat (or other grain) was placed upon a threshing floor; and the oxen were driven, treadmill style, around the floor until their hooves had beaten out the grain. No Jew, in the light of the law of Moses, could muzzle the ox and prevent his eating during his work on the floor. Pagans, of course, muzzled the ox to prevent his eating any of the grain.

The prohibition in Deuteronomy occurs in a section where human relations, rather than the treatment of animals, is under consideration; and from this it appears that the human application of the principle was primary, even in Deuteronomy. As Morris said, "It may well have been meant figuratively from the first."[8] In any event, Paul applied it with full force to the question of supporting preachers of the gospel.

---

[7]Donald Guthrie, *The New Bible Commentary* (Grand Rapids: Wm. B. Eerdmans Publishing Company, 1970), p. 1062.

[8]Leon Morris, *op. cit.*, p. 134.

Fourth Argument

Verse 11, *If we sowed unto you spiritual things, is it a great matter if we shall reap your carnal things?*

As Grosheide noted, "*Carnal* is not here identical with *sinful*; the contrast is between the heavenly and the earthly, between the spiritual and the material."[9] "What was earthly support in comparison with the riches of the gospel?"[10]

Verse 12, *If others partake of this right over you, do not ye yet more? nevertheless we did not use this right; but we bear all things, that we may cause no hindrance to the gospel of Christ.*

Fifth Argument

The right pointed out in this verse is the superior right of one who planted and nourished a congregation over the claims of others who came afterward; and, by their admission of the claims of many teachers who succeeded Paul, they were bound to admit the prior rights of the founder of their congregation. This writer has known of ministers of the gospel whose labors had planted churches, but who were neglected and denied adequate support at a later period when those congregations had flourished and become prosperous; and something of this same abuse was taking place in Corinth. Despite this, Paul, even then, was not willing to be supported by any gifts from Corinth.

"That we may cause no hindrance to the gospel . . ." In order to disarm any evil thought to the effect that Paul was preaching the word of God for money, the grand apostle chose rather to suffer privation and hardship.

Sixth Argument

Verse 13, *Know ye not that they which minister about sacred things eat of the things of the temple, and they that wait upon the altar have their portion with the altar?*

---

[9]F. W. Grosheide, *The New International Commentary* (Grand Rapids: Wm. B. Eerdmans Publishing Company, 1953), p. 207.

[10]J. W. McGarvey, *op. cit.*, p. 91.

Paul doubtless had in mind the sacred things of the temple in Jerusalem, but his words have even a wider application, including the universal practice of all the world in such matters, the same things being true of the pagan temples as well as of the temple of the Jews.

It may well be that Paul's mention, only a moment previously, of not being a "hindrance" to the gospel, was precisely what prompted the thought of the rich emoluments and perquisites of all priests, pagan and Jewish, and of the "hindrance" which the conduct of such priests certainly causes.

Barclay gave a detailed account of all the profitable benefits which Jewish priests claimed under the temple system, pointing out that, at a time when the average family had meat only once a week, many of the priests were suffering "from an occupational disease caused by eating too much meat."[11] They had grown indolent, wealthy, and disdainful of the poor. Paul would not be *like them.*

Nevertheless, Paul did not deny, but rather affirmed, the propriety of the servants of temples living from the temple revenues, the application being that ministers of the gospel should live from the revenues of the churches.

Seventh Argument

Verse 14, *Even so did the Lord ordain that they that proclaim the gospel should live of the gospel.*

Most commentators believe that Paul here had reference to the Lord's statement that "The laborer is worthy of his hire" (Luke 10:7); but it might be true that "They that proclaim the gospel should live by the gospel" is a verbatim statement of the Lord himself, being another quotation from the Lord found exclusively in Paul's writings, another example of the same thing being in Acts 20:35: "It is more blessed to give than to receive." There is no logical reason why this may not be another such statement of the Lord himself.

---

[11]William Barclay, *The Letters to the Corinthians* (Philadelphia: The Westminster Press, 1954), p. 89.

In any case, here was the climax of Paul's argument that ministers of the gospel should be supported by the churches. He summed it all up as having been "ordained," that is, "commanded" by the Lord Jesus Christ himself; and it makes no difference if the reference is to such a passage as Luke 10:7, or to a specific order of the Lord; it is true either way, or both ways.

The balance of the chapter deals with a further explanation on Paul's part of why he had renounced on his own behalf a right of so much consequence to the growth of the church in all ages. The nobility, self-denial, altruistic motivation and benevolent love of others are set forth in the following verses.

Verse 15, *But I have used none of these things: and I write not these things that it may be done in my case; for it were good for me rather to die, than that any man should make my glorying void.*

Why did Paul take such a viewpoint? He clearly foresaw that, in so doing, he would rob Satan of any excuse to allege that the eternal gospel of Christ had first been advocated by men seeking their own gain. He would simply rather die than to give the devil any such opportunity to slander the truth.

"Glorying . . ." has reference to glorying in a gospel freely proclaimed without cost to those who heard it. The genius of the holy apostle was profoundly correct in such a discernment; and, through his own self-denial and sacrifice, he placed all subsequent generations of men under a debt of appreciation and gratitude.

Verse 16, *For if I preach the gospel, I have nothing to glory of; for necessity is laid upon me; for woe is unto me, if I preach not the gospel.*

"Woe unto me . . . if I preach not . . ." It is to be feared that many ministers of the present day are lacking the essential compulsion which moved the apostle. As Barnes said:

> Men who leave the ministry and voluntarily devote themselves to some other calling when they might preach, never had the right spirit. A man whose heart is

> not in the ministry, and who would be as happy in any other calling, is not fit to be an ambassador of Christ.[12]

What an indictment of one's life must it be for him to turn away from preaching the truth of God to a perishing world in order to avoid inconvenience, poverty, deprivation and hardship, and with a view to possessing a greater share of the earth's wealth, honor and privilege! It is to be feared that the spirit of the apostle Paul is as rare upon earth now as it was then.

Verse 17, *For if I do this of mine own will, I have a reward: but if not of mine own will, I have a stewardship entrusted to me.*

"If I do this of mine own will . . ." This probably refers to "preaching the gospel without financial support," as indicated by the consequence, "I have a reward." Above, it was pointed out that this reward consisted of thwarting Satan in a most important particular, the same being stated in the verse immediately following.

"I have a stewardship entrusted to me . . ." Shore's discernment of the meaning here appears to be correct. He said that if Paul's preaching the gospel (without charge) was not a thing voluntarily done, then, in that case, "he would be merely a steward, a slave doing his duty."[13] Throughout this passage, it is clear that Paul aimed at going beyond all duty and obligation. The phrase "over and beyond the call of duty" finds its noblest application in the person of Paul the apostle.

Verse 18, *What then is my reward? That, when I preach the gospel, I may make the gospel without charge, so as not to use to the full my right in the gospel.*

"The gospel without charge . . ." This was Paul's reward, to be able to preach the gospel without charge to dying men. It is not to be denied that a commendable pride existed in his heart. As Wesley said:

---

[12]Albert Barnes, *Notes on the NT* (Grand Rapids: Baker Book House, 1949), p. 164.

[13]T. Teignmouth Shore, *Ellicott's Commentary on the Whole Bible* (Grand Rapids: Zondervan Publishing House, 1959), p. 320.

> There is perhaps no passage in the apostle's letters where there are more admirably revealed at once the nobility, delicacy, profound humility, dignity, and legitimate pride of this Christian character. Serving Christ cannot give him matter of joy except insofar as he has the consciousness of doing so in a condition of freedom.[14]

Verse 19, *For though I was free from all men, I brought myself under bondage to all, that I might gain the more.*

From this it is clear that it was not *merely* a matter of justifiable pride that Paul should have insisted on making the gospel free; but it was related to thwarting Satan, as noted under verse 15, above, and for the purpose of procuring a more abundant harvest in the gospel. Moreover, there can be little doubt that Paul's selfless actions actually did result in a mighty increase in the numbers of those accepting the truth. In all ages, there are men of little minds who suppose that every servant of the gospel is more interested in the pecuniary rewards of his work than in the salvation of souls; and, alas, it must be confessed that many times the conduct of preachers themselves supports such allegations.

"Under bondage to all . . ." This has the same ring as Paul's "debtor both to Greeks and barbarians" (Rom. 1:14). He accepted for himself the obligation of preaching the gospel "to the whole creation."

Verse 20, *And to the Jews I became as a Jew, that I might gain Jews; to them that are under the law, as under the law, not being myself under the law, that I might gain them that are under the law.*

"I became as a Jew . . ." has the meaning that Paul did not then any longer consider himself as a Jew, except in an accommodative sense. At a time when it is being alleged that Jews do not have to give up their Jewry to become Christians, it is significant here that Paul did, in some very real sense, consider that he was no longer a Jew. If not, he could not have declared that "to the Jews he became as a Jew."

---

[14]Godet as quoted by John Wesley, *One Volume NT Commentary* (Grand Rapids: Baker Book House, 1972), in loco.

"Not being myself under the law . . ." This is "a remarkable statement which emphasizes how completely Paul had broken with the law of Moses."[15] This is one of the strongest statements in his writings.

On all matters of innocence or indifference, Paul accommodated himself to the life-style of those whom he hoped to win for the gospel. In keeping with such conduct, he ate with Gentiles without raising any question of where they had purchased the meat; and when in the homes of Jews, Paul avoided flaunting any of the liberty which he enjoyed in Christ.

This accommodation to the viewpoint of others was the master strategy of Paul, reminding us of the notable instance from the life of the Saviour, who, at the well of Samaria, sought the common ground with the woman who had come to draw water. Jesus approached her in the common circumstance that both were thirsty. See CJ, p. 114. This conformity to the views of others on Paul's part, however, was limited to incidental or indifferent things; for Paul made it clear in the next verse that he was *always* under the law of Christ.

Verse 21, *To them that are without law, as without law, not being without law to God, but under law to Christ, that I might gain them that are without law.*

This was the limitation which was never waived or relaxed. Whatever adaptation marked Paul's conduct, it never involved disobeying the word of the Lord, or violating his allegiance to the law of Christ.

Verse 22, *To the weak I became weak, that I might gain the weak: I am become all things to all men, that I may by all means save some.*

David Lipscomb's comment on this is:

> Paul accommodated himself to the prejudices and preferences of men so far as he could without sacrificing truth and righteousness, in order to win them to Christ . . . He did this not that he might be personally popular

---

[15]S. Lewis Johnson, Jr., *Wycliffe Bible Commentary* (Chicago: Moody Press, 1971), p. 616.

with any man, but that by doing so he might throw no obstacle in the way of their giving the gospel a fair hearing.[16]

For example, Paul felt no obligation whatever to keep the forms and ceremonies of the law of Moses; yet he observed and kept such things in circumstances where his failure to do it would have antagonized the Jews, and in cases where their observance did not violate the spirit of the new law in Christ Jesus. Thus, Paul shaved his head; but there is no record that he ever *ate* the Jewish Passover. As he said, "Christ is our passover."

"That I may save some . . ." As Johnson said, "This does not remove salvation from the hands of God";[17] and, when it is declared in the word of the Lord that men should "save themselves" (Acts 2:40), it is likewise true that their doing so cannot remove salvation from God's hands. When a man is baptized unto the remission of his sins, it does not make him his own saviour; because, when one obeys the gospel, he saves himself in the sense that he does that without which not even God can save him. In that same sense, not even God could save sinners without the preaching of the word; and by preaching the word, Paul, in that sense, saved men.

Verse 23, *And I do all things for the gospel's sake, that I may be a joint partaker thereof.*

Adam Clarke translated this, "I do all this for the sake of the prize, that I may partake of it with you."[18] Paul's use of the word "prize" in the verse immediately following also seems to indicate that it was the prize of eternal life which he had in view here. At any rate, he at once elaborated an illustration taken from the Isthmian games, in which the attainment of the prize was the goal of all participants.

Verse 24, *Know ye not that they that run in a race run all, but one receiveth the prize? Even so, run that ye may attain.*

---

[16]David Lipscomb, *Commentary on First Corinthians* (Nashville: The Gospel Advocate Company, 1935), p. 137.

[17]S. Lewis Johnson, Jr., *op. cit.*, p. 616.

[18]Adam Clarke, *Commentary on the Whole Bible* (New York: Carlton & Porter, 1831), Vol. VI, p. 239.

There are important differences, as well as similarities, in such a contest as Paul referred to here. Analogies are: (1) to win; a man must contend legally, being properly enrolled in the contest, suggesting that a Christian must contend along with others *in the church*, and not as some kind of free-lance operator; (2) discipline is required (Heb. 12:1); (3) some win; others do not win; (4) a host of spectators views the contest (Heb. 12:1); (5) patience is necessary; (6) the winner receives the prize. The contrasts are: (1) only one may win an earthly race; all may win the heavenly; (2) the earthly reward is but a trifle; the heavenly reward is eternal life.

"The prize . . ." Johnson objected to interpreting this as eternal life, declaring that "The apostle had in mind service and rewards, and not salvation and eternal life."[19] However, it is probable that such comments are derived from the necessity some scholars feel to soften the implications of "castaway" or "rejected" in verse 27. The "prize" in which Paul hoped to participate with all Christians could hardly be anything else, other than eternal life.

Regarding the Games

Barnes gives an excellent summary of the Greek contests which prompted Paul's comparison in this and following verses. There were four great celebrations: (1) the Pythian at Delphi, (2) the Isthmian at Corinth, (3) the Nemean in Argolis, and (4) the Olympian at Elis, on the southern bank of the Alphias river. Some of these were celebrated every four years (hence the word Olympiad), but others, such as the Isthmian, were celebrated every two years; and the Pythian were celebrated every three years, or as some say, every five years. In any case, there was hardly any year in which one or more of these celebrated contests did not occur.

The prizes given in these various games were usually garlands bestowed upon the victors, being constructed of the leaves of olive, pine, apple, laurel, or even parsley, their worth being totally symbolical.[20] It was for such worthless prizes that

---

[19]S. Lewis Johnson, Jr., *op. cit.*, p. 617.
[20]Albert Barnes, *op. cit.*, pp. 169-171.

men endured all kinds of rigorous training and hardship; but it is a far different kind of prize that may be won by the Christian.

Verse 25, *And every man that striveth in the games exerciseth self-control in all things. Now they do it to receive a corruptible crown; but we an incorruptible.*

See under preceding verse for note on the nature of the "corruptible" crown bestowed upon the winner in the Greek games. In focus here is the dedication and discipline which men enforced upon themselves in order to win such prizes.

"But we an incorruptible . . ." This is the phrase that requires "prize" in preceding verses to be understood as eternal life, that being the *only* incorruptible crown, all others being sure to perish with time and using. This is the reward which is called "the crown of righteousness," which shall be bestowed upon the faithful by the Lord himself "at that day," that is, the judgment day (2 Tim. 4:8). It is the "crown of glory that fadeth not away," which shall be given to the redeemed "when the chief Shepherd shall be manifested" (1 Peter 5:4). It is the "crown of life" (Rev. 2:10).

Throughout this chapter, Paul was showing the Corinthians, and all Christians, that the inconveniences, hardships, disciplines and self-denial which were accepted by men striving to win in such a contest as the games, should far more willingly be endured and accepted by those intent upon the eternal reward. Specifically, they were not to flaunt their liberty in such a manner as to discourage others.

Verse 26, *I therefore run, as not uncertainly; so fight I as not beating the air.*

This indicates that "The whole of this chapter has been a vindication of Paul's self-denial,"[21] the object of it being the persuasion of the Corinthian boasters of their "liberty" to follow Paul's example by denying themselves all indulgence at the expense of the faith of their weaker brethren.

"Beating the air . . ." is a reference to boxers who missed with their punches and so lost the fight. "Uncertainly . . ." has

---

[21]T. Teignmouth Shore, *op. cit.*, p. 291.

reference to contestants in a race who, through lack of training, wobbled to defeat, not victory.

Verse 27, *But I buffet my body, and bring it into bondage: lest by any means, after that I have preached to others, I myself should be rejected.*

"Buffet my body . . ." is metaphorical and does not refer to any type of flagellation such as was practiced by ascetics as a means of religious discipline. It indicates that every Christian, as Paul did, should exercise the sternest self-control over the body, its desires and appetites being a powerful source of temptation in all men.

"I myself should be rejected . . ." As Foy E. Wallace, Jr., said: "The translators (in this place) were evidently attempting to circumvent the possibility of apostasy."[22] There is no excuse for rendering the word here (*adokimos*) as either "rejected" (RV) or "disqualified" (RSV). It means "reprobate" and is so translated elsewhere in the NT (Rom.1:28; 2 Cor.13:5,6,7; 2 Tim.3:8; Titus 1:16). It is thus crystal clear that the apostle Paul, even after the world-shaking ministry of the word of God which characterized his life, considered it possible that he himself could become reprobate and lose the eternal reward. It was for the purpose of avoiding that possibility that he buffeted his body, walked in the strictest discipline, and devoted every possible effort to the service of the Lord. His example should put an end to all thoughts of "having it made" as a Christian and being certain to win 'eternal life apart from the most faithful continuance in God's service.

We must therefore refuse interpretations of this passage such as that of Morris, who said, "Paul's fear was not that he might lose his salvation, but that he might lose his crown through failing to satisfy his Lord."[23] Clearly it was such a view as this that led to the mistranslation of verse 27; but the truth is available and clear enough for all who desire to know it.

---

[22]Foy E. Wallace, Jr., *A Review of the New Versions* (Fort Worth: The Foy E. Wallace Jr., Publications, 1973), p. 435.

[23]Leon Morris, *op. cit.*, p. 140.

The hope of eternal life is not sealed in a single glorious moment in one's experience of conversion; but it is a life- long fidelity to the risen Lord, the running of life's race all the way to the finish line. As De Hoff wrote:

> Not until every thought and imagination of man's heart is brought into subjection is his conversion complete. In this sense, conversion goes on as long as we live; and we are finally free from sin only when the day dawns and the shadows flee away, and we stand justified in the presence of God with the redeemed of all ages.[24]

Farrar's analysis of this verse is as follows:

> The word "reprobate" here rendered "a castaway" (AV) is a metaphor derived from the testing of metals, and the casting aside of those which are spurious. That Paul should see the necessity for such serious and unceasing effort shows how little he believed in saintly works of "supererogation, over and above what is commanded." "When the cedar of Lebanon trembles, what shall the reed by the brookside do?"[25]

It might be added that this passage also shows how little Paul believed any such doctrine as the "final perseverance of the saints," called also "the impossibility of apostasy."

---

[24]George W. De Hoff, *op. cit.*, p. 78.

[25]F. W. Farrar, *Pulpit Commentary* (Grand Rapids: Wm. B. Eerdmans Publishing Company, 1950), Vol. 19, p. 291.

CHAPTER 10

In this chapter, and through verse 1 of the next, Paul completed his answer to the triple question regarding the permissibility of Christians (1) sitting down at idol feasts, (2) purchasing meat in the common markets, and (3) being guests where facts about the origin of the meat were unknown.

The very first word in this chapter demands that a close connection with the previous two chapters must be recognized; and it is deplorable that the RSV omitted that word, ignoring it completely. That word is "for"; and such a perversion of the sacred text was, as Farrar said, "due to the failure to understand the whole train of thought."[1] Also, it may be suspected that the omission of this authentic connective could be related to the critical bias which would make this chapter "the relic of a previous epistle."[2] It is now recognized, however, that such a view is concocted out of "no sufficient evidence."[3] The understanding of Paul's full line of thought in these chapters also explodes any notion that two different positions are advocated by the apostle in chapters 8 and 10.

It will be recalled that in chapter 8, the apostle effectively blasted the conceit and arrogance of his Corinthian questioners by warning them that (1) knowledge puffs up, but does not build up (v. 1), (2) those who thought they knew, actually knew nothing as they should have known (v. 2), (3) their actions defiled the consciences of the weak (v. 7), (4) such "liberty" was a stumblingblock to the weak (v. 9), (5) sitting down in an idol's temple encouraged idol worship (v. 10), (6) through their conduct the weak perished (v. 11), and (7) their actions were not merely sins against brethren but a "sin against Christ" (v. 12). In this light, it is ridiculous to make chapter 8 to be in any manner permissive with regard to the worship of idols.

---

[1]F. W. Farrar, *Pulpit Commentary* (Grand Rapids: Wm. B. Eerdmans Publishing Company, 1950), Vol. 19, p. 322.
[2]*ISBE* p. 713.
[3]*Ibid.*

The cautious manner of Paul's dealing with the question in chapter 8, however, was to make a distinction between the legitimate claims of Christian liberty and the heartless abuse of the principle. Having fully made that distinction in chapter 8, and also having reinforced his own example in such matters by explaining his forbearance in the matter of financial support in chapter 9, Paul in this chapter returned to make an unqualified demolition of the thesis that any Christian could have anything whatever to do with idol worship.

Verse 1, *For I would not, brethren, have you ignorant, that our fathers were all under the cloud, and all passed through the sea.*

At the end of chapter 9, Paul had hinted that it was possible, even for himself, to be a "castaway," after preaching to others, requiring the conclusion that even he (who had as much "knowledge" as any of the Corinthians, and who knew all about Christian liberty) took the most vigorous precautions against sinning, and that such precautions required him to give up everything such as the indulgences of the Corinthians.

Apparently, the inherent error in the philosophical Corinthians was the impression that the Lord's Supper and Christian baptism had made them immune to any contamination from the idol feasts, especially in the light of their presumed "knowledge" that idols were actually nothing anyway. Paul refuted this by reference to the allegorical nature of historic Israel, many of them, in fact most of them, being lost despite their covenant relationship to God.

"For . . ." This connective requires the understanding that this section of the epistle is a continuation of the argument in previous chapters. See in chapter introduction.

"I would not have you ignorant . . ." was a favorite expression with Paul. He used it in 1 Corinthians 12:1, 2 Corinthians 1:8, Romans 1:13, 11:25, and in 1 Thessalonians 4:13, as well as here. It is not likely that Paul thought his readers would have been ignorant of the history of Israel, but rather that they would not have been aware of the typical nature of that history.

"Our fathers . . ." Many of the Corinthians were not of Jewish extraction, and therefore the reference here regards

Israel as the spiritual ancestry of all Christians. As Russell said, "The OT was used in the Christian church, and even Gentile converts were expected to be familiar with it."[4] See Romans 9:6, Galatians 3:27-29, etc.

"All under the cloud . . . all passed through the sea . . ." The word "all," repeated five times in these first four verses, emphasizes the fact that the entire Jewish people enjoyed the high privilege of covenant relationship with God, being fed miraculously, and that they were thus constituted as God's chosen people. Some of the Corinthians seem to have regarded the fact of their being baptized into Christ as some kind of endowment that made them immune from dangers, or in some manner exempt from sin even while indulging themselves at idol feasts. By the analogy of what happened historically to Israel, Paul would teach them that high privilege does not mean immunity from sin and death.

Verse 2, *And were all baptized unto Moses in the cloud and in the sea.*

By this bold comparison, Paul made the marvelous deliverance of Israel through the Red Sea from the pursuing armies of Pharaoh as a figure, or type, of Christian baptism. It should be carefully noted that the figure in evidence here is not baptism, that being the reality of which the great deliverance of Israel was the figure. Nowhere in the NT is baptism ever referred to as any kind of ' 'figure" or "sign." "The voluntary character of that baptism is suggested by the aorist middle,"[5] as in Acts 22:16, Acts 2:38, where the meaning is "have yourselves baptized."[6]

Bruce presented the analogy between Israel and Christians thus:

> Their (the Christians') baptism is the antitype of Israel's passage through the Red Sea; their sacrificial feeding on Christ by faith is the antitype of Israel's

---

[4]John William Russell, *Compact Commentary on the NT* (Grand Rapids: Baker Book House, 1964), p. 419.

[5]Paul W. Marsh. *A New Commentary* (Grand Rapids: Zondervan Publishing House, 1969), p. 394.

[6]W. E. Vine, *An Expository Dictionary of NT Words* (Old Tappan, N. J.: Fleming H. Revell Company, 1940), p. 97.

> nourishment with manna and the water from the rock; Christ the living Rock is their guide through the wilderness; the heavenly rest before them (the Christians) is the counterpart to the earthly Canaan which was the goal of the Israelites.[7]

As the next verse indicates, there is also a reference to the Lord's Supper in Paul's analogy.

Verse 3, *And did all eat the same spiritual food.*

Just as Israel's commitment "unto Moses" by their passage through the sea corresponded to the Christian's baptism, their being fed with "spiritual food," that is, food of supernatural origin, as in the manna, and the water from the rock, corresponded to the Christian's eating the flesh of Christ and drinking his blood in the manner of John 6:54-58. John Wesley said that this spiritual food was "typical of the bread which we eat at Christ's table."[8] Dummelow noted that "Only here in the NT are the two Sacraments mentioned side by side,"[9] giving three reasons why the term "spiritual food" was used in this verse: (1) it was miraculous; (2) it was typical; and (3) it assured them of God's presence.

Verse 4, *And did all drink the same spiritual drink: for they drank of a spiritual rock that followed them: and the rock was Christ.*

"Rock that followed them . . ." This is not to be understood as Paul's reference to the Jewish legend about a literal rock that followed the Israelites in their wanderings. The rock to which Paul referred here was clearly stated: "The rock was Christ." The miracle of Moses' bringing forth water from the rock in the wilderness (Ex. 17:5ff) provided literal water for Israel; but much more than that is in evidence here. As Marsh said, "The rock was Christ, not 'is' or 'is a type of' . . . and this is a clear statement of the pre-existence of Christ."[10]

---

[7]F. F. Bruce, *The Epistle to the Hebrew* (Grand Rapids: Wm. B. Eerdmans Publishing Company, 1967), p. 62.

[8]John Wesley, *One Volume NT Commentary* (Grand Rapids: Baker Book House, 1972), in loco.

[9]J. R. Dummelow, *Commentary on the Holy Bible* (New York: The Macmillan Company, 1937), p. 907.

[10]Paul W. Marsh, *op. cit.*, p. 394.

One of the most beautiful and instructive titles of Christ in all the Bible is "Christ the Living Stone"; and for a full discussion of this, see CR, pp. 352-357.

In these first four verses, the broad outlines of the great allegory of fleshly Israel are laid down; and a little further attention is due to it. As De Hoff declared: "The story of the Israelites and their journey from Egypt into Canaan is a type of our journey from the Egypt of sin into the everlasting Canaan."[11]

THE GRAND ANALOGY OF ISRAEL

Egypt is a type of sin and bondage.
God's sending Moses to deliver them is a type of God's sending Christ to deliver us from the degrading slavery of sin.
Pharaoh is a type of the devil.
The compromises he offered Moses are like the compromises Satan still suggests to Christians.
Moses is the most eloquent type of Christ in all the Bible (see CH, pp. 67-69).
Israel's crossing the Red Sea is typical of Christian baptism.
Their spiritual food is typical of the Lord's Supper.
Israel's entering the wilderness is typical of the Christian's entering the church.
The wilderness is a type of the church.
That Israel sinned is typical of the sins and rebellions of Christians.
The majority of them failed to enter Canaan; and this is typical of "the many" Christians who will not be saved eternally.
Canaan is a type of heaven.
Some of Israel entering Canaan is typical of the final victory of Christians who shall enter into the joy of the Lord.
That some of them "fell" is typical of Christians who fall away and are lost.
God's providential care of Israel in the wilderness is typical of his providential care of Christians till "the end of the world."

---

[11]George W. De Hoff, *Sermons on First Corinthians* (Murfreesboro, Tenn.: The Christian Press, 1947), p. 79.

The fact of Israel's being "baptized" and having the Lord's Supper (in the analogy) did not make them immune to sin and death, as Paul was teaching here; and the same is true of Christians now.

Canaan was entered when Israel crossed Jordan, making Jordan a type of death, beyond which Christians enter heaven.

The dangers which beset Israel in the wilderness are typical of the dangers confronting Christians during their probation.

They were tempted to commit fornication, even as the Corinthians were being tempted, and by the same means, through the licentious celebrations of idol worship.

Other analogies in this remarkable allegory may be pointed out, but the above is sufficient to show the extensive parallel between the fleshly and the spiritual Israels.

Verse 5, *Howbeit with most of them God was not well pleased: for they were overthrown in the wilderness.*

Of all that great host who passed through the Red Sea and witnessed God's mighty act of delivering them from slavery, all of them except Caleb and Joshua failed to enter Canaan (Num. 14:30-32). This brief, pungent verse is the apostle's summary of one of the most tragic and pathetic failures of all history. Passing over, except for the brief references in the first four verses, the startling parallels between fleshly and spiritual Israel, Paul here called attention to the pitiful defeat of an entire generation in the wilderness and made their overthrow a warning to the Corinthians and the Christians of all generations of the dreadful consequences of disobedience.

Verse 6, *Now these things were our examples, to the intent we should not lust after evil things, as they also lusted.*

The blunt meaning here is that Christians should not suppose that their having been baptized into Christ and having been made partakers of the Lord's table, nor the fact of their sharing high privileges of spiritual life in God's kingdom, could endow them with any immunity to sin, a conceit which it seems some of the Corinthians had.

"Were our examples . . ." Farrar believed that these words might also be rendered, "Now in these things, they also proved to be figures of us";[12] but the meaning is the same either way. After having been totally and completely "saved" from Egyptian slavery, they were lost and rejected; and, corresponding to that, Christians who are completely and totally saved may fall into sin and lose their hope of eternal life.

"Lust after evil things . . ." Although the technical meaning of "lust" is "to desire either good things or bad things,"[13] its use in the holy scriptures is invariably a reference to illicit and harmful desire. The inspired author James identified this inward desire ever burning in men's hearts as the embryonic source of all sin. To paraphrase James, "Lust has a child, which is sin; and then sin also has a child, which is death" (James 1:12-15). Self-denial is the soul's rejection of all unlawful desire. The surrender to Christ is the subordination of all selfish desire to the will of the Lord. The lust after evil things is the first of five rebellious actions of fleshly Israel; and, enumerating them one by one, Paul demanded that Christians avoid committing them.

Verse 7, *Neither be ye idolaters, as were some of them; as it is written, The people sat down to eat and drink, and rose up to play.*

The scriptural quotation here is Exodus 32:6; and thus the idolatry Paul mentioned was that of Israel's worshiping the golden calf. The mention of idolatry almost in the same breath with "lust" (v. 6) shows the close connection, the one leading to the other, indicating that idolatry depended for its motivation upon the gratification of fleshly lusts. It is of great significance that in the incident thus cited by Paul, the OT specifically revealed that the people "were naked" (Ex. 32:25); and this may not be dismissed as a mere reference to their *spiritual* nakedness!

"Sat down to eat . . . rose up to play . . ." The "playing" was not some innocent diversion, or game, this being a reference to the wild naked dances which concluded the idol feasts. As Wesley said, "(the word play) means to dance in honor of their

---

[12]F. W. Farrar, *op. cit.*, p. 323.
[13]Donald S. Metz, *Beacon Bible Commentary* (Kansas City: Beacon Hill Press, 1969), p. 405.

idol."[14] McGarvey declared that the kind of playing in view here "was familiar to the Corinthians who had indulged in such licentious sportfulness"[15] in such temples as those of Bacchus, Poseidon and Aphrodite (Venus).

Verse 8, *Neither let us commit fornication, as some of them committed, and fell in one day three and twenty thousand.*

Notice the list of sins: (1) we should not lust after evil things; (2) neither be idolaters; (3) neither let us commit fornication. The whole sequence was the normal procedure in idol worship.

"In one day three and twenty thousand . . ." Numbers 25:9 gives the number who fell as 24,000; and many have been perplexed by this, even Lipscomb saying, "Why this discrepancy I am not able to explain."[16] The explanation is in the words "in one day," a phrase not in the OT narrative. Paul's 23,000, therefore, did not include those slain by the judges before this "one day." It will be recalled that, before the plague broke out, God through Moses had commanded the judges of Israel to "hang all the heads of the people" who had condoned and encouraged the worship of Baal-Peor, the idol god of the Moabites, especially the Moabitish women who had used the device of idol worship to seduce the Israelites to commit fornication. Putting the two figures together, in which there is no discrepancy whatever, it is clear that the judges hanged a thousand men in connection with this disaster which are not counted in Paul's 23,000 who perished in *one day*. Guthrie pointed out a Jewish tradition which confirms this explanation. He said, "Jewish tradition ascribed 1,000 deaths to the action of the judges described in Numbers 25:5."[17] Another pseudocon bites the dust!

Verse 9, *Neither let us make trial of the Lord, as some of them made trial, and perished by the serpents.*

"Make trial of the Lord . . ." refers to provoking the Lord through disobedience and murmuring against his benign

---

[14]John Wesley, *op. cit.*, in loco.

[15]J. W. McGarvey, *Commentary on 1 Corinthians* (Cincinnati: Standard Publishing Company, 1916), p. 100.

[16]David Lipscomb, *Commentary on First Corinthians* (Nashville: The Gospel Advocate Company, 1935), p. 149.

[17]Donald Guthrie, *The New Bible Commentary* (Grand Rapids: Wm. B. Eerdmans Publishing Company, 1970), p. 1064.

government, in a sense "testing" the Lord to see whether or not he will punish the disobedient. The OT background of this admonition is found in Numbers 21:5, 6. Significantly, all sin and disobedience of God fall into the category of making "trial" of him. The particular sins of Israel mentioned here were those of speaking against God and Moses and complaining of the manna.

"The Lord . . ." Many ancient authorities read "Christ" instead of "Lord" (RV margin); and, as Barnes observed, "It cannot be denied that the more natural construction is . . . 'Christ' . . . rather than 'God.'"[18] As the reference is to a time before Christ came, however, the translators rendered it "Lord," thus avoiding the difficulty. The point is not crucial, because, as a matter of fact, they made trial of both God and Christ. The view preferred here is that Paul meant "Christ," the same being another reference to his pre-existence, and indicating that our Lord's pre-incarnation activity included that of shepherding the chosen people in the wilderness. It was not Christ, however, who spake the law to Israel, for Hebrews 1:1 makes it clear that God did that through the prophets, and not through his Son.

Verse 10, *Neither murmur ye, as some of them murmured, and perished by the destroyer.*

The sin of murmuring rounds out the five: lusting, idolatry, fornication, making trial of God, and murmuring.

"Neither murmur ye . . ." For a more detailed comment on this vice, see CA, pp. 121-122. The murmurers are the complainers, fault-finders, objectors and critics who, alas, form a part of every congregation that ever existed. The attitude represented by such behavior is not a minor or negligible "fault" but an atrocious sin, standing in sequence here as the climax involving even greater guilt than idolatry and fornication; for it would certainly seem to be true that Paul arranged these in ascending order of magnitude.

Verse 11, *Now these things happened unto them by way of example; and they were written for our admonition, upon whom the ends of the ages are come.*

---

[18]Albert Barnes, *Notes on the NT* (Grand Rapids: Baker Book House, 1949), p. 185.

"Now these things happened . . ." This is a bold testimony to the OT record, which contains not legends, myths or traditions, but what "happened."

"By way of example . . ." This same thought was expressed in verse 6; and under verse 4, above, is given a list of analogies in the great allegory of fleshly Israel, the type of spiritual Israel. Romans 15:4 has much the same teaching, indicating that the OT is for the "learning" of Christians, and making it clear that the OT is a legitimate part of the teaching which applies to every Christian, only with this limitation, that all of its forms and ceremonies and *types* have been replaced by the great realities of the new covenant.

"Upon whom the ends of the ages are come . . ." This is similar in thought to "this is the . . . last days" (Acts 2:16, 17) mentioned by Peter on Pentecost, and a number of other similar references in the NT; and the usual interpretation is to refer these to the final dispensation of God's grace, the Christian age, which at that time was only beginning. In this interpretation, the meaning is that the present dispensation is terminal, which is believed to be true of course; but the words have a more immediate application to the end of the Jewish dispensation which had already occurred in the crucifixion of Christ; but that terminus of the whole Mosaic age would shortly be marked by the destruction of the Jewish state, the city of Jerusalem and the temple. It is not incorrect to see this also in Paul's words here. It was indeed the "ends of the ages" shortly to be fantastically demonstrated before their eyes in 70 A.D.

As Barnes truly observed, "This by no means denotes that the apostle believed the world would soon come to an end."[19]

Verse 12, *Wherefore let him that thinketh he standeth take heed lest he fall.*

Whether taken alone or in context, this verse may not be referred to anything else other than to the danger of apostasy, which is an ever-present *possibility* for all of the saved in Christ as long as they are under the probation of earthly

---

[19]*Ibid.*, p. 186.

existence. We shall not take occasion here to demonstrate the lengths to which scholars have gone in their vain efforts to edit such a thought out of it. Unless there is a real and present danger of falling away so as to be lost, the message of this whole chapter is meaningless. "The history of Israel not only showed the mere possibility of apostasy, but demonstrated its actual reality and the sad prevalence of it."[20]

Verse 13, *There hath no temptation taken you but such as man can bear: but God is faithful, who will not suffer you to be tempted above that ye are able; but will with the temptation make also the way of escape, that ye may be able to endure it.*

"No temptation . . . but such as man can bear . . ." The notion of temptations being irresistible was not allowed by Paul. "Any temptation that comes to us is not unique! others have endured it, and others have come through it."[21]

"God . . ." The agency of God himself is in view in this passage. All temptation, while allowed by God, is also controlled by him; and the Father will simply not allow a child of God to be tempted above what he is able to bear. In the wise providence of God, he has made a way out of every temptation; and, as Barclay noted, "There is the way out, and the way out is not the way of surrender, and not the way of retreat, but the way of conquest in the power of the grace of God."[22]

This instruction regarding "the way of escape" seems to have been given by Paul to alleviate any undue discouragement caused by the blunt and dreadful warning in verse 12. The fact that many may, and do, apostatize cannot mean that they were overwhelmed by irresistible temptations, but that they neglected to take "the way of escape."

Verse 14, *Wherefore, my beloved, flee from idolatry.*

This is Paul's dramatic summary of the whole epistle from 8:1 to this place, tying the whole passage together as one ardent and sustained plea against any indulgence whatever, by any persons whatever, including both the weak and those

---

[20]J. W. McGarvey, *op. cit.*, p. 102.
[21]William Barclay, *The Letters to the Corinthians* (Philadelphia: The Westminster Press, 1954), p. 100.
[22]*Ibid.* p. 101.

who thought of themselves as "strong," and demanding absolutely that they "flee from idolatry." The meaning of that is to get as far away from it as possible. Such dillydallying with idolatry as that being engaged in by the "knowledge" party in Corinth was the most stupid kind of folly. Their acceptance of any kind of participation in the idol feasts was a violation of their status as participants in the Lord's Supper; and Paul's saying, "I speak as to wise men," in the next verse, far from complimenting them on their wisdom, is a bitter irony spoken in rebuke of their phenomenal spiritual density.

Verse 15, *I speak as to wise men; judge ye what I say.*

"Wise men . . . (?)" To these who were sitting down in the temples of idols and criticizing the "weak" who would not do likewise, these who were boasting of their "liberty" and declaring that "all things were lawful" for Christians, Paul's remark here has the weight of "All right, you smart people, listen to this."

Verses 16-17, *The cup of blessing which we bless, is it not a communion of the blood of Christ? The bread which we break, is it not a communion of the body of Christ? seeing that we who are many are one bread, one body: for we all partake of the one bread.*

"The cup of blessing . . ." This was one of the four cups which marked participation in the Jewish passover (see CL, pp. 467-468), being the final one, over which the patriarch pronounced a blessing at the end of the passover. "It is here transferred to the chalice of the Eucharist."[23]

"Which we bless . . ." Paul's use of the plural "we" reveals "his representing the entire company present, and not as individually possessed of some miraculous gift."[24] The superstition that the one presiding at the Lord's table performed any function that could change the nature of the elements of bread and wine did not arise till a much later time. The thought of this whole verse is that participants in the Lord's supper were unified and bound together in one spirit. Their taking the

---

[23]F. W. Farrar, *op. cit.*, p. 324.
[24]T. Teignmouth Shore, *Ellicott's Commentary on the Whole Bible* (Grand Rapids: Zondervan Publishing House, 1959), p. 324.

supper was a declaration that "They had the same object of worship, the same faith, the same hope, etc., with others whom they joined in such a religious act."[25]

Nothing may be made of the fact that Paul mentioned the cup first in this passage, a circumstance which probably resulted from the fact that, "In the heathen feasts, the libation came before the food."[25] Also, there is the obvious intention of the apostle to dwell at greater length upon the bread. The great principle behind Paul's remarks here is the truth that "Partaking of a religious table, whether Christian, Jewish or heathen, involves fellowship with the being to whom it is directed,"[26] as well as with the participants themselves. This great principle was not even guessed at by the Corinthians who partook of the idol feasts.

"In almost all nations, the act of eating together has been regarded as a symbol of unity and friendship."[27] This is even more true with reference to eating a sacred meal such as the Lord's supper.

Verse 18, *Behold Israel after the flesh: have not they that eat the sacrifices communion with the altar?*

"The question is not the intention of the actor, but the import of the act, and the interpretation universally put upon it."[28] Paul thus removed the evaluation of idol worship altogether from the consideration of any "intention" in the heart of the worshiper, the act itself being universally understood as worship either of God or of idols. Here again the question of "What is worship?" demands consideration; and it is a principle laid down dramatically in scripture that worship is "an action," not some kind of subjective feeling. For full discussion of this see in CA, pp. 208-210. The subjective feelings of Jewish worshipers made no difference whatever; if they brought their sacrifices, they had communion with the altar and were invariably accounted as worshiping God.

---

[25]James Macknight, *Apostolical Epistles and Commentary* (Grand Rapids: Baker Book House, 1969), p. 160.

[26]S. Lewis Johnson, Jr., *Wycliffe Bible Commentary* (Chicago: Moody Press, 1971), p. 620.

[27]Albert Barnes, *op. cit.*, p. 191.

[28]David Lipscomb, *op. cit.*, p. 155.

Verse 19, *What say I then? that a thing sacrificed to idols is anything, or that an idol is anything?*

The Hebrew idiom here is to be understood as a negative, such use of the interrogative being common in the NT. In Paul's view, the idol was actually nothing at all; and the intention of the "knowledge" group in Corinth was nothing at all; but none of this made any difference with the fact that actions engaged in the worship of idols were sinful.

Verse 20, *But I say, that the things which the Gentiles sacrifice, they sacrifice to demons, and not to God: and I would not that ye should have communion with demons.*

"To demons . . ." Despite the fact of an idol; being nothing at all, there is, nevertheless, a Satan in the world, and a great number of malignant spirits, perhaps even fallen angels, who are used by the evil one to attain his goals regarding human corruption and destruction. The device of the idol is used by Satan as a means of destroying men's souls; and Paul brings such facts as these into sharp focus here. One of the great blind spots in modern thinking regards the very existence of Satan as a person; but the most universally prayed prayer on earth says, "Deliver us from the evil one." Paul here identified such things as idol feasts at a theater where the forces of Satan are operative. Men refuse to believe this at their peril.

"The essence of the matter lay in the participation in idol worship, which was a reversion to heathenism."[29] As Alford said, "Heathendom being under the dominion of Satan . . . he and his angels are in fact the powers honored and worshiped by the heathen, however little they may be aware of it."[30] "Demons are the real force behind all pagan religion; attested not only by the OT and the NT, but by missionary experience. Idolatry is a medium through which satanic power is particularly manifest."[31]

Verse 21, *Ye cannot drink the cup of the Lord, and the cup of demons: ye cannot partake of the table of the Lord, and of the table of demons.*

---

[29]Donald S. Metz, *op. cit.*, p. 410.
[30]*Ibid.*
[31]Paul W. Marsh, *op. cit.*, p. 396.

"Ye cannot . . ." has the weight of "I forbid you to . . ." Of course, it was not a physical impossibility for some to lead such double lives; and it may be inferred that some in Corinth were actually partaking of both; but it was a sin, the words here indicating that it was morally impossible to do such a thing.

Verse 22, *Or do we provoke the Lord to jealousy? are we stronger than he?*

Even in the OT, idol worship was spoken of as provoking the Lord to jealousy; and, as Macknight said, "This is an allusion to Exodus 20:5, where, after prohibiting the worshiping of images, God adds,"I the Lord thy God, am a jealous God!"[32]

"Are we stronger than he? . . ." This carries the thought, "Do you really wish to be an enemy of God?" Jesus gave a parable of one who contemplated going to war with one stronger than himself in Luke 14:32. The thought there is particularly applicable here. See CL, p. 319.

Verse 23, *All things are lawful; but not all things are expedient. All things are lawful; but not all things edify.*

"All things are lawful . . ." The total absence from this passage of any mention of behavior which might, under any circumstances, be considered "lawful" raises a question of how these words should be understood. If this was the watchword of the "knowledge" party in Corinth, and if they had been pressing Paul for permission to engage in idol worship, which seems likely, then the words here are spoken by way of identifying those to whom these stern words were addressed.

Verse 24, *Let no man seek his own, but each his neighbor's good.*

This does not forbid conduct which is in keeping with enlightened self-interest, but requires that every action shall also be weighed in the light of its effect upon one's fellow Christians. The purely selfish person is by definition non-Christian.

Verse 25, *Whatsoever is sold in the shambles, eat, asking no question for conscience' sake.*

---

[32]James Macknight, *op. cit.*, p. 163.

In verse 21, Paul had commanded, "I forbid you to partake of idol feasts"; but there were two other questions which had troubled the Corinthians, a second being whether or not to eat meat from the common markets, where thc likelihood was strong that the meat had been sacrificed to idols. The apostolic answer to this second question was: "Pay no attention to the possibility of its having been sacrificed to idols, there being no intrinsic change whatever wrought in the meat by such an act." Paul reinforced this by an OT quotation in the next verse.

Verse 26, *For the earth is the Lord's, and the fulness thereof.*

This meant that the meat did not really belong to an idol, no matter if it had been sacrificed. It may therefore be eaten in gratitude as a gift from the Lord, and having no connection at all with an idol. This is a quotation from Psalm 24:1, emphasizing that nothing that men might do can change the ownership of that which intrinsically belongs to God, not merely by the right of creation, but also by the right of maintenance.

Verses 27-28, *If one of them that believe not biddeth you to a feast, and ye are disposed to go; whatsoever is set before you, eat, asking no question for conscience' sake. But if any man say unto you, This hath been offered in sacrifice, eat not, for his sake that showed it, and for conscience' sake.*

This was Paul's answer to the third question, which regarded eating as a guest in the home of an unbeliever. Paul's command was full of reason and consideration. The Christian was not to raise any question whatever about the meat served; but, on the other hand, if the meat was definitely identified by "any man" as having been offered to idols, then the Christian should not indulge in it. Thus, by his firm and unequivocal answer to the three solemn questions propounded by the Corinthians, Paul enforced the absolute abstinence on the part of Christians from anything that was identified as a sacrifice to an idol. Where does that leave the "all things are lawful" proposition?

Before leaving this, the words of Farrar should be noted:

> How gross was the calumny which asserted that Paul taught men to be *indifferent* about eating things sacrificed to idols! He taught indifference only in cases where

> idolatry could not be directly involved in the question. He only repudiated the idle superstition that the food became *inherently* tainted by such a consecration when the eater was unaware of it.[33]

Verses 29-30, *Conscience, I say, not thine own, but the others; for why is my liberty judged by another conscience? If I partake with thankfulness why am I evil spoken of for that for which I give thanks?*

It will be remembered that Paul frequently had resort to the old diatribe manner of presenting his arguments, in which a question is raised from the viewpoint of the opponent and then devastated with a concise reply. Something of that is certainly in evidence here; and Metz caught the spirit of these verses perfectly, thus:

> Paul writes as though he hears an objection from one of the "enlightened" Corinthians. *Living Letters* paraphrases it thus: "But why, you may ask, must I be guided by what someone else thinks? If I can thank God for the food and enjoy it, why let someone spoil everything just because he thinks I am wrong?" In verse 31, Paul replies, "Well, I'll tell you why."[34]

Verse 31, *Whether therefore ye eat, or drink, or whatever ye do, do all to the glory of God.*

The overriding question which must determine all that any Christian does is the question of whether or not his actions will build up, edify, strengthen and encourage the church of Christ; and if any action whatsoever falls short of such utility to bless and honor God's kingdom, then it is forbidden to the child of God. God's glory is paramount; human appetite and convenience have no weight whatever when opposed to God's glory. Paul was a great leader who refused to do anything that might hinder men outside the church or alienate those within it.

Verses 32-33, *Give no occasion of stumbling, either to Jews, or to Greeks, or to the church of God: even as I also please all men in all things, not seeking mine own profit, but the profit of many that they may be saved.*

---

[33]F. W. Farrar, *op. cit.*, p. 325.
[34]Donald S. Metz, *op. cit.*, p. 412.

"Give no occasion of stumbling . . ." This is the apostolic order. If our human brethren, either in or out of the church, may be offended by any action, that action for the true Christian is proscribed and forbidden. We are not living the Christian life for the purpose of blessing ourselves, merely, but for the purpose of saving as many immortal souls as possible.

"That they may be saved . . ." This was the passionate desire of the holy apostle; and everything was subordinated to that goal. What a revival would break out upon earth today if all those who profess to follow Christ should adopt such a rule of conduct.

Chapter 11, verse 1, *Be ye imitators of me, even as I also am of Christ.*

This is included in the next chapter, but the logical connection of it is at the conclusion of Paul's words in chapter 10. Paul often used the admonition to be "imitators" of himself, always with the limitation of the qualifier, "as he followed the Lord," whether expressly stated or not. He gave the same command in 1 Corinthian 4:16, Philippians 3:17, and in 1 Thessalonians 1:6.

CHAPTER 11

This and the following three chapters are usually construed as Paul's corrective admonition regarding the "worship services"; but since the first paragraph (vv. 1-16) undoubtedly refers to social customs, there being even some doubt of its application to any worship service whatever, there is no need for adherence to such an outline. Throughout this epistle, the apostle Paul dealt with miscellaneous church conditions and disorders, making it nearly impossible to fit the epistle into any form of classical outline.

The first paragraph regards the veiling of women (1-16), and the second teaches concerning the Lord's supper (17-34).

Regarding the Veiling of Women

Paul's teaching here is the basis of diametrically opposed views, Lipscomb holding that "Whether the woman prays in the closet at home, or in the assembly, she should approach God with the tokens of her subjection to man on her head."[1] Johnson limited the ruling to the worship meeting, saying, "This alone is in view."[2] He interpreted the words here as "Paul's ruling that women must cover their heads during the meeting."[3] This writer admires and respects the immortal Lipscomb; but, in his comment above, the words "tokens of her subjection to man" betray a basic misunderstanding of this difficult passage. If Paul really meant that women should be veiled, then no fancy little hat will do it. This student of the Scriptures is adamantly opposed to tokenism and would just as soon accept "token baptism" as a "token veil." As Marsh said:

> One thing is certain; within the context of our contemporary culture, the modern western hat — decorative, attractive, and often obstructive — cannot be said to

---

[1]David Lipscomb, *Commentary on 1 Corinthians* (Nashville: The Gospel Advocate Company, 1935), p. 167.

[2]S. Lewis Johnson, Jr., *Wycliffe Bible Commentary* (Chicago: Moody Press, 1971), p. 622.

[3]*Ibid.*

> compare with the veil, either in appearance, function or purpose.[4]

As McGarvey said, "In western countries a woman's hat has never had any symbolism whatever."[5] The notion that any kind of hat, in the modern sense of that word, can in any manner be construed as a "token veil" is founded in neither reason nor scripture; and to get that simple fact in focus is to go a long way to understanding this subject.

Eldred Echols, Professor of Bible, South Africa Bible School, Benoni, South Africa, summed up an extensive study of this problem by the Bible faculty with the following conclusion:

> The dogmatic position that 1 Corinthians 11 requires a woman to wear a hat at a religious service is linguistically and historically impossible. To enjoin it as an obligation upon Christian women is dangerously presumptive, since it is not based upon Biblical authority. On the other hand, there is not the slightest reason why any Christian woman should not wear a hat at church or elsewhere if she wishes to do so. Nevertheless, she should not be deceived into imagining that her hat has any bearing upon first century doctrine or practice.[6]

References to key words in the exegesis below will further elaborate the facts supporting Echols' conclusion. This writer wholeheartedly concurs in this conclusion and also with that of McGarvey who wrote: "The problem in western assemblies is how best to persuade women to take their hats off, not how to prevail upon them to keep them on!"[7]

"Drawings in the catacombs do not bear out the assumption that Christian women wore veils at services in the early church."[8] The extensive art of the Middle Ages, however, invariably portrays the women as fully veiled; but, of course,

---

[4]Paul W. Marsh, *A New Commentary* (Grand Rapids: Zondervan Publishing House, 1969), p. 397.

[5]J. W. McGarvey, *Commentary on 1 Corinthians* (Cincinnati: Standard Publishing Company, 1916), p. 113.

[6]Eldred Echols, *Private Manuscript*, circulated throughout the area of Benoni, South Africa by the faculty of the Bible School. Other references to this will be attributed to EE. This writer is indebted to John H. Banister, Dallas, Texas, for this manuscript.

[7]J. W. McGarvey, *op. cit.*, p. 113.

[8]EE.

this was derived largely from the Roman Catholic culture of that era. In fact that culture may be viewed as the source of the custom of wearing hats (by women) in church services in the present times, the same having been accepted in Reformation and post-Reformation times without critical reappraisal because more urgent issues commanded the attention of scholars.

Despite the conclusion accepted by this commentator to the effect that Paul does not here require women to wear hats at church, it is felt that Barclay went much too far in saying that "This is one of these passages which have a purely local and temporary significance."[9] On the contrary, Paul's teaching here is invaluable and relevant to all generations with regard to the Christian's relation to the culture in which he lives.

Before proceeding to a line-by-line study of this paragraph, one other colossal fact should be noted, that being the word "custom" which appears in verse 16, at the end of the paragraph. Paul did a similar thing in Romans 8:1, where the word "now" flies like a banner, demanding that the antithesis "then" be understood as a description of what he treated in chapter 7. See CR, pp. 262,263, 278. The word "custom" as used in verse 16 clearly identifies the subject under consideration in this paragraph as the customs of the times, and not as an apostolical treatise on what either men or women should wear in religious services, except in the degree that the one had a bearing upon the other. Sex differentiation as indicated by hair-length is outlined; and it is hair, not clothes, of which Paul spoke:

Verse 1 was discussed at the end of chapter 10.

Verse 2, *Now I praise you that ye remember me in all things, and hold fast the traditions, even as I delivered them to you.*

Traditions of men are not necessarily binding, but the holy traditions delivered by the apostles of Christ were of the highest authority. For a considerable part of the first century, there existed many written documents of the Christian religion (Luke 1:1); but such written documents were extensively

---

[9]William Barclay, *The Letters to the Corinthians* (Philadelphia: The Westminster Press, 1954), p. 107.

supplemented by the word-of-mouth teaching which was promulgated by apostles and eyewitnesses of the inception of Christianity. See CMK, pp. 3, 4.

"Hold fast the traditions . . ." "This ordinarily means 'handed down from generation to generation'; but here it refers to the doctrine orally delivered by the apostles to the churches in the first Christian generation."[10] In view of the meaning here, the old AV rendition of "ordinances" is better than "traditions," despite the fact of the latter being the literal meaning.[11]

Verse 3, *But I would have you know that the head of every man is Christ; and the head of the woman is the man; and the head of Christ is God.*

In the threefold step from woman to man to Christ to God, it may appear surprising that Paul began with the center stop; but there seems to have been a design in this. Paul, who was about to speak of the subordination of woman to her husband, would first speak to man with a reminder that he himself is subordinated to Christ the Lord. In Ephesians 5:22-33, Paul made it abundantly clear that the subjection of wives to their husbands was coupled with the sternest commandments with regard to the husband's duty to the wife.

In the current era, there are those who would set aside the apostolical authority regarding the question of the subordination of the wife to her husband; but the wisdom of the ages and also the word of God concur in teaching the necessity that every organism must have a head; and there cannot be any denial that in God's basic unit of all civilization and all progress, which is the family, the head must be either the man or the woman; and God here commanded man to fulfill that function of being the head of the family. If history has demonstrated anything, it is the truism that a matriarchal society is, by definition, inferior.

"The head of Christ is God . . ." The equality of Christ with the Father is everywhere apparent in scripture, as Paul

---

[10]John William Russell, *Compact Commentary on the NT* (Grand Rapids: Baker Book House, 1964), p. 421.

[11]F. W. Farrar, *Pulpit Commentary* (Grand Rapids: Wm. B. Eerdmans Publishing Company, 1950), p. 361.

himself said in Philippians 2:6; but, even so, the Godhead itself could not function in the project of human redemption without the subordination of the Son *for that purpose*. Just so, the subordination of woman to her husband does not set aside the equality of both male and female "in Christ," but it is for the purpose of making the family a viable and successful unit. This verse makes the "headship of the man over the woman parallel to the leadership of God over Christ."[12] Thus the same equality, unity of purpose and unity of will, should exist between a man and his wife as exists between the Father and the Son.

Verse 4, *Every man praying or prophesying, having his head covered, dishonoreth his head.*

"Having his head covered . . ." Here is where the misunderstanding of this passage begins. This clause, as rendered in the popular versions, is commentary, not Bible. As Echols noted:

> "Having his head covered" is a commentary, not a translation. Lenski translated the sense correctly: "having something down from his head." What the "something" is is neither stated nor implied in verse 4.[13]

The logical understanding of this would refer it to "long hair," being long enough to hang down from the head, as clearly indicated by the apostles' words a moment later: "If a man have long hair, it is a dishonor to him" (v. 14).

The ancients accepted Paul's dictum on this and went so far as to define the length of hair that was considered an infraction of Paul's words.

> The hair of the head may not grow so long as to come down and interfere with the eyes .. cropping is to be adopted . . . let not twisted locks hang far down from the head, gliding into womanish ringlets.[14]

Significantly, the words "hang far down" strongly resemble Paul's words "having something down from his head." The above is from Clement of Alexandria and was written in the second century.

---

[12]J. W. McGarvey, *op. cit.*, p. 109.
[13]EE.
[14]Clement of Alexandria, in *Ante Nicene Fathers* (Grand Rapids: Wm. B. Eerdmans Publishing Company, 1956), Vol. II, p. 286.

The notion that Paul in this place referred to the *tallith* (shawl), or *yarmelke* (skull cap) worn by Jewish worshipers is refuted by the fact that the Greek NT does not indicate in this verse an artificial covering of any kind.[15] This does not mean, however, that Paul would have approved of the use of either in Christian worship. "For Paul such a covering probably symbolized that the Jewish male continued in spiritual darkness, from which Christians had been liberated."[16] We may therefore interpret this verse as a simple admonition that it was a disgrace for any long-haired Christian male to participate in praying and prophesying; and this interpretation certainly harmonizes with verse 14. History has certainly vindicated this view; because universal human behavior has departed from it only in isolated instances and for relatively very short periods of time.

"Every man . . ." It is wrong to understand this in the generic sense as "every man or woman." Russell said:

> There are two Greek words for "man"; one for man as a human being; the other contrasting man with woman or child; the latter form is used for man in every instance in this chapter (vv. 3-16).[17]

Verse 5, *But every woman praying or prophesying with her head unveiled dishonoreth her head; for it is one and the same thing as if she were shaven.*

"Every woman praying or prophesying . . ." As Lipscomb said:

> In all the history of Christ and the apostles no example is found of women speaking publicly or leading in public prayer, although they were endowed with miraculous gifts, and did prophesy and teach in private and in the family circle.[18]

However, McGarvey construed this passage as an example of "women when exercising the prophetic office in the church." Macknight took another view (see below). For further discussions, see under 14:34, below.

---

[15]EE.
[16]Paul W. Marsh, *op. cit.* p. 397.
[17]John William Russell, *op. cit.*, p. 421.
[18]David Lipscomb, *op. cit.*, p. 163.

> We may suppose that the Corinthian women affected to perform such offices in the public assemblies on pretence of their being inspired; and, although Paul did not here condemn that practice, it does not follow that he allowed it, or that it was allowed in any church.[19]

"With her head unveiled . . ." The word here rendered "unveiled" is *akatakaluptos*.[20] "There is no intrinsic meaning in this word which suggests either the covering material or the object covered; it is simply a general word."[21] *Katakaluptos* means covered completely. *Akatakaluptos* means not completely covered. Thus again, the passage falls short of mentioning any kind of garment. To suppose that Paul here meant "mantle" or "veil" or any such thing is to import into this text what is not in it. We have seen that he was speaking of "hair" in verse 4; and that is exactly what he is speaking of here. "Not completely covered" would then refer to the disgraceful conduct of the Corinthian women in cropping their hair, after the manner of the notorious Corinthian prostitutes; which, if they did it, was exactly the same kind of disgrace as if they had shaved their heads. It is crystal clear that Paul is not speaking of any kind of garment; because he said in verse 15, below, "For her hair is given her *instead of a covering*."[22] (See under verse 15.) Only in verse 15 does Paul mention any kind of garment (*peribolaion*) and even there he stated that the woman's hair took the place of it.

"Dishonoreth her head . . ." Understanding the "unveiled" in the preceding clause as a reference to cropping her hair explains this. Any man's wife adopting the style of the notorious "priestesses" on the Acro Corinthus would bring shame and dishonor upon her "head," that is, her husband, who would thus be scandalized in the conduct of his wife. Also, from this, it is clear that in verse 4, man's "head," which is Christ, is the one dishonored there. Thus the thing which concerned Paul here was the arrogant adoption of the hair-style (by women) of the shameless priestesses of Aphrodite.

---

[19]James Macknight, *Apostolical Epistles and Commentary* (Grand Rapids: Baker Book House, 1969), p. 172.

[20]W. E. Vine, *An Expository Dictionary of NT Words* (Old Tappan, N. J.: Fleming H. Revell Company, 1940), p. 174.

[21]EE.

[22]NG.

Is there any lesson for modern Christians in this? Indeed there is. Any time that Christian men or women adopt styles, whether of clothing or hair, which are widely accepted as immoral, anti-social, anti-establishment, or in any manner degrading, such actions constitute a violation of what is taught here.

Verse 6, *For if a woman is not veiled, let her also be shorn: but if it is a shame for a woman to be shorn or shaven, let her be veiled.*

Here again the sense of this place is destroyed by the traditional rendition "veiled." No artificial covering of any kind has thus far been mentioned by Paul in this chapter, nor will there be any reference to any kind of garment or artificial covering until verse 15, below, where it is categorically stated that her hair is given her "instead of" any other covering. Paul is only repeating here the obvious truth that for a woman to adopt the Aphrodite hair style was the same thing as being shaven. The shaving of any woman's head was considered either a sign of deep mourning, or a fitting punishment for adultery; and the overwhelming inference here is not that the Corinthian women had thrown off the oriental style "veil" that obscured almost all of the female person, there being no evidence at all that first-century Christian women ever wore such a thing, but that they had adopted the chic hair-styles of the women of Aphrodite. Can it be believed that Paul was here pleading for the Corinthian women to put on "veils" in the style of present-day Moslems, when he was about to say in verse 15, below, that their hair had been given them "instead of" such a covering? It is the flagrant mistranslation of this passage which has obscured the truth and confused millions of students of it.

Verses 7-9, *For a man indeed ought not to have his head veiled, forasmuch as he is the image and glory of God: but the woman is the glory of the man. For the man is not of the woman; but the woman of the man: for neither was the man created for the woman; but the woman for the man.*

"Ought not to have his head veiled. . ." See under verse 4 for the true meaning which is that "a man ought not to have anything hanging down from his head," an obvious reference to long hair, as more thoroughly explained above. Whatever "covered" means in verse 4 must also be the meaning of "veiled" in this verse. Moreover, the fact that Paul is speaking of something fundamental and intrinsic in human appearance, and not merely about some kind of clothing, is inherent in the reasons assigned to support his words. In these verses, the big thing in view is the eternal propriety of woman's submission to her husband, a subject already in Paul's mind, from the reference to "man as the head of woman" (v. 3). The facts of creation reveal that (1) woman was taken out of man, (2) she was given to man, (3) she was created for man, and (4) she was intended to be the glory of man. The scandalous behavior of the Corinthian women had contravened God's purpose in all of these things, hence the mention of them here.

Charles Hodge stated in connection with these verses:

> In this way does the NT constantly authenticate, not merely the moral and religious truths of the OT, but its historical facts; and makes the facts the grounds or proofs of great moral principles.[23]

Verse 10, *For this cause ought the woman to have a sign of authority on her head, because of the angels.*

This verse should be read without the words "a sign of," the same being not in Paul's writings at all, but having been merely added by translators to help out with what they conceived to be the meaning of the passage. As Farrar said, "A great deal of irrelevant guesswork has been written on this verse."[24] We shall not trouble the reader with any of the wild guesses concerning the danger that women without veils might tempt some of the angels attending church and seeing them, or any such speculations. The simplest explanation (since Paul was speaking of the proper subordination of woman) is that this is a reminder that the "angels who kept not their first estate" lost heaven; and it is not far-fetched to draw the analogy that those precious angels called women should not go beyond the limitations imposed upon them by their creation.

---

[23]Charles Hodge, *An Exposition of the First Epistle to the Corinthians* (Grand Rapids: Wm. B. Eerdmans Publishing Company, 1974), p. 210.

[24]F. W. Farrar, *op. cit.*, p. 362.

"Authority upon her head . . ." Scholars do not agree on the exact meaning implied by the use of "authority" here; but it is clear that Paul referred to the woman's head being properly covered; but it is of the utmost importance to note that *the nature of that covering* is not here specified. The opinion of this writer is that the reference means she should not have her hair cropped. Even in such a regulation as that, the implication is that the prohibition is not absolute, but qualified. The sin was not in cutting off hair, but in cutting it off in such a manner as to obscure the sexes or to imitate the shameless prostitutes of the pagan temples.

Verses 11-12, *Nevertheless, neither is the woman without the man, nor the man without the woman, in the Lord. For as the woman is of the man, so is the man also by the woman; but all things are of God.*

Despite the fact of Paul's speaking on the subordination of woman in God's order of created beings, he was careful here to point out what kind of subordination he was speaking of. Man and woman are mutually dependent upon each other, each enjoying unique prerogatives and blessings under the will of God, as Paul stressed in Ephesians 5:22-33, etc. While true enough that the first woman was made out of man, it has been true of all others since then that they are born of woman. The natural relationship between men and women, like everything else, is ordained of God. Johnson believed that the point of emphasis here is that "The man must always remember that he exists by woman, and that both are of God."[25]

Verse 13, *Judge ye in yourselves: is it seemly that a woman pray unto God unveiled?*

As Farrar said, "This is an appeal to the decision of their instinctive sense of propriety."[26] Johnson believed that "seemly" here should be read "proper."[27] It should be noted again that "unveiled" here has no reference at all to what is commonly referred to as a "veil." The word is exactly the same as the one used in verse 5.[28] A covering of some kind is meant;

---

[25]S. Lewis Johnson, Jr., *op. cit.*, p. 623.
[26]F W. Farrar, *op. cit.*, p. 363.
[27]S. Lewis Johnson, Jr., *op. cit.*, p. 624.
[28]W. E. Vine, *op. cit.*, p. 175.

but the Greek text leaves totally out of sight anything that would enable this to be identified as some kind of artificial covering, or man-made garment. See under verse 5. The instinctive judgment of men is much more easily associated with their approval of long hair for a woman than with the approval of some kind or style of clothing. The fallibility of human instinct in that whole area of concern is proved by the new styles accepted every spring!

Verse 14, *Doth not even nature itself teach you, that if a man have long hair, it is a dishonor to him?*

As Johnson observed, "The fact of short hair for men and long hair for women is a divine suggestion in nature itself."[29] It is quite evident throughout this whole paragraph that Paul is talking about "hair," not clothes! If such is not the case, such a verse as this is totally out of place. The judgment of history as well as the NT confirms Paul's words here are true. Men may deny it if they please; but the sacred text and the usage of centuries are against any such denial.

Verse 15, *But if a woman have long hair, it is a glory to her: for her hair is given her for a covering.*

"It is a glory to her . . ." This would have been the ideal place for Paul to have said that a mantle thrown over a woman's head and shoulders is a glory to her, if he ever had such a thing in mind. On the contrary, it comes out here, as it does in every verse in the whole passage, his subject was "hair"!

"Her hair is given her for a covering . . ." Here again is an enormous mistranslation; and one may only wonder at the efforts of commentators to make this conform to the misinterpretations they have foisted upon this innocent passage. For example, Johnson declared that "This does not mean that her hair is her covering";[30] but a glance at any interlinear Greek NT will reveal the meaning instantly. Nestle gives it, "instead of a veil."[31] The Emphatic Diaglott has "Her hair is given her

---

[29]S. Lewis Johnson, Jr., *op. cit.*, p. 624.
[30]*Ibid.*
[31]NG.

instead of a veil."[32] Echols emphatically stressed this expression "instead of" as follows:

> The idea conveyed by "instead of" is that if the noun preceding this preposition is available, the noun following the preposition is not required. Therefore, the conclusion is quite inescapable that, if a woman's hair conforms to apostolic standards of propriety, she requires no artificial covering.[33]

But of paramount importance in this verse is the noun *paribolaion*, here rendered "veil." This is the one noun in the whole passage that unmistakably refers to a head covering. Thayer's Greek-English Lexicon of the NT translates it, "a covering thrown around, a wrapper." This is the "veil" which has already been imported into the passage five times; but this is Paul's first reference to anything of the kind; and, significantly, it is mentioned in the same breath with woman's hair which is given to her "instead of" any such covering.

The only conceivable situation in which it may be inferred that Paul expected women to wear the kind of mantle, or veil, spoken of here, would be one in which a woman's hair had been lost, from disease, accident, or something of that kind. Echols thought that "instead of" in this verse "forces us to accept the alternative that, if a woman's hair does not fulfill its proper function, then she should wear a mantle or hood."[34] However, this seems to be an unnecessary conclusion, since the natural modesty of almost any person would lead to the wearing of a head covering in such a circumstance.

Verse 16, *But if any man seemeth to be contentious, we have no such custom, neither the churches of God.*

"If any man seemeth to be contentious..." This was Paul's way of saying, "Look, we do not intend to argue this question endlessly; the whole matter is already solved by the type of behavior which marks God's churches everywhere." This is grounds for holding that in this whole passage it is decorous conduct with which Paul is concerned, since it touched on the

---

[32]ED.
[33]EE.
[34]EE.

all-important question of the proper submission of women to their husbands, and was also related to the prevailing opinion of the people in that community.

This whole passage affirms the necessity for Christians to have a decent respect for the opinions of mankind, and not to flaunt social customs of any kind merely for the sake of being different. As McGarvey said, "One who follows Christ will find himself conspicuously different from the world, without practicing any tricks of singularity."[35]

Questions on Above Verses

If Paul meant "hair," why did he use the word "covered"? The answer is that in the vocabulary of the OT "to uncover the head" was to shave off the hair. When Nadab and Abihu sinned (Lev. 10:1ff), God commanded Aaron not to "uncover his head" in mourning at their death; and this meant not to cut off his hair (the customary sign of mourning). Job shaved his head when he learned his children were dead (Job 1:20). Many examples of this usage could be cited; but as Echols noted: "Wherever the expression 'uncover the head' occurs in the Hebrew OT, it means 'remove the hair.'"[36] The culture of that era as well as the environment at Corinth suggests that some of the Corinthian women (in the church) were violating decent rules of conduct, not by discarding the mantle (*peribolaion*) which there is no evidence that any of them were wearing, but by adopting the cropped hair of Aphrodite's priestesses. It is even likely that some of them had been converted and had neglected to change their hair styles. Furthermore, it must be evident to all who think about it that when Paul said in verse 4 that a man praying or prophesying with his head "covered" dishonored his head, he simply *could not* have referred to any man's wrapping himself up in the type of mantle that was called a veil in those days. That type of veil (or mantle), as far as history reveals, was never worn by men in any circumstance. Therefore the fault Paul sought to correct in verse 4 was not that of men veiling themselves like women, but that of sporting indecently long hair.

---

[35]J. W. McGarvey, *op. cit.*, p. 110.
[36]EE.

What was the veil, actually, that was worn in those days? It was a large loose mantle which the woman wrapped around her head and face, leaving only the eyes visible, and sometimes only one eye. The word "veil" used by our translators is extremely misleading. Ruth's veil, for example, held six measures of barley! (Ruth 3:15). Although Hebrew women did not always wear veils, they seem to have done so for harvesting, as in the case of Ruth.

Was the mantle (veil) a symbol of modesty and submission? It came in time to be so considered; but there was certainly a time when such a garment (designed to obscure the person) was considered the attire of a harlot. Note the following:

> And she (Tamar) put her widow's garments off, and covered her with a veil, and wrapped herself, and sat in an open place, which is by the way to Timnath; for she saw that Shelah was grown, and she was not given unto him to wife. When Judah saw her, he thought her to be an harlot; because she had covered her face. And he turned in unto her by the way (Gen. 38:14-16).

Is there any word in this whole passage that unmistakably means the type of veil under consideration? Yes, the word *peribolaion* in verse 15 refers to that type of covering; and this is the only word in the whole passage that does so; but this is also the verse where Paul said the Lord had given woman her hair "instead of" any such garment!

What is Paul's subject in these verses? Whatever it was, it could not have been the type of veil or mantle that obscures the person of women, that having been mentioned only once. On the other hand *hair* is mentioned three times, *shaved* or *shorn* is mentioned four times; and, in this light, it appears certain that Paul's subject here was *hair*. One could not speak of a mantle's being shorn or shaved.

How could this passage have been so long misunderstood? Echols' explanation is as good as any. He said:

> A clear understanding has been obscured by ambiguous English translations, as well as by established custom. There can be little doubt that the custom itself

derived largely from Roman Catholic practice during the Middle ages.[37]

CONCERNING THE LORD'S SUPPER

The balance of this chapter (17-34) deals with abuses in the Corinthian congregation with regard to the proper observance of the Lord's Supper and the "love feast" which usually preceded it in the primitive church.

Verses 17-18, *But in giving you this charge, I praise you not, that ye come together not for the better but for the worse. For first of all, when ye come together in the church, I hear that divisions exist among you; and I partly believe it.*

"When ye come together . . ." is a reference to the formal assembly of the congregation for worship as a body, the corporate worship, as it is sometimes called.

"Not for the better but for the worse . . ." Not merely were their assemblies so disordered and perverted as to deny all benefit to the worshipers, but they were actually productive of harm, so much so that those attending were actually worse off for having participated.

"When ye come together in the church . . . divisions . . ." Paul had already discussed the shameful schisms, or parties, that had become prevalent in Corinth; and it seems here that he is referring to the intrusion of this party spirit into the worship itself, but especially to the manifestation of that spirit in the common meal that in those times was held before the Lord's Supper and in close connection with it. As Alexander Campbell said:

> There can be no doubt that the Eucharist at this period (shortly after Pentecost) was preceded uniformly by a common repast, as when the ordinance was instituted. Most scholars hold that this was the prevailing usage in the first centuries after Christ; and we have traces of this practice in 1 Corinthians 11:20ff.[38]

---

[37]EE.

[38]Alexander Campbell, *Acts of the Apostles* (Austin: Firm Foundation Publishing House, 1858), p. 18.

Verse 19, *For there must be also factions among you, that they that are approved may be made manifest among you.*

A glimpse of the divine mind is in this. Christians who become upset and discouraged because of schisms, factions and other disorders in the church make a tragic mistake. As God used Satan in the Paradise of Eden to test the progenitors of the human race, he still tests the faith of all Christians. Church difficulties provide an opportunity for Christians to demonstrate that they are genuine followers of the Lord. God never intended that any man should move through life in a constant environment of encouragement and spiritual delight. There is a place in the experience of every Christian where "the rubber meets the road"; and his response to unfavorable, or even tragic, situations will determine whether or not he is "approved" of God. It should always be remembered that "many are called, but few are chosen."

Verse 20, *When therefore ye assemble yourselves together, it is not possible to eat the Lord's Supper.*

"It is not possible to eat the Lord's Supper . . ." This cannot mean that it was physically impossible, but that it was morally impossible. The abuses of the *Agape*, or love feast, which preceded the holy communion were so grave as to contravene any true participation in the sacred supper.

"The Lord's Supper . . ." Morris said, "*Kurakon*, translated "the Lord's," is found only here and in Revelation 1:10 in the NT."[39] Thus, only here does the expression "The Lord's Supper" appear in the NT. There is no doubt, however, that the expression was, at the date of this epistle, the usual manner of referring to this solemn rite. Farrar observed that "The fact that there is no article in the Greek shows the early prevalence of this name for the Eucharist."[40]

It is rather amazing that Barnes made a deduction from this verse to the effect that the Lord's Supper should be observed in the evenings, not in the mornings of the Lord's Days. He said:

---

[39]Leon Morris, *Tyndale Commentary* (Grand Rapids: Wm. B. Eerdmans Publishing Company, 1958), p. 158.

[40]F. W. Farrar, *Pulpit Commentary* (Grand Rapids: Wm. B. Eerdmans Publishing Company, 1950), p. 364.

> It is called *supper*, indicating the evening repast; it was instituted in the evening; and it is most proper that it should be observed in the after part of the day. Churches have improperly changed to the morning . . . a custom which has no sanction in the NT; and which is a departure from the very idea of a supper.[41]

Barnes' deduction should be rejected, because there is no hint in the NT that *the time of day* for the observance of this rite was ever the subject of any apostolical decree. *The day* is indicated, but not the time of day. Moreover, Pliny's letter to the emperor Trajan, shortly after the beginning of the second century, stated that the Christians were "accustomed to meet before daybreak."[42] From these considerations, it is clear that "The Lord's Supper" has reference to the hour of its institution, and not to the hour of its observance by Christians.

Verse 21, *For in eating each one taketh before other his own supper; and one is hungry, and another is drunken.*

The abuse at Corinth was compound. The *Agape*, or love feast, which in early times preceded the Lord's Supper, had at Corinth been shamelessly mixed with the sacred rite to the extent of the total corruption of both. The so-called love feast was somewhat like the "dinners on the grounds" which were a feature of rural congregations throughout America in this century. However, at Corinth, the rich who brought bountiful provisions for such affairs were not sharing with the poor who had been able to bring little or nothing. Some were actually having a big feast and then returning home before the others arrived. Drunkenness and gluttony were prevalent, in addition to the pitiless disregard of the poor and needy. It may be presumed that the emblems of the Lord's Supper might have been distributed by each group to themselves at the conclusion of their feasts; but by so doing they did not eat "one bread" with their brethren, thus having no fellowship with them and totally circumventing the purpose of the Lord's Supper. An analysis of such disorders shows that:

---

[41]Albert Barnes, *Notes on the NT* (Grand Rapids: Baker Book House, 1949), p. 211.

[42]Henry Bettenson, *Documents of the Christian Church* (New York and London: Oxford University Press, 1947), p. 6.

1. The various groups did not eat at the same time.
2. Each group ate its own provisions, instead of sharing in the "one bread" (10:17).
3. Some ate too plentifully; some ate nothing at all, for there was nothing left.
4. Some were "drunken"; and there is no need to soften the meaning of this. "Grotius gives *drunken* the milder, and Meyer the stronger sense."[43]
5. The corruption of the Lord's Supper by such practices was complete; and, according to Farrar, "This abuse led to the separation of the Agape from the Holy Communion,"[44] and to the ultimate discontinuation of the former.

Verse 22, *What, have ye not houses to eat and drink in? or despise ye the church of God, and put them to shame that have not? What shall I say to you? shall I praise you? In this I praise you not.*

"Have ye not houses to eat and drink in . . ." It should be carefully noted that Paul did not here condemn a congregation's eating upon the occasion of their formal coming together for worship, nor eating in any building or location where such meetings were held. What he condemned was their intemperance, disregard of the need of others, and their shameless mixing of the Lord's Supper with a common meal. The *kind of eating and drinking* they were doing belonged properly at home and not at church. He condemned their abuse of sacred privilege in the strongest terms. It is also incorrect to infer from this that Paul thought that it was proper for them to eat and be "drunken" at home!

Verse 23, *For I received of the Lord that which also I delivered unto you, that the Lord Jesus in the night in which he was betrayed took bread.*

This is the fourth time in the NT that the institution of the Lord's Supper is recorded. Some scholars deny that Paul received a direct revelation on this subject; but if he was

---

[43]J. W. McGarvey, *op. cit.*, p. 115.
[44]F. W. Farrar, *op. cit.*, p. 364.

merely repeating what he had received from other apostles; it is hard to see why he would have said:

"I received of the Lord . . ." Wuest wrote that:

> Paul had doubtless heard the account of the institution of the Lord's Supper from the eleven, but he also had it by revelation from the Lord (1 Cor. 11:23). He received his gospel by direct revelation in Arabia.[45]

Leon Morris and F. W. Farrar, with many others, concur in this view.

Verse 24, *And when he had given thanks, he brake it, and said, This is my body, which is for you: this do in remembrance of me.*

"Had given thanks . . ." In Matthew and Mark, reference to this act says, "Having blessed it"; but Luke has it as here. As Hodge declared: "The two expressions mean the same thing. Both express the act of consecration, by a grateful acknowledgment of God's mercy and invocation of his blessing."[46]

"He brake it.." From this it is clear that "the breaking of the bread ought not to be abandoned, as in the case when *wafers* are used."[47] Some have supposed that breaking the bread contradicts (by symbolism) the fact that not a bone of Jesus was broken (John 19:36)! but the breaking of a bone is not the same as the breaking of the body. The spear that pierced Jesus' side certainly broke his "body," but did not break any bone. The AV, of course, has "This is my body which is *broken*"; and the meaning is certainly in the passage, deriving from "he brake it." Thus the meaning is true, despite the fact of the word "broken" not being in the best manuscripts.

"This do in remembrance of me . . ." For more explicit comment on the commemorative aspect of the Lord's Supper, see Nature of the Lord's Supper, under verse 34.

Verses 25-26, *In like manner also the cup, after supper, saying, This cup is the new covenant in my blood: this do, as*

---

[45]Kenneth S. Wuest, *Wuest's Word Studies from the Greek NT* (Grand Rapids: Wm. B. Eerdmans Publishing Company, 1973), Vol. III, p. 224.

[46]Charles Hodge. *op. cit.*, p. 224.

[47]F. W. Farrar, *op. cit.*, p. 365.

often as ye drink it, in remembrance of me. For as often as ye eat this bread, and drink the cup, ye proclaim the Lords' death till he come.

"After supper . . ." This phrase is invaluable in that it shows why two cups were mentioned, one before the bread and the other afterward, in Luke 22:17-20. The first cup Luke mentioned was the fourth cup of the simulated passover meal, which Paul here called "supper" with the strongest implications that it was in no sense the Passover itself (except by accommodation), the same being called the "cup of joy." Both the bread and the wine of the Lord's Supper were given "after supper," and in that order, the bread first, the cup afterward. See CL pp. 467, 468.

"This cup is the new covenant in my blood . . ." This means the same thing as "This is my blood of the covenant" (Matt. 26:26); and in Paul's statement here, it is absolutely clear that the meaning in Matthew in no sense favors the crass literalism of such doctrines as transubstantiation or consubstantiation, no semblance of any such thing being suggested here. The student should consult the sacred text and the comments in the other three NT reports of this event: CM, pp. 429ff; CMK, pp. 306ff; and CL, pp. 467ff.

Regarding the superstition that the emblems of the Lord's Supper are, in their consecration, literally changed to the body or flesh and blood of Christ, Hodge gave this pertinent comment:

> It is only by denying all distinctions between matter and spirit, and confounding all our ideas of substance and qualities, that we can believe that wine is blood, or bread flesh.[48]

"For as often as ye eat this bread, and drink the cup . . ." Regarding the proper time of observance for the Lord's Supper, the NT teaches that it was observed upon the first day of the week, the first day of *every* week, and *not upon any other* days of the week. This passage is therefore no permit to take it any time we please. See CA, pp. 385, 386, and 517.

---

[48]Charles Hodge, *op. cit.*, p. 225.

"Eat this bread and drink this cup . . ." Apostolical practice makes it certain that communion under one kind, that is, taking *either* the bread or the wine without the other, was never encouraged or allowed in the NT. Furthermore, Paul's use of "or drink this cup" in verse 27 is not a denial of this. As Farrar said, "What he meant there was that it was possible to partake in a wrong spirit either of the bread or of the cup."[49]

"Ye proclaim the Lord's death till he come . . ." As Dummelow said, the Lord's Supper is "a living sermon."[50] Thus the instructive nature of this solemn rite is stressed. See Nature of the Lord's Supper, below. The word for "proclaim" here is *katangello.* Morris gave the meaning as "announce" or "proclaim," saying that "It means that the solemn observance of the service of Holy Communion is a vivid proclamation of the Lord's death."[51]

"Till he come . . ." The Lord's Supper faces in two directions, back to Calvary and forward to the Second Advent, being retrospective in regard to one and prospective with regard to the latter. The Second Advent is a major doctrine of Christianity; and it is fitting that it should be honored in this pivotal ordinance.

Verse 27, *Wherefore whosoever shall eat the bread or drink of the cup of the Lord in an unworthy manner, shall be guilty of the body and the blood of the Lord.*

Due to the rendition in the AV, "eateth and drinketh unworthily," many Christians have erroneously concluded that their "unworthiness" forbade their observance of the supper; but this is not true at all. The rendition here makes the meaning clear that it is not the "worthiness" of the participant which is in view, but the "worthiness" of his manner of partaking of it. Indeed, who was ever worthy to eat the flesh and drink the blood of the Son of God? The moment any man might suppose that he was "worthy" to do such a thing, the presumption itself would deny it. Nevertheless, there is a real danger here. If any person shall partake of this solemn rite

---

[49]F. W. Farrar, *op. cit.*, p. 365.

[50]J. R. Dummelow, *Commentary on the Holy Bible* (New York: The Macmillan Company, 1937), p. 912.

[51]Leon Morris, *op. cit.*, p. 162.

without discernment of the event it memorializes, or without regard to the obligations imposed by it, or without any consistent effort to partake of it continually and faithfully throughout his life, or until the Lord comes, or without the due reverence and appreciation due such an ordinance — then such a person becomes guilty of the body and the blood of Jesus, the meaning of this being that he, in a spiritual sense, has become a crucifier of the Lord himself.

"Or drink of the cup . . ." See under preceding verse.

Verse 28, *But let a man prove himself, and so eat of the bread, and drink of the cup.*

"Before taking part in such a service, the very least we can do is to conduct a rigorous self-examination."[52] The word used here means "to test" and was used of the testing of metals. The point is that no Christian should observe the Lord's supper in any casual or flippant manner, treating it as something ordinary. It is the central ordinance of Christianity; and the believer's fidelity to it, or infidelity, is fraught with eternal consequences.

Verse 29, *For he that eateth and drinketh, eateth and drinketh judgment to himself, if he discern not the body.*

"Judgment . . ." may also be rendered "damnation" or "condemnation," in any event meaning consequences both serious and eternal.

"Discern not the body . . ." This may be indefinite by purpose on Paul's part. It would apply either to the precious body of Christ sacrificed upon Calvary for all men, or the church which is his spiritual body, the offense being the same either way the text is read. Significantly, it was the failure of the Corinthians that they disregarded the spiritual body (Despise ye the church of God?); and it is a fact that unfaithfulness at the Lord's table in all generations has been one of the most prevalent and hurtful means of despising God's church. Countless souls are continually guilty of this very thing. The apostle here warned of drastic penalties incurred by such negligence.

---

[52]*Ibid.*, p. 163.

Verse 30, *For this cause many among you are weak and sickly, and not a few sleep.*

This has usually been interpreted to mean that physical sickness and death had been visited upon the sinful Corinthians, due to their shameful perversion and abuse of the Lord's Supper; and while it must be allowed that in that age of the church, God did send visitations of divine wrath against wrongdoers, as in the case of Ananias and Sapphira, and perhaps also the incestuous man mentioned earlier in this epistle; nevertheless, the conviction here is that, if that had been in Paul's mind, he could hardly have said that "some sleep," sleep being too mild a word to use with reference to victims of divine wrath.

The meaning which appears to be most likely is that Paul was speaking of those who had become spiritually weak and sickly, some no doubt having perished spiritually. If that was meant, then the condition of those asleep was terminal and irrevocable, being the same as that evident in Mark 3:29, Hebrews 6:6, 1 Timothy 5:6, 2 Peter 2:20, I John 5:16, 1 Thessalonians 5:19. For a dissertation on the unpardonable sin, see CMK, pp. 65-67. The condition of those asleep was no different from that of Ananias and Sapphira; and therefore Paul's gentle word "sleep" would appear to have been spoken in tenderness and regret.

Johnson noted that wherever "sleep" is used of death in the NT, it refers to the death of Christians, inferring from this that these "had not lost their salvation, but the privilege of service on earth."[53] Such a conclusion seems precarious to this writer. There is an echo of Calvinism in such a viewpoint.

Verses 31-32, *But if we discerned ourselves, we should not be judged. But when we are judged, we are chastened of the Lord, that we may not be condemned with the world.*

In these verses, it seems quite clearly indicated that Paul was still speaking of the weak and sickly Christians and of them that "slept." Thus, the implications would be that through the scourge of physical illness, resulting in death for

---

[53]S. Lewis Johnson, *op. cit.*, p. 626.

some and severe sickness for others, God was chastening the people with an ultimate purpose of their salvation in view. It is therefore quite difficult to support a dogmatic opinion with regard to the meaning of verse 30. One thing may be definitely learned from it; *that* is the dreadful consequences of unfaithfulness at the Lord's table.

Farrar's paraphrase of this is as follows:

> If we were in the habit of discriminating between spiritual and common things, we should not be undergoing this sign of God's displeasure; but the fact that his judgments are abroad among us, is for our further moral education, and to save us from being finally condemned with the world.[54]

Verse 33, *Whereas, my brethren, when ye come together to eat, wait for one another.*

This writer still remembers the occasions in his boyhood, when church never started on time, because "tarry ye one for another" from the AV was interpreted to mean that church could not begin till all the members were present. Sometimes this resulted in quite sensational delays! What Paul said here, of course, was that the affluent should not bring their provisions and eat them all before the poor arrived, the primary application of this, it seems, being to the *Agape*, and not to the Lord's Supper which followed it. The relevance of the passage still holds. Considerations of love and helpfulness should always be extended to brothers by brothers in Christ, even to the tardy.

Verse 34, *If any man is hungry, let him eat at home; that your coming together be not unto judgment. And the rest will I set in order whensoever I come.*

This was the apostolical order that resulted in the separation of the Agape from the Lord's Supper and the eventual discontinuation of the former. The Lord's Supper was here elevated to a position higher than that of merely satisfying the appetites. The hungry should eat at home. Nevertheless, the beauty of the *Agape*, as practiced in the primitive church, has

---

[54]F. W. Farrar, *op. cit.*, p. 366.

always enthralled and captivated the imagination; and there can be little doubt that meals served in the present times by churches "on the grounds," in their buildings, or in parks and public places, are vestigial recurrences of that once glorious custom which perished in the shameful abuses at Corinth. It was the selfishness, greediness and lust of the natural man insufficiently subdued by the indwelling Spirit which perverted, and by that perversion destroyed an age of loving innocence. The church, it seems has never been able to recapture that lost innocence. Observations of the dinners served by congregations through many years have afforded this writer many occasions to note the ease with which the Corinthian perversions invade and destroy such dinners.

Nature of the Lord's Supper

The central ordinance of Christianity is the Lord's Supper, standing in a metaphor as a summary of the whole Christian religion: "Except ye eat the flesh and drink the blood of the Son of man ye have no life in you" (John 6:53). See CJ, pp. 186-188. The nature of this precious rite is discerned in seven words, as follows:

1. Retrospective. It looks back to Calvary, bringing to the worshiper's mind the night of betrayal, agony, blood and tears, and the awful scenes of the crucifixion itself. Christians who have been "baptized into his death" (Rom. 6:3) find in this solemn ceremony a recurring participation in Christ's death. Upon that fixed interval recurring every Lord's Day, the child of God turns his thoughts and meditations back to the cross, in his heart living with the Saviour those awful events of his Passion, reviewing over and over again the scenes and circumstances which marked the Lord's supreme act of atonement for the sins of the whole world. Christ died for our sins; and it is that historical event which anchors and perpetuates the Lord's Supper; and thus the historicity of Christ's death and resurrection is demonstrated and proved throughout all times and places by this sacred rite.

2. Prospective. The ancient pagan god of war was the two-faced Janus (from whence the name of the month January), facing in both directions, forward and backward. In a far more

wonderful manner, the Lord's Supper faces toward Calvary in retrospect, and also toward the Second Advent, prospectively. When the Manhattan Church of Christ constructed a new building in New York City, the custom of writing the words, "Do this in remembrance of me" on the Lord's table, was expanded by adding the words, "This do ye till I come." Thus the essential expectation inherent in the holy supper was scripturally recognized. Unless Christ is coming again, all true meaning of the Lord's Supper disappears; for there is in every proper observance of it the conviction of that time when the skies will be bright with the coming of the Son of God the second time apart from sin to reward the righteous and to bring about the summation of all things.

3. Introspective. In Paul's writings in this chapter, the necessity of every man's examining himself is affirmed (v. 28). It is in that rigorous self-examination which should mark every man's participation in the Lord's Supper that the introspective nature of it is seen. One's life, his sincerity, his devotion, dedication and love for the Lord who redeemed him at such awful cost should all appear within the thoughts of the participant. How can any wickedness bear the light of such an introspective searching?

4. Commemorative. "In remembrance of me," Jesus said (v. 25). The Lord's Supper is one of the great memorials to the event of the Dayspring's visitation from on high, the Lord's baptism and the Lord's day being two others. What a memorial is this! No tower of stone or marble palace, no tablet or inscription, no name conferred on cities or places, no granite obelisk or shining monument could ever have a fraction of the effectiveness of this worldwide memorial of the Lord's Supper. It has now been observed by Christians on more than 100,000 successive Lord's Days; nor is there any possibility that there will ever be a single Sunday till the end of time when it will not be observed by people who love the Lord and await his Second Advent. Under Judaism, men remembered their sins; in Christ they remember their Redeemer who has forgiven their sins (Jer. 31:31-35).

5. Instructive. "Ye proclaim the Lord's death till he come." If one wishes to preach a sermon of redemption to a dying

world, let him faithfully observe this sacred supper. Jesus himself identified it as a proclamation. If one would instruct dying men to turn their hearts to the cross of Christ, the way to do it is to exhibit unvarying fidelity to this Christian duty. Books are cast aside, sermons forgotten, solicitous words ignored; but no man can ignore the example of a faithful life with regard to the Holy Communion of the body and the blood of Christ. The weakness of churches in this generation may not so much be attributed to weak preaching (although there is plenty of that), but to weak living on the part of her members. The man who neglects or abandons the Lord's Supper has hidden his light, stifled the message of salvation and denied his Lord.

6. Corrective. Implicit in the self-examination mentioned under 3 above, is the requirement that elements of personal life out of harmony with the high professions of Christianity will be recognized and corrected. This is inherent in the meaning of "Let a man prove himself." Faithful adherence to the duty of observing the Lord's Supper will either remove one's sins, or one's sins will remove him from frequenting the Lord's table.

7. Separative. This ordinance, more than any other, reveals who is saved and who is not saved. Here is the spiritual device of the Lord himself which separates the wheat from the chaff. Christ himself said, "Except ye eat the flesh of the Son of man and drink his blood, ye have not life in yourselves" (John 6:53); and men may scream about this if they please, but it is the truth. Go to church. The saints and the sinners alike sing the hymns; the believer and the infidel alike hear the sermon respectfully; the sons of light and the sons of darkness give of their money; the saved and the lost bow their heads for the prayers; but when the emblems of the Lord's Supper appear, a separation is made. The NT reveals that here is an ordinance so important that the whole world is polarized by it, Christians being quite properly identified as those who faithfully observe it, and non-Christians identified as those who take it not. Oh yes, to be sure, this ordinance *alone* is not the terminator; but the importance of it is such that Christ himself used it as a

metaphor of the whole Christian religion. "He that eateth my flesh and drinketh my blood hath eternal life; and I will raise him up at the last day" (John 6:54). For more on this, see CJ, pp. 186-188.

CHAPTER 12

This and the following two chapters were written to correct disorders which had arisen in the Corinthian church over the question of spiritual gifts, especially with regard to envy and strife over the relative importance of various gifts. The great test of all spirituality is its relation to Christ and his spiritual body the church. So-called "gifts" that led to the denunciation of Christ or any conduct that contravened the will of Christ were not of God, but of the devil. "Gifts" that take people away from the church are not of God's Spirit at all, but are derived from the evil one (vv. 1-3). There is diversity in the unity of the church, since the Lord has not given the same gifts to all Christians (vv. 4-11). The great metaphor of "the body" is developed as a figure of Christ's spiritual body, the church (vv. 12-31).

Verse 1, *Now concerning spiritual gifts, brethren, I would not have you ignorant.*

The word "gifts" is supplied; and this does no violence to the text, since it may not be denied that the "gifts" were very much in Paul's thoughts. The setting of the entire Corinthian letter should be noted.

> Before the NT was completed, while it was still being written, in certain places and at certain times, God gave special miraculous manifestations of the Holy Spirit's help of the churches.[1]

It is with such miraculous gifts that this and the following chapters are concerned. As Kelcy said:

> These gifts were necessary in the days of the infancy of the church when as yet the body of perfectly revealed truth was incomplete. They were temporary measures designed for a special purpose.[2]

---

[1]Henry H. Halley, *Bible Handbook* (Grand Rapids: Zondervan Publishing House, 1927), p. 548.

[2]Rayond C. Kelcy, *First Corinthians* (Austin: R. B. Sweet Co., Inc., 1967), p. 55.

The trouble was that in Corinth "The whole idea of the gifts of God's Spirit had degenerated, most of them being ignored, and the one being stressed above all others was speaking in tongues."[3] Thus most of these three chapters deals with that phenomenon. However, there are beautiful insights into many other things as well.

Verse 2, *Ye know that when ye were Gentiles ye were led away unto those dumb idols, howsoever ye might be led.*

There is a reminder to the Corinthians here that just as they had been carried away (led away) into idolatry, there was another danger that some were being "carried away" with charismatic gifts! The impotence of idol worship also appears in this. As Wesley paraphrased it, "Ye were led by the subtlety of your priests."[4] "Literally, they were led about like a condemned prisoner."[5] As Morris noted:

> There is something pathetic about idol worship. The heathen are pictured, not as freely following the gods their intellects have fully approved, but as under constraint, helpless, men who know no better.[6]

Verse 3, *Wherefore, I make known unto you, that no man speaking in the Spirit of God saith, Jesus is anathema; and no man can say, Jesus is Lord, but in the Holy Spirit.*

The genuine test of true spirituality turns upon the attitude of the soul toward the Lord Jesus Christ. It is astounding that some of the tongue speakers in Corinth had (presumably) blasphemed the name of the Lord himself, "anathema" meaning accursed! If this seems astonishing, then let it be compared with certain "charismatics" of our own times who deny many of the fundamental doctrines of Christianity "in the name of Christ"! As Russell pointed out, Paul did not refer to those alone who actually used the words "Jesus is anathema," but to

---

[3]Donald S. Metz, *Beacon Bible Commentary* (Kansas City: Beacon Hill Press, 1968), p. 424.

[4]John Wesley, *One Volume NT Commentary* (Grand Rapids: Baker Book House, 1972), in loco.

[5]Donald S. Metz, *op. cit.*, p. 425.

[6]Leon Morris, *Tyndale Commentary* (Grand Rapids: Wm. B. Eerdmans Publishing Company, 1958), p. 425.

all those who practice "what amounts to the same thing."[7] To deny or renounce Christ's teaching would be the equivalent error.

"Jesus is Lord . . ." The sure mark of spirituality is the soul's confession of Jesus as Lord (Rom. 10:9), coupled with the exhibition of a life in harmony with such a profession.

The immaturity of the Corinthian church is evident in the fact of their seeking some shortcut to spiritual excellence. This is precisely the motivation, it would seem, of many in various ages who have aspired to miraculous manifestations, thinking that in these they achieved genuine spirituality. It should be noted in this connection that Corinth was the most carnal of all the churches mentioned in the NT; and it was precisely there that "a church had mostly gone to tongues."[8]

Various Spiritual Gifts Enumerated

Verse 4, *Now there are diversities of gifts, but the same Spirit.*

"Here the apostle called the supernatural endowments of the first Christians *gifts*, because they were foretold under that name (Ps. 68:18; Eph. 4:8)."[9] They are also referred to in the several terms of Hebrews 2:4 as "signs and wonders, and manifold powers, and gifts of the Holy Spirit, according to his own will." All such supernatural wonders were scheduled to disappear (13:8); and their unique purpose was that of "confirming" the word of God (Mark 16:20), certainly not that of flattering the ego of Corinthian charismatics.

"Diversities . . ." This is used nowhere else in the NT.[10] Likewise the word "gifts" is "a typically Pauline word, used only once by any other NT writer (1 Peter 4:10)."[11] It is derived from *charismata*, whence the term "charismatic." another

---

[7]John William Russell, *Compact Commentary on the NT* (Grand Rapids: Baker Book House, 1964), p. 423.

[8]A. B. Bruce, *St. Paul's Conception of Christianity* (New York: Charles Scribner's Sons, 1898), p. 247.

[9]James Macknight, *Apostolical Epistles and Commentary* (Grand Rapids: Baker Book House, 1969), p. 194.

[10]Paul W. Marsh, *A New Commentary* (Grand Rapids: Zondervan Publishing House, 1969), p. 401.

[11]*Ibid.*

form of the word being *charis* (grace). thus these were "grace-gifts." The big point Paul made here is that all gifts came from the same Spirit. Significantly, verses 4-6 speak of "same Spirit . . . same Lord . . . same God," giving a strong trinitarian emphasis.

Verse 5, *And there are diversities of ministrations, and the same Lord.*

Verse 6, *And there are diversities of workings, but the same God, who worketh all things in all.*

The mere fact of some of the Corinthian Christians having one gift and others another gift really made no difference, since it was the same godhead working through all of them. Unlike the numerous idols of the pagans, the one true God is a unity, a unity which was denied by the parties and divisions in Corinth; and these words were written with a view to restructuring the broken unity.

Verse 7, *But to each one is given the manifestation of the Spirit to profit withal.*

"To profit withal . . ." "This means that they were for the common good; the spiritual gifts were to benefit others"[12] Charismatic gifts were being utilized by the Corinthians for self-promotion, especially the more spectacular and showy gifts like tongue speakings. This, of course, was totally wrong and contrary to God's purpose.

Verse 8, *For to one is given through the Spirit the word of wisdom; and to another the word of knowledge, according to the same Spirit.*

Here begins Paul's enumeration of those miraculous gifts with which God endowed certain men in the primitive period of the church's history.

"The word of wisdom . . ." "This was the doctrine of the gospel, communicated by inspiration, . . . peculiar to the apostles, and enabling them to direct religious faith and practice infallibly."[13] This is mentioned first because it was first chronologically and first in importance.

---

[12]Donald S. Metz, *op. cit.*, p. 427.
[13]James Macknight, *op. cit.*, p. 195.

"The word of knowledge . . ." This was the gift of that superior order of prophets, among whom were Barnabas, Stephen and Paul himself. As Macknight pointed out, it was this class of persons who unraveled the mystery hidden before times eternal, who discovered the deep secrets hidden in the ancient scriptures regarding the call of the Gentiles, the rejection of Israel, the salvation of all men through the faith and obedience of Christ, etc. Paul received divine knowledge with reference to all these things; Barnabas apparently discerned the mystery of the new name and Paul as the name bearer; and Stephen unlocked the mystery of the Jewish temple, revealing that, from its inception, it represented a departure from God's will.

Verse 9, *To another faith, in the same Spirit; and to another gifts of healings, in the one Spirit.*

The list of miraculous endowments continues here. "Faith" is the endowment of all Christians, but more than faith ordinary is meant here.

> It has a special meaning here. It must mean a faith that has special, visible results, a faith that enables one to do miracles (Matt. 17:20; 1 Cor. 13:2).[14]

Lipscomb identified faith here as "that which enabled one to remove mountains, as Jesus said, enabling one to exert power."[15]

"Gifts of healings . . ." As Hodge said, "This evidently refers to the miraculous healing of diseases."[16] There were many examples of this recorded in Acts, as for example when Paul healed Publius and many others on Malta (Acts 28:8,9). In this connection, it is clear that not even Paul used such a gift for the indiscriminate healing of all who were sick. There was a divine purpose in miracles, that being confirmation of the word of God. Significantly, Paul did not heal Timothy (1 Tim. 5:23), nor Trophimus (2 Tim. 4:20). As Johnson said of the gifts of healing in view here:

---

[14]F. W. Grosheide, *The New International Commentary* (Grand Rapids: Wm. B. Eerdmans Publishing Company, 1953), p. 286.

[15]David Lipscomb, *Commentary on 1 Corinthians* (Nashville: The Gospel Advocate Company, 1935), p. 182.

[16]Charles Hodge, *An Exposition of the First Epistle to the Corinthians* (Grand Rapids: Wm. B. Eerdmans Publishing Company, 1974), p. 247.

> They are not to be confused with the work of so-called divine healers today. The gift of healing provided restoration of life, which is beyond the power of 'divine healers' (see Acts 9:40; 20:9).[17]

Verse 10, *And to another working of miracles; and to another prophecy; and to another discernings of spirits: to another divers kinds of tongues; and to another the interpretation of tongues.*

Five other miraculous gifts are enumerated here, making nine mentioned in this paragraph.

"Working of miracles . . ." It appears that miracles would be a greater gift than healings, mentioned above them; but McGarvey thought that these included miracles of judgment such as those executed upon Elyinas, Ananias and Sapphira, saying that "The miracles of mercy stand higher in God's esteem than those which execute his judgments and mete out punishment."[18]

"Prophecy . . ." Gifts of prophecy, including the ability to foretell future events, were the endowment of certain Christians in the apostolical age; and there would appear to have been two orders of these, the higher including those mentioned under verse 8, and others whose ability concerned the prediction of events such as those prophesied by Agabus (Acts 11:28; 21:11).

"Discernings of spirits . . ." This was a gift enabling its possessor to identify and expose false teachers. Presumably this gift was held by all of the apostles and prophets of the new dispensation as well as by other persons not so generally known.

"Divers kinds of tongues . . ." The nature of the tongue speaking Paul discussed in these chapters has been the subject of much disagreement. Many of the older commentators have held that only one kind is mentioned in the NT, that being the miracle of Pentecost in which the apostles spoke in tongues

---

[17]S. Lewis Johnson, Jr., *Wycliffe Bible Commentary* (Chicago: Moody Press, 1971), p. 628.

[18]J. W. McGarvey, *Commentary on 1 Corinthians* (Cincinnati: The Standard Publishing Company, 1916), p. 123.

and were understood by all who heard them, each in his own language. McGarvey and Lipscomb both understood it thus. Nevertheless, there appears to be insurmountable difficulties in such an understanding of what is in view here. "Kinds of tongues" forbids the idea of there having been only one kind; and, besides that, the special gift of interpreting tongues mentioned a moment later and the absolute necessity of having an interpreter (as mentioned in 14:27,28) make it impossible to identify the "tongues" discussed here with the miracle of Pentecost. There was no interpreter then! For those who might be interested in a further examination of the interpretation that only the speaking of foreign languages unknown to the speaker (but spoken miraculously) is meant here, James Macknight treats it extensively. John Peter Lange, Adam Clarke, Matthew Henry, and John Calvin all held this view; and despite the reluctance of this student to disagree with such giants of exegesis, in conscience it must be done. The lack of any need to interpret on Pentecost, plus the opinion of outsiders that the tongue speakers were "mad" (14:23); plus the fact that there were many of them engaging in this activity all at once, requiring Paul to restrict it to one at a time (14:27); plus the impression that inevitably comes from reading the entire context — all of these things support the conclusion that the phenomenon was different from that of Pentecost.

Why was it? Why did not Paul condemn it out of hand, instead of containing it by a series of regulations clearly designed to discourage and diminish it? We do not certainly know. Yet we shall hazard the opinion that whatever purpose of the divine mind was fulfilled by it, the Corinthians had contravened it by their shameless distortion and abuse of it.

"Interpretation of tongues . . ." This is perhaps the key to understanding the whole passage. Through the influence of God's Spirit some could speak languages they had never learned; but for this to do any good at all, someone was required to interpret what was said, the ability to do so being the "gift" in view here. Furthermore, such a thing raises all kinds of questions. Some have supposed that both gifts of tongues and interpretations were held by the same individual; but, if that is so, why did not such an individual speak in the proper language to begin with? On the other hand if the gifts were not joined in one individual, then only on the mission field could there have been any utility whatever in it. Perhaps it was this abuse of a genuine gift God had intended for missionary work, making it a plaything and diversion in an established church, which was the thing being done in Corinth. Despite abuses, however, there was a genuine gift, which appears from Paul's words that he "spoke with tongues more than ye all" (14:18), and also his admonition, "forbid not to speak with tongues" (14:39). Paul's firm declaration, however, to the effect that he certainly would not speak with tongues in Corinth (14:6ff) would strongly indicate that whatever the gift was, it did not belong in the assembly of Christians; and this agrees with the dogmatic statement that tongues were a sign "not to them that believe, but to the unbelieving" (14:22). From this, it has to be inferred that any tongue speaking Paul did, it was in the mission field, and for the purpose of reaching people whose language he did not know. The fact of Paul's doing such a thing at all, coupled with his refusal to do it in the presence of believers, emphasizes the limited nature of the gift and also refutes the conceit that what he did was merely ecstatic jabbering. The Corinthians had probably prostituted the gift to that low level; but Paul would never have done so. The fact of his having used the gift himself, however, and the knowledge of its true utility (in certain limited circumstances, and for that age only), were doubtless the facts underlying his refusal to denounce and forbid the thing altogether.

The conclusion, therefore, is valid, which may be summarized thus:

All of the nine gifts in view here were miraculous.

All disappeared completely at the end of the apostolical age.

The mess at Corinth was a mingling of the true gift of tongues with emotional and psychologically induced ecstatic utterances, which were not miraculous at all but nonsense.

A further element of the disorder was the perversion and prostitution of the true gifts (on the part of a few), making it a device of self-glorification.

It was this mixture of genuine and false elements which made it impossible for Paul to condemn the false without appearing also to condemn the true gift. Remember, he was not present, but was writing a letter.

Therefore, he laid down the rules which would eliminate and destroy the false, but which would leave undisturbed the true gift.

Thus, there were *three kinds* of tongues in NT times: (1) those spoken by the apostles on Pentecost, (2) the gift of tongues in this passage which required an interpreter, and (3) the false tongues which had invaded Corinth.

Paul had the true gift of verse 10 here; but it may never be supposed that he engaged in the non-sensical blabberings affected by the Corinthian tongue speakers.

The nine miraculous gifts mentioned here are: (1) wisdom, (2) knowledge, (3) faith, (4) healings, (5) miracles, (6) prophecy, (7) discernments of spirits, (8) tongues, and (9) interpretation of tongues.

Is the true gift of speaking in tongues on earth today? The answer has to be negative. What is admittedly true of all other gifts in this list may not be denied as true of the eighth and ninth also. A more extensive examination of this entire question is found in chapter 14.

Wonderful as was the true gift of tongues, it cannot fail to be significant that it appears last in Paul's list, both here and in verse 30. Why? Perhaps it was the fact of its being so easily counterfeited. In those days, as now, anybody could do it, not the real thing, of course, but the counterfeit. This is not intended as a denial of the sincerity of some who practice this; but the sincerity of its advocates has never been a reason *sole* for accepting any proposition, religious or otherwise.

Verse 11, *But all these worketh the one and the same Spirit, dividing to each one severally even as he will.*

Paul's evident purpose in this was to discourage the inordinate over-valuation of some gifts above others, the humble teacher of the word of God being no less honorable than the holder of some more spectacular gift. He at once presented the marvelous metaphor of "the body" to prove that *there are no unimportant members*; because the Spirit of God has created, endowed and maintains them all.

THE ONE BODY

Verse 12, *For as the body is one, and hath many members, and all the members of the body, being many, are one body; so also is Christ.*

The great Pauline teaching that the church comprises the spiritual body of Christ is among the most important teachings revealed to men. God's device of accounting men righteous is that of forming them into a corporate unity, of which Christ is head, all the saved being members of it, the body itself being identified as "Christ," and therefore partaking of the perfect righteousness of the Son of God himself. God saves men, not by injecting righteousness into them (on the grounds of their faith and/or obedience), but by transferring them "into Christ," identifying them "as Christ," and making them, in fact, to be Christ. By this heavenly device, man becomes truly righteous and thus saved, not as John Doe, but as Christ. Faith and obedience of the gospel are the conditions antecedent to God's transfer of sinners into Christ, baptism being the action through which God effects the actual entry into Christ; but neither the faith of the sinner nor any act of obedience is the ultimate ground of his redemption, that all-important ground being the perfect faith, obedience and righteousness of the Christ himself. For full discussion of this, see CR, pp. 118-126. Any man failing to fulfill the prior conditions of being "in Christ" is not a part of the body in view here, as evidenced in the next verse.

Verse 13, *For in one Spirit were we all baptized into one body, whether Jews or Greeks, whether bond or free; and were all made to drink of one Spirit.*

"In one Spirit were we all baptized . . ." Throughout the NT, Christian baptism is revealed to be one of the two essential elements of the new birth, without which no man may see the kingdom of God. These are: obedience to the ordinance of baptism and the reception of the Holy Spirit. Jesus joined these two essential elements by his requirement that men be "born of the water and of the Spirit" (John 3:5ff). Peter joined them on Pentecost by the command that all men should "repent and be baptized... and . . . receive the Holy Spirit" (Acts 2:38ff). There is no doubt whatever that Paul's words here refer to the same twin essentials of the new birth, the same being a prior condition of participation in the body of Christ.

"In one Spirit . . ." As Kelcy said, 'This is actually 'by one Spirit,' making the Holy Spirit the agent or administrator of baptism."[19] In a similar way, Christ was named as the actual administrator of the rite of baptism, even though his disciples actually did the baptizing (John 4:1, 2). The unity of the godhead makes it correct to refer any action ordained and commanded by God, to the Father, the Son, or the Holy Spirit; and when the action is obeyed, it is proper to say that any one of them did it. This truth does not exclude the reception of the indwelling Spirit in Christian hearts, as Paul dogmatically emphasized that in the very next clause, "made to drink of one Spirit."

"We were all baptized . . . and were all made to drink of one Spirit . . ." As Metz correctly noted, "the word 'baptized' relates to the actual act of baptism."[20] The mention of the Spirit as the administrator of baptism in this verse provoked Hodge to declare that the baptism in view, therefore, is "the baptism of the Holy Ghost!"[21] If that is true, it would make Paul here declare that all of the Corinthians were baptized in the Holy Ghost, or had received the Holy Spirit baptism! Who could believe such a thing? It is true of course that all of them had themselves baptized, and in consequence had all received the gift ordinary of the Holy Spirit, common to all Christians; but to suppose that those carnal Corinthians had "all" participated in the baptism of the Holy Spirit is impossible. Of course, the design of many scholars is to get water baptism out of this text altogether; but that is also impossible.

"All made to drink of one Spirit . . ." This refers to the reception of the ordinary gift of the indwelling Spirit by the Corinthians in consequence of primary obedience to the gospel. "There is no evidence that all the disciples at Corinth, or any of them, had been baptized in the Holy Spirit"[22]

Verse 14, *For the body is not one member, but many.*

---

[19]Raymond C. Kelcy, *op. cit.*, p. 57.
[20]Donald S. Metz, *op. cit.*, p. 432.
[21]Charles Hodge, *op. cit.*, p. 255.
[22]David Lipscomb, *op. cit.*, p. 186.

The spiritual body of Christ, like the human body, is composed of many members, having various functions, and some "from the human viewpoint" being of lesser or greater honor; but, by the very fact of being "of the body," each member is necessary, partaking of the destiny of the whole body.

Verses 15-17, *For if the foot shall say, Because I am not the hand, I am not of the body; it is not therefore not of the body? And if the ear shall say, Because I am not the eye, I am not of the body; is it not therefore not of the body? If the whole body were an eye, where were the hearing? If the whole were hearing, where were the smelling?*

The great lesson is that various members of Christ's spiritual body have many various talents, perform many different services, some (in the eyes of men) receiving distinctions and honors; but no member of the holy body should be envious of any other. All are necessary; all are genuinely a part of the sacred whole. The differences among Christians are similar to the differences in nature, in which arena there is infinite diversity, not even two snowflakes ever having been exactly alike. This is according to God's will. In the current era, men are apparently determined that all shall be alike; but this can never be. In some limited political sense, perhaps, it may be affirmed that "all men are created equal"; but as a matter of simple fact, the opposite is true. Wolfgang Amadeus Mozart at the age of five years composed a concerto in one sitting and then played it from memory![23]

Robertson suggested that in this passage men "should observe the difference in the Christian doctrine of unity and equality, and the world's idea of leveling all to one standard."[24]

Verses 18-21, *But now hath God set the members each one of them in the body, even as it pleased him. And if they were all one member, where were the body? But now are they many members, but one body. And the eye cannot say to the hand, I have no need of thee: or again the head to the feet, I have no need of you.*

---

[23]Helen L. Kaufmann, *The Story of Mozart* (New York: Grosset and Dunlap, Publishers, 1955), p. 18.

[24]Robertson as quoted by John Wesley, *op. cit., in loco.*

"As it pleased him . . ." God made people different, each person being unique; and there were never two "equal" people on earth. This may displease men, but it pleased God, that being his holy purpose so to do.

"But one body . . ." Since the figure here represents the corporate body of Christians on earth, it must be accepted as God's purpose that "they all should be one" (John 17:21), even as Christ prayed. The shattered unity of Christianity is due not to the will of God, but to the devices of Satan.

"I have no need of thee . . . I have no need of you . . ." The thought of Paul in this passage is that the learned, the famous, the talented and the honorable cannot possibly do without the rest of the body. The nation could get along without its philosophers and politicians much better than it could get along without its farmers and plumbers. The same principle holds in the church.

Verses 22-24, *Nay, much rather, those members of the body which seem to be more feeble are necessary: and those parts of the body, which we think to be less honorable, upon these we bestow more abundant honor; and our uncomely parts have more abundant comeliness; whereas our comely parts have no need: but God tempered the body together, giving more abundant honor to that part which lacked.*

"Necessary . . . together . . ." These are the big words that show the mutual dependence and indispensability which characterize the relationship of every member of the body of Christ to every other member. There is even a sense in which the "less honorable" are more abundantly honorable. Eisenhower reprimanded a general in the army for speaking of a soldier as "just a private," adding that "The private is the man who wins the war." This is exactly what Paul was saying here.

Verse 25, *That there should be no schism in the body; but that the members should have the care one for another.*

As Dummelow expressed it, "What is true of the human body, through the nervous connection of all of its parts, should be true of the church."[25]

---

[25]J. R. Dummelow, *Commentary on the Holy Bible* (New York: The Macmillan Company, 1937), p. 913.

Verse 26, *And whether one member suffereth, all the members suffer with it; or one member is honored, all the members rejoice with it.*

This means that "All the members will feel involved in the misfortune or prosperity of fellow-Christians."[26] If a brother suffers any kind of sorrow or loss, those who are really Christians will share in the hurt; and whatever honor, success or joy may come to a brother in Christ, the same should be an occasion of rejoicing on the part of all his Christian brothers.

Verse 27, *Now ye are the body of Christ, and severally members thereof.*

As Farrar interpreted this, "Paul did not mean that the Corinthian church was a member in the body of all the churches, but that each Christian is a member of the body of Christ."[27] Johnson added that:

> There is no definite article (ye are body of Christ); and this does not refer to the local church at Corinth, for there are not many bodies, a thought contrary to the context. Rather, it points to the quality of the whole, which each of them individually helps to constitute.[28]

Verse 28, *And God hath set some in the church, first apostles, secondly prophets, thirdly teachers, then miracles, then gifts of healings, helps, governments, divers kinds of tongues.*

"Apostles and prophets . . ." The preeminence of these is apparent in all Paul's writings. See Ephesians 2:19. There is a conscious ranking of offices and functions of the Lord's church in this passage, as indicated by "firstly... secondly . . . thirdly . . . then." It is significant that teachers of God's word are ranked next to the highest. It is of no consequence that the order of "miracles" and "healings" is reversed, due to their similarity.

"Helps . . . governments, divers kinds of tongues . . ." Dummelow thought that "helps" refers to the office of deacons and

---

[26]Donald Guthrie, *The New Bible Commentary* (Grand Rapids: Wm. B. Eerdmans Publishing Company, 1970), p. 1068.

[27]F. W. Farrar, *Pulpit Commentary* (Grand Rapids: Wm. B. Eerdmans Publishing Company, 1950), Vol. 19, p. 399.

[28]S. Lewis Johnson, Jr., *op. cit.*, p. 630.

"governments" to that of the presbytery. It is significant that "divers kinds of tongues" is placed last. That which had so captured and carried away the Christians at Corinth was here made to be the lowest in God's scale of values.

"Governments . . ." This reference to church government should not be downgraded nor overlooked. Church organization was not something that men contrived and added in the post-apostolical era. "God set some in the church," including elders of the church. Acts bears witness to the fact that apostolical churches did not exist without elders, except for the briefest time after their founding (Acts 11:29; 14:23).

The "miracles" in view in this passage ceased; but from this it might not be inferred that the office of elders also ceased. As Hodge said, "The evidence that an office was intended to be permanent was the command to appoint to the office"[29] those possessing the qualifications. No such continuity pertains either to the miracles, the apostles, the prophets, the healings, or the speaking in tongues.

Verses 29-31, *Are all apostles? are all prophets? are all teachers? are all workers of miracles? have all gifts of healings? do all speak with tongues? do all interpret? But desire earnestly the greater gifts. And moreover a most excellent way show I unto you.*

The tragedy at Corinth was that a few who had the genuine gift of tongues were displaying it for purposes of their own vanity in the public assemblies of the congregation. where it was never intended to be used, being absolutely unnecessary and unneeded there; and then, to compound the evil, there were evidently a great many others who were getting in on the action by exhibiting a kind of tongue speaking (called ecstatic utterances) which had absolutely nothing to do with the Holy Spirit, having only one utility, that of flattering the practitioners of it and bringing down the scorn of the whole community upon the whole church. With marvelous diplomacy, Paul avoided condemning "tongues" abstractly, for that might have been to reflect upon those who really possessed the gift; but he promptly gave orders which diminished and

---

[29]Charles Hodge, *op, cit.*, p. 263.

removed the objectionable conduct altogether. However, before he would give those orders (chapter 14), he would show them "a most excellent way." That way was the way of love, love itself being one of the fruits, indeed the first fruit, of the Holy Spirit in the lives of Christians (Gal. 5:22). The immortal words of the thirteenth chapter comprise the apostle's exhortation for the Corinthians to walk in the way of love.

CHAPTER 13

Barclay said, "For many, this is the most wonderful chapter in the NT";[1] but as McGarvey said, "It has been admired by all ages, but, unfortunately, practiced by none!"[2] A sample of the marvelous praise which has been heaped upon this chapter is the following:

> It is a glorious hymn or paean in honor of Christian love, in which St. Paul rises on the wings of inspiration to the most sunlit heights of Christian eloquence. Like Psalm 45, it may be entitled "A Psalm of Love."[3]

There are elements of misunderstanding, however, in the view that "This passage found in the middle of a protracted argument suggests that we have here the result of a sudden burst of inspiration!"[4] Not part of, but *all* that Paul wrote was inspired of God. Furthermore, this whole chapter may not be separated from the argument in the preceding and following chapters; for itself is part of the argument, a very telling part of it.

The chapter falls easily into three divisions: (1) the absolute necessity of love (1-3), (2) the characteristics of love (4-7), and (3) the permanence of love (8-13). Despite this classification, verse 13 evidently stands apart. The disorders of the Corinthian church are continually in view. Both the positive and negative attributes of love in verses 4-7 are clearly the opposites of conditions among the Corinthians. Also, such words as "tongues . . . prophecy . . . knowledge . . . faith so as to move mountains cannot be understood, except as references to the miraculous gifts at Corinth. This chapter should never be construed as merely an abstract teaching on love, parentheti-

---

[1]William Barclay, *The Letters to the Corinthians* (Philadelphia: The Westminster Press, 1954), p. 131.

[2]J. W. McGarvey, *Commentary on 1 Corinthians* (Cincinnati: The standard Publishing Company, 1916), p. 127.

[3]F. W. Farrar, *Pulpit Commentary* (Grand Rapids: Wm. B. Eerdmans Publishing Company, 1950), Vol. 19, p. 422.

[4]T. Teignmouth Shore, *Ellicott's Commentary on the Whole Bible* (Grand Rapids: Zondervan Publishing House, 1959), p. 387.

cally inserted. The situation at Corinth was still the center of Paul's attention here.

Verse 1, *If I speak with the tongues of men and of angels, but have not love, I am become sounding brass, or a clanging cymbal.*

"Tongues of men and of angels . . ." No affirmation is made here regarding the language of angels. Hodge paraphrased this as "all languages, human or divine."[5] That the speech of angels should have been brought in here could have derived from Paul's own experience in which he was caught up into heaven and heard words "unspeakable, unlawful to utter" (2 Cor. 12:4). There is also an assumption here that "angels are superior in all respects to men."[6] Thus, Paul made his argument more overwhelming with the contrast between the tongues of angels and the distressing tongues of Corinth.

"But have not love . . ." Three Greek words for "love" are *eros* (erotic love), *philo* (affection), and *agape*, the latter being the word here. "The word was not classical Greek. No heathen writer had used it."[7] Yet it was in the Greek language and was used in the LXX. Thus the Spirit chose a word for Christian love which was free of the sensual overtones of more common Greek words. *Agape* is considered to be one of the grandest words in the NT.

"Sounding brass, or a clanging cymbal . . ." The cacophanous pretense of heathen worship included the clashing and banging of gongs and cymbals and the braying of brass trumpets. Barclay identified such noises as characteristic "especially of the worship of Dionysus and Cybele."[8] Paul teaches two things by this: (1) that the exhibitions of the Corinthian tongue speakers were of the same significance as heathen worship and (2) that both were noisy, empty and worthless.

---

[5]Charles Hodge, *An Exposition of the First Epistle to the Corinthians* (Grand Rapids: Wm. B. Eerdmans Publishing Company, 1974), p. 266.

[6]Albert Barnes, *Notes on the NT* (Grand Rapids: Baker Book House, 1949), p. 242.

[7]F. W. Farrar, *op. cit.*, p. 422.

[8]William Barclay, *op. cit.*, p. 181.

Verse 2, *And if I have the gift of prophecy, and know all mysteries and all knowledge; and if I have all faith, so as to remove mountains, but have not love, I am nothing.*

"Prophecy ... knowledge ... faith so as to move mountains ..." These are to be added to "tongues" mentioned in verse 1, all of them being miraculous gifts which had caused so much trouble at Corinth.

"All faith ..." Although this refers to a miraculous gift, faith is never to be viewed as appearing in various varieties, being of one kind only. In all the word of God, there is no mention of several kinds, or even two kinds of faith. It is always the *amount of faith* which is determinative. True to that fact, Paul is not here speaking of some special kind of faith, but of "all faith," meaning the superlative *amount*, not some special "kind." No greater misunderstanding exists among religious people today than the notion that there is any such thing as "saving faith," understanding it as a special quality or variety of faith that inevitably procures salvation.

Paul's words here are a sufficient refutation of the popular heresy regarding "faith alone" or "saving faith." "All faith" cannot mean anything less than faith in its superlative degree (degrees of faith being often mentioned... "little faith ... great faith ... etc."); and if certain "kinds of faith" contrary to all scripture, should be supposed as existing, there would be no way to exclude them from being included in Paul's sweeping words "all faith." Significantly, not even "all faith" can avail any man of salvation unless his heart is filled with love of man and of God. This obvious truth has resulted in some of the exegetes placing a false construction upon "love" as Paul used it here, making it to mean "God's love of men," not their love of God. Throughout this chapter it will be observed that it is love of humanity as a reflection of the love which Christians have for God which is being discussed. See under verse 13.

"Prophecy ..." The miraculous gift of prophecy belonged to Balaam, but his having love neither of God or Israel caused his ruin. Caiaphas as God's high priest uttered prophecy; but his loveless heart made him an enemy of God (John 11:51; Num. 24:1ff; 31:8).

"All faith so as to remove mountains ..." While true enough that removing mountains was a well-known Jewish metaphor for solving difficult problems (see Matt. 17:20; Luke 17:6, especially the comment in CL, pp. 370-371), it is clearly the miraculous manifestation of faith that is meant here. As Wesley said, "This means the highest degree of miracle-working faith."[9]

Judas Iscariot was cited by David Lipscomb as being an example of faith to perform miracles, but with no love of Christ. "Judas had faith to work miracles (Matt. 10:1); but he did not possess love, betrayed the Lord, and went to his own place."[10]

Verse 3, *And if I bestow all my goods to feed the poor, and if I give my body to be burned, but have not love, it profiteth me nothing.*

"Bestow all my goods . . ." "The Greek word here means to feed others by giving them morsels of food,"[11] giving the meaning of giving away all the giver's property a little bit at a time so as to reach the greatest possible number.

"My body to be burned . . ." Coining as it did before the savage persecutions in which Christians were burned for their faith, this is surprising, being perhaps prophetic. Some have supposed that Paul was here thinking of the Hebrew children (Dan. 3:23), and Barclay thought it possible that Paul "referred to a famous monument in Athens called 'The Indian's Tomb.' It honored an Indian who had burned himself in public."[12]

Whatever may have prompted Paul's words here, the lesson is clear, that no liberal giver nor fanatical ascetic may be assured of eternal life without the all-important, indispensable virtue of love. In the days of the persecutions, some were tempted to seek martyrdom as a sure means of attaining eternal life; but a proper regard for what Paul said here would have discouraged such a thing.

Paul in these first three verses did not mention all of the miraculous gifts, but the most respected; and thus what is said

---

[9]John Wesley, *One Volume NT Commentary* (Grand Rapids: Baker Book House, 1972), in loco.
[10]David Lipscomb, *Commentary on 1 Corinthians* (Nashville: The Gospel Advocate Company, 1935), p. 194.
[11]T. Teignmouth Shore, *op. cit.*, p. 338.
[12]William Barclay, *op. cit.*, p. 132.

here of the examples chosen applied with equal force to all the others.

Verse 4, *Love suffereth long, and is kind; love envieth not; love vaunteth not itself, is not puffed up.*

Patient endurance and active good are qualities of love. Paul enumerated fifteen qualities of love in verses 4-7; but this is far from being a methodical dissertation on love as an abstract subject. The qualities cited here have the utility of contrasting with the extraordinary gifts so coveted at Corinth; and they are presented here as exactly opposed to the characteristic of the puffed-up Corinthians. As Hodge said:

> Those traits of love are therefore adduced which stood opposed to the temper which they exhibited in the use of their gifts. They were impatient, discontented, envious, inflated, selfish, indecorous, unmindful of the feelings or interests of others, suspicious, resentful and censorious.[13]

Verses 5-7, *Does not behave itself unseemly, seeketh not its own, is not provoked, taketh not account of evil; rejoiceth not in unrighteousness, but rejoiceth with the truth; beareth all things, believeth all things, hopeth all things, endureth all things.*

The true meaning of all of these qualities is seen in their opposites as cited by Hodge (under verse 4).

"Seeketh not its own . . ." Barclay rendered this "Love does not insist upon its rights."[14] He also stated that "It would be the key to almost all the problems which surround us today, if men would think less of their rights and more of their duties."[15] The essential selfishness in all human nature has been exploited politically in this generation, and the ultimate fruits of unbridled selfishness are yet to be reaped.

"Believeth all things . . ." As Johnson said, "This does not include gullibility, but means rather that the believer should not be suspicious."[16]

---

[13]Charles Hodge, *op. cit.*, p. 269.
[14]William Barclay, *op. cit.*, p. 185.
[15]*Ibid.*
[16]S. Lewis Johnson, Jr., *Wycliffe Bible Commentary* (Chicago: Moody Press, 1971), p. 632.

Verses 8-10, *Love never faileth: but whether there be prophecies, they shall be done away; whether there be tongues, they shall cease; whether there be knowledge, it shall be done away. For we know in part, and we prophesy in part; but when that which is perfect is come, that which is in part shall be done away.*

Beginning here, and to the end of the chapter, it is the permanence of love, as contrasted with the supernatural gifts which were so highly treasured by the Corinthians, which is stressed. And before moving to declare that all of these things which had so dazzled and inflated the Corinthians were soon to end, Paul had just outlined the glory and desirability of Christian love, the same being the "most excellent way" mentioned in 12:31b. But here he made the unqualified declaration of the end of supernatural gifts in the church. It may only be hoped that the Corinthians got the point better than many of the modern commentators.

"Love never faileth . . ." As in the RSV, "Love never ends."

"Prophecies . . . shall be done away . . ." This cannot mean that prophecies shall be contradicted by events, but as Hodge said, "The gift (of prophecy) shall cease to be necessary, and therefore shall not be continued."[17]

"Tongues . . ." shall cease . . ." This means that the *true* gifts of tongues would cease. In many generations after those days, the gift of so-called "tongues" would flourish at intervals throughout the history of Christendom; but Paul's words here absolutely deny any authenticity whatever to the so-called charismatics of the present day. True, it is only said here that "tongues *shall* cease"; but there is no reason whatever to believe that this least of all supernatural gifts should have survived when supernatural knowledge, divine prophecy, and the gift of miracle-working faith perished; which, of course, they did. Any authentic speaking in tongues is here restricted by the apostle Paul to the age of miracles; and when that ceased, the tongues ceased, except for the affectations of those who indulge, from whatever motives, the counterfeit "tongues" of the present day.

---

[17]Charles Hodge, *op. cit.*, p. 271.

The very fact of Paul's showing "the more excellent way" declared that the supernatural gifts would soon pass away, otherwise that generation would not have needed the instruction. Those gifts at Corinth had a purpose. In that day in Corinth, no man had a copy of the NT; therefore it was necessary that supernaturally endowed men should teach and lead them; but today, "No preacher or teacher has any message from God unless he gets it from the Bible."[18]

During the childhood age of the church, miracles authenticated the message of the inspired preachers (Mark 16:20). Miracles were to confirm the word of God. "No miracle today could confirm the word of God; it is already confirmed. Men need simply to believe and obey it."[19]

The burden of proof must rest upon those who suppose the age of miracles is still upon us. If there are super-natural gifts, where are they? The contradicting claims of religious bodies pretending to work miracles are mutually destructive. This writer believes that there are no miracles being performed today by any persons whomsoever. Paul said they would cease; and they have ceased! That there are marvelous providences, so singular and astonishing as to startle men, is not surprising; for it may not be denied that God is still working in the world, and especially in his kingdom; but that quality of miracles bearing witness as a confirmation of God's word is not discernible in such merciful providences. What about the answer to prayer? Yes indeed God answers prayer, and sometimes in the most astonishing ways; but such a thing bears no likeness to the supernatural and visible wonders of the apostolical age.

The character of men pretending to perform miracles in this generation refutes their claims. They get rich doing it; but the apostles never took money for healing anyone.

As Foy E. Wallace stated it:

> The miraculous endowments designated *spiritual* gifts have *failed*, have *ceased*, have *vanished away* and are

---

[18]George W. De Hoff, *Sermons on First Corinthians* (Murfreesboro, Tenn.: The Christian Press, 1947), p. 96.
[19]*Ibid.*

> therefore no longer in force. All such powers were temporary and provisional and cannot now be exercised.[20]

There is a meaning in such words as "cease . . . fail... vanish away," not merely of continuing no longer, but of being superseded by something else. As Russell noted, "Tongues prophecies, and . . . knowledge shall be superseded."[21] Despite the fact of Russell's taking a dispensational view of this passage, his idea of "superseded" is correct. And what was to supersede the tongues, etc.? It was the inspired writing of the New Testament. Thus, the fact of the appearance of that which was to do the superseding proved the near approach of the time for it to occur. In a sense, this Epistle superseded the tongues of Corinth.

"When that which is perfect is come . . ." The great problem before Paul was the instruction and guidance of the church in Corinth; and the most acceptable view of what might be called "perfect" in connection with that problem would be the completed canon on the NT. McGarvey understood it as "the recorded word."[22] Kelcy called it"The body of truth fully revealed."[23] De Hoff identified it as "The NT."[24] The comparison which Paul at once made contrasted the childhood age of the church with the church's maturity, not the present dispensation with the ultimate condition of the saints in heaven; and this demands that the expression "that which is perfect" must be associated, not with conditions in heaven, but with the maturity of the church; and that condition is met only by referring the words to God's completed revelation, the Bible.

A great many commentators insist upon referring "that which is perfect" to conditions in heaven, as for example in the following:

> This anticipates the Parousia, the culmination of the age. To suggest that "the perfect" refers to the completion

---

[20]Foy E. Wallace, Jr., *A Review of the New Versions* (Fort Worth: Foy E. Wallace, Jr., Publications, 1973), p. 435.

[21]John William Russell, *Compact Commentary on the NT* (Grand Rapids: Baker Book House, 1964), p. 426.

[22]J. W. McGarvey, *op. cit.*, p. 132.

[23]Raymond C. Kelcy, *First Corinthians* (Austin: R. B. Sweet Co., Inc., 1967), p. 61.

[24]George W. De Hoff, *op. cit.*, p. 96.

> of the Canon of Scripture fails to find any support in the biblical usage of perfect . . . Such an interpretation exists to explain the absence of certain *charismata* in many churches today.[25]

Regarding the "biblical usage" of "perfect," it should be noted that even of the OT it was said, "The law of the Lord is perfect converting the soul" (Ps. 19:7); thus "perfect" most assuredly is applied to the revealed word of God; and such being true of the OT makes it even more applicable to the NT. As for the absence of "certain *charismata*" in present-day churches, it may be dogmatically affirmed that "*all charismata*" is absent from all present-day churches, with the exception of counterfeit tongues affected by certain groups, the behavior of whom invariably demonstrates their so-called "manifestations" as being contrary to the orders of the Holy Spirit, unscriptural and thus bearing no resemblance whatever to the genuine gift which existed in the times of the apostles.

"That which is in part shall be done away . . ." Failure to see that "*miraculous* knowledge, tongues, prophecies, etc." called in these chapters "spiritual gifts," are to be identified with the things in part that shall be done away involves interpreters in an impossible position. Take ordinary "knowledge," is this to be done away with when we get to heaven? Certainly not. Later, at the end of the chapter, Paul gives a glimpse of eternity, but not here. The things in part which were soon to be done away were the supernatural gifts of the infancy age of the church. "Paul considered the days of spiritual gifts as the process by which the goal of maturity should be reached."[26] As Lipscomb said it:

> These gifts were to continue in the church to guide and instruct it until the completed will of God was made known. They were to serve a temporary purpose; then when their office was fulfilled, they were to pass away and give place to the revealed will of God..[27]

---

[25]Paul W. Marsh, *A New Commentary* (Grand Rapids: Zondervan Publishing House, 1969), p. 404.

[26]Raymond C. Kelcy, *op. cit.*, p. 62.

[27]David Lipscomb, *op. cit.*, p. 200.

The pattern of many commentators is like that of Macknight who paraphrased this thus:

> When the perfect gift of complete illumination is bestowed on all in heaven, then that which is partial, namely, the present gifts of knowledge and prophecy, shall be abolished as useless.[28]

However, who can believe that Paul was trying to control the outrageous situation in Corinth by assuring them that all of those miraculous gifts would disappear when they all got to heaven? The perfect illustration of what he really means was childhood giving way to maturity, stated in the very next line.

Verse 11, *When I was a child, I spake as a child, I felt as a child, I thought as s child; now, that I am become a man, I have put away childish things.*

Can this be anything if not a suggestion that the Corinthians should stop being children and grow up? In case any of them might have missed the point, he added a bit later, "Brethren, be not children in mind" (14:20). Furthermore, the admonition was given in the same breath with Paul's statement that five intelligible words were worth more than ten thousand words in an unknown tongue!

Verse 12, *For now, we see in a mirror, darkly; but then face to face: now I know in part; but then shall I know fully even as also I was fully known.*

In this there surely must be a glimpse of eternal things; and it evidently occurred to Paul in connection with what he had just said of the childhood age of the church giving way to maturity, applicable to the current era of that day; but like many other examples in the Bible, it has a secondary reference to something much more remote. (Other examples of this same type of thing are in Matthew 2:15, 2:18 . . . See comment in CM, pp. 18-19.) We may therefore refer the words about seeing through a mirror darkly, and knowing "in part" to the present dispensation of God's grace, and the words about being "face to face" (presumably with the Lord) and knowing "fully" may be understood as descriptive of conditions in eternity. That there

---

[28]James Macknight, *op. cit.*, p. 219.

is, in fact, just such an emphasis in this verse 12, is proved by Paul's prompt return to the "now" in the final verse immediately after this. A failure to observe this limitation of verse 12 is fatal to any true interpretation of this passage.

"In a mirror darkly . . ." Ancient mirrors were of polished metal, easily tarnished, and any image was only dimly seen. Paul himself referred even to the Christ as "the image of God" (2 Cor. 4:4; Col. 1:15); and although it would be sinful and incorrect to suppose any deficiency in the blessed Saviour, mortal life is limited. Nothing is dim about Christ as God's image except the tarnished mirrors by which mortal men behold it. There shines in these words the essential need for men to walk by faith; because what they may "see" even under the best of circumstances must be described as seeing "darkly." See CH, pp. 209-210.

"Then face to face . . ." In the resurrection, we shall behold the face of the Beloved. "We know that if he shall be manifested, we shall be like him; for we shall see him even as he is'" (1 John 3:2).

"Now I know in part . . ." Note the temporal "now"; and note also that Paul was not referring to the Corinthians who knew far less than he did; for it is of himself that this is said. What a shocking rebuke of intellectual arrogance is this! The greatest mind of the apostolical age, other than that of Christ himself, here stressed the partial and incomplete nature of that whole body of revelation which Paul, more than any other, delivered to mankind. "The permanent danger of intellectual eminence is intellectual snobbery,"[29] as Barclay said; but there is surely an antidote for it in such a passage as this.

Verse 13, *But now abideth faith, hope, love, these three; and the greatest of these is love.*

"But now . . ." This means "in this present state." "If we give it any other sense, as though Paul said, 'now to sum all things up,' then we have him saying that faith, hope and love are eternal."[30] As Barclay said, the stress in this verse regards

---

[29]William Barclay, *op. cit.*, p. 131.
[30]J. W. McGarvey, *op. cit.*, p. 133.

"the supremacy of love,"[31] not its permanence which was treated in verse 8 in this paragraph. "Now" in this verse meant that Paul had returned to the present situation after the digression to speak of eternal things in verse 12, which should be treated, actually, as a parenthesis. Shore and many others insist that "*Now* is not here temporal, but logical";[32] but this viewpoint should be rejected, as James Macknight declared:

> The clause "now abideth" implies that these graces (faith, hope and love) are not always to abide; at least the graces of faith and hope shall not abide; for seeing that faith is the persuasion of things hoped for (Heb. 11:1), and hope that is seen is not hope (Rom. 8:24); in heaven, where all the objects of our faith and hope are put in our possession, there can be no place for either.[33]

By the above comment, Macknight clearly construed the "now" of this verse as temporal, that is, a reference to the time present. All of the clever arguments adduced to show how we shall still have faith and hope in heaven fall to the ground in the light of the truth that both faith and hope deal with uncertainties, and there shall be no uncertainties in the eternal world.

"Abideth . . ." here has the force of saying that the miraculous spiritual gifts shall not abide; and, of course, they did not; nor do they exist now. It is in this dispensation that faith, hope and love abide; but what is especially stressed, "Love is the greatest" of the trio.

"And the greatest of these is love . . ." It is an unqualified disaster for advocates of the "faith only" theory that love should here be ranked ahead of faith; and, consequently, it is usually interpreted as meaning "God's love of men," not men's love of God and of each other. Thus Guthrie commented on this verse, "greater than these is the love (of God)."[34] Throughout the chapter, it has been made clear that love as a virtue of men, not as an attribute of God, is meant. It is true, of course, that

---

[31]William Barclay, *op. cit.*
[32]T. Teignmouth Shore, *op. cit.*, p. 839.
[33]James Macknight, *op. cit.*, p. 221.
[34]Donald Guthrie, *The New Bible Commentary* (Grand Rapids: Wm. B. Eerdmans Publishing Company, 1970), p. 1069.

the love in Christian hearts has been shed abroad in their hearts by the Holy Spirit; but by the virtue of that very fact it becomes a Christian virtue.

Why Love Is the Greatest Thing

Love is the fulfillment of the law, which was never true of faith (Rom. 13:10).
Love outranks faith in the power to motivate men.
Love includes obedience (John 14:15), which is not true of faith or hope.
Love is the heart of the Great Commandment to love God and one's neighbor (Mark 12:28-31).
Love shall abide eternally, whereas both faith and hope shall not, except in some exceptional sense.
Love, if lacking in the heart, would be a sufficient deficiency to prevent one's salvation, even if he possessed "all faith" (v. 2).
Love works the greatest miracle of transformation in human hearts, distinguishing it from faith, which exists in some pretty cold fish!

There is no wonder, then, that Paul extolled the virtue of love in his wonderful efforts to correct the puffed-up Corinthians. This chapter may be viewed as one of the most important in scripture, not merely for the truly marvelous things said of love, but also for the firm word therein regarding the cessation of the miraculous age. For further comments on "miracles" and why they ceased, see CH, pp. 42-44.

Concerning the subject of love, there is none other that so fascinates and inspires the hearts of men; for this gift ranks first among the fruits of the Holy Spirit (Gal. 5: 22ff). There is even a sense in which it is a continuing "miracle" throughout the church age, not any less than the "confirming miracles" of the apostolical period, merely different. It is the signature of God himself in the hearts of all the redeemed.

God's Signature

Love is God's imprimatur
  Upon the human heart,
A glorious investiture,
  His image to impart.

Love is chief of all the graces,
  The royal prothonotary,
Assigning each and all their places
  In God's economy.

It is the precious bridal song,
  The prothalamion hymn
Of Jesus Bride, the ransomed throng
  Who have believed in him.

Upon the entire human race,
  To prove them born above,
The Father stooped his name to trace.
  The signature is Love.

—James Burton Coffman
New York City, November 27, 1965

CHAPTER 14

In this the third chapter of Paul's writings specifically related to tongue speaking and other spiritual gifts, the full thrust of his purpose is revealed. It is the conviction of this writer that nothing in the history of the church has been any more misunderstood than this chapter. One can only be amazed at the near-universal acceptance of the idea that what those Corinthians were doing was actually *caused by* the Holy Spirit! This is viewed as totally wrong with regard to all of the conduct which demanded Paul's attention.

THE GENUINE GIFT OF TONGUES

It may not be denied that there was a *real* gift of tongues belonging to some in Corinth, although this chapter does not give us much information on how that genuine gift operated. Many commentators believe that the *legitimate* gift of tongues at Corinth was no different from what it was on Pentecost; and there is a considerable weight of evidence to support this. Paul and Luke were friends; and the use of the same word to describe God's gift is used here which is used in Acts 2; and, since Acts was written by Luke at a time after Paul wrote the Corinthians, "It would seem logical that Luke would have noted the distinction between the two phenomena, if any existed."[1]

However, Paul taught that there was a genuine gift of "interpretation of tongues" (12:10): and this has the effect of denying the gift at Corinth any identity with the miracle of Pentecost, where no interpreter was needed.. Furthermore, Paul allowed that when an interpreter was present, along with other prescribed conditions, the gift at Corinth might properly be used (14:27). From this, it seems mandatory to view the genuine gift at Corinth as different from that of Pentecost, and

---

[1]S. Lewis Johnson, Jr., *Wycliffe Commentary* (Chicago: Moody Press, 1971), p. 634.

also of far less importance, even that genuine gift (at Corinth) being by Paul ranked last among spiritual gifts.

The genuine gift (at Corinth) was never exercised by Paul, who surely had the gift (14:18), in public assemblies of the church, at least as far as the record goes, and based upon his stated refusal to use it at Corinth (14:6ff). Paul's use of the gift, it is generally agreed, was either privately or in some missionary effort, there being utterly no word of either in the NT. Certainly, he didn't do it in church assemblies. The question persists regarding the authenticity of those Corinthian tongues. Can it be supposed that the Holy Spirit which led Paul to hide his gift and never use it publicly — can we suppose that the same Holy Spirit was moving in those Corinthians? No!

Whatever the genuine gift was (at Corinth), there is simply no glimpse whatever of it in this chapter. The genuine gift had to be either identical with that of Pentecost, or a far lesser thing given for the encouragement of individuals and to be used privately (14:4). It is the conviction here that the genuine gift to the Corinthians was precisely that, a demonstration of tongues for personal edification, not in the sense of learning anything, but as proof that he who had it enjoyed possession of the Holy Spirit. The need for an interpreter of the true gift proves that the possessor of it would not have known what he said, unless, of course, he also had the gift of interpreting tongues.

Does this true gift come into view in the Corinthian assemblies? Yes, but only to the extent that it had been perverted by dragging it into the public worship. However, the overwhelming certainty presses upon us that the visible tongues of Corinth were totally sinful and contrary to the will of God, being either (1) a prostitution of a private gift for public glory in the case of the true gift, or (2) a sensational orgiastic counterfeit demonstration having no connection whatever with the Holy Spirit.

This mingling of the true (even though perverted as to purpose and use) tongues with the false is evidently the reason for Paul's tenderness in dealing with this sin. He simply did not wish to say anything that would discourage those souls who had indeed received of God the private gift of tongues for their encouragement. Since we today are dealing with a far different situation, it is proper to speak much more plainly of those bastard tongues at Corinth.

THE FALSE GIFT OF TONGUES

By the above title is meant the counterfeit, faked and pretended gift of tongues. As Billy Graham said of tongues in the United States at this present time (March 26, 1976), "There is much that is counterfeit . . . tongues are no evidence that a person has been baptized in the Holy Spirit."[2] It is clearly evident that the genuine gift of tongues, whether like those at Pentecost or at Corinth, perished with the age of miracles, and that all of the tongue speaking of this generation is spurious. Graham was correct about the "counterfeit" aspect of it. Barclay also observed this and suggested how it comes about:

> It (the true gift) was a dangerous gift . . . greatly admired, and the possessor was very liable to develop a certain spiritual pride in his gift . . . The very desire to possess it produced, at least in some, a kind of self-hypnotism and a kind of deliberately induced hysteria which issued in a completely false and deluded and synthetic speaking in tongues.[3]

The phenomenon called tongue speaking can be faked; this writer has seen it faked; and the simple truth is that anybody can fake it. Such a thing, of course, can also be produced through the influence of a kind of mob psychology which is sometimes evidenced in religious groups. There is no understanding of this chapter without taking into account the falsity of those Corinthians tongues, but at the same time not denying a legitimate gift as then existing and having been prostituted to unholy ends. This indeed posed a delicate problem. How could the darnel be pulled up without rooting up the wheat? Paul's method of doing so was a marvel. He simply issued

---

[2]Billy Graham, as quoted in *Christianity Today* (Washington, D. C.: Today's Publications, Inc., 1976), Vol. XX, Number 13.

[3]William Barclay, *The Letters to the Corinthians* (Philadelphia: The Westminster Press, 1954), p. 142.

apostolical orders that would inevitably, if followed, diminish and destroy the bastard gift, while at the same time cautioning "not to forbid to speak in tongues" (v. 39). Metz said, "It was difficult to distinguish the valid gift (of tongues) . . . from an invalid expression of personal exultation."[4] It should be remembered, however, that the disappearance of apostolical miracles has removed the necessity of confusion with regard to tongue speaking. The only kind that has ever existed since the age of the apostles has been the kind Billy Graham called "counterfeit."

Why has the phenomenon of counterfeit tongues persisted? It has been produced by people who earnestly desire to do it, and who have been led to believe it is scriptural because of the inaccurate and misleading words in many of the "translations" of the NT in vogue today. For the prime example of this, see under verse 16:18 in the Gospel of Mark, and comment in CMK, pp. 363-367. Such persons are sincere, to be sure, but sincerely wrong.

However, there is another force operative in the tongue speakings of post-apostolical times, and that is satanic instigation. The pride, vainglory, envy, strife, factionalism, etc., which marked the original outbreak of counterfeit tongues was of Satan; and it may not be doubted that the evil one is still active in such things as the recurring appearance of tongue speaking throughout Christian history.

Verse 1, *Follow after love; yet desire earnestly spiritual gifts, but rather that ye may prophesy.*

"Follow after love . . ." seems to connect with what was said in chapter 13. "This clause belongs to the preceding chapter."[5]

"Desire spiritual gifts . . . prophesy . . ." The spiritual gift of prophecy was largely a teaching gift (v. 3), but also included, at least in some cases, the ability to foretell future events. It was the teaching phase Paul stressed here, indicating that teaching was a much more desirable activity than tongue speaking.

---

[4]Donald S. Metz, *Beacon Bible Commentary* (Kansas City: Beacon Hill Press, 1968), p. 447.

[5]Adam Clarke, *Commentary on the Whole Bible* (New York: Carlton & Porter, 1831), Vol. VI, p. 273.

This gift, like all the infancy-age miracles, ceased. There are no miraculously endowed teachers today, despite Satan's having induced a few to fake even this.

Verse 2, *For he that speaketh in a tongue speaketh not unto men, but unto God; for no man understandeth; but in the spirit he speaketh mysteries.*

"Speaketh not unto men . . ." This refers to the true gift of tongues as manifested in Corinth and has the information that it was *privately* utilized. Any other, besides the possessor, was never to hear it done. God of course could hear.

"No man understandeth . . ." This probably means that, even if another heard it, he would not be able to understand it; and it appears that the speaker also could not understand it, unless he had the gift of interpretation. If there was an interpreter, then others might be permitted to hear both the tongue and the interpretation.

In view here is the almost total uselessness of this gift in the area of instructing the church, even the true gift.

Verse 3, *But he that prophesieth speaketh unto men edification, and exhortation, and consolation.*

Even the utility of the gift of prophecy was here said to perform the same services usually associated with ordinary teaching. This shows how unspectacular it was as compared with tongues.

Verse 4, *He that speaketh in a tongue edifieth himself; but he that prophesieth edifieth the church.*

"Edifieth himself . . ." The true gift of tongues benefited not others but the tongue speaker himself. Since not even he understood what was said ("no man understandeth"), the nature of that edification would appear to have been the confirmation to him (by the gift) of his having received the Holy Spirit. No man today could need any such confirmation because the NT makes it clear that all believers who repent and are baptized into Christ enjoy the promise of the sacred scriptures that they will in consequence of their obedience and subsequently to their obedience receive the Holy Spirit (Acts 2:38ff); and that word is all the confirmation that any true believer really needs.

"He that prophesieth edifieth the church . . ." The word from which the Pauline expression "edifieth" is translated is related to the building up of an edifice; and Paul demanded that *everything* ("all things, v. 26) bc done unto edification of the church. This requirement alone demanded the omission of tongues from all church services.

Verse 5, *Now I would have you all speak with tongues, but rather that ye should prophesy: and greater is he that prophesieth than he that speaketh with tongues, except he interpret, that the church may receive edification.*

"I would have you all speak with tongues . . ." The true gift was referred to here; but even of it the apostle said that teaching and edifying the church constituted a far better thing.

"Except he interpret . . ." Despite Paul's mention of the interpretation of tongues as a genuine gift, the possibility in view here that even the tongue speaker himself might possess it, it does not appear in this chapter that any of the Corinthians were said to have this gift. Only the possibility that they might have it is indicated.

"Greater is he that prophesieth . . ." The teacher did more good and was therefore greater than the tongue speaker.

Verse 6, *But now, brethren, if I come unto you speaking with tongues, what shall I profit you, unless I speak to you either by way of revelation, or of knowledge, or of prophesying, or of teaching.*

"What shall I profit you . . ." means "I shall not profit you in any manner at all," if I come to you speaking in tongues. This was Paul's refusal to speak in tongues in the Christian assembly at Corinth; and it is safe to assume that he never did so anywhere else. The only way that even an apostle could benefit his hearers was by preaching to them.

"By way of revelation . . ." refers to what was revealed in scripture.

"Or of knowledge" refers to the spiritual gift of knowledge which Paul assuredly had.

"Or of prophesying . . ." refers to intelligible teachings given by the Holy Spirit to Paul as a spiritual gift.

"Or of teaching . . ." refers to ordinary teaching of what was learned from others, orally or through study of their writings.

Here again the essentially private nature of the true gift of tongues is implicit and demanded by the context.

Verse 7, *Even things without life, giving a voice, whether pipe or harp, if they give not a distinction in the sounds, how shall it be known what is piped or harped?*

If such an illustration as this has any meaning, it has to be that uninterpreted tongues are as noisy, disagreeable, useless, cacophanous and worthless as a kitten on the keys of a piano. Paul, of course, made the comparison with instruments known in his day.

Verse 8, *For if the trumpet give an uncertain voice, who shall prepare himself for war?*

The meaning of this is exactly the same as in verse 7, the repetition of the thought using another illustration was for emphasis. Uninterpreted tongues were as disastrous as the efforts of a military bugler whose unintelligible blasts could not be distinguished either as a call to charge, a call to retreat, or a call to go to bed!

Verse 9, *So also ye, unless ye utter by the tongue speech easy to be understood, how shall it be known what is spoken? for ye will be speaking into the air.*

The force of verses 7-9 is that the false tongues of Corinth were unintelligible nonsense, having no meaning whatever, being nothing more than jabberings of orgiastic demonstrators; and here was the delicate part of the whole situation, the *uninterpreted* manifestations of the genuine gift itself resembled the false tongues so perfectly that no one on earth could have told any difference! It was a master stroke of the devil that he had prevailed upon some who had the true gift to bring it into the public worship; and therefore, when Paul condemned the false, his care not to discourage the true variety of tongues resulted in an occasion of misunderstanding of this subject for centuries afterward. What Paul said here is applicable to both varieties of tongues, both kinds being forbidden in public worship, the true kind because it was not interpreted and had no business in the public worship to start with, and the false kind because it was nothing but pure nonsense anyway.

The essential thing to see is the close likeness in appearance of the two kinds of tongues; and this is paramount as an indication that the true tongues of Corinth were unlike those of Pentecost.

Verses 10-11, *There are, it may be, so many kinds of voices in the world, and no kind is without signification. If then I know not the meaning of the voice, I shall be to him that speaketh a barbarian, and he that speaketh will be a barbarian unto me.*

These verses are a recapitulation of the argument in verses 7-9, the conclusion being that any kind of jargon or gobbledegook, such as tongues, which cannot be understood by the hearers, is condemned.

"Barbarian . . ." in ancient times meant merely one who did not speak Greek. Paul encountered some of these "barbarians" on his mission tours, namely, at Malta and at Lycaonia (Acts 14:11); and significantly Paul did not understand the dialect of the Lycaonians, this being another reason to suppose that Paul's gift of tongues did not include the gift of speaking in languages he had never learned, but was rather for private encouragement.

Verse 12, *So also ye, since ye are zealous of spiritual gifts, seek that ye may abound unto the edifying of the church.*

The teacher of the word of God is the true hero, not the tongue speaker. It is simply incredible that the people affecting to speak in tongues could really imagine that they are doing any good. One humble teacher of the word of God does more good than a thousand tongue speakers, even if their alleged "gift" should be accepted as genuine. Why then should intelligent people bother with it, or be impressed with it, or make any excuses whatever for it? This whole section of this chapter (vv. 1-12), if it had any purpose at all, was to get rid of tongue speaking in the assemblies of the church in Corinth, with the delicate purpose of Paul, always in view, not to discourage any real gift that might have existed there.

Verse 13, *Wherefore let him that speaketh in a tongue pray that he may interpret.*

"That he may interpret . . ." Again, no certainty that any interpreters existed at Corinth appears here. Paul's admonition that they should pray to be able to interpret is, on the contrary, a declaration that they could not interpret.

Verse 14, *For if I pray in a tongue, my spirit prayeth, but my understanding is unfruitful.*

As Lipscomb said with reference to this and verse 15:

> Neither the AV nor the RV is correct here. The thought evidently is, "I will sing as the Spirit directs or inspires, and I will sing in a language that those who hear can understand." . . . The following verse shows clearly that Paul's meaning is: "I will pray and sing by the inspiration of the Spirit, and in a language that they will understand to their profit."[6]

The inference that must be made from this and the next verses is that the tongue speakers had even taken over the songs and prayers of the public worship! Of course, Paul would not countenance anything of that kind.

The quotation of these verses in the sense of people singing and praying in the public services "with the spirit and the understanding" is based upon an incorrect discernment of their meaning. It is not the subjective understanding of the participant that is meant, but the objective purpose of conveying understanding to others.

Verse 15, *What is it then? I will pray with the spirit, and I will pray with the understanding also: I will sing with the spirit, and I will sing with the understanding also.*

"What is it then? . . ." McGarvey understood this is idiomatic for "What is the conclusion of the argument?"[7] We might state the argument as this: "Therefore, let's have no more of this tongue business in the songs and prayers; let everything be done in a language everybody can understand."

Verses 16-17, *Else if thou bless with the spirit, how shall he that filleth the place of the unlearned say the Amen at the giving*

---

[6]David Lipscomb, *Commentary on First Corinthians* (Nashville: The Gospel Advocate Company, 1935), p. 208.

[7]J. W. McGarvey, *Commentary on First Corinthians* (Cincinnati: The Standard Publishing Company, 1916), p. 137.

of thy thanks, seeing he knoweth not what thou sayest? For thou verily givest thanks well, but the other is not edified.

"Say the Amen . . ." It was customary from the earliest times for Christians to say Amen to the public prayers and thanksgivings of the church. Any use of a tongue in such prayers contravened the purpose of congregational participation in the public prayers; and it is an error, therefore, to suppose that the Holy Spirit was guiding those tongue speakers to do anything of that kind. The Blessed Spirit never operated against the will of God. Therefore, we view Paul's words, "Verily givest thanks well!" as absolutely sarcastic, meaning that no matter how "well" they thought they were giving thanks, the Holy Spirit was opposed to what they were doing, on the simple grounds that the rest of the congregation would not know "what thou sayest." It is the failure to see the essential sin of that whole tongue speaking outburst (of both kinds) which has blinded men to the teaching of this chapter. To suppose that the Holy Spirit was actually guiding those ostentatious leaders of the public prayers, or songs, so that they were doing so in tongues, is absolutely an impossibility.

Verse 18, *I thank God, I speak with tongues more than ye all.*

This is the verse, beyond all others, that is supposed to take the lid off tongue speaking and to legitimatize it for all generations; but this cannot be. We have already noted that Paul never used the gift in the presence of others, or in church assemblies. Furthermore, Paul's speaking in tongues "more than ye all" is tremendously significant. His speaking in tongues was genuine, a true gift, to edify himself; the "gifts" he was correcting were (1) either the misused genuine gifts, or (2) the affectations of the tongue counterfeiters; well, actually both of these were condemned.

What then was the apostle's purpose in bringing up the fact that he himself spoke in tongues? Bruce gave the probable explanation thus:

> His speaking with tongues belonged to the sphere of his private devotions. We should not have known of his possessing this gift (even in this passage) were it not that his possessing it in an exceptional degree gave him the

undeniable right to put it in its place in relation to other spiritual gifts.[8]

If Paul had not possessed the gift, some of his critics would have responded merely by saying, "Well, you know nothing about it." As it was, Paul's possession of the gift superlatively enabled him to pour a pitcher of ice water over the whole practice. Bruce further commented on what Paul did here, saying, "(This was) a master-touch which leaves the enthusiasts completely outclassed and out-maneuvered on their own ground."[9]

The tongue speaking fraternity cannot claim Paul as an advocate of their practices, there being no record whatever that he ever did it in the presence of another human being; and, besides, his gift was the real thing!

Verse 19, *Howbeit in the church I had rather speak five words with my understanding, that I might instruct others also, than ten thousand words in a tongue.*

Well, there it is! Anyone in possession of God's Spirit would have exactly the same attitude; but no, the tongue speakers would rather speak ten thousand words in tongues than five words that anybody could understand!

"In the church . . ." "This of course refers to the Christian assembly."[10] All of Paul's tongue speaking was apparently done in private devotions.

Verse 20, *Brethren, be not children in mind: yet in malice be ye babes, but in mind be men.*

No new paragraph begins here, such a division being arbitrary and incorrect. There is a continuation of the thought of the foolishness of tongue speaking. The three phases of mortal life: babes, children and men were intended to explain the whole matter of spiritual gifts, belonging as they did to the infancy and childhood age of the church, and not to its maturity. This is therefore a call for the Corinthians to stop

---

[8]F. F. Bruce, *Answers to Questions* (Grand Rapids: Zondervan Publishing House, 1972), p. 99.

[9]*Ibid.*

[10]Leon Morris, *Tyndale Commentary* (Grand Rapids: Wm. B. Eerdmans Publishing Company, 1958), p. 196.

chasing after tongues and to grow up spiritually. As McGarvey said it:

> All Christians who mistakenly yearn for a renewal of those spiritual gifts, should note the clear import of these words of the apostle, which show that their presence in the church would be an evidence of weakness and immaturity, rather than of fully developed power and seasoned strength.[11]

In this connection, see also 13:8-11, above.

Verse 21, *In the law it is written, By men of strange tongues and by the lips of strangers will I speak unto this people; and not even thus will they hear me, saith the Lord.*

Paul here quoted Isaiah 28:11, where strange tongues were a chastisement for the unbelief of God's people, in that they were made to hear God's voice speaking to them in the unknown tongue uttering harsh commands given by the foreign invader. As Metz said:

> Paul now introduces an extremely sober note. Whereas the Corinthians regarded speaking in tongues as something to be desired, Paul pointed out that it might be a sign of God's displeasure and punishment.[12]

Verse 22, *Wherefore tongues are for a sign, not to them that believe, but to the unbelieving: but prophesying is for a sign, not to the unbelieving, but to them that believe.*

Tongues in a church are not a sign of God's blessing at all, any more than the foreign tongue of the invader was a blessing of God in Jerusalem, but just the opposite! Tongues in a church? Not as long as there is a single believer in it! The notion that speaking in tongues is to convert unbelievers is foreign to this text. It does just the opposite of converting unbelievers, with the result that they turn aside in disgust, as Paul stated in the very next verse.

"Prophesying a sign . . . to them that believe. ." The fact of Paul's calling it a "sign" for believers instead of saying that it was merely for the benefit of believers indicates that the

---

[11]J. W. McGarvey, *op. cit.*, p. 132.
[12]Donald S. Metz, *op. cit.*, p. 45O.

miraculous endowment of certain teachers in the primitive church is in view. It must have been of great value to have such directly inspired teachers in that age of the church (the infancy age); and the foolishness of the Corinthians is seen in their astounding preference for the showy gift of tongues, instead of honoring and preferring a gift that could have blessed and benefited.

Verse 23, *If therefore the whole church be assembled together and all speak with tongues, and there come in men unlearned or unbelieving, will they not say that ye are mad?*

Far from being an instrument of converting unbelievers, or being some kind of sign that would help unbelievers to believe, tongues in a public assembly were a positive hindrance, resulting not in the conversion of any but in the judgment against Christians to the effect that they were all crazy. It should be carefully noted that what was true of the counterfeit tongues in this respect was also true of any genuine tongues exercised without an interpreter's presence to tell what was said. And if this was true in those days, how much more is it true today, generations and centuries after the true gift disappeared altogether.

Incidentally, it is quite obvious that the assemblies of the early Christians were open meetings, free to be attended by any who might wish to do so.

Verse 24, *But if all prophesy, and there come in one unbelieving or unlearned, he is reproved by all, he is judged by all.*

"If all prophesy . . ." This answers to "if all speak with tongues" in the preceding verse; but what is meant in both cases is a reference to "all who participate publicly," instead of being an affirmation that all were speaking at one time. However, despite the absence of that thought from this particular verse, it was true of the tongue speakers that they were all speaking at once. This is a mandatory conclusion based on Paul's order that the speakers should speak "one at a time," or "in turn" (v. 27).

"Reproved by all, . . . judged by all . . ." has reference to the power of a decently ordered service featuring intelligible speakers to move the unregenerated to accept the gospel, as stated in the next verse.

Verse 25, *The secrets of his heart are made manifest; and so he will fall down on his face and worship God, declaring that God is among you.*

Many in all ages have prostrated themselves before God in worship and in prayers, and the admissibility of this as legitimate is plain enough in this verse. There is no rule, however, that this must always be done.

"Fall down on his face and worship God . . ." "Power to make unbelieving visitors fall down on their faces and worship God, O for such today, instead of dead formalism on one hand and irreverent monkey business on the other!"[13]

Verse 26, *What is it then, brethren? When ye come together, each one hath a psalm, hath a teaching, hath a revelation, hath a tongue, hath an interpretation. Let all things be done unto edifying.*

The spontaneous, informal nature of the early church services is clearly visible. There could have been no set program in advance, with even the words that men would say written down a week ahead. There cannot be any doubt that formalism, which is the current religious style, and which certainly corrected the shameful disorders like those at Corinth, has nevertheless left many a congregation in a state of abiosis.

"Psalm . . ." probably refers to a song, or hymn composed by the worshiper during the previous week, or at least one he had learned. There were no hymn books or congregational singing, except tunes sung in unison; and four-part harmony had not been invented. A very early description of Christian worship stated that "they sang by turns a hymn to Christ as God";[14] and there can hardly be any doubt that this was true.

"Teaching . . ." would refer to the instruction of ordinary, uninspired teachers; and in this, it corresponds roughly to preaching in the present time.

---

[13]Henry H. Halley, *Bible Handbook* (Grand Rapids: Zondervan Publishing House, 1927), p. 549.

[14]Henry Bettensen, *Documents of the Christian Church* (New York & London: Oxford University Press, 1947), p. 6.

"Revelation . . ." is a reference to the words of an inspired, miraculously endowed teacher who had "the gift of prophecy" as used in this chapter.

"Tongue . . ." would mean, not the counterfeited non-sensical "utterings" of the fakers, but the real gift (with the great big IF stated in verse 29, IF there was an interpreter). The frequency in this chapter of that condition coming into view, always with the uncertainty of "may" or "if" connected with it, strongly suggests that there might not have been very many interpreters at Corinth.

"Interpretation . . ." This was mentioned along with "tongue" to bind the two inseparably together; and it seems plausible that by this inclusion Paul did not mean to certify the fact of there actually being interpreters of tongues in Corinth, but rather as a device of eliminating tongues altogether *unless* this condition was fulfilled (having an interpreter). Certainly the fact is plain enough that there was a *possibility* of no such interpreter being present; and therefore Paul gave the order that if none indeed was present, tongues were not to be used under any circumstances (vv. 28-28).

"Let all things be done unto edifying . . ." This has the weight of "no tongues in any case," except, of course, if such might have been duly interpreted by an inspired interpreter.

Verses 27-28, *If any man speaketh in a tongue, let it be by two, or at most three, and that in turn; and let one interpret: but if there be no interpreter, let him keep silence in the church; and let him speak to himself, and to God.*

There are a number of rules in these two verses which must be observed whenever tongues may be used. These are:

1. No more than three may speak in a tongue on any given occasion.
2. All tongue speaking must be done "in turn," that is, by persons speaking one at a time.
3. On no occasion may tongues be used unless an interpreter is standing by to tell the audience every word that was spoken.

To these prohibitions, there must be added a number of others which are given in this chapter, including these:

4. Everything must be done unto edifying, and tongues do not edify.
5. Love is a better thing to practice than speaking in tongues.
6. Five intelligible words are to be preferred to ten thousand in an uninterpreted tongue.
7. Under no circumstances let the women do it (v. 34), interpreter or no interpreter.
8. Greater is the teacher than the tongue speaker.
9. Uninterpreted tongues will cause outsiders to say, "Ye are mad."

An analysis of the above apostolical rules on tongue speaking will emphasize the importance of the inspired interpreter, the gift of interpretation itself being one of the miraculous gifts; and Paul's statement in this verse 28 that, "If there be no interpreter, let him keep silence in the church," still leaves the possibility that there were not any in Corinth who had that gift. This might very well have been Paul's way of putting the terminator on tongues without discouraging any who might really have had the genuine gift. Certainly, the lack of authentic interpretation in the present times raises the most serious questions and goes far to prove the invalid nature of that which passes for tongue speaking today. Has any revelation been delivered to mankind since the days of the apostles by means of the gift of tongues duly interpreted? If so, where is it? Has there ever been preserved any of this supernatural wisdom that is said to be imparted to men by means of tongues? If so, who has ever heard a single word of it? If it is a fact that God is speaking in such a manner to men today, and that there are interpreters who might tell what is spoken, why has it not been published, in order for all men to be able to share in it?

The things spoken by alleged interpreters who are conveying present-day messages received through tongues are nothing new, being for the most part garbled and confused bits of teaching gleaned piecemeal from smatterings of religious texts, being in no sense whatever any such thing as a coherent and enlightening communication from Almighty God. In a word, all the post-apostolical tongue speakings for nineteen centuries have not contributed one authentic sentence to the revealed will of God, like that in the NT. If this does not condemn the whole monstrous aberration, then how on earth could it be condemned? The blunt, dogmatic apostolic answer to tongue speakings is just this: *but if there be no interpreter!* We know there are no authenticated holders of this gift today; and the strong suggestion persists in this whole chapter that there were none of that class in Corinth.

"Speak to himself and to God . . ." This stresses the private nature of the true gift; and the apostolical order for it not to be used in church (without an interpreter) removed the only possible reason why the counterfeiters were faking it, making it impossible for them to accumulate any flattery or "glory" from the display of their "abilities" publicly.

Verses 29-32, *And let the prophets speak by two or three, and let the others discern. But if a revelation be made to another sitting by, let the first keep silence. For ye all can prophesy one by one, that all may learn, and all may be exhorted; and the spirits of the prophets are subject to the prophets.*

In a word, these four verses lay down practically the same rules for the prophets as those applying to those having the tongues (of either kind). There were not to be over three on any one occasion; two may not speak at once; and if one prophet was interrupted by another, that was the end of the first prophet's message! This would have made for shorter services, since the probable result was that they could run through the maximum number of three rather quickly under those rules!

"The spirits of the prophets are subject to the prophets . . ." means that any true prophet could control his speaking; there was not any such thing as an irresistible compulsion for any *true* prophet to speak. Rules like these carry the strong implication that some at Corinth had claimed otherwise.

Putting together all of Paul's regulations, the conclusion persists that there were also false prophets engaging in the free-for-all orgiastic demonstrations going on in Corinth. Certainly, in the case of the tongue speakers: (1) they were all speaking at once, (2) perhaps dozens were participating every Sunday, and (3) such a thing as interpreting what was spoken in tongues had been ignored altogether.

Verse 33, *For God is not a God of confusion, but of peace.*

This adds another dimension to Paul's picture of the Corinthian assembles: they were scandalous examples of utter and complete confusion. Was God the author of it? Certainly not! Is he the author of similar confusion in our own times? Certainly not! Who is the author of such confusion? Both then and now the author is Satan.

Verse 34, *As in all the churches of the saints, let the women keep silence in the churches: for it is not permitted them to speak; but let them be in subjection, as also saith the law.*

Before dealing with this as it may be applied in all generations, it should first be observed that the primary meaning has to be, "Do not let the women speak in tongues under any circumstances." This command comes right in the middle of an extensive treatise on tongue speaking; and to blow this up to a universal law that no woman might open her mouth in a church service is simply contrary to all reason. As Glenn Wallace once paraphrased this: "As for tongue speaking, don't let the gals do it at all!" This applied even if an interpreter was present.

"It is not permitted unto them to speak . . ." That is, it was not permitted for them to speak in tongues, that having been the subject Paul was discussing. Significantly, even in these times of the alleged reappearance of this gift, it is almost invariably the women who catch on to it first, and later their husbands. Thus Pat gets it from Shirley, Tom gets it from Mabel, etc., just like Adam took the forbidden fruit from the hands of Eve.

"But let them be in subjection, as also saith the law . . ." This prohibition was directed against the arrogant leadership of some of the Corinthian women in the promotion of a fad, that of speaking in tongues. Their vigorous advocacy of it had cast them in a role of immodesty and rebellion even against their husbands, hence Paul's rule as stated here. It was this sinful usurpation of their husbands' status as head of the family which was the essence of their wrongdoing. Not so much their voices being heard in a Christian assembly, but the rejection of lawful authority, is the thing suggested by Paul's statement that the Law of Moses forbade it.

The impossibility of reconciling the radically opposed views of scholars and commentators on this passage has the effect of sending us back to the OT, to which Paul appealed in this verse.

Upon the occasion of the creation and fall, God said to Eve, "Thy desire shall be to thy husband, and he shall rule over thee" (Gen. 3:16). Even prior to that, Eve was designated as a "help" suitable for man (Gen. 2:18). Thus, from the very beginning the authority of the family was vested in the man. The Corinthian women had violated that intention and Paul immediately assigned two reasons for forbidding the action (speaking in tongues publicly) which frustrated God's purpose.

These reasons were: (1) The OT gave man the authority over the family. as in verses cited above, and (2) the customs of the age made it shameful for a woman to speak in public. The first of these reasons, of course, is the greater, the other having been removed by the customs of subsequent ages. Some would do away with these rules altogether on the grounds that there is "neither male nor female" in Christ Jesus (Gal. 3:28); but, as McGarvey declared, "This is unwarranted; for while the gospel emancipated woman, it did not change her natural relation"[15] in the hierarchy of the family. From this, it is to be inferred that rule (1) is still operative in the sense in which it is applied in the OT. Paul's appeal here to the OT proves this. What then was the force of the rule under the old covenant?

1. Many exceptions to the rule were allowed and approved by God.

(a) Miriam the prophetess, the sister of Aaron, took a timbrel in her hand; and all the women went out after her (Ex.15:20).

(b) And Deborah, a prophetess, the wife of Lapidoth, she judged Israel at that time . . . and the children of Israel came up to her for judgment (Judg. 4:4, 5).

(c) So Hilkiah the priest . . . went unto Huldah the prophetess, the wife of Shallum . . . and they communed with her (2 Kings 22:14).

---

[15]J. W. McGarvey, *Commentary on First Corinthians* (Cincinnati: The Standard Publishing Company, 1916), p. 143.

Clearly, the prophetesses of the OT exercised their gift publicly, even the priests and the king being subject to what they said.

Is it any different in the NT? Note the following:

(a) And there was one Anna, a prophetess, the daughter of Phanuel . . . which departed not from the temple... and spake of him (Christ) to all them that looked for redemption in Jerusalem (Luke 2:36-38).

(b) The apostle Peter, on Pentecost, cited the OT scriptures which prophesied that in the times of the new covenant, "Your sons and your daughters shall prophesy" (Acts 2:17).

From these passages from both testaments, it is clear that the total exclusion of women from any public speaking did not occur, nor was the action of such women construed as "usurping authority" over a man. Anna spoke openly in the temple to everybody; and all Israel went "up to Deborah" for judgment.

The whole tenor of the Bible, therefore, forbids the arbitrary enforcement of Paul's "Let your women keep silent" beyond the theater of its first application. Again from McGarvey:

> The powers of woman have become so developed, and her privileges have been so extended in gospel lands, that it is no longer shameful for her to speak in public; but the failing of one reason is not the cessation of both. The Christian conscience has therefore interpreted Paul's rule rightly when it applies it generally and admits of exceptions.[16]

Of course, the gift of prophecy is no longer found in the church; but again to quote McGarvey:

> The gift of prophecy no longer exists; but, by the law of analogy, those women who have a marked ability, either for exhortation or instruction, are permitted to speak in the churches. . . . The law is permanent, but the application of it may vary. If man universally gives woman permission to speak, she is free from the law in this respect.[17]

---

[16]*Ibid.*
[17]*Ibid.*

McGarvey's comment written during the previous century cannot be set aside as a mere catering to current trends.

In this context, it is not amiss to point out that the appearances of prophetesses in both OT and NT seem to have been simultaneous with periods of decadence and spiritual lethargy.

George W. De Hoff, a current church leader and a scholar of great discernment, vigorously supported McGarvey's position on this question, saying:

> No verse in the Bible teaches that women must teach God's word *at home*, or *in private*, those limitations having been added by false teachers. Any teaching that does not usurp authority over a man does not violate this passage.[18]

Some things, however, are forbidden to women in the Christian religion. By scriptural definition, a woman may not be an elder of the church, nor a deacon, nor an evangelist. Phoebe (Rom. 16:1) was not a deacon in any official sense. See comment on this in CR, pp. 508-510. Churches presuming to appoint deaconesses do so without scriptural authority, and without any guidelines as to the needful qualifications.

Women may not be appointed to the eldership of a church, because, like most men, they are unqualified. None of them may be "the husband of one wife," etc. Moreover the essential authority of the eldership is such that a woman's place in it would violate the primal law regarding her lawful subordination to her husband. To make a woman an elder would indeed "usurp authority over a man," in fact all the men of her congregation. The idea of "teaching a man" as a violation of that law is, however, far-fetched. Did Priscilla usurp authority over Apollos when she (and her husband) taught him the word of God (Acts 18:24ff)?

Women may not be evangelists. The notable violations of this during our own times have in no sense cast any reflections upon the wisdom of this rule, but rather have confirmed it as

---

[18]George W. De Hoff, *Sermons on First Corinthians* (Murfreesboro, Tenn.: The Christian Press, 1947), p. 99.

divine. The office of the evangelist is one of authority in the name of God; and as De Hoff expressed it:

> She cannot be an evangelist for the reason that an evangelist must rebuke with all authority, the very thing the inspired apostle Paul has forbidden her to do (1 Tim. 2:11, 12); but women who are faithful Christians may certainly teach God's word in Bible classes, at home or in the meeting house.[19]

What is said of women being elders, deacons or evangelists is also true of their being "preachers" in any sense whatever; because it is the duty of all preachers to be evangelists, even if their preaching sometimes gives little evidence of respecting their commission. Every preacher or evangelist is commanded to "Reprove, rebuke, exhort, with all longsuffering and teaching" (1 Tim. 4:2).

Verse 35, *And if they would learn anything, let them ask their husbands at home: for it is shameful for a woman to speak in the church.*

The women under consideration in this order were married, nothing whatever being said of widows, spinsters or the unmarried; and they were also ignorant, as indicated by "if they would learn anything." To make this a universal rule for all women is to ignore the limitations evident in the passage. As McGarvey said, "To understand the passage we should know the ignorance, garrulity and degradation of Oriental women."[20] This was addressed to abuses of the formal worship by women of a certain class in an ancient culture. See under verse 34, above. What about the woman whose husband is an ignoramus, an unbeliever, or an open enemy of God and all religion; should she comply with this rule? Until it is affirmed that *she* should, it is a sin to make this rule universal.

Verse 36, *What, was it from you that the word of God sent forth? or came it from you alone?*

This was Paul's sarcastic denunciation of the pretensions of the Corinthians, having the impact of "Surely, you people could not believe that you are some kind of Mother Church!"

---

[19]*Ibid.*, p. 100.
[20]J. W. McGarvey, *op. cit.*, p. 143.

Verse 37, *If any man thinketh himself to be a prophet, or spiritual, let him take knowledge of the things which I write unto you, that they are the commandment of the Lord.*

All Christians of all ages should heed this verse. Difficult as some of Paul's intentions may be for men to discern, the unqualified inspiration of this chapter, and the entire epistle, must be received. Tongue speakers may not set aside the rules designed to control and eliminate tongues; but it is equally true that churches may not set aside the limitations imposed upon women in the realm of authority, in evangelism, and in holding offices of authority in the church.

Verse 38, *But if any man is ignorant, let him be ignorant.*

As Kelcy pointed out, "There is good textual authority for rendering this verse as the RSV does: "If anyone does not recognize this, he is not recognized."[21]

Verses 39-40, *Wherefore my brethren, desire earnestly to prophesy, and forbid not to speak with tongues. But let all things be done decently and in order.*

"To prophesy . . ." While still refusing to forbid tongues categorically, for fear of wounding some with the real gift, Paul again stressed the superiority of teaching, commanding here that the brethren should desire to teach, not to speak in tongues.

"Forbid not to speak with tongues . . ." Throughout this chapter, it has been stressed that the existence of actual gifts of tongue speaking and interpretation made it impossible to declare all such things out of order. Despite this forbearance, there never was a church anywhere which could practice tongue speakings while observing Paul's rules, which inevitably diminished them to the vanishing point; and which, after the cessation of miraculous gifts, eliminated them altogether.

"Let all things be done decently and in order . . ." This is the golden rule for organizing and conducting public worship services of the church in all ages. The first announcement of it came in a situation where it was drastically needed; and,

---

[21]Raymond C. Kelcy, *First Corinthians* (Austin: The R. B. Sweet Co., Inc., 1967), p. 69.

despite the fact that over-formalization may occur from an over-zealous enforcement of it, it is the failure to enforce it at all which distinguishes many so-called "free" religious groups today.

CHAPTER 15

When darkness falls upon the day of life, when death has come, and when men gather around a grave, then it is that they turn to this immortal chapter, where are recorded the title deeds of man's highest hope, the Christian gospel's promise of eternal life. Light from this chapter dispels the darkness surrounding the grave; its message reassures the sorrowful, redefines the meaning of life itself and writes upon the tomb the blessed words, "Asleep in Jesus." It speaks at every funeral.

Apostolical power and inspiration charge every word of this chapter with everlasting significance, which has been neither dimmed nor eroded by the passing of nineteen centuries. Even the mysteries of it, which men may not fully understand, have power to quicken the human spirit and rekindle the fires of faith. The dimensions of this heavenly message are so vast that finite man may neither completely comprehend nor intelligently deny it; thus leaving every man the moral option of trusting the Father's promise or turning to the blackness of total despair. It is the voice of God the Father of mankind that speaks to men here; and, for all who listen, it promises that nothing can harm the Father's child, that there is no need to fear, and that even life's sorrows, infirmities and sufferings are not without purpose, and that none of life's labors are in vain "in the Lord."

Concerning the Resurrection, Both Christ's and Ours

Practically all of this chapter is devoted to teaching concerning the resurrection, Barnes giving the following outline of it:[1]

I. The dead will be raised (1-34).

A. The resurrection of Christ proves it (1-11).

---

[1]Albert Barnes, *Notes on the NT* (Grand Rapids: Baker Book House, 1949), p. 280. Numerous challenges were made in this outline.

1. The scriptures foretold it (1-4).
2. Eyewitnesses attested it (5-11).

B. To deny the resurrection is absurd (12-34).

1. If the dead rise not, it would mean Christ did not (13).
2. It would follow that preaching was useless (14).
3. It would mean faith was worthless (14).
4. It would mean that the apostles were liars (15).
5. It would deny all possibility of salvation from sin (16-17).
6. It would mean that the righteous dead were lost (18).
7. It would mean all believers in Christ were to be pitied (19).
8. It would mean that even the rite of baptism for the dead, as practiced by the heathen, was absurd (29).
9. It would mean that sufferings and privations of the apostles were vain and useless (31-34).

C. An illustration of the reasonableness of the doctrine of the resurrection (introduced parenthetically, as often in Paul's writings) (20-28).

1. But now hath Christ been raised up (20). Paul could not wait till the conclusion of his argument, but dogmatically declared the truth of the resurrection.
2. As death came to all through one person (Adam), it is fitting that the resurrection should come through one (21-22).
3. The order of the resurrection is given (23-28).

II. Regarding the nature of the bodies that shall be raised up (35-41).

A. It is like grain that is planted (36-38).
B. It is like different kinds of flesh (39).
C. It is like different kinds of celestial bodies (40-31).
D. It is described as:

1. Incorruptible (42).
2. Glorious (43).
3. Powerful (43).

4. A spiritual body (44).
5. It is like the risen body of Christ (45-50).

III. What shall become of those who remain alive at the Second Advent? (55-57).

A. The answer is that they shall be changed in an instant, and thus participate in the resurrection just like others.

IV. The practical application of the doctrine of the resurrection (55-58).

A. It places the Christian in a position of strength, the great victory already having been won (55-57).
B. All of the Christian's energies should be devoted fully to the service of God, being assured that his labor is not in vain "in the Lord" (58).

While it may be questioned that "This chapter is more important than any other part of this epistle,"[2] it is nevertheless true that the sacred scriptures have attained some kind of a climax in the verses of this chapter.

Verse 1, *Now I make known unto you, brethren, the gospel which I preached unto you, which also ye received, wherein also ye stand.*

It is rather tragic that the Corinthians required that someone remind them of the fundamental facts of the Christian gospel, at a time so soon after they had heard it, obeyed it, and were enjoying the blessings of salvation derived from it. As Hodge declared, "Certain false teachers at Corinth had denied the resurrection."[3] There is no profit in trying to identify these false teachers. Satan always has an advocate in every community; and those of Jewish background could have been contaminated by the Sadducees, while those of Greek origin could have cited a hundred of their philosophers who despised any such doctrine as the resurrection of the dead (Acts 17:32).

Verse 2, *By which also ye are saved, if ye hold fast the word which I preached unto you, except ye believed in vain.*

---

[2]*Ibid.*
[3]Charles Hodge, *An Exposition of the First Epistle to the Corinthians* (Grand Rapids: Wm. B. Eerdmans Publishing Company, 1974), p. 308.

Two clauses in this verse reiterate the principle that even for those already saved, it is yet required of them that they "hold fast the word," and that otherwise even their glorious beginning is a total loss. Many commentators move quickly to soften the meaning here, saying that "*Believed in vain* does not indicate loss of salvation as a possibility";[4] but it is clear enough that the passage cannot possibly mean anything else but the loss of salvation for those who hold not fast the word.

Verse 3, *For I delivered unto you first of all that which also I received: that Christ died for our sins according to the scriptures.*

"First of all . . ." This means "First in importance, not in time, the doctrine of the resurrection being primary, cardinal, central and indispensable."[5]

"That which I also received . . ." Wesley was no doubt correct in the conviction that this meant "I received from Christ himself; it was not a fiction of my own."[6] To be sure, Paul had contact with other apostles whose testimony corroborated his own; but there can be no meaning here to the effect that Paul was merely repeating what he had heard from others.

"Christ died for our sins . . ." Volumes of truth are embedded in this. Christ's death was not a mere murder, designed and carried out by his enemies; but it was a conscious laying down of his life for the sins of mankind. The great atonement is in view here.

"According to the scriptures . . ." "The double appeal to the scriptures (vv. 3,4) in so brief a statement is deliberate and important."[7] The magnificent prophecies of the OT which so accurately foretold the death of the Son of God are so important that they deserved and received mention even ahead of the apostolical testimony about to be cited. As to what scriptures

---

[4]S. Lewis Johnson, Jr., *Wycliffe Bible Commentary* (Chicago: Moody Press, 1971), p. 639.
[5]David Lipscomb, *Commentary on First Corinthians* (Nashville: The Gospel Advocate Company, 1935), p. 221.
[6]John Wesley, *One Volume NT Commentary* (Grand Rapids: Baker Book House, 1972), in loco.
[7]David Lipscomb, *op. cit.*, p. 222.

were meant, Psalm 16:10, Isaiah 53:10, Hosea 6:2, Jonah 2:10 (see Matt. 12:40), Zechariah 12:10 and 13:7 are among them, besides all of the typical things such as the sin offering and the passover sacrifices.

Verse 4, *And that he was buried; and that he hath been raised on the third day according to the scriptures.*

This dogmatic declaration of the death, burial and resurrection of Christ was written while the *majority of that generation* in which it occurred were still alive (v. 6); and the presence of many enemies who denied it but who were powerless to produce any evidence against it, makes this an argument of eternal power and dependability. In fact all of the evidence in this chapter shows that even the enemies who were denying the resurrection (as a general thing) were compelled to admit the resurrection of Christ, because Paul adduced the latter as proof of the former!

Farrar extolled the apostolic witness of the resurrection in this passage by observing that:

It is a complete summary.
It includes material which is not in the gospels.
It appeals to ancient prophecies.
It shows the force of the evidence which convinced the apostles.
It appeals to many eyewitnesses still living.
It was written within 25 years of the events themselves.[8]

"And that he was buried . . ." This is one of three NT references to the burial of Christ, except in the gospels, the other two being Acts 2:29 and 13:29. "It blasts the swoon theory; he really died; and it leads naturally to the empty tomb, a witness for the resurrection which has never been effectively denied."[9]

"Hath been raised the third day . . ." The scripture which affirmed Jesus would rise on the third day is Jonah 1:17 (Matt. 12:40). For discussion of the day Jesus was crucified and the related question of "the third day," see CMK, pp. 341-348.

---

[8]F. W. Farrar, *The Pulpit Commentary* (Grand Rapids: Wm. B. Eerdmans Publishing Company, 1950), Vol. 19, p. 484.
[9]S. Lewis Johnson, Jr., *op. cit.*, p. 639.

"According to the scriptures . . ." See under preceding verse.

Verse 5, *And that he appeared to Cephas; then to the Twelve.*

"Cephas . . ." is the name for Peter; and one significant thing is that the Lord made a special appearance to the apostle who had denied him, giving hope to all who fall, and showing that the Lord is tender and merciful to forgive our sins (see Luke 24:34). Some have criticized Paul for omitting the appearances to the women (John 20:14); but those do not belong here, since they were "evidential to the apostles, rather than to the world,"[10] and came at a time when the apostles themselves were in a state of shock and unbelief.

"Then to the Twelve . . ." This is a reference to the office of the Twelve, and the fact of Jesus' appearances being to ten on one occasion and eleven on another is a mere quibble of no importance at all.

Verse 6, *Then he appeared to about five hundred brethren at once, of whom the greater part remain until now, but some are fallen asleep.*

No infidel can get rid of this testimony. The generation that witnessed this wonder could not deny it; and the subsequent objections of unbelievers are refuted by the simple fact of their total ignorance of what took place, except as attested by the eyewitnesses. Many scholars, as Dummelow, identify this appearance to over five hundred as identical with "the mountain appearance in Galilee (Matt. 28:16ff)."[11] It could, however, have been another not reported in the gospels, just as the appearance to James, given a moment later, is also not given in the gospels.

"The greater part remain . . ." This "is of the highest evidential value,"[12] because it was written by one who would rather have died than to tell a lie, and who could not possibly have been guilty of making a statement that could have been refuted by any enemy of the truth.

---

[10]F. W. Farrar, *op. cit.*, p. 484.

[11]J. R. Dummelow, *Commentary on the Holy Bible* (New York: The Macmillan Company, 1937), p. 917.

[12]F. W. Farrar, *op. cit.*, p. 484.

"Some are fallen asleep . . ." Reference to death as a sleep originated with Jesus himself and was quickly adopted by Christians when speaking of the beloved dead. See CJ, p. 275.

Verses 7-8, *Then he appeared to James; then to all the apostles; and last of all, as to the child untimely born, he appeared to me also.*

"James . . ." This appearance is nowhere else mentioned in the NT. Macknight identified this James as "James the less, author of the NT book of James and a brother of our Lord."[13] As the apostle James was already dead at the time of Paul's writings, it seems probable that Paul would have been referring to the other James, who was also called an apostle in a secondary sense. He presided over the church in Jerusalem, as recorded in Acts. Jerome recorded a curious legend to the effect that James had made a vow that he would neither eat nor drink till he had seen Jesus risen from the dead, and that Jesus, appearing to him, said, "My brother, eat thy bread, for the Son of man is risen from the dead."[14] Jesus' brothers did not, at first, believe in him (John 7:3).

"Last of all . . ." does not mean that Jesus appeared to no other afterward, because he also appeared to John at a much later time (Rev. 1:16ff). It has the meaning of "last in this list which I am giving.',

"Untimely born . . ." The word here is used of an abortion and "denotes the violent and unnatural mode of Paul's call to the apostleship."[15] Although himself one of the witnesses of Christ's resurrection, Paul here dissociated himself from the Twelve as being conscious of his own unworthiness from having persecuted the church.

Verse 9, *For I am the least of the apostles, that am not meet to be called an apostle, because I persecuted the church of God.*

As Kelcy said, "This verse is explanatory of verse 8."[16] The extent of Paul's persecutions were probably much more exten-

---

[13]James Macknight, *Apostolical Epistles and Commentary* (Grand Rapids: Baker Book House. 1969), p. 256.

[14]Jerome as quoted by Farrar, *op. cit.*, p. 484.

[15]David Lipscomb, *op. cit.*, p. 224.

[16]Raymond C. Kelcy, *First Corinthians* (Austin: R. B. Sweet Co., 1967), p. 70.

sive than the glimpses of them which appear in the NT might indicate.

Verse 10, *But by the grace of God I am what I am: and his grace which was bestowed upon me was not found vain; but I labored more abundantly than they all: yet not I, but the grace of God which was with me.*

Despite the deep humility expressed in verse 9, Paul nevertheless did not depreciate the glory and dignity of his calling. "The whole verse is a maintenance of official dignity as an apostle."[17]

"More abundantly than they all . . ." Paul's labors were the most extensive of any of the apostles, and the most fruitful. Such rewards of his efforts Paul ascribed not to himself but to the grace of God.

Verse 11, *Whether then it be I or they, so we preach, and so ye believed.*

The gospel Paul preached was one and the same as that preached by all the others, the point here being that it made no difference whether from himself or others the message had been received. It was one message only, with the same result of salvation no matter who preached it.

"We preach . . ." There are two words in the NT for preaching. This one means "We proclaim, or herald."[18] The other is "prophesy" and refers to spiritual teaching and instruction.

Verse 12, *Now if Christ is preached that he hath been raised from the dead, how say some among you that there is no resurrection of the dead?*

The certainty of Christ's resurrection was so solidly embedded in the convictions of the apostolic church that Paul made it to be here an argument proving the resurrection generally of all the dead, a hope stubbornly denied by the Greek philosophers (Acts 17:32). As Hodge declared, this verse proves that some of the Corinthians were denying the general resurrection

---

[17]T. Teignmouth Shore, *Ellicott's Commentary on the Whole Bible* (Grand Rapids: Zondervan Publishing House, 1959), p. 346.

[18]F. W. Farrar, *op. cit.*, p. 485.

for all Christians (and all men), while admitting through necessity the resurrection of Christ. Paul affirmed the resurrection of Christ as proof of the resurrection of all. This is the first in a series of arguments proving the validity of the Christian hope of the resurrection. The philosophical conceit which Paul laid to rest by these arguments was: "The Greek idea of the immortality of the soul . . . that after death the soul escaped from the body to be absorbed into the divine or continue a shadowy existence in the underworld."[19]

Verse 13, *But if there is no resurrection of the dead, neither hath Christ been raised.*

If there is no resurrection for all, then the resurrection of Christ itself is meaningless.

Verse 14, *And if Christ hath not been raised, then is our preaching vain, your faith also is vain.*

The absolutely fundamental nature of the resurrection of Christ and the legitimate corollaries derived from it are affirmed here. So-called "modernists" who pretend to be Christians while denying the resurrection are not Christian at all in any NT sense.

Verse 15, *Yea, and we are found false witnesses of God; because we witnessed of God that he raised up Christ: whom he raised not up, if so be that the dead are not raised.*

As McGarvey said, "It was not an issue of truth or mistake, but of truth or falsehood."[20] There can be no middle ground in judging the words of that group of men who bore witness to Christ's resurrection and then went up and down the ancient empire sealing the testimony with their life's blood. It was either truth, or it was a bold calculated lie which perpetrated upon mankind the greatest hoax of all time; and the known character and behavior of the blessed apostles makes it impossible to believe the second alternative.

"He raised up Christ . . ." Christ's resurrection is viewed in the NT as having been accomplished by the Son himself (John

---

[19]Donald Guthrie, *The New Bible Commentary* (Grand Rapids: Wm. B. Eerdmans Publishing Company, 1970), p. 1071.

[20]J. W. McGarvey, *Commentary on First Corinthians* (Cincinnati: Standard Publishing Company, 1916), p. 149.

10:18), and by the Holy Spirit (Rom. 8:11). The whole godhead was active in it.

Verse 16, *For if the dead are not raised, neither hath Christ been raised.*

Of course, the denial of any such thing as the resurrection included the resurrection of Christ with that which was denied; but there is more to this than that. The whole purpose of Christ's entry into our earth life with its sufferings and death, consummated by his glorious resurrection, was the purpose of conquering death upon behalf of all humankind; and, if such a thing as the resurrection of men was impossible, Christ would never have undertaken the mission at the outset. As Shore expressed it:

> In other words, if there be no resurrection, the only alternative is atheism, for otherwise one would have to believe that, though there is a God who is wise and just, yet the purest and greatest life that was ever lived is no better in the end than the life of a dog.[21]

Verse 17, *And if Christ hath not been raised, your faith is vain; ye are yet in your sins.*

Believing in the resurrection of Christ is absolutely mandatory for all who hope for salvation; and this applies equally to all individuals, institutions and even churches which deny it. There is no redemption apart from the belief that Jesus Christ is the Son of God, inclusive of the doctrine of the resurrection and many other necessary deductions from the prime fact of our Lord's divinity.

Verses 18-19, *Then they also that have fallen asleep in Christ have perished. If we have only hoped in Christ in this life, we are of all men most pitiable.*

The otherworldliness of Christianity shines in this. The great proposition that undergirds Christianity is that the saved shall be forever with the Lord in that upper and better world where all the problems of earth shall be solved in the light and bliss of heaven. Christianity is not to be advocated merely upon the premise that it is good psychology, or that it

---

[21]T. Teignmouth Shore, *op. cit.*, p. 347.

leads to a better life in the present world, however true these tangential benefits might be. As Barnes said, "This does not mean that Christians are unhappy, or that their religion does not produce comfort."[22] Despite the present benefits of serving Jesus Christ, including the undeniably superior virtues that are inculcated in it, and the personal joy of believing, the proposition Paul lays down here is that nobody can be truly better off from believing and advocating a lie. In the midst of all this reasoning on the resurrection, Paul discarded his line of argument for a moment, and thundered once more the apostolical oracle of Christ's resurrection (vv. 20-28).

Verse 20, *But now hath Christ been raised from the dead, the firstfruits of them that are asleep.*

The only historical fact that could have produced the phenomenon known as Christianity was that cited here, the resurrection of Christ. There are no intelligent explanations aside from this. The very existence of Christianity is proof enough that Christ actually arose from the dead. Only the spiritually blind or willfully evil mind may deny it.

"The firstfruits of them that are asleep . . ." It is this connection of Christ's resurrection with all that is implied and prophesied by it that should be noted. See under verse 16, above. One of the great Jewish festivals was just approaching, in which the firstfruits of the harvest were waved before the Lord; and, as surely as the first sheaves of the harvest carried a pledge of that harvest, so the resurrection of Christ carried a pledge of the resurrection of all men.

Verse 21, *For since by man came death, by man came also the resurrection of the dead.*

One great truth evident in the Bible is that men would never have been subject to death, if it had not been for the sin of Adam. By that one man's sin, death has fallen upon all men. The analogy pointed out in this verse is that, in view of death's having resulted from one man's sin, it is not unreasonable that the resurrection of all men should come about through one man's resurrection, that of Christ himself.

---

[22]Albert Barnes, *op. cit.*, p. 291.

Verse 22, *For as in Adam all die, so also in Christ shall all be made alive.*

This spells out the analogy stated in the previous verse. All who ever lived on earth shall rise from the dead, the wicked and the righteous alike, and all of this as a consequence of Christ's resurrection. Some would limit the "all" to them that are in Christ, leaving the wicked without any prospect of resurrection; but the total teaching of both OT and NT is against such a view. Daniel 12:2 and John 5:28, 29 teach the resurrection of all men, both the wicked and the righteous; and this, of course, is the obvious sense of "all" here which means the same in both clauses. As Barnes said, other interpretations are contrived "through reasoning and theology."[23]

Verse 23, *But each in his own order: Christ the first-fruits; then they that are Christ's, at his coming.*

"Each in his own order . . ." The word rendered order is a military word, "denoting a company."[24] Christ outranks his followers, who in turn outrank the unbelieving.

"At his coming . . ." The Second Advent will be the occasion of the general resurrection of both wicked and righteous, despite the affirmation that the "dead in Christ shall rise first" (1 Thess. 4:16). Both shall occur on the same occasion (Matt. 25:31ff); and the separation of the wicked from the righteous will take place then.

Verse 24, *Then cometh the end, when he shall deliver up the kingdom to God, even the Father; when he shall have abolished all rule and all authority and power.*

"The end . . ." means the end of the world, an event mentioned elsewhere in the NT, as in Matthew 28:20, 2 Peter 3:10, etc. See CM, p. 527.

"He shall have delivered up the kingdom . . ." The Second Advent will not be the beginning of the reign of Christ but the end of it. Millennial expectations predicated upon the supposition that Christ will reign on earth with his saints after the Second Advent cannot be harmonized with this.

---

[23]*Ibid.*, p. 295.

[24]W. E. Vine, *An Expository Dictionary of NT Words* (Old Tappan, N. J.: Fleming H. Revell Company, 1940), *in loco.*

"Shall have abolished all rule, authority, power . . ." The word "abolished" here does not in any manner suggest that all inimical powers opposed to Christ will submit to his will and obey the gospel at some time prior to the end, but that they will be abolished! Speculations by religious teachers on "how" this will be accomplished are certain to be wrong.

Verse 25, *For he must reign, till he hath put all enemies under his feet.*

This has the weight of saying that "Christ must keep on reigning till he hath put down all enemies," with the necessary deduction that he is now reigning over his kingdom which is the church.

Verse 26, *The last enemy that shall be destroyed is death.*

The general resurrection will thus occur at a time after the full and total authority of Christ has been demonstrated.

Verse 27, *For he put all things in subjection under his feet. But when he saith, All things are put in subjection, it is evident that he is excepted who did subject all things unto him.*

"For, He . . ." refers to God. The quotation is from Psalm 8:6 (LXX). "The words, spoken of man in general, are here transferred to the federal Head of humanity, the ideal and perfect God-man, Jesus Christ."[25] See CH, pp. 45-49.

"He is excepted . . ." "All things subjected to Christ" did not mean, of course, that God was subject to the Saviour, all beings of the godhead constituting a sacred unity.

Verse 28, *And when all things have been subjected unto him, then shall the Son also himself be subjected to him that did subject all things unto him, that God may be all, in all.*

It is a gross error to see this passage as reducing in any manner the status of Jesus Christ and his "equality with God" (Phil. 2:6), the thing in view here being the end of Christ's mediatorial office. At the time of his kingdom being united with godhead in heaven, the need of those special devices which were necessary in human redemption shall have disappeared. This verse marks the end of the digression which Paul

---

[25]F. W. Farrar, *op. cit.*, p. 487.

began back in verse 20. He at once resumed his argument to show the absurdity of unbelief in the resurrection of the dead.

Verse 29, *Else what shall they do that are baptized for the dead? If the dead are not raised at all, why then are they baptized for them?*

This is branded by many as a very difficult verse; but the proper regard of the third person plural pronouns in this verse makes it easy. Paul here used an *argumentum ad hominem*, that is, an argument based upon what men were doing, indicating clearly enough that some persons known to the Corinthians were practicing a baptism for the benefit of the dead; but the one thing that makes it impossible to suppose that Paul approved of such a thing is the use of the third person pronouns. There are no examples in the NT of the practice of Christians being designated as what "they" do. Concerning Christian baptism, for example, it is always "we" or "you" who were baptized and addressed in the first or second persons, never in the third person. It is still "they" not "we" who baptize for the dead!

With reference to the practice itself, nothing is known of Christians ever doing such a thing till far later in the Christian era; and, even then, it is most likely that a misinterpretation of Paul's words here was a contributing factor. Hodge flatly declared that nothing was ever known of Christians doing such a thing "before the second century."[26] Invariably throughout history, the Christian community has condemned this practice as heretical, there not being a word in the whole NT that countenances such a thing. Only the revival of the practice by the Mormons in our own times has appeared as an exception. The whole concept of proxy baptism is contradictory to biblical teaching.

The objection that Paul would not have referred to such a practice without indicating his disapproval is not well founded. In this same epistle (8:10), Paul mentioned "sitting at an idol's temple" without condemning it. Besides that, the use of any practice (for argument's sake) may be, even today, referred to without the speaker's approval of it. This writer once heard a

[26]Charles Hodge, *op. cit.*, p. 337.

pioneer preacher discoursing on the resurrection, and he said, "The Indians bury a dog and a spear with the fallen warrior; and why should they do that, if there is no resurrection?" That was exactly the *argumentum ad hominem* that Paul used here. Furthermore, Paul had already promised that he would correct certain unspecified disorders at Corinth when he returned personally to visit them (11:34); and it may be taken as certain that baptism for the dead was one of them. There are all kinds of fanciful "explanations" of the baptism mentioned here; but with reference to any of them which denies that somebody at Corinth was doing it, the plain meaning of the apostle's language here (as attested by dozens of scholars) refutes them.

Verse 30, *Why do we also stand in jeopardy every hour?*

If the apostles had not been extremely sure of the resurrection, why would any of them have endured such hardship and sufferings, even unto death? This argument is unanswerable.

Verse 31, *I protest by that glorying in you, brethren, which I have in Christ Jesus our Lord, I die daily.*

> Such a life as St. Paul's, both as regards the spiritual battles in his own soul, and the ceaseless conflict with enemies around him, was indeed a daily dying.[27]

"That glorying in you . . ." Farrar affirmed that the real meaning of this is, "by my glorying in you."[28] Paul's one reason for earthly glorying was the conversion of men to Christ. His "hope, and joy and crown of rejoicing" was the conversion of men and the establishment of churches (Rom. 15:16).

Verse 32, *If after the manner of men I fought with beasts at Ephesus, what doth it profit me? If the dead are not raised, let us eat and drink, for tomorrow we die.*

"Fought with beasts at Ephesus . . ." Scholars are divided on whether to construe this metaphorically as a reference to great persecutions and dangers Paul endured at Ephesus, or as mention of an event in which the apostle actually did so. There is no way to know, for plausible and weighty arguments may

---

[27]T. Teignmouth Shore, *op. cit.*, p. 349.
[28]F. W. Farrar, *op. cit.*, p. 488.

be deployed on either side of the question. The feeling here is that this refers to actual conflict; and Luke's not mentioning it does not deny it. There were several shipwrecks that Luke did not mention, along with many other hardships of the grand apostle. Besides that, there is a glimpse of some mortal danger to Paul from which he was saved by Priscilla and Aquila (Rom. 16:4), for which the Gentile churches throughout the Roman Empire gave thanks to God; and that mystery could be related to this. In any case, the point should not be forgotten: what was the profit of such danger and suffering endured for the sake of Christianity, if there is no resurrection of the dead?

"Eat and drink, for tomorrow we die . . ." This was Epicureanism; and Paul's words here may be construed as saying that paganism is as good as Christianity if the doctrine of the resurrection is denied.

Verse 33, *Be not deceived: Evil companionships corrupt good morals.*

Scholars identify this statement with the works of Menander, a heathen poet; but some believe the expression had passed into the Greek language as proverb. Paul's use of it here was to warn the Corinthians against any toleration of the evil teachers who were denying the resurrection; for the toleration of them was certain to have corrupted some of the church. The truth spoken is timeless and applicable to all who ever lived in any generation.

Verse 34, *Awake to soberness righteously, and sin not; for some have no knowledge of God: I speak this to move you to shame.*

Barnes said this means, "Arouse from your stupidity on this subject!"[29] The toleration of the skeptical teachers was a public disgrace to the church.

Verse 35, *But some will say, How are the dead raised? and with what manner of body do they come?*

This is more than a diatribe which frequently marked Paul's style; it is a conscious answer directed to allegations and questions actually being pressed at Corinth. Of course, it is no

---

[29]Albert Barnes, *op. cit.*, p. 309.

objection to the hope of a resurrection that men are not able to explain it; and in conscience it must be admitted that Paul did not explain it in this great passage. He did, however, prove that it is no more marvelous than many other things, some known and some unknown to men. See discussion of "How Can These Things Be?" in CJ, pp. 89-90.

Verse 36, *Thou foolish one, that which thou thyself sowest is not quickened except it die.*

The continual miracle of seedtime and harvest is not less glorious than the miracle of the ultimate resurrection, only different. Paul's reference to planting seeds that produce something far different from the seeds, yet identified with the seeds, is similar to Christ's use of the same analogy in John 12:24, where he applied it to his own death and resurrection. Can anyone understand the principle of seeds dying, growing, and producing a crop? Certainly not. Jesus himself said, "Thou knowest not how!" (Mark 4:26-29). Thus, what Paul means by this is simply that the existence of the common miracle of seeds should enable the believer to receive as truth Christ's promise of the resurrection.

"Thou foolish one . . ." It is worth noting that the word *more*, meaning "fool," is a different word from "the one that was forbidden by the Lord."[30]

Verses 37-38, *And that which thou sowest, thou sowest not the body that shall be, but a bare grain it may chance of wheat, or of some other kind; but God giveth it a body even as it pleased him, and to each seed a body of its own.*

The Greek word for "body" in these verses, and in 40, 41, is *soma*,[31] which is the same word used for a man's body. One may take a handful of various seeds which are superficially very much alike; but when they are planted an amazing difference appears. This is God's doing, "as it pleased him"; and Paul's argument must be allowed as valid, that the God who does such a thing as that also has the power to provide man with a resurrection body.

---

[30]T. Teignmouth Shore, *op. cit.*, p. 350.
[31]W. E. Vine, *op. cit., in loco.*

The Greeks despised the body; but it is everywhere respected in the NT. The mocking Greeks at Corinth denied the possibility of a resurrection, pointing out the impossibility of reassembling all the atoms of the body destroyed by fire, lost at sea, or disintegrated into dust; but the Christian holds that it is no more difficult for God to give one *another body* than it was to give him the one he now enjoys.

Verse 39, *All flesh is not the same flesh: but there is one flesh of men, and another flesh of beasts, and another flesh of birds, and another of fishes.*

It is the infinite power and diversity of God's creative ability which is stressed by these words. There is hardly any environment upon the face of the earth, sky, land or sea, which is not inhabited by creatures that God has made and sustained through the ages. Some creatures live in the depth of the sea under pressure and temperature conditions which would be fatal to a man in an instant; and so it is throughout the whole creation. As Barnes observed, "It is not necessary therefore to suppose that the body which shall be raised shall be precisely like that which we have here."[32]

Verses 40-41, *There are also celestial bodies, and bodies terrestrial: but the glory of the celestial is one, and the glory of the terrestrial is another. There is one glory of the sun, and another glory of the moon, and another glory of the stars; for one star differeth from another star in glory.*

The same meaning is apparent in these lines as in those above. "Can it be thought strange if there should be a difference between our bodies when on earth and when in heaven?"[33] God who has wrought all of the wonders of the sidereal creation, as well as all the wonders on earth, is most certainly able to perform what has been promised with regard to the resurrection. How filled with conceit and unbelief must be that mortal man, who is himself the creature made by an infinite God, and who must soon stumble into a grave, but who has the arrogance and pride to busy himself formulating

---

[32]Albert Barnes, *op. cit.*, p. 312.
[33]*Ibid.*, p. 313.

postulates about what may be possible or not for Almighty God! By such a sin Satan himself fell into condemnation.

Verses 42-44, *So also is the resurrection of the dead. It is sown in corruption; it is raised in incorruption: it is sown in dishonor; it is raised in glory: it is sown in weakness; it is raised in power: it is sown a natural body; it is raised a spiritual body. If there is a natural body, there is also a spiritual body.*

Incorruptible, glorious, powerful and spiritual shall be the new body given in the resurrection; and these qualities of it are contrasted with the corruption, dishonor and weakness of the natural body at the moment of its being "sown', in death. Paul does not say here that there is any "maybe" connected with this teaching; this reveals what is to be; and the certainty of the spiritual body's arrival at the due time in the unfolding of the Father's will is attested and prophesied by the very existence of the natural physical body itself. "If there is a natural body, there is also a spiritual body!" Men may disbelieve it if they please, but that unbelief will neither prevent nor delay the fulfillment of God's will, having no consequence at all, except in the effect it shall have upon the destiny of them that disbelieve.

Verse 45, *So also it is written, The first man Adam became a living soul. The last Adam became a life-giving spirit.*

For an extended discussion of the similarities and contrasts between Adam I and Adam II, see CR, pp. 205-212. Of course, there were far more contrasts than similarities between Adam and Christ; but the position that each holds as head of the natural creation (of man) on the one hand, and head of the spiritual creation on the other is similar.

The passage Paul quoted here is Genesis 2:17. "Living soul" is what Adam *became*; God had breathed into his nostrils the breath of life; but through disobedience Adam became this lower thing, the merely natural man. Through Christ, however, man may enjoy that higher existence which God intended from the first.

Verse 46, *Howbeit that is not first which is spiritual, but that which is natural; then that which is spiritual.*

The time sequence here applies to men now, their first existence being merely physical, the natural life derived from the great prognitor Adam in whose "image" (Gen. 5:3) all men are born. God made Adam in God's image; but after the fall, it appears that men were not born in God's image (except in a limited sense), but in the image of the fallen ancestor. Hereditary depravity is not in this, but there is certainly some kind of limitation, or tendency.

"First . . . that which is natural . . ." "This is a general law; seed-time precedes harvest; and the physical is preparatory for the spiritual."[34]

"The last Adam . . ." Johnson correctly viewed this expression as having been coined by Paul, "to indicate that there can be no third representative man, sinless, and without human father, as were both Christ and Adam.[35] G. Campbell Morgan loved to preach on "Christ, God's Last Word to Man."[36]

Verses 47-49, *The first man is of the earth, earthy: the second man is of heaven. As is the earthy, such are they also that are earthy: and as is the heavenly, such are they also that are heavenly. And as we have borne the image of the earthy, we shall also bear the image of the heavenly.*

The second man is of heaven . . ." This epic declaration is meaningless unless it teaches the preexistence of Christ, his unity with God the Father, and the virgin birth by which he identified himself with the earthy. God created Adam, but he was still earthy, having been made of the dust of the earth; but Christ had ever been with the Father. As Jesus expressed it, "I came forth and am from God" (John 8:42). And again, "I am from above: ye are of this world; I am not of this world" (John 8:23). One can only marvel at the type of scriptural illiteracy which cannot find the virgin birth in Paul, John and other portions of the NT.

"The earthy . . ." All men bear the likeness of Adam (Gen. 5:3).

---

[34]Paul W. Marsh, *A New Commentary* (Grand Rapids: Zondervan Publishing House, 1969), p. 412.

[35]S. Lewis Johnson, Jr., *op. cit.*, p. 644.

[36]G. Campbell Morgan, *God's Last Word to Man* (Old Tappan, N. J.: Fleming H. Revell Company, 1936).

The Nature of the Resurrection Body

"We shall also bear the image of the heavenly . . ." As certainly as men are like Adam and have the same physical nature that Adam possessed, that certain are they to bear the image of Jesus Christ and to possess, ultimately, exactly the same kind of spiritual body that Jesus displayed after the resurrection. A little is known of Jesus' body after the resurrection, despite the fact that it is but *little.* (1) He had flesh and bones. (2) He could appear and disappear at will through closed or locked doors. (3) He could ascend or descend. (4) He could vanish out of sight. (5) He could even change his appearance (Mark 16:12). (6) He could be recognized or not, at will. (7) He was not merely a spirit (Luke 24:39). By the words of this clause, Paul clearly stated that just as our physical bodies are like that of Adam, our spiritual bodies shall be like that of Christ. Significant also is the fact that Christ was the same person after the resurrection as he was before, indicating that there shall be no loss of personality in the resurrection state.

Verse 50, *Now this I say, brethren, that flesh and blood cannot inherit the kingdom of God; neither doth corruption inherit incorruption.*

"Flesh and blood . . ." has reference to man's present state; and this is no comment at all upon the composition of the resurrection body. Jesus had flesh and bones (Luke 24:49). This merely says that in man's mortal state, it is impossible for him to enjoy eternal life.

Verses 51-52, *Behold, I tell you a mystery: We shall not all sleep, but we shall all be changed, in a moment, in the twinkling of an eye, at the last trump: for the trumpet shall sound, and the dead shall be raised incorruptible, and we shall be changed.*

"We shall not all sleep . . ." There is nothing in this passage to support the notion that Paul believed the end to be in his own lifetime. Some of the Thessalonians got that impression from Paul's teaching; but he at once wrote them another letter to dispel such a foolish notion and to point out that great epochs of time were to unfold before the final day. By this word, Paul merely meant those living at the time of the Second Advent would undergo an instantaneous change.

"We shall all be changed . . ." Johnson and many others find grounds here for what they call "a partial rapture of the church";[37] but the meaning of "all" appears to be far too comprehensive to support such a view.

"In a moment . . ." Bruce approved the rendition "moment" in this place, calling it "perfectly correct."[38] He further said:

> The Greek word *atomos* (whence our word *atom*) means "incapable of being cut"; and Paul used it here to indicate a division of time so brief that it cannot be subdivided farther, a "split second" if you like.[39]

"The trumpet shall sound . . ." No man may say exactly what this is; but it is clear enough that God would have no need of any literal trumpet. Zechariah said, "The Lord God shall blow the trumpet" (9:14); and the symbolism would appear to be the same as when one might say, "Well, the boss blew the whistle on that practice," meaning, of course, that he stopped it. Something like that is meant here. Jesus mentioned the final day in these words: "And he shall send forth his angels with a great sound of a trumpet, and they shall gather together the elect, etc." (Matt. 24:31). Note that it was not a trumpet, but "the great sound of a trumpet." See also 1 Thessalonians 4:16. There will come the time when God will blow the trumpet on this world of ours and summon all men to the judgment of the great day.

"I tell you a mystery . . ." This term in the NT ordinarily refers to some secret hitherto unknown, but now revealed through the word of God. For a discussion of NT mysteries, see CM, p. 189, also an entire book on *The Mystery of Redemption.*[40]

Verse 53, *For this corruptible must put on incorruption, and this mortal must put on immortality.*

The certainty of the change to spiritual bodies in the resurrection is here affirmed by the use of the imperative

---

[37]S. L. Johnson, Jr., *op. cit.*, p. 645.
[38]F. F. Bruce, *Answers a Questions* (Grand Rapids: Zondervan Publishing House, 1972), p. 100.
[39]*Ibid.*
[40]See CMY in list of abbreviations.

"must" which has such significant usage in the NT. See CM, pp. 275-276.

Verses 54-55, *But when this corruptible shall have put on incorruption, and this mortal shall have put on immortality, then shall come to pass the saying that is written, Death is swallowed up in victory. O death, where is thy victory? O death, where is thy sting?*

This passage recalls the words from Hosea:

> I will ransom them from the power of the grave; I will redeem them from death. O death, I will be thy plagues; O grave, I will be thy destruction (Hosea 13:14, AV).
>
> I will ransom them from the power of Sheol; I will redeem them from death: O death, where are thy plagues? O grave, where is thy destruction? (RV).

Nearly two thousand years have passed since this apostolical lightning split the midnight darkness surrounding the tomb; and even yet there is never a day passes in any city anywhere which fails to shout this message over the dead. In Houston, where these lines are being written, it is certain that a hundred times this very week these words have echoed in the chapels and cemeteries where men gather to bury the dead; and so it is all over the world when Christ is known.

Victory in the presence of death! If men wonder why the holy faith in Jesus Christ continues from age to age, let them find at least a part of the answer in these immortal words before us.

Verse 56, *The sting of death is sin; and the power of sin is the law.*

"Sting of death is sin . . ." Sin brought death into the world as a consequence. However enticing and beautiful sin may appear to be, there is a stinger in it, as discovered by Adam and Eve, and all of their posterity.

"The strength of sin is the law . . ." As Dummelow said:

> This is true because the law reveals sin and, indeed, intensifies its power, without giving power to overcome it (Rom. 7:7-13; 8:2,3).[41]

---

[41]J. R. Dummelow, *op. cit.*, p. 920.

See CR, pp. 265-264, for discussion of the law and its relation to sin. Paul here briefly mentioned the subject that he treated at length in Romans chapter 7.

Verse 57, *But thanks be to God who giveth us the victory through our Lord Jesus Christ.*

> Oh sing unto Jehovah a new song;
> For he hath done marvelous things:
> His right hand, and his holy arm, hath wrought salvation! (Ps. 98:1).

"Through our Lord Jesus Christ . . ." In the NT this always has reference to being "in Christ" as in the next verse where Paul said "in the Lord." God's way of saving men is by their being transferred "into Christ," identified with Christ, and thus saved "as Christ." As Farrar summarized it, "Paul's hope of the resurrection rests, like all his theology, on the thought that the life of the Christian is life 'in Christ.' "[42] See CR, pp. 318ff.

Verse 58, *Wherefore, my beloved brethren, be ye stedfast, unmovable, always abounding in the work of the Lord, forasmuch as ye know that your labor is not in vain in the Lord.*

"Beloved brethren . . ." It is remarkable how frequently Paul used this term of endearment and affection. Not even the gross sins and mistakes of the sensual and carnal Corinthians could diminish his love for them nor his loving persuasion helping them to conform more perfectly to the will of Christ.

"Be ye stedfast . . ." Paul expected Christians to be able to "take it." He wrote the Ephesians, "Stand therefore" (Eph. 6:14); and the admonition is the same here. Through the ages, there has been no more necessary virtue than the ability to be steadfast amidst changing scenes and times, despite temptations and sorrows, and without regard to every "wind of doctrine" that creates some little stir among men.

"Unmovable . . ." The Christian is to be unmovable not in prejudice, but in faith.

"Abounding in the work of the Lord . . ." Far from advocating an easy way of salvation by merely believing, Paul

---

[42]F. W. Farrar, *op. cit.*, p. 493.

demanded and encouraged that the redeemed should abound continually in the Lord's work. He commanded the Philippians to "work out your own salvation with fear and trembling" (1:12). He established a pillar of truth, both at the beginning of Romans (1:5) and at the end of it (16: 26), stressing the "obedience of faith." He, like every true Christian, would have been outraged by any notion to the effect that people are "saved by faith alone."

"Your labor is not in vain . . ." What is done for Christ and his kingdom is work for God; all else is idleness. "Why stand ye here idle all day?" was the question Jesus burned into men's consciences (Matt. 20:6). They were not idle in the sense of doing nothing, but in the sense of not doing the only thing that mattered; and, alas, it must be feared that the same is true of many today.

"In the Lord . . ." This expression, or its equivalent, appears 169 times in the writings of the apostle Paul; and by that fact, it may be claimed that this is the most important phrase Paul ever wrote, because he repeated it more than any other. Salvation is "in the Lord" and nowhere else. Every man should ask himself the question, "Am I in the Lord?" As to how this relation is established, the sacred scriptures leave no doubt whatever. Men are baptized "into Christ" at a time subsequent to their having believed on the Lord Jesus Christ and having repented and confessed his name (Acts 2:38; Rom. 6:3; Gal. 3:27). There is no other way to be "in the Lord."

The conclusion of this chapter reveals it as a prime motivation of Christian service. It is unfortunate, in a sense, that its marvelous teachings are stressed almost exclusively at funerals.

CHAPTER 16

Paul abruptly left off speaking of the glorious resurrection and plunged into practical matters, giving instruction with regard to the projected contribution for the poor in Jerusalem (1-8), recommending their acceptance of Timothy, and writing a five-point summary of the whole epistle (9-13). He concluded with various greetings (14-20), and his personal salutation and signature (21-24).

Verse 1, *Now concerning the collection for the saints, as I gave order to the churches of Galatia, so also do ye.*

The proposed beneficiaries of this collection were the poor Christians in Jerusalem; and Paul had busied himself extensively in the advocacy and promotion of this gathering of funds for their relief. A number of very important considerations are suggested by this.

The reasons behind Paul's engagement in the fund-raising were as follows: (a) It had been strongly recommended at the so-called council in Jerusalem (Gal. 2:10). (b) It was drastically necessary from a humanitarian viewpoint. The persecutions that arose around the martyrdom of Stephen had left many in a state of dire need. As Adam Clarke said, "The enmity of their countrymen to the gospel of Christ led them to treat those who professed it with cruelty, and spoil them of their goods."[1] Furthermore, the excessive generosity of many during the days of that so-called communism (Acts 2:45) had brought practically the whole church to a state of destitution. Communism, even of the benevolent and non-violent kind practiced in the primitive church, has never been capable of producing anything except poverty, as attested this very day by the economic conditions of the whole Communist world. (c) As Lipscomb noted, "There was also Paul's effort to soften the prejudices of the Jewish Christians against their Gentile

---

[1]Adam Clarke, *Commentary on the Whole Bible* (New York: Carlton & Porter, 1831), Vol. VI, p. 296.

brethren."[2] (d) It was a way of demonstrating the unity of the Church. As Barclay put it, "It was a way of teaching the scattered Christians that they were not (merely) members of a congregation, but members of the church."[3] (e) It was a way of stressing giving as a vital doctrine of Christianity. (f) It was an implementation of the principle that Christians are saved to serve. (g) It was a way of strengthening the givers in the faith of Christ.

One reason for that collection, as alleged by some, is not valid. Farrar said, "It was the only way the Gentile churches could show their gratitude to the mother church!"[4] It was not Jerusalem, however, but Antioch, which was, in a sense, the mother church of the Gentile congregations; and in the light of Paul's statement that the real "mother" church is "the Jerusalem which is above" (Gal. 4:26), it is apparent that the Mother Church virus which has plagued humanity had not been any particular motivation of Paul's collection.

There could be another thing in the stress of this operation. as revealed in the NT, and that is the need for minsters of the very highest rank (Paul was an apostle) to engage at times in fund raising, a thing many of the so-called elite are stubbornly prone not to do!

"The churches of Galatia . . ." Paul's similar admonition to the Galatians is not found in the NT book of that name: and therefore it had been conveyed "either by messenger, or by a letter not preserved."[5] Any thoughtful student must allow that Paul's known letters must be only a fraction of all that he wrote, but, nevertheless, a fraction preserved to us by the infallible power of the Holy Spirit. The Galatian churches here mentioned were "those of Pisidia, Antioch, Iconium, Derbe, and Lystra (Acts 13:14, 14:13)"[6]

---

[2]David Lipscomb, *Commentary on First Corinthians* (Nashville: The Gospel Advocate Company, 1935), p. 248.

[3]William Barclay, *The Letters to the Corinthians* (Philadelphia:. The Westminster Press, 1954), p. 181.

[4]F. W. Farrar, *Pulpit Commentary* (Grand Rapids: Wm. B. Eerdmans Publishing Company, 1950), Vol. 19, p. 549.

[5]J. R. Dummelow, *Commentary on the Holy Bible* (New York: The Macmillan Company, 1937), p. 921.

[6]*Ibid.*

Verse 2, *Upon the first day of the week let each one of you lay by him in store, as he may prosper, that no collections be made when I come.*

"Upon the first day of the week . . ." The astounding remark by Farrar that "This verse can hardly imply any religious observance of the Sunday"[7] is to be rejected. That is exactly what it does imply. Macknight translated this clause, "On the first day of every week";[8] Grosheide declared the meaning to be "On every Sunday";[9] and Hodge said it means, "The collection was to be made every Lord's day."[10] Pliny's letter to Trajan bears testimony to the fact that the Christians of his day (prior to his death in 113 A.D.) were accustomed to meet on "an appointed day";[11] and here that appointed day is somewhat inadvertantly identified by the apostle Paul as every Sunday.

There is no fact connected with Christianity any more certain than the apostolical custom of worship services every Lord's day. Beginning with the very day of our Lord's resurrection, and continuing upon successive Sundays thereafter (John 20:18,24,26), worship was observed by the apostles. A careful study of Acts 20:6,7, 21:4 and 28:14 discloses not merely that the worship and observance of the Lord's supper took place on Sundays, but also that the Lord's supper was never observed by the apostolic church on any other day. See CL, p. 517. Added to that testimony is the undeniable meaning of the verse before us.

"Let each one of you lay by him in store . . ." It is generally admitted that every Christian was to participate in the giving, but "by him" has given the commentators a lot of trouble. Thus Johnson thought it was "a reference to the home-giving

---

[7]F. W. Farrar, *op. cit.*, p.549.

[8]James Macknight, *Apostolical Epistles and Commentary* (Grand Rapids: Baker Book House, 1969), p. 291.

[9]F. W. Grosheide, *The New International Commentary* (Grand Rapids: Wm. B. Eerdmans Publishing Company, 1953), p. 398.

[10]Charles Hodge, *First Epistle to the Corinthians* (Grand Rapids:. The Wm. B. Eerdman, Publishing Company, 1974), p. 363.

[11]Henry Bettensen, *Documents of the Christian Church* (New York & London: Oxford University Press, 1947), p. 6.

was to be private giving."[12] The word "home" is not in the Greek text, nor is such an idea to be found there. As Lipscomb and many others have noted, "The idea that the storing was to be at home is incompatible with the idea that 'no collections be made when I come.'"[13] "The words do not mean to *lay by at home*, but to *lay by himself*."[14] This indicates that the amount of giving was to be determined by the man *himself*, not by any tax or suggestion from others. The word rendered "in store" means "putting in the treasury . . . the common treasury, not every man's own house."[15]

As one studies some of the so-called modern translations of this place, it is clear that they are not translations in any sense, but human commentary substituted for the word of God. Even the RSV is seriously at fault in handling this passage. As Wallace said, "They changed Paul's words from 'lay by him in store' to 'put something aside and save'; but in 1952 they revised their own rendition to 'store up'"[16]

For its hermeneutical value, the following list of Greek words translated "giving" or its equivalent are compiled from William Barclay:

Logia (1 Corinthians 16:1) means "a special collection" (Churches which do not like special appeals, take note).
Charis (1 Corinthians 16:3) means bounty or "free gift freely given."
Koinonia (2 Corinthians 8:4; 9:13; Romans 15:6) means "fellowship."
Daakoma (2 Corinthians 8:4; 9:1, 12, 13) means practical Christian service." Our word "deacon" is related to it.
Hadrotes (2 Corinthians 8:20) means "abundance."
Eulogia (2 Corinthians 9:5) means "bounty" in the sense of what is given joyfully
Leitiurgia (2 Corinthians 9:12) means giving of money or services voluntarily, especially some large gift.
Eleemosune (Acts 24:17) is the Greek word for "alms." Our word "eleemosynary" as applied to charitable institutions comes from this.
Prosphora (Acts 24:17) means "offering or sacrifice." Thus what is given to the needy, or to the church, is a sacrifice or offering to God.

---

[12]S. Lewis Johnson, Jr., *Wycliffe Bible Commentary* (Chicago: The Moody Press, 1971)' p. 646.
[13]David Lipscomb, *op. cit.*, p. 249.
[14]Charles Hodge, *op., cit.*, p.364.
[15]*Ibid.*
[16]Foy E. Wallace, Jr., *A Review of the New Versions* (Fort Worth: The Foy E. Wallace, Jr., Publications, 1973), p. 436.

This impressive list is a testimony to the importance of giving as laid down in the NT; and any preacher will find such a catalogue as this helpful and stimulating.

A concluding line on this verse is from Hodge:.

> The only reason that can be assigned for requiring the thing to be done on the first day of the week, is that on that day the Christians were accustomed to meet, and what each one had laid aside from his weekly gains could be treasured up, i.e., put into the common treasury of the church.[17]

"As he may prosper . . ." This does not mean that only the prosperous should give, but that every man, in the extent of his prosperity, should give to the proposed collection.

In the whole matter of Christian giving, these verses indicate that (1) all should participate, (2) according to the ability of each, and (3) that it should be done regularly and continually.

Verse 3, *And when I arrive, whomsoever ye shall approve, them will I send with letters to carry your bounty unto Jerusalem.*

Paul did not propose to take charge of the contribution himself, suggesting here that men duly appointed by the congregations should with proper screening and recommendation be dispatched with the money to its destination. The care of the apostle to avoid all appearance of improper conduct in such a thing should be noted. He avoided all such suspicion of misappropriation of the funds. A list of the seven faithful men appointed to carry the money is found in Acts 20:4, along with a list of the various congregations they represented.

Verse 4, *And if it be meet for me to go also, they shall go with me.*

Macknight thought that Paul here "insinuated his inclination"[18] to favor an invitation to be in the group conveying the funds; and, of course, as it turned out, he was included. The

---

[17]*Ibid.*
[18]James Macknight, *op. cit.*, p. 293.

notion that Paul meant that "if the amount was large enough"[19] he would be willing to go seems to be unjustified.

Verse 5, *But I will come unto you, when I shall have passed through Macedonia; for I pass through Macedonia.*

This evidently indicates a change in Paul's plans to visit Corinth; because in 2 Corinthians 1:15ff, there seems to be a critical attitude accusing the apostle of vacillating; but his postponement of his visit was founded in the highest wisdom. He would give them a little time to get their house in order before he came.

Verse 6, *But with you it may be that I shall abide, or even winter, that ye may set me forward on my journey whithersoever I go.*

The intention of spending some time at Corinth was fulfilled. "This he afterward found himself able to do" (Acts 20:2,3).[20]

"Set me forward on my journey . . ." This is not a hint that he would expect to receive traveling expenses, rather having reference to the custom of the Christians accompanying departing guests for some distance at the time of their leaving, as in Acts 15:3, 17:15, and Romans 15:24.

Verses 7-9, *For I do not wish to see you now by the way; for I hope to tarry a while with you, if the Lord permit. But I will tarry at Ephesus until Pentecost; for a great and effectual door is opened unto me, and there are many adversaries.*

"I do not wish to see you . . ." The reason given was that he desired a longer visit than was possible at present; but this was also related to the deplorable conditions at Corinth. A short visit would not give sufficient time for working out all of the problems; besides, given time for the letter he was writing to have its effect, there might be fewer problems to solve at a later time.

"If the Lord permit . . ." Paul's plans were made like those of any other Christian, subject to the sovereign will of God; and

---

[19]Charles Hodge, *op. cit.*, p. 365.
[20]John William Russell, *Compact Commentary on the NT* (Grand Rapids; Baker Book House, 1964), p. 434.

this was fittingly recognized by the apostle. The notion that the Holy Spirit was directing on a day-to-day basis every move that Paul made is surely denied by these words.

"At Ephesus until Pentecost . . ." Pentecost was one of the three great national feasts of the Jews which fell in the May-June period. For full discussion of Pentecost, see CA, pp. 31-35.

"A great and effectual door . . ." The marvelous opportunity for Paul at Ephesus was one of the reasons assigned for his intention of staying longer.

"And there are many adversaries . . ." To some men, this hardly would have appeared as a reason for staying; but Paul reasoned that where Satan had stirred up great opposition to the truth, there must also be great opportunities for saving men. The bold and dauntless courage of Paul shines in a remark like this. There are many NT accounts of the enemies he encountered and vanquished (Acts 20:19; 19:23, etc.).

Verse 10, *Now if Timothy comes see that he be with you without fear; for he worketh the work of the Lord, as I also do.*

"Without fear . . ." Paul's concern that Timothy might encounter some cause of fear at Corinth might have sprung from the fierce partisanship in the church there, or from the youth, inexperience and timidity of Timothy, or even from a combination of both.

"The work of the Lord, as I also do . . ." No higher recommendation could have been written for anyone than this. The Noble Timothy was a loyal and able helper of the apostle throughout his ministry.

Verse 11, *Let no man therefore despise him. But set him forward on his journey in peace, that he may come unto me: for I expect him with the brethren.*

This was a command that the Corinthians should accord full honors to the apostle's helper, a duty that probably needed to be brought to their attention. Factionalism always results in the neglect of obvious duties. Paul expected Timothy to rejoin him at Ephesus within a short time.

Verse 12, *But as touching Apollos the brother, I besought him much to come unto you with the brethren: and it was not at all his will to come now; but he will come when he shall have opportunity.*

This verse is significant in showing that Paul and Apollos were on friendly terms with each other and that neither Paul nor Apollos was in any manner responsible for the ugly factions that had grown up around their names at Corinth. Paul's desire that Apollos should go to Corinth might have been prompted by the thought that he could give valuable aid in correcting the Corinthian disorders. Also, as some believe, it is possible that communications to Paul from Corinth had requested Apollos to come. Despite their love and affection for each other, however, Apollos was not a pupil of Paul's and felt justified in denying the apostle's request, but promising to go later.

Verses 13-14, *Watch ye, stand fast in the faith, quit you like men, be strong. Let all that you do be done in love.*

As McGarvey declared, "In these brief . . . phrases, Paul sums up the burden of this entire epistle."[21]

"Watch ye . . ." Although originally directed as an admonition to Corinth, this is a timeless duty of all Christians. The things they were to watch against were (1) the danger of division, (2) the deception of false teachers, (3) the atheistic denials of the resurrection, (4) the failure of love of the brethren, etc.

"Stand fast in the faith . . ." It is deplorable that the RSV renders this "Stand firm in your faith"; for what Paul plainly meant was that they should not depart from the Christian faith. This is the marching order for every Christian of all ties and places. Paul himself gave this the highest priority, saying near the end of life that "I have kept the faith" (2 Tim. 4:7).

"Quit you like men . . ." This carries the weight of "Stop acting like spiritual infants, quarreling, boasting and indulging yourselves without discipline!" Many church problems are due to pure infantilism on the part of members who do not grow up spiritually.

---

[21]J. W. McGarvey, *Commentary on First Corinthians* (Cincinnati:. The Standard Publishing Company, 1916), p. 164.

"Be strong . . ." Strength is manifested by courageous and unwavering loyalty to the word of God, by the resistance of temptation, by fleeing from it, by regular and faithful attendance at worship service, by constant and liberal giving, by loving consideration of the rights, opinions and needs of others, and by the repudiation of the world's value judgments.

"Let all that ye do be done in love . . ." This summarizes the teaching of the whole 13th chapter. A constant and unfeigned love of the Lord, of his church as a whole, and of its individual members is the mark of a strong Christian. Love is "the greatest" because it is always marked by obedience. See under 13:13.

Verse 15, *Now I beseech you, brethren (ye know the house of Stephanas, that it is the firstfruits of Achaia, and that they have set themselves to minister unto the saints.)*

Evidently, Stephanas had been baptized while traveling at Athens; for Paul's first visit to Achaia (at Athens) resulted in the baptism of Dionysius, Damaris, "certain men" and "others"; thus the name of Stephanas must be added to those. Here it appears that later his entire house (as many as were adults) had also obeyed the gospel. The position advocated by some to the effect that Paul depreciated the results at Athens (Acts I7:34) is rejected. It is far more likely that Stephanas was among the "certain men" mentioned by Luke.

"Have set themselves to minister . . ." Farrar recorded a curious opinion that Stephanas, Fortunatus and Achaicus were "perhaps slaves of the household of Chloe";[22] and that this paragraph might have been written to protect them against the wrath of the Corinthians due to their having delivered to Paul an account of disorders in Corinth (1:11). The origin of that supposition is not known. In any case, the men mentioned (especially the household of Stephanas) were giving diligent service to the church; and Paul ordered them respected.

Verse 16, *That ye also be in subjection unto such, and to every one that helpeth in the work and laboreth.*

---

[22]F W. Farrar, *op. cit.*, p. 551.

Evidently there was some basis for fearing that this advice was needful; and the surmise that they might have been slaves could be correct, as there were many slaves among the churches of that era.

Verse 17, *And I rejoice at the coming of Stephanas and Fortunatus and Achaicus: for that which was lacking on your part they supplied.*

"Fortunatus . . ." This man is nowhere else mentioned in the NT; but Clement of Rome (30-100 A.D.) credited him with having been one of the messengers by whom Clement sent a letter (The First Epistle of Clement) to the Christians at Corinth.[23]

"They supplied . . ." Dummelow paraphrased the thought as "Their visit has made up for your absence."[24]

Verse 18, *For they refreshed my spirit and yours: acknowledge ye therefore them that are such.*

It is not clear, exactly, what Paul meant by the statement that these men "refreshed" (past tense) the spirit of the Corinthians in the same manner of his own refreshment by their visit; but the interpretation of Meyer as quoted by Hodge may be correct: "You owe (to them) whatever in my letter serves to refresh you."[25]

"Them that are such . . ." has reference to all persons of good will and Christian character who, by their very presence on earth, serve to refresh and encourage the followers of Christ the Lord.

Verse 19, *The churches of Asia salute you. Aquila and Prisca salute you much in the Lord, with the church that is in their house.*

"Aquila and Prisca . . ." See CR, pp. 511-13 for comment on this distinguished couple. The whole world of Gentile Christians were under a debt of thanks to them for having saved Paul's life, an event of which absolutely nothing is known; but

---

[23]Clement of Rome in *Ante-Nicene Fathers* (Grand Rapids: Wm. B. Eerdmans Publishing Company), Vol. I, p. 21.

[24]J. R. Dummelow, *op. cit.*, p. 921.

[25]Charles Hodge, *op. cit.*, p. 371.

the NT affords several splendid glimpses of this remarkable Christian couple.

"And the church that is in their house . . ." Prisca and Aquila, to follow the order Paul himself sometimes used, were of sufficient wealth and generosity to provide a meeting place for Christians in their residence, a thing they did both in Rome and at Ephesus. Russell said that "It is probably that there were as yet no special buildings for Christians";[26] in fact, Barclay went much further, declaring that "It is, in fact, not until the third century that we hear about a church building at all!"[27]

"The churches of Asia salute you . . ." This is a reference to the proconsular province of Asia, and not to the continent.

Verse 20, *All the brethren salute you. Salute one another with a holy kiss.*

"A holy kiss . . ." Why did this lovely custom, which certainly prevailed in those times, disappear? As Barclay said: "(1) It was liable to abuse, and (2) it was liable to misinterpretation by heathen slanders, and (3) the church itself became less and less of a fellowship."[28]

This custom is mentioned in 2 Corinthians 13:12, Romans 16:16, and in 1 Peter 5:14; and the feeling persists that the third reason cited by Barclay, above, is the principal cause of its disappearance. Christians do not always love one another as they should. Yet it must also be allowed that the apostolical order of such a thing was related to the customs of the times and should not be construed as binding in times and cultures as diverse from theirs as is ours.

Verse 21, *The salutation of me Paul with mine own hand.*

This was Paul's authentication of the epistle, his signature. Paul's letters were usually written by a secretary, an amanuensis, probably Sosthenes in the case of this epistle (1:1). Tertius wrote Romans (16:22); and Paul also wrote the salutation and signature of 2 Thessalonians (3:17), indicating that an unnamed amanuensis wrote that epistle also.

---

[26]John William Russell, *op. cit.*, p. 435.
[27]William Barclay, *op. cit.* p. 187.
[28]*Ibid.*, p. 188.

Verses 22-23, *If any man loveth not the Lord, let him be anathema. Marana tha. The grace of the Lord Jesus Christ be with you.*

"Anathema . . ." means a thing accursed, leading to the necessary deduction that a refusal to love the Lord makes one an enemy of God.

"Marana tha . . ." The comment of F. F. Bruce on this expression is as follows:

> If this word is divided as *Marana tha*, it means "Our Lord come"; but if we divide it *Marana tha*, it means "Our Lord has come." It is an Aramaic phrase which found its way into the liturgy of the church from its earliest days.[29]

The point to be emphasized is that this expression just as easily means "Our Lord has come" as it does the other proposition, "Our Lord come." There is no need whatever, then, to accept as binding the latter meaning as indicated in RV, RSV, and other versions, leading to the hurtful and erroneous idea that the apostles believed the Second Advent was at hand. Phillips translated this, "May the Lord come soon."

It is far preferable to divide the word *Maran atha*, as in the King James Version, giving the true meaning that "Our Lord has come in his incarnation." The scholars who prefer the other division are influenced by some of the literature (unbiblical) of ancient times in which the other division is the usual one; but Bruce explained that, by early post-apostolic times, these verses had become a kind of liturgy used at the Lord's table; and in *that usage*, it had reference to the Lord's coming to be with his followers in the assembly, as he had promised (Matt. 18:20). Thus, upon examination of this, it is certain that there is no reference whatever in this word to the Second Advent.

"The grace of the Lord Jesus Christ be with you . . ." For a discussion of this characteristically Pauline greeting, see CR, p. 13. This beautiful greeting, which Paul so frequently used, was not enough in this first epistle to Corinth. Paul had

---

[29]F. F. Bruce, *Answers to Questions* (Grand Rapids: Zondervan Publishing House, 1972), p. 100.

written some of the sternest rebukes in the holy scriptures, and he had borne down upon them with all of his apostolical power to force a correction of their shameful abuses; therefore, he would not close with the usual greeting, adding to it an affirmation of his love for every one of them.

Verse 24, *My love be with you all in Christ Jesus. Amen.*

"In Christ Jesus . . ." This phrase beyond all others is the badge and signature of the gospel Paul preached. The whole book of Ephesians, practically, is founded upon the conception inherent in this phrase which so abounds in his writings. If one is "in Christ" and if one is "found in him" (Phil. 3:9), salvation is assured and heaven is certain! It was that relationship to the Corinthians as his fellow-members of Christ's spiritual body to which Paul appealed in this final loving word. Amen.

BIBLIOGRAPHY

The following authors and sources were quoted in the comments on 1 Corinthians:

Barclay, William, *The Letters to the Corinthians* (Philadelphia: The Westminster Press, 1954).

Barnes, Albert, *Notes on the New Testament* (Grand Rapids: Baker Book House, 1949).

Bettenson, Henry, *Documents of the Christian Church* (New York & London: Oxford University Press, 1947).

Bruce, A. B., *St. Paul's Conception of Christianity* (New York: Charles Scribner's Sons, 1898).

Bruce, F. F., *The Book of Acts* (Grand Rapids: Wm. B. Eerdmans Publishing Co., 1954).

Bruce, F. F., *Answers to Questions* (Grand Rapids: Zondervan Publishing House, 1972).

Bruce, F. F., *Epistle to the Hebrews* (Grand Rapids: Wm. B. Eerdmans Publishing Company, 1967).

Campbell, Alexander, *Acts of the Apostles* (Austin: Firm Foundation Publishing House, 1858).

Clarke, Adam, *Commentary on the Whole Bible* (New York: Carlton & Porter, 1831).

Clement of Alexandria, *Ante-Nicene Fathers* (Grand Rapids: Wm. B. Eerdmans Publishing Co., 1956).

Clement of Rome, *Ante-Nicene Fathers* (Grand Rapids: Wm. B. Eerdmans Publishing Co., 1956).

Craig, Clarence Tucker, *Interpreter's Bible* (New York: Abingdon Press, 1953).

De Hoff, George W., *Sermons on First Corinthians* (Murfreesboro, Tenn.: The Christian Press, 1947).

De Welt, Don, *Acts Made Actual* (Joplin, Mo.: College Press, 1958).

Dummelow, J. R., *Commentary on the Holy Bible* (New York: The Macmillan Company, 1937).

Echols, Eldred, Private Manuscript: *The Head Covering of First Corinthians 11,* prepared by faculty and Bible students of South Africa Bible School, Benoni, South Africa, 1968. Abbreviated EE.

Emphatic Diaglott (Brooklyn: International Bible Students Association).

Farrar, F. W., *Pulpit Commentary* (Grand Rapids: Wm. B. Eerdmans Publishing Co., 1950).

Goodspeed, Edgar J., *The New Testament, An American Translation* (Chicago: The University of Illinois Press 1923).

Grosheide, F. W., *The New International Commentary* (Grand Rapids: Wm. B. Eerdmans Publishing Co., 1953).

Guthrie, Donald, *The New Bible Commentary* (Grand Rapids: Wm. B. Eerdmans Publishing Co., 1970).

Halley, Henry H., *Bible Handbook* (Grand Rapids: Zondervan Pub. House, 1927).

Hillyer, Norman, *The New Bible Commentary,* Revised (Grand Rapids: Wm. B. Eerdmans Publishing Co., 1967).

Hobbs, Herschel H., *An Exposition of the Gospel of Luke* (Grand Rapids: Baker Book House, 1966).

Hodge, Charles, *An Exposition of the First Epistle to the Corinthians* (Grand Rapids: Wm. B. Eerdmans Publishing Co., 1974).

International Standard Bible Encyclopaedia (Chicago: The Howard-Severance Company, 1915). Abbreviated ISBE.

Johnson, S. Lewis, Jr., *Wycliffe Bible Commentary* (Chicago: Moody Press, 1971).

Kaufmann, Helen L., *The Story of Mozart* (New York: Grossett & Dunlap, Publishers, 1955).

Kelcy, Raymond C., *First Corinthians* (Austin: R. B. Sweet Company, Inc., 1967).

Lange, John Peter, *Commentary on Acts* (Grand Rapids: Zondervan Publishing House, 1866).

Lipscomb, David, *Commentary on First Corinthians* (Nashville: The Gospel Advocate Company, 1935).

Mackay, John, *God's Order* (New York: The Macmillan Company, 1953).

Macknight, James, *Apostolical Epistles and Commentary* (Grand Rapids: Baker Book House, 1969).

McGarvey, J. W., *Commentary on First Corinthians* (Cincinnati: Standard Publishing Company, 1916).

Marsh, Paul W., *A New Commentary* (Grand Rapids: Zondervan Publishing Company, 1969).

Marshall, Alfred, *The Nestle Greek Text with a Literal English Translation* (Grand Rapids: Zondervan Publishing House, 1958).

Metz, Donald S., *Beacon Bible Commentary* (Kansas City: Beacon Hill Press, 1968).

Morgan, G. Campbell, *God's Last Word to Man* (Old Tappan, N. J.: The Fleming H. Revell Company, 1936).

Morris, Leon, *Tyndale Commentary* (Grand Rapids: Wm. B. Eerdmans Publishing Company, 1958).

Russell, John William, *Compact Commentary on the New Testament* (Grand Rapids: Baker Book House, 1964).

Shore, T. Teignmouth, *Ellicott's Commentary on the Whole Bible* (Grand Rapids: Zondervan Publishing House, 1959).

Vine, W. E., *An Expository Dictionary of New Testament Words* (Old Tappan, N. J.: Fleming H. Revell Company, 1940).

Wallace, Foy E., Jr., *A Review of the New Versions* (Fort Worth: The Foy E. Wallace, Jr., Publications, 1973).

Wesley, John, *One Volume Commentary* (Grand Rapids: Baker Book House, 1972).

West, Kenneth S., *Word Studies from the Greek New Testament* (Grand Rapids: Wm. B. Eerdmans Publishing Company, 1973).

INDEX

*Indicates special article on subject thus marked.

2
Corinthians

INTRODUCTION

Reference is made to the introduction to 1 Corinthians, since all that is said there with reference to the authorship and authenticity of that epistle is also true of this.

Authorship: "That the Second Epistle is a genuine work of the apostle Paul has seldom been seriously disputed."[1] Furthermore, even in the instances in which radical scholars have questioned its authenticity, the result has been the discredit of themselves, rather than the erosion of the confidence with which the Christians of all ages have received both these epistles as absolutely canonical and authentic works of the blessed Paul. "That the apostle Paul was the author of what is now known as 2 Corinthians is not a matter of dispute in reputable scholarly circles."[2] Both external and internal evidence of its genuineness are overwhelmingly sufficient. "It would be difficult to find a composition more convincingly impressed with the personality of its author."[3]

Date: Hughes gave the date of 2 Corinthians as "the autumn of 57 A.D."[4] Macknight favored "the summer of 57 A.D."[5] Lipscomb set it in "the latter part of 57 A.D."[6] The discovery of the fragment of a limestone tablet at Delphi in 1905, fixing the date of Gallio's coming to Corinth as proconsul in the year 51 A.D.[7] has led to an adjustment of the usually accepted date for 2 Corinthians. As Tasker said, "The Second Epistle to the Corinthians was almost certainly written in the late autumn of A.D. 56."[8]

---

[1]J. R. Dummelow, *Commentary on the Holy Bible* (New York: The Macmillan Company, 1937), p. 924.

[2]Philip E. Hughes, *Paul's Second Epistle to the Corinthians* (Grand Rapids: Wm. B. Eerdmans Publishing Co., 1962), p. xv.

[3]*Ibid.*

[4]*Ibid.*

[5]James Macknight, *Apostolical Epistles with Commentary* (Grand Rapids: Baker Book House, 1969), Vol. II, p. 308.

[6]David Lipscomb, *Second Corinthians* (Nashville: Gospel Advocate Co.), p. 13.

[7]Jack P. Lewis, *Historical Backgrounds of Bible History* (Grand Rapids: Baker Book House, 1971), p. 154.

[8]R. V. G. Tasker, *The Second Epistle of Paul to the Corinthians* (Grand Rapids: Wm. B. Eerdmans Publishing Co., 1958), p. 15.

Unity of 2 Corinthians: The irresponsible speculations and denials of radical scholars in the first half of this century are no longer of any significance. As Hughes pointed out, there was a time when to question the unity of 2 Corinthians "was to be very much in the fashion, but now a swing back to the traditional view of the letter's integrity is noticeable."[9] Hughes went on to name a number of the outstanding scholars of today who declared that "2 Corinthians is beyond doubt a unity."[10] There has never existed even the slightest evidence to the contrary. The epistle has come down through history as a unit; and the fulminations of critics who based their theory of a chopped-up letter containing fragments of other documents solely upon internal characteristics of the epistle have been repeatedly refuted and frustrated. Tasker summed it up by saying, "It is our duty to approach the Second Epistle to the Corinthians as a unity."[11]

How many letters? First Corinthians refers to a letter Paul had written, and which had been misunderstood (5:9), a letter which was lost, no copy of it having survived. Beyond this, however, this student is not willing to go to the extent of postulating another lost letter, usually referred to by scholars as "the severe letter." The theory of such a letter is founded upon a misreading of 2:5-9; and for a discussion of this see the notes under those verses. That 1 Corinthians itself may be identified as the "severe letter" of 2:5-9 and 7:8 is evident in the fact that many of the wisest scholars have been doing so for many generations. Even some who have postulated the "severe letter" as being another lost document have candidly admitted that such a postulation "is not necessary."[12] Again, it should be reiterated that no evidence of any kind has ever been discovered that lends the slightest credibility to the existence of a lost "severe letter." The true instincts of faith in Christ lead automatically to the rejection of the kind of wild guessing which marks the works of critical scholars trying to support a hypothesis. Once the imagination of the lost severe letter is accepted as a fact, then the explanations of what was in it

---

[9]Philip E. Hughes, *op. cit.*, p. xxi.
[10]*Ibid.*, p. xxii.
[11]R. V. G. Tasker, *op. cit.*, p. 35.
[12]*Ibid.*, p. 18.

surpass all the boundaries of likelihood or reason. All of the dogmatic assertions of what was "probably" in that lost letter may be set aside as having no value whatever. They are not even good reading.

Occasion of writing: All that is certainly known of the occasion for the writing of 2 Corinthians is that it was written about a year after 1 Corinthians. After the riot at Ephesus, Paul found it necessary to leave there for Macedonia; but, in spite of the fact that wonderful opportunity opened to him at Troas, where he had stopped en route, his anxieties regarding the situation in Corinth began to press upon him very heavily. It may be assumed that he had received some news at intervals after the 1 Corinthian letter had been delivered; but the question of whether or not they would obey his commands still remained in Paul's mind. The mention of the expected coming of Titus to Troas, where Paul had hoped to meet him, indicates that Titus might have been working with the situation at Corinth for some time; but, as preachers often do, Titus had neglected to write Paul any real news of what had taken place. Paul, therefore, could not settle down for a preaching tour in Troas; but, instead, he decided to strike out through Macedonia in search of his brother Titus. He met him, supposedly at Philippi, learned the glad news of the obedience of the Corinthians, and promptly wrote 2 Corinthians. Paul's supposed reference to "the severe letter" in 7:8 is quite applicable to the severe admonitions and apostolical condemnations in the canonical first letter; and it is a thousand times more reasonable to suppose that the matchless words of that inspired epistle produced the change at Corinth than to attribute their repentance to some speculative "bawling out" administered in a letter supposedly lost.

Is the "severe" letter incorporated in this Second Epistle, beginning at 10:1? Absolutely no! The very existence of any "severe" letter must be denied, as Hughes so ably demonstrated; and the hypothesis that it did exist is worthless as the basis for another hypothesis to the effect that a considerable fragment of it became a part of 2 Corinthians. In this monstrous hypothesis built upon another hypothesis, the radical critics have elaborated an absurdity. It would seem that the fallacy of 2 Corinthians being a "scissors and paste" job, like those of modern critics, was concocted out of utter ignorance or total disregard of the way in which ancient manuscripts were produced. How foolish is the notion that "some leaves of one letter got mixed up with another"; when, as a matter of fact, Paul's letters were written on parchment in the form of a roll; and there were no "leaves"! As Munch said of the alleged interpolation beginning at 10:1, "This assumption will not hold water."[13]

Criticisms of Paul: It is clear that 2 Corinthians was Paul's response to vicious and untruthful slanders alleged against him by false teachers and savage partisans at Corinth. These will be noted in the text of the commentary as the evidence of them occurs; but this summary of them should be kept in mind: (1) some questioned his credentials as a true apostle; (2) they alleged vacillation and cowardice on his part, due to his change of plans; (3) they hinted charges of irregularity in his handling the collection for the poor in Jerusalem; (4) they charged him with conscious inferiority, citing the fact that he did not preach for pay; (5) they demeaned his personal appearance and made fun of his sermons, etc., etc. It is not hard to see in such evil slurs the hand of the Jewish hierarchy in Jerusalem. They never missed any opportunity of pursuit and harassment of their former sheriff who became the most gifted of apostles.

Nature of the epistle: There is no doubt that this letter creates and sustains an emotional impact nowhere exceeded in the NT. It is a letter of "profound spiritual riches."[14] F. W. Farrar stated that:

> As *hope* is the keynote of the Epistles to the Thessalonians, *joy* of that to the Philippians, *faith* of that to the Romans, *heavenly things* to that of the Ephesians, *affliction* is the predominant word and thought in the Second Epistle to Corinthians.[15]

Paul was a man of absolute integrity; and, as an apostle of Christ, one of the most gifted who ever lived. When such a man

---

[13]Johannes Munck, *Paul and the Salvation of Mankind* (London, 1958), pp. 170ff.

[14]Philip E. Hughes, *op. cit.*, p. xxxv.

[15]F. W. Farrar, *The Second Epistle to the Corinthians*, Pulpit Commentary (Grand Rapids: Wm. B. Eerdmans Publishing Co., 1950), Vol. 19, *2 Cor.*, p. ii.

was subjected to the attack of vicious and unprincipled enemies, his very soul was outraged. The pouring out of his impassioned defense in this letter is as eloquent and moving a dissertation as was ever penned upon earth. Even beyond that, the fire of his inspiration illuminates every line of it.

Outline: The epistle falls naturally into three divisions. Chapters 1-7 stress the joy and relaxation that Paul felt upon receiving the good news of the success of his corrective efforts in Corinth. Chapters 8-9 are principally concerned with the promotion of the collection for the poor saints in Jerusalem. Chapters 10-13 contain Paul's impassioned and vehement defense of his apostleship. The logical unity of these three sections will become starkly evident as they are studied.

Abbreviations: These are the same as those already listed in the introduction to 1 Corinthians.

CHAPTER 1

After the salutation (vv. 1-2), this chapter is wholly given to Paul's affirmation of his absolute sincerity and integrity. As Hughes said, "The import of verses 3-11 seems to have been missed by many commentators."[1] In the very forefront of Paul's defense regarding his coming to Corinth stands this amazing record of his affliction which had made it *impossible* for him to come. Therefore, this record of that dreadful happening in Asia is a definite and convincing refutation of all charges of insincerity on his part. Verses 12-14 have the dogmatic answer that in the case of the apostle Paul, "There were no hidden actions in his life . . . there were no hidden motives in his life . . . and there were no hidden meanings in any of his words."[2] A further explanation of the necessities which had entered into certain changes in his plans was given in verses 15-24.

Verse 1, *Paul, an apostle of Christ Jesus through the will of God, and Timothy our brother, unto the church of God which is at Corinth, with all the saints that are in the whole of Achaia.*

"Paul, an apostle . . ." In nine of the thirteen (fourteen) epistles of Paul, the affirmation of his apostleship stands in the salutation. Thus, as Lipscomb said, "He used it (the title of apostle) in all but five of his letters."[3] (Lipscomb counted Hebrews as Pauline.) No title of Paul was given in either of the Thessalonians or Hebrews. To the Philippians he spoke of himself and Timothy as "servants of Jesus Christ"; and to Philemon he called himself "a prisoner of Jesus Christ." It was most appropriate that in this epistle, wherein a major section concerns the vindication of his rights as an apostle, and to a community where his authority was being challenged, this

---

[1]Philip E. Hughes, *Paul's Second Epistle to the Corinthians* (Grand Rapids: Wm. B. Eerdmans Publishing Co., 1962), p. 9.

[2]William Barclay, *The Letters to the Corinthians* (Philadelphia: The Westminster Press, 1954), p. 194.

[3]David Lipscomb, *Second Corinthians* (Nashville: The Gospel Advocate Co.), p. 19.

bold declaration of his apostolical authority should stand at the very beginning.

"Timothy our brother . . ." Sosthenes stands in the salutation to the Corinthians in the first epistle, as Timothy was not at that time with Paul. It may be assumed that Sosthenes was not present when this letter was sent. Timothy had aided in the evangelization of Corinth when the church was founded there; but he did not share any apostolical authority with Paul in this letter. Timothy was a faithful and devoted helper of the apostle; but the contrast between "an apostle of Jesus Christ" and "our brother" is meaningful.

"The church of God which is at Corinth . . ." In view of all the disorders and sins which beset the Christians who received this letter, it may be asked, How, in conscience, could Paul refer to them as the "church of God"? John Calvin's explanation is as good as any that has come down through history. He said:

> Paul discerned among them the doctrine of the gospel, baptism and the Lord's Supper . . . They retained the fundamental doctrine, adored the one god, and invoked in the name of Christ; and since they placed the confidence of their salvation in Christ, and had a ministry that was not altogether corrupted, the church still continued to exist there.[4]

It is apparent everywhere in the NT that the legitimacy of congregations and Christians alike depended more upon the ideals and intentions of their heart than upon any perfection in the realization of them. All Christians should take encouragement from this.

"With all the saints . . ." This is a common designation for Christians in the NT; but it should be understood more as a description of what they should have been than as a description of what they were. As Carver put it:

> Paul does not address his readers as saints because they have realized in life the full implications of the

---

[4]John Calvin, *Commentary on First Corinthians* (Grand Rapids: Wm. B. Eerdmans Publishing Co., 1949 reprint), Comment on 1 Cor. 1:2.

> name, but simply because they authentically belong to Christ as a body of believers.[5]

However, there is also in this word a prospect of the ultimate destiny of every Christian. Whatever the shortcomings now, there is certain to come the hour when every child of God shall be presented "without blemish" and "perfect in Christ" (Col. 1:28). It is in that manifest destiny of ultimate perfection that a true Christian, regardless of mistakes, is authentically a "saint." Of course, there is absolutely nothing in this word that is connected with the pretensions of this historical church in the so-called canonizing of dead people. The saints at Corinth were very much alive.

"That are in the whole of Achaia . . ." The geographical area of Achaia had two meanings. In the classical sense, "It meant only the northern strip of the Peloponnesus; as a Roman province the name included both Hellas and the Peloponnesus."[6] In fact, it included "the whole area south of the province of Macedonia."[7] In this probably lies the explanation of why Stephanas was called the "firstfruits of Achaia" (1 Cor. 16:15), whereas it would appear that "Donysius, Damaris and others" were the first-fruits (Acts 17:34). Concerning what Paul meant by Achaia in this passage, McGarvey thought it was the whole province, basing his conclusion upon the use of the word "whole."[8]

Verse 2, *Grace to you and peace from God our Father and the Lord Jesus Christ.*

"Grace to you and peace. . ." Broomall has an excellent comment on this, as follows:

> In the protocol of salvation, recognized even in a salutation, *grace* always precedes *peace*. The former is the basis and the foundation of the latter. Therefore, the

---

[5]Frank G. Carver, *Beacon Bible Commentary* (Kansas City: Beacon Hill Press, 1968), Vol. 8, p. 500.

[6]F. W. Farrar, *Pulpit Commentary* (Grand Rapids: Wm. B. Eerdmans Publishing Co., 1950), Vol. 19, 2 Cor., p. 1.

[7]Philip E. Hughes, *op. cit.*, p. 5.

[8]J. W. McGarvey, *Second Epistle to the Corinthians* (Cincinnati: The Standard Publishing Company, 1916), p. 169.

order cannot be changed. No man can have peace who has not previously experienced divine grace.[9]

"God our Father and the Lord Jesus Christ . . ." "It should be noticed that the deity of Christ is plainly implied by the language of this verse."[10] He is linked on an equality with God as the source of grace and peace. Furthermore Jesus Christ is distinguished by the title "Lord." "This is the very term (*Kyrios*) which is used in the Septuagint version of the OT to translate the sacred four-letter name of God (*Yahweh*)."[11] See further discussion of this title in CL pp. 8-10.

Verse 3, *Blessed be the God and Father of our Lord Jesus Christ, the Father of mercies and God of all comfort.*

"Father of our Lord Jesus Christ . . ." This is not a denial of the deity of Christ implied in the previous verse; but it brings to view the incarnation, during which the son-ship of our Lord was predominant.

"Father of mercies . . ." It is the mercy of God, more than any other attribute, which has captured the imagination of mankind. Every chapter in the Koran, except one, begins with the words, "In the name of God the Merciful, the Compassionate."

"God of all comfort . . ." "The word *comfort*, either as a verb or a substantive, occurs ten times in verses 3-7."[12] As a matter of truth, God is the God of everything beautiful and desirable. He is the God of patience and of comfort (Rom. 15:5), the God of glory (Acts 7:2), the God of hope (Rom. 15:33), the God of peace (Rom. 15:33), and the God of love and peace (2 Cor. 13:11).

Verse 4, *Who comforteth us in all our affliction, that we may be able to comfort them that are in any affliction, through the comfort wherewith we ourselves are comforted of God.*

"Affliction . . ." Here is introduced the word which flies like a banner over the entire epistle. The word with its synonym "suffering" occurs eight times in this paragraph.

---

[9]Wick Broomall, *Wycliffe Bible Commentary* (Chicago: Moody Press, 1971), p. 651.
[10]Philip E. Hughes, *op. cit.*, p. 7.
[11]*Ibid.*
[12]F. W. Farrar, *op. cit.*, p. 2.

"That we may be able to comfort . . ." Inherent in Paul's statement here is the fact that only those who have suffered are able to comfort others. Also, it is God who is the source of all comfort, except that which is merely superficial; and even those purely human sources of comfort are themselves related to the nature of God.

"Who comforteth us . . ." One of the great comforts Paul had received and which he acknowledged here "seems to have resulted from the good reports brought from Corinth by Titus. "[13] Paul's 1 Corinthians letter had accomplished his purpose; the Corinthians had repented; and Paul was comforted in the knowledge that the crisis in Corinth had passed.

Before leaving this verse it should be pointed out that in the AV the word "comfort" is rendered "consolation" in several places. Farrar called the variations "needless"; and, although granting that they were well intentioned, he said:

> They arose from a false notion of style, a deficient sense of the precision of special words, and an inadequate conception of the duties of faithful translation, which requires that we should as exactly as possible reflect the peculiarities of the original, and not attempt to improve upon them.[14]

It is precisely in this conceit of "improving" the word of God that many of the "modern" translations are unqualified failures. The instance cited by Farrar from the AV is fortunately rare in that version; but many of the current so-called "translations" are nothing but commentary, and in countless examples unwholesome and inaccurate commentary.

Verse 5, *For as the sufferings of Christ abound unto us, even so our comfort also aboundeth through Christ.*

"The sufferings of Christ . . ." These may not be understood as the usual hardships and tribulations of life, but as sufferings, oppositions, threatenings and dangers resulting directly from the sufferer's engagement in the service of the Lord. Christ promised his apostles that they would suffer terrible

---

[13]John William Russell, *Compact Commentary on the NT* (Grand Rapids: Baker Book House, 1964), p. 439.

[14]F. W. Farrar, *op. cit.*, p. 2.

persecutions in the course of their ministry; and Paul certainly sustained his share of them, and even more. See chapter 11:23ff.

Verse 6, *But whether we are afflicted, it is for your comfort and salvation; or whether we are comforted, it is for your comfort, which worketh in the patient enduring of the same sufferings which we also suffer.*

"For your comfort and salvation . . ." All of the hardships endured by the apostle were for the sake of the eternal salvation of his converts. This is the motivation which even yet supplies the energy for many faithful ministries of the gospel. Whatever earthly hardships and persecutions attend the work, either of ministers or others, the goal of saving souls from eternal death is paramount.

"The same sufferings . . ." In this Paul acknowledged that the Corinthians themselves were under the same hatred and opposition of Satan that he himself endured.

"Patient enduring . . ." The Christian answer to the devil's opposition, however manifested, is patient endurance. Steadfastness is the prime requirement of all Christian living.

Verse 7, *And our hope for you is stedfast; knowing that, as ye are partakers of the sufferings, so also are ye of the comfort.*

This says that all sufferings received in the service of Christ are also certain to receive the comfort of Christ, the sufferings and the comfort being inseparably linked together. "We suffer with him, that we may be glorified with him" (Rom. 8:17). "If we endure, we shall also reign with him" (2 Tim. 2:12).

Verse 8, *For we would not have you ignorant brethren, concerning our affliction which befell us in Asia, that we were weighed down exceedingly, beyond our power, insomuch that we despaired even of life.*

"Which befell us in Asia . . ." Although it is impossible for us to know exactly what it was that befell Paul in Asia, it is as Hughes said, that a commentator "is bound to examine such information as the text affords."[15]

---

[15]Philip E. Hughes, *op. cit.*, p. 16.

THE AFFLICTION IN ASIA

McGarvey followed the reasoning of such commentators as Calvin, Paley, Olshausen and others in identifying this affliction as the riot at Ephesus, described by Luke (Acts 19:23-20:1). However, the narrative in Acts appears to indicate that Paul escaped without any suffering at all. Furthermore, "I would not have you ignorant" in this verse seems to say that the knowledge of this affliction would be news at Corinth; and as Ephesus was only 200 miles from Corinth, we may not suppose that such a riot as that described in Acts would have been unknown at Corinth. The intercourse between the two cities was too constant and sustained for that.

Tertullian authored the earliest comment that has come down through history; and he stated that Paul in this passage referred to his fighting wild beasts at Ephesus, stating that Paul "enumerated it to induce an unfaltering belief in the resurrection of the flesh."[16] Besides the question of whether or not Paul's fighting wild beasts was physical or metaphorical, there is also the fact that Paul had already mentioned that episode (whatever it was) in the first epistle (15:32).

Charles Hodge thought Paul might have referred in general terms to "plots and attempts against Paul's life." Windisch thought it may have been an attempt to lynch Paul. Hoffmann applied the reference to a shipwreck (11:25), one not reported by Luke. Stanley and Rendell suppose that it may have been the agonizing anxiety concerning the state of the church in Corinth. Many commentators explain it as some terrible illness from which Paul recovered.

Among so many learned opinions, another, whether learned or not, can do no harm. It is believed by this writer that reference is here made to some terrible danger from which Paul was delivered, but which remains unreported in the NT. That such an awful danger did in fact exist is proved by Paul's crediting Priscilla and Aquila with having saved his life, placing the Gentile churches of the whole Roman empire in debt to them for "laying down their own necks" on his behalf

---

[16]Tertullian, *Ante-Nicene Fathers, On the Resurrection of the Flesh*, xlviii (Grand Rapids: Wm. B. Eerdmans Publishing Co., 1957), Vol. III, p. 582.

(Rom. 16:4). This event of their saving Paul's life was extensively known among the Gentile churches everywhere; and when Paul later arrived at Corinth, he surely gave them all the details of it. Just why the details were not given for us is not known; but there was possibly something sensitive about it that made it dangerous, at least for a while, to elaborate the details. See CR, p. 512.

Verse 9, *Yea, we ourselves have had the sentence of death within ourselves, that we should not trust in ourselves, but in God who raiseth the dead.*

Paul treasured the awful experience through which he had passed for the great lesson which it reinforced; namely, that one's trust should never be in himself but in the Lord, even God who raises the dead. By this reference to raising the dead, there is brought into view the passage in Hebrews 11:19, in which Abraham's offering of Isaac was enabled through his confidence that God was able to raise the dead, giving incidental support to the view that the author of Hebrews and the author of this passage are one and the same person. Where else in all the Bible is Abraham's reliance upon God's ability to raise the dead even hinted at? And how did Paul know it? He himself had trusted God in the same manner when death loomed as a certainty, and at a time when many of God's promises to the blessed apostle were as yet unfilled.

Verse 10, *Who delivered us out of so great a death, and will deliver: on whom we have set our hope that he will also still deliver us.*

"So great a death . . ." How could anyone refer to any ordinary fatal illness in terms like these? The implication is overwhelming that something extraordinary was involved; and common fatal diseases are not extraordinary.

"Will deliver . . ." Paul could not have meant that he still had remnants of the "fatal infection"; but rather that whatever danger might beset him in the future, he would still confidently rely upon God to deliver him.

Verse 11, *Ye also helping together on our behalf by your supplication; that, for the gift bestowed upon us by means of many, thanks may be given by many persons on our behalf.*

"Ye also helping . . ." This is not a declaration that the Corinthians had helped, by their prayers, Paul's deliverance from the affliction in Asia, just mentioned; although, in a general sense, their constant prayers on Paul's behalf certainly had a part in it. The second clause shows that Paul expected their participation in the thanksgiving for his deliverance.

"By means of many . . ." The gift of Paul's deliverance had resulted from the participation of many people, among whom, no doubt, were Priscilla and Aquila; and it was appropriate that many people, including the Christians in Corinth, should participate in the thanksgiving.

Before leaving the record of this episode, it should be remembered that the sensational event of Paul's deliverance from the terrible affliction in Asia was reason enough, *prima facie*, to refute the insinuations of Paul's enemies at Corinth to the effect that his delay in visiting them was irresponsible.

Verse 12, *For our glorying is this, the testimony of our conscience, that in holiness and sincerity of God, not in fleshly wisdom but in the grace of God, we behaved ourselves in the world, and more abundantly to you-ward.*

This verse is Paul's affirmation of total sincerity and godliness in all of his dealings with the Corinthians. He gloried in the fact of the absolute integrity and uprightness of his behavior among them. He had not indulged in the tricks and devices of "fleshly wisdom." His actions were open before God and themselves; there were no hidden deeds of darkness and dishonesty on his part.

Verse 13, *For we write no other things unto you, than what ye read or even acknowledge, and I hope ye will acknowledge unto the end.*

Furthermore, there were no hidden things in his writings. If his enemies had perpetrated the slander that his writings were deceptive, or that he wrote one thing and meant another, this verse nailed their accusations as falsehoods. The very fact of Paul's answering them is proof that slanders were made.

"Unto the end . . ." These words should be translated "fully," as thoroughly explained by Hughes.[17] The widespread error to the effect that Paul thought the end of the world was just around the corner probably lay at the base of the mistranslation. As Allo said:

> Those who wish to understand this in an eschatological sense are not only misled by the mistaken idea that Paul and the Corinthians were expecting the end of the world as near at hand . . . they also commit a serious error of literary judgment in failing to notice the intentional antithesis between *know* and *know fully*, as here, and as in 1 Corinthians 13.12.[18]

Verse 14, *As also ye did acknowledge us in part, that we are your glorying, even as ye are also ours, in the day of our Lord Jesus.*

"In part . . ." The significance of this is that "a portion of the church believed him to be sincere and consistent, though there was a faction that denied it."[19]

"In the day of our Lord Jesus . . ." This is a glance at the final day of judgment at the Second Coming of our Lord. All of the affairs of the Christian's daily life must be evaluated in the light of that final reckoning.

Verses 15, 16, *And in this confidence I was minded to come first unto you, that ye might have a second benefit; and by you to pass into Macedonia, and again from Macedonia to come unto you, and of you be set forward on my journey to Judaea.*

Paul's first purpose was to go via Corinth to Macedonia, and thence via Corinth again to Judaea; but in 1 Corinthians 16:5, he wrote that this plan had given way to another, and that he proposed to go to Macedonia first. This was apparently the basis of the slander that Paul could not make up his mind, or that he was deceitful. If the plan made originally could have been carried out, it would have meant a double visit to Corinth, described by Paul here as "a second benefit."

---

[17]Philip E. Hughes, *op. cit.*, p. 27.

[18]E. B. Allo, *Saint Paul: Seconde Epitre Aux Corinthiens* (Paris, 1956), *in loco.*

[19]David Lipscomb, *op. cit.*, p. 30.

"Set forward on my journey . . ." This is a reference to the early custom of members of the congregation accompanying the apostle part of the way upon occasions of his departure, as in Acts 15:3, 20:38, 21:5 and in Romans 15:24.

Verse 17, *When I therefore was thus minded, did I show fickleness? or the things that I purpose, do I purpose according to the flesh, that with one there should be the yea yea and the nay nay?*

Paul's argument is simply that: Surely I cannot be accused of fickleness merely upon the basis of changes in my plans! He further declared that he had made his plans in good faith, changing them only when there appeared good and sufficient reasons for doing so. Incidentally, there is a glimpse in this of the fact that even so Spirit-filled a person as the blessed apostle was compelled to make future plans, not upon the basis of direct inspiration, but upon the basis of sober, practical good judgment. Some of the charismatics of our own times should take note of this.

"According to the flesh . . ." is a reference to plans made without sincerity, or for the purpose of deception. There is one sense in which all of a Christian's plans for the future are made "in the flesh," that is, without the benefit of inspiration.

"Yea yea and nay nay . . ." This is an idiom for double talk, insincerity, and deception.

Verse 18, *But as God is faithful, our word toward you is not yea and nay.*

Paul's promises were sincerely made; and there was no deception whatever. How could the promises of an apostle through the will of God be otherwise?

Verse 19, *For the Son of God, Jesus Christ, who was preached among you by us, even by me and Silvanus and Timothy, was not yea and nay, but in him is yea.*

"By me and Sylvanus and Timothy . . ." These were with Paul in the founding of the church at Corinth; and the very fact of their having preached the truth that is in Christ Jesus made it morally impossible for them to have engaged in the kind of petty deceptions alleged against him by his foes.

"In him is yea . . ." "Yea and nay" continues to be used here as an idiom of fraud and deception. In Christ there is neither fraud nor deception; but in him is yea; and in this context "yea" is an idiom for utmost truth, sincerity and integrity. This verse means that integrity is the hallmark of every Christian. Being "in Christ" is one and the same thing as being absolutely honest, truthful and straightforward in all communications of every kind. In the light of this, is it not true that some who may claim to be so are not really "in Christ" at all?

"Sylvanus . . ." This is the same person identified as Silas in Acts 15:32, 40, who was one of the prophets of the early church, and also a companion of Paul on the second missionary tour. He was with Paul in jail at Philippi and throughout that exciting tour.

Verse 20, *For how many soever be the promises of God, in him is the yea: wherefore also through him is the Amen, unto the glory of God through us.*

"In God is yea . . . and the Amen . . ." There is a profound inference in this verse to the effect that disbelieving God's chosen apostle Paul is a denial of the truth and righteousness of the Father himself. Paul said, in these words, "Believe me; believe God." No sterner or more dogmatic affirmation of his apostleship could be imagined.

"The Amen . . ." God will not only honor his promises, which are invariably true; but he will sum them up with a heavenly Amen. God's word is the last word. God is the Amen; but so also is Christ. "These things saith the Amen, the faithful and true witness" (Rev. 3:14). Thus, "The Amen is through him who is himself the Amen"[20] Many of our Lord's most solemn pronouncements began with "Amen, Amen, I say unto you . . . etc." This is translated, "Verily, verily, I say unto you." This was a most arresting manner of declaring for those who heard him the absolute authority and immutability of Jesus' teachings.

---

[20]Philip E. Hughes, *op. cit.*, p. 37.

Verses 21,22, *Now he that establisheth us with you in Christ, and anointed us, is God; who also sealed us, and gave us the earnest of the Spirit in our hearts.*

Three things in these verses, (1) the anointing, (2) the sealing, and (3) the giving of the earnest are all references to one action, that of conversion, by which the believer is united with Christ "in Christ." This action, as evident on Pentecost, was a compound act of obedience: believing, repenting, being baptized, receiving the gift of the Holy Spirit. After discussing various theories on this, Hughes stated that:

> It is more satisfactory to identify the anointing, sealing, and giving of the earnest with the single event of baptism, and the continuous establishing with the other and constantly repeated NT sacrament of the holy communion.[21]

"Establishes us with you . . ." Paul affirmed in this the essential unity of all Christians, himself as well as the Corinthians, "in Christ." By virtue of unity with Christ and "in Christ," there is no fraud, insincerity or deception in any Christian, apostle or otherwise, all such evils being fundamentally opposed to their very nature in the Lord.

"Sealed us . . . earnest of the Spirit . . ." The earnest (or token) of the Holy Spirit is identified with "the Holy Spirit of promise" (Eph. 1:13) and is the invariable inheritance of all who obey the gospel of Christ. For further discussion see CR, p. 124. Even the Corinthians possessed the earnest of the Holy Spirit, despite their delinquency in so many particulars.

Verses 23, 24, *But I call God for a witness upon my soul, that to spare you I forbare to come to Corinth. Not that we have lordship over your faith, but are helpers of your joy: for in faith ye stand fast.*

"I call God for a witness . . ." Some call this an oath; but others deny it. Even God himself, for a righteous purpose, "interposed with an oath" (Heb. 6:17); and Paul's appeal to God as witness in this passage would seem to indicate that the prohibition of Christ in Matthew 5:34ff should not be applied to

---

[21]*Ibid.*, p. 44.

the kind of oath (if it is an oath) in evidence here. Certainly, it would appear that courts of justice should be allowed to administer oaths, even to Christians. See more on this in CM, p. 67.

"To spare you, I forbare to come . . ." Here Paul finally got around to the dogmatic reason why he changed some of his plans of going to Corinth. The situation was so bad there that he considered it profitable and righteous to wait a while until they had more time to repent of their sins. An earlier confrontation might have resulted in thwarting God's will among them. As these words stand in the RV, they seem to imply that Paul had not yet gone to Corinth (after the founding of the church); but Tasker pointed out that a permissible translation is, "I came not any more,"[22] thus avoiding a denial of the "painful visit" which was probably made between the writing of the two epistles.

"Not that we have lordship . . ." Paul's statement that he would "spare" the Corinthians by delaying another visit could have had implications of apostolical authority not intended by Paul; therefore he at once entered a disclaimer of any "lording it over" God's heritage. Not even an apostle might do such a thing as that (1 Peter 5:3).

> There is then no scriptural warrant for hierarchical domination or lordship in the church of Christ. Absolute authority is not vested in any supposed apostolic office or succession, but in the person and office of Christ.[23]

Not even the apostle Peter, upon whom such an overwhelming burden of overlordship has been imposed during the historical progression of Christianity, did not consider himself as an ecclesiastical overlord any more than did Paul (1 Peter 5:2).

"For in faith ye stand fast . . ." The literal Greek rendition gives this as "In the faith ye have stood firm."[24] The meaning is clearly that the Corinthians are continuing in the Christian religion; and there is no statement in the passage about

---

[22]R V. G. Tasker, *The Second Epistle of Paul to the Corinthians* (Grand Rapids: Wm. B. Eerdmans Publishing Co., 1958), p. 50.

[23]Philip E. Hughes, *op. cit.*, p. 49.

[24]*The Emphatic Diaglott* (Brooklyn: Watch Tower Bible and Tract Society).

salvation being "by faith." Translators never miss an opportunity to plug the favorite heresy of "salvation by faith only"; and despite the fact that they no longer dare to add the word "only," that is definitely intended as the meaning in such renditions as this.

The chapter break here is right in the middle of Paul's line of thought. Chapter 1 should have ended at verse 14, or have been extended through 4 of chapter 2.

CHAPTER 2

The apostle Paul wrote much like some people talk; one thing led to another; and he often digressed from a line of thought, coming back to it only after a parenthetical discussion of something else. This trip through 2 Corinthians is as exciting as a drive down Oak Creek canyon, with one sensational view following another. Paul concluded his explanation of the change in his plans (vv. 1-4), recommended leniency to the Corinthians in a disciplinary problem (5-11), touched on his waiting for Titus at Troas (12-13), and penned a masterpiece regarding the nature of gospel influence, drawing a rather rough analogy from the spectacle of a Roman triumph.

Verse 1, *But I determined this for myself, that I would not come again to you with sorrow.*

Regardless of how little we know of any sorrowful visit Paul had paid the Corinthians, the plain meaning of several passages in this letter demands the conclusion that it was made and that it cannot be identified with the original visit which led to the founding of the church. Paul wrote: "This is the third time I am ready to come to you (12:14); and he repeated it, "This is the third time I am coming to you" (13:1). Even the verse before us contributes to the certainty that Paul had already made two visits to Corinth when 2 Corinthians was written; because it is very difficult to imagine that Paul here referred to his original visit to Corinth, which had resulted in one of the most successful preaching experiences of his whole life and the gathering of a mighty congregation of believers. No; there had to have been another visit, a sorrowful visit.

"Come again to you with sorrow . . ." But, cannot this have the meaning of, "My second visit to you should not be a sad one," rather than "I would not pay you a second sad visit"? Theodoret, Farrar and other learned commentators say that it can, and that "The notion of three visits to Corinth, one unrecorded, is a needless and mistaken inference."[1] Despite this, Paul's double mention of his proposed visit as the "third" one (cited above) declares the certainty of a second one already made. The thing that upsets the commentators is that no one knows anything about that second visit, except as indicated here, that it was a sad one. We admire the frank honesty of David Lipscomb who said, "But this (13:1) with 12:14, makes it clear that he made a visit of which we have no record."[2] Extreme caution should be used, however, in accepting the wild and irresponsible assertions of some recent exegetes with regard to "what happened" at that unrecorded visit. It is the ridiculous postulations of some on what took place at that visit that have made it impossible for some scholars to admit that it took place; and, as regards the *kind of visit* alleged and in which Paul "was insulted,"[3] etc., etc. That *visit* did not occur, being nothing but the fruit of a fertile imagination!

The silence of Luke in Acts with regard to that "second visit" "should not be taken as being in conflict with the natural interpretation of what Paul said here; many things are omitted by Luke."[4]

Regarding the question of when that other visit (the second) took place, this too is a disputed problem. Hughes, Alford, Denney, Lightfoot, Zahn, Sanday and many others regard it as having occurred before 1 Corinthians was written, rejecting out of hand the proposition that it took place in the interval between the two Corinthian letters of the NT. After reading all of the material available on the question, this writer simply does not know when it took place, but finds no fault with placing it between the letters, *if* at the same time we reject totally the speculative allegations of imaginative critics whose arrogant assertions of what took place at that meeting are pure nonsense. How could any responsible scholar tell what happened at a meeting which might have happened before either

---

[1]F. W. Farrar, *Pulpit Commentary* (Grand Rapids: Wm. B. Eerdmans Publishing Co., 1950), vol. 8, 2 Cor., p. 36.

[2]David Lipscomb, *Second Corinthians* (Nashville: The Gospel Advocate Co., 1936), p. 169.

[3]William Barclay, *The Letters to the Corinthians* (Philadelphia: The Westminster Press, 1954), p. 201.

[4]Philip E. Hughes, *Paul's Second Epistle to the Corinthians* (Grand Rapids: Wm. B. Eerdmans Publishing Co., 1962), p. 52.

of the Corinthians was written, and of which not one authentic syllable is anywhere recorded, either in the NT or anywhere else? Reluctant as arrogant scholarship may be to confess that it does not know, the certain fact of total ignorance on this point must be respected by all who regard the truth.

Verse 2, *For if I make you sorry, who then is he that maketh me glad but he that is made sorry by me?*

Farrar's discernment of the meaning here is this: "Paul was unwilling to pain those who gladdened him, and therefore would not pay them a visit which could only be painful on both sides."[5]

Verse 3, *And I wrote this very thing, lest, when I came, I should have sorrow from them of whom I ought to rejoice, having confidence in you all, that my joy is the joy of you all.*

"I wrote this very thing . . ." This is most suitably understood as a direct reference to 1 Corinthians 16:5ff where he told the Corinthians of his revised itinerary."[6] Some have referred these words to the "lost letter"; but such a reference is arbitrary. Besides, the understanding of these words as a reference to First Corinthians "has been the understanding of the church through many centuries."[7] Hughes, wise comment on this place is:

> The further we are removed in time from the original events, the more we should, as a matter of principle, hesitate to entertain novel theories in the face of a strong tradition of interpretation and in the absence of anything fresh in the way of external evidence. In a case of this kind, the probability is all in favor of the earlier exegesis being correct rather than the later conjecture.[8]

Verse 4, *For out of much affliction and anguish of heart I wrote unto you with many tears; not that ye should be made sorry, but that ye might know the love which I have more abundantly unto you.*

This continues to be a reference to 1 Corinthians, nor can this be construed as any sort of proof of a second lost letter

---

[5]F. W. Farrar, *op. cit.*, p. 36.
[6]Philip E. Hughes, *op. cit.*, p. 56.
[7]*Ibid.*
[8]*Ibid.*

between the canonical Corinthians. The notion that 1 Corinthians could not have been written out of "anguish of heart" betrays a total insensitivity to the things which most assuredly can cause anguish of heart to any Christian, especially to the apostle who had converted them and had such love for them. The conditions at Corinth, described in 1 Corinthians, were exceedingly deplorable. Incest, heartless lawsuits by the members before pagan judges, drunkenness at the Lord's table, arrogant self-seeking among the members, denials of the resurrection, warring, loveless factions, etc., etc. "Any one of these things was sufficient to cause Paul real distress and the severest grief."[9] McGarvey also understood this verse as a reference to 1 Corinthians.

Verse 5, *But if any hath caused sorrow, he hath caused sorrow, not to me, but in part (that I press not too heavily) to you all.*

The traditional interpretation of this makes it a reference to the incestuous person of 1 Corinthians 5:1-8. McGarvey saw in verses 3,5 above a plain hint of the connection between the two passages, since, he said, "By referring to 1 Cor. 4:21, 5:1, it will be seen that the threat of correction at his coming and the case of the incestuous person were twin thoughts in his mind."[10] Although this writer began these studies in 2 Corinthians with the firm conviction that the offender mentioned in this passage is not the same as the incestuous person of 1 Corinthians 5: 1ff, extensive study of the question has inclined more and more to the traditional view that they are one and the same.

For nineteen centuries, the almost unanimous position of scholars was that of accepting the two offenders as the same person; and no hard evidence of any kind has been discovered that could refute it. Some made the deduction that "deliverance to Satan" in 1 Corinthians likely caused the death of the incestuous person, but such a deduction cannot be proved. In the light of this passage in 2 Corinthians, if applied to him, he did not die. As was pointed out in the comment on 1

---

[9]*Ibid.*

[10]J. W. McGarvey, *Second Epistle to the Corinthians* (Cincinnati: Standard Publishing Company, 1916), p. 177.

Corinthians 5:1ff, there are many things about that episode which are simply unknown and unknowable.

In all history, until very recent times, only one voice was ever raised in denial of the identity of the two offenders as one; and that was that of Tertullian who lived only about a hundred years after the times of Paul. Yet, even in his case, it appears that the universally held conviction of that time was denied by nobody except Tertullian; and he was able to offer no proof whatever to support it. As Hughes reasoned:

> If Tertullian had had any knowledge of a tradition or even hypothesis that a scandalous affront had been offered either to Paul or his deputy Timothy after the delivery of First Corinthians, or that Paul had paid an intermediate visit to Corinth during which his authority had been treated with contempt, and that he had afterward written an intermediate letter demanding the punishment of the offender, it is incredible that he should not have welcomed it as a corroboration of his own view that Paul did not here refer to the incestuous man.[11]

How strange it is that Tertullian's denial of the identity of these two offenders as being the same person should itself have become the most positive evidence of the very thing he denied. The ways of the Lord are not the ways of men. After considering this ancient voice from the subapostolic age, this writer feels the utmost confidence in receiving the long sustained opinion that the same offender appears in both passages. A corollary of this is the rejection of the notion that Paul's second visit occurred between the Corinthian letters, and also that of "the severe letter" being anything other than a reference to the canonical 1 Corinthians.

"He hath caused sorrow, not to me . . ." Paul could not possibly have said this about some buffoon's contemptuously insulting him in the public assembly at Corinth, which is the gist of most of the speculative descriptions of that alleged meeting.

"But in part . . . to you all . . ." The scandalous conduct of the incestuous person was a public disgrace to the whole

---

[11]Philip E. Hughes, *op. cit.*, p. 62.

church; and to suppose that such an affront to Christian morality had not caused deep sorrow to the whole church is to suppose an impossibility. Paul too was sorry; but the scandal was not an affront to him, but a public calamity to the whole church. Every minister can recall incidents of great moral failure in a congregation and the heartache that inevitably came upon the whole congregation as a result.

"In part . . ." indicates that not all of the congregation grieved; some "puffed up" libertarians did not have enough sense of Christian morality to cause them any grief whatever.

Verse 6, *Sufficient to such a one is this punishment which was inflicted by the many.*

The tact and consideration of Paul are evident in his unwillingness even to mention either the name of the offender or to identify the shameful sin of which he was guilty.

"Inflicted by the many . . ." This indicates that, according to his instructions (1 Cor. 5:4), the whole congregation had dealt with the offender in a public gathering. There was no way to ease sin like that out of the church privately.

"Sufficient . . ." This requires the understanding that the guilty man had put away his father's wife, acknowledging his sin, and returning to the congregation with a plea for forgiveness.

Verses 7, 8, *So that contrariwise ye should rather forgive him and comfort him, lest by any means such a one should be swallowed up with his overmuch sorrow. Wherefore, I beseech you to confirm your love toward him.*

"Forgive . . . comfort him . . ." The notion of some, going all the way back to Tertullian, that the man's sin was in any sense unforgivable is founded on a lack of perceiving the fact that the blood of Jesus Christ is more than sufficient to the cleansing of "all sin" (1 John 1:7), even of Christians. As a matter of truth, the incestuous person was hardly any greater sinner than many of the other Corinthians (1 Cor. 6:8-11). The failure to believe Paul was here speaking of the incestuous person also stems from the failure to view a sin forgiven as being something infinitely removed from a sin unforgiven.

"I beseech you to confirm your love toward him . . ." Nothing could be more unbecoming to a church, or to Christians, than to withhold forgiveness from a penitent Christian needing and asking it. It should be noted that Paul's request that forgiveness be extended is made in this letter and that there is no mention of a prior request to that effect.

Verse 9, *For to this end also did I write, that I might know the proof of you, whether ye are obedient in all things.*

The "painful visit" and "severe letter" theorists have misread this verse. "To this end also did I write . . ." refers to the clauses following and not to the request of forgiveness, that is, the proof of obedience, which should be referred to his order of discipline for the incestuous man. Of course, if "to this end" is made to refer to a request for forgiveness for the offender, it would demand the postulation of an intermediate letter, there being no request of forgiveness for the offender in 1 Corinthians, as there had been no repentance at the time 1 Corinthians was written. Thus, another supposed "proof" of the intervening "severe letter" is nothing but an improper reading of this verse.

Verses 10, 11, *But to whom ye forgive anything, I forgive also: for what I also have forgiven, if I have forgiven anything, for your sakes have I forgiven it in the presence of Christ; that no advantage may be gained over us by Satan: for we are not ignorant of his devices.*

Titus had informed Paul of the successful issue of the order of discipline enforced upon the incestuous man, only with the exception that some of the church seemed unwilling to forgive and reinstate him. Paul added the record of his own forgiveness of the man's sin, "in the presence of Christ" as an added inducement to making his forgiveness and reinstatement complete.

"His devices . . ." The device of Satan which surfaces in this paragraph is that of a super-piety that will not forgive offenders even when they have put away their sin, repented, and asked forgiveness. This device is still being used by the devil.

Verses 12, 13, *Now when I came to Troas for the gospel of Christ, and when a door was opened unto me in the Lord, I had no relief for any spirit, because I found not Titus my brother: but taking my leave of them, I went forth into Macedonia.*

"I had no relief . . ." Paul had gone to Troas after the riot at Ephesus (on his way to Macedonia) as recorded in Acts 20:1; and, from what is said here, it is clear that great opportunities for the gospel strongly inclined Paul to take advantage of those opportunities; but the anxious uncertainty that he felt because of the still unresolved situation in Corinth made it impossible for him to remain. Titus' meeting with him there, as evidently planned, did not occur; and as almost a year had passed since his epic letter had been sent (1 Corinthians), he decided to press on into Macedonia in the hope of meeting Titus on the way. That reassuring meeting with Titus came to Paul's mind as these words were written; and the news was so encouraging that he burst into an extended expression of praise and thanksgiving to God, forming a rather lengthy parenthesis between this mention of Titus and the resumption of his line of thought again in 7:5.

Verse 14, *But thanks be to God, who always leadeth us in triumph in Christ, and maketh manifest through us the savor of his knowledge in every place.*

Triumph Metaphor

Suddenly, in the light of the good news brought by Titus, Paul sees the glorious triumph of the gospel through him; and he compared it to a glorious triumph, like those for Roman emperors, with Christ as the great Conqueror and himself as a captive participating in it and sharing in the glory of it.

The Corinthians knew about triumphs, for the triumph of L. Mummius over the conquest of Corinth was one of the most splendid spectaculars the world had ever seen; and then in A.D. 51, only five or six years before 2 Corinthians was written, Claudius had celebrated his triumph over the Britons; "and their king Caractacus had been led in the procession, but his life was spared."[12]

Such a triumph always featured the conquering here, whose many captives were led behind, some to be freed, others to be slaughtered as a feature of the spectacle; and Paul's appeal to

[12]F. W. Farrar, *op. cit.*, p. 30.

the triumph metaphor envisioned Christ as the great Conqueror who leads all men, whether they will or not; Paul's view of himself in this was that of his being willingly led in the train of Christ and expecting to receive his mercy at last. "The haughty Cleopatra had said, 'I will not be led in triumph'";[13] and there are many like that with regard to Christ.

Verses 15, 16, *For we are a sweet savor of Christ unto God, in them that are saved, and in them that perish; to the one a savor from death unto death; to the other a savor from life unto life. And who is sufficient for these things?*

Vast quantities of incense were burned along the route of a Roman triumph; and those who were in the heroic procession found the meaning of that odor an assurance of their death on the one hand, or of their life, if they were spared, on the other hand. The overwhelmingly delicious odor that marked the triumph meant death for some, life for others. Paul here affirmed that it is like this with the gospel. It saves some, destroys others. In a similar way, the parables of Jesus enlightened some, but hardened and destroyed others. Not the gospel, but men's response to it, is the determinator.

McGarvey pointed out the extremely significant phrases "from death" and "from life" as used in this passage. To the unbelieving, the news of the gospel is from one who was crucified and is dead; so, for them, it is an odor from death unto death, even eternal death; but to Christians, the news (odor) is "from life," that is, from One who is alive forever more. Hence, the news of the gospel is "from life unto life" in them that are saved.[14]

Paul's use of this analogy is somewhat loose, for he made several applications of it. In 1 Corinthians 4:9, he pictured the apostles as bringing up the rear of the triumphal procession, which was the position of those appointed to die in the arena. Nevertheless, this is one of the most effective and instructive analogies in the Pauline writings.

"Who is sufficient for these things . . . ?" The meaning of this is: "What kind of ministry could be adequate for such a

---

[13]*Ibid.*
[14]J. W. McGarvey, *op. cit.*, p. 181.

task?"[15] And Paul's unhesitating reply is, "Ours is!" And why is the ministry of Paul the apostle sufficient for such heavenly usage? The answer is thundered in the next verse being this, that he was preaching the pure gospel of God without adulteration like that practiced by the false apostles and teachers who were hindering the Corinthians.

Verse 17, *For we are not as the many, corrupting the word of God: but as of God, in the sight of God, speak we in Christ.*

"Corrupting the word of God . . ." The figure here is originally that of a tavernkeeper who mixes poor wine with good to increase his profits."[16] In such a comparison as this, two things appear: (1) there is the disclosure of the true motive of false teachers who are in the gospel business for the profit they can make for themselves, and (2) there is the usual method of such teachers, that of adding to the gospel substances that are no part of the true gospel with the intention of making it more acceptable to sinners who rebel at the true gospel.

As Carver said of this:

> The first leads to the second. To approach the ministry with motives of personal profit, ambition, or vanity, is already to adulterate it. He who makes the word serve his advantage rather than being a servant of the word changes the very character of the gospel.[17]

Paul's quadruple affirmation of the integrity of his own ministry is the profound declaration that it was conducted (1) in sincerity, (2) of God, that is, by his direct authority and order, (3) in the sight of God, that is, openly and in view of all men as well as in the sight of God, and (4) in Christ, which means, as a pure and faithful member of the spiritual body of Christ (the church), and in full compliance with all Christian duties.

---

[15]Frank G. Carver, *Beacon Bible Commentary* (Kansas City: Beacon Hill Press, 1968), p. 519.
[16]*Ibid.*
[17]*Ibid.*

CHAPTER 3

An excellent outline of this chapter is by Farrar:[1]

Paul spoke of letters of commendation (vv. 1-3); his sufficiency as of God (vv. 4-6); the new covenant is more glorious than the one given to Moses (vv. 7-11); Paul's ministry needs no veil on the face (vv. 12-13); the veil still darkens Israel (vv. 14-15); the veil is done away in Christ (vv. 16-18).

Verse 1, *Are we beginning again to commend ourselves? or need we as some, epistles of commendation to you or from you?*

As Lipscomb said, "Against the usage of such letters in general, Paul here says nothing."[2] Rather, Paul is either replying to some allegation of the false teacher who might have inferred that nobody recommended Paul, or he is consciously hedging against a similar charge that he anticipated. "It is not necessary to deduce from this verse, as many do, that the charge of self-praise had already been leveled against Paul."[3] The type of deduction usually made from this verse is that "They had sneered at him for always commending himself."[4] Those who would use this passage as a prohibition of such recommendations as church letters are misapplying it. "We are not dealing simply with letters attesting that the bearers are church members in good standing."[5] There are the following examples from the NT of what might be entitled church letters:

1. The book of Philemon, a letter on behalf of Onesimus.
2. Acts 18:27, a letter on behalf of Apollos.
3. Acts 15:23f, a letter on behalf of Paul, Silas and others.

---

[1]F. W. Farrar, *Pulpit Commentary* (Grand Rapids: Wm. B. Eerdmans Publishing Company, 1950), p. 56.

[2]David Lipscomb, *Second Corinthians* (Nashville: The Gospel Advocate Company, 1937), p. 47.

[3]R. G. V. Tasker, *The Second Epistle of Paul to the Corinthians* (Grand Rapids: Wm. B. Eerdmans Publishing Company, 1958), p. 59.

[4]E. H. Plumptre, *Ellicott's Commentary* (Grand Rapids: Zondervan Publishing House, 1959), Vol. VII, p. 370.

[5]F. F. Bruce, *Answers to Questions* (Grand Rapids: Zondervan Publishing House, 1972), p. 101.

4. 2 Corinthians 8:23, a letter on behalf of Titus.
5. 1 Corinthians 16:10, a letter on behalf of Timothy.
6. Romans 16:1f, a letter on behalf of Phoebe.

When Paul had entered upon his mission of persecution to Damascus, he requested letters from the high priest (Acts 9:2); and from the above examples from the NT, it appears that the Jewish custom of granting credentials to legitimate members of the faith was brought over into the Christian religion. It was quite necessary to do this, because "Even Lucian, the pagan satirist, noted that any charlatan could make a fortune out of the simple-minded Christians, because they were so easily imposed upon."[6]

Nevertheless, Paul was in a different category and needed no letters from any person or church to commend him. He had wrought mighty miracles among the Corinthians and elsewhere; and the very existence of their congregation proved the genuineness of his apostleship. Not so with regard to some of those false teachers at Corinth, who, having no genuine worth of any kind, had nevertheless supplied themselves with "letters."

"As some . . ." Paul's reference to false teachers at Corinth, is in irony, "which is pointed by the effective, almost sarcastic, use of anonymous 'some.'"[7] Clines pointed out that the words are *de rigeur*, "a favorite term of his for his opponents,"[8] as in 10:2, Galatians 1:7, and 1 Timothy 1:3. Some of such characters had actually "penetrated the Corinthian church on the strength of these bills of clearance for the profitable marketing of their merchandise in spiritual things."[9]

Verse 2, *Ye are our epistle written in our hearts, known and read of all men.*

"Ye are our epistle . . ." The Corinthian church, in a figurative sense, was Paul's letter of recommendation.

---

[6]William Barclay, *The Letters to the Corinthians* (Philadelphia: The Westminster Press, 1954), p. 208.
[7]Philip E. Hughes, *Paul's Second Letter to the Corinthians* (Grand Rapids: Wm. B. Eerdmans Publishing Co., 1962), p. 85.
[8]David J. A. Clines, *New Testament Commentary* (Grand Rapids: Zondervan Publishing House, 1969), p. 422.
[9]Philip E. Hughes, *op. cit.*, p. 85.

"Written in our hearts . . ." The RSV has "written in your hearts" which is probably the better rendition. Clines called the RSV "preferable" in this place,[10] despite the fact of its manuscript support being weaker. In context, the Corinthians are the letter; and since all men can read it, it would have to be written in their heart rather than Paul's for this to be possible. Had it been written in Paul's heart only, who could have read it? The heart of the formerly reprobate Corinthians, now converted, however, was where the writing had taken place. Such changes as had taken place in them (due to a change in heart) upon their conversion were indeed visible to the whole world of that period. "The metaphor is that the Corinthian church was itself the epistle of Christ";[11] and Paul's laying claim to the epistle as his is a reference to his having established their congregation through the preaching of the gospel. In verse 5, Paul made it clear that in the higher sense he considered God to be the true author of the epistle, that is, of the conversions at Corinth.

Verse 3, *Being made manifest that ye are an epistle of Christ, ministered by us, written not with ink, but with the Spirit of the living God; not in tables of stone, but in tables that are hearts of flesh.*

"An epistle of Christ, ministered by us . . ." is a clarification of "Ye are our epistle" in the preceding verse. Paul's position was the same in this as that of the apostles who passed out the bread when Jesus fed the five thousand, the apostles being not the chef on that occasion but the waiters. So here, Paul wrote the epistle in the sense of preaching the gospel; but the true author was Christ who gave the gospel. Plumptre's explanation is that "Paul had been the amanuensis of that letter; but Christ had been the real writer."[12]

"Written not with ink . . ." This merely forces the conclusion that Paul was using "epistle" in a figurative sense. He was not speaking of any ordinary letter written with ink upon a parchment.

---

[10]David J. A. Clines, *op. cit.*, p. 422.

[11]Foy E. Wallace, Jr., *A Review of the New Versions* (Fort Worth: Foy E. Wallace, Jr., Publications, 1973), p. 437.

[12]E. H. Plumptre, *op. cit.*, p. 370.

"Spirit ... tables ... hearts ..." God had written the Decalogue with his finger upon tables of stone; but in the new covenant, of which Paul now began to speak, not God's finger, but Gods' Spirit did the writing. Note the plural of "hearts," a plain reference to the many Christians at Corinth, and supporting the interpretation that Paul's letter was written upon their hearts, not upon his own. There can be no doubt of Jeremiah's great prophecy of the new covenant (31:31ff) being in the background of Paul's thoughts in this passage.

Verse 4, *And such confidence have we through Christ to God-ward.*

"The changed lives at Corinth confirm Paul's confidence of his divine appointment."[13] Thus, not merely all men, but Paul himself also could read the proof of his apostolical commission in the great harvest of souls won for the Lord in Corinth. How natural, therefore, it was for him to point out to others what was so starkly clear to himself.

Verse 5, *Not that we are sufficient of ourselves, to account any thing as from ourselves; but our sufficiency is from God.*

See under verses 2 and 3. Although claiming the Corinthians as his epistle, he wished to make it clear that the true author is God, and that to him all of the glory belongs, hence the repetition of this thought here. Back in 2:16, Paul's implied answer to the question, "Who is sufficient for these things?" was to the effect that he and the other apostles were sufficient because they preached the true word of God and did not adulterate it. In that sense, of course, they were sufficient; but here Paul registered the great truth that only God is truly sufficient.

Verse 6, *Who also made us as sufficient ministers of a new covenant; not of the letter, but of the spirit: for the letter killeth, but the spirit giveth life.*

Having acknowledged God as the all-sufficient, Paul at once reemphasizes his own apostolic sufficiency for the preaching of God's new covenant.

---

[13]Norman Hillyer, *The New Bible Commentary, Revised* (Grand Rapids: Wm. B. Eerdmans Publishing Co., 1970), p. 1078.

Letter and Spirit

"Not of the letter, but of the spirit . . ." Both in this and in the final clause of this verse, the RSV has perpetrated a gross error in capitalizing "Spirit" in order to make it mean "Holy Spirit" in both clauses, an error slavishly followed in *Good News for Modern Man, Phillips NT, The NEB*, and others. While it is true, of course, that the blessings of the new covenant may be enjoyed only by those who have received the blessed Holy Spirit, there is no reference to that here. As Hughes said, "It is unlikely that a direct reference to the Spirit is intended."[14] "The contrast in verse 6 is not between the outward and inward sense of scripture, but between the outward and inward power of the Jewish and Christian dispensations."[15] As Tasker put it, "Paul is distinguishing the new covenant from the old by using the contrasted categories of spirit and letter, life and death."[16] Farrar gave the meaning as "Not of the law, but of the gospel."[17] Paul's usage of this same expression in Romans 2:28f speaks of a true Jew as one who is a Jew in heart, *in the spirit, not in the letter*. There is no need to multiply evidence that Paul used the same expression here exactly as he used it there.

It is equally evident, as Hughes noted, that "This verse is not concerned with any supposed distinction between two different senses of scripture, the literal and the spiritual."[18] It is precisely in such a supposed distinction that much error flourishes, and has flourished for centuries. William Tyndale mentioned it in his day:

> Some preach Christ, and prove whatsoever point of faith thou wilt, as well out of a fable of Ovid or any other poet, as out of St. John's gospel or Paul's epistles. Yea, they are come to such blindness, that they not only say that the literal sense profiteth not, but also that it is hurtful and noisome, and killeth the soul.[19]

---

[14]Philip E. Hughes, *op. cit.*, p. 101.
[15]J. W. McGarvey, *Second Epistle of Paul to the Corinthians* (Cincinnati: The Standard Publishing Co., 1916), p. 184.
[16]R. V. G. Tasker, *op. cit.*, p. 62.
[17]F. W. Farrar, *op. cit.*, p. 58.
[18]Philip E. Hughes, *op. cit*, p. 99.
[19]*Ibid.*

Hughes added that such erroneous ideas were always supported by people quoting this very passage.[20]

Any persons denying a Christian duty or rejecting an ordinance of God, such as baptism, on the premise that "spiritual" baptism is meant, etc., etc., are finding in Paul's remark here something that was never in it.

Verses 7, 8, *But if the ministration of death, written and engraven on stones, came with glory, so that the children of Israel could not look stedfastly upon the face of Moses for the glory of his face: which glory was passing away: how shall not rather the ministration of the spirit be with glory?*

Ministration of Death

The old covenant, deficient on account of man's sins, was nevertheless attended at its inception by glorious manifestations of God's power and majesty, including the radiance of Moses' face mentioned here (see Ex. 34:29-35). Paul's argument is simply this, that if even the old covenant, called here the ministration of death, was attended by such glory, how much more glorious is the gospel of Christ, or the new covenant. Of deep interest is Paul's view of history, especially that of Israel, which he interpreted as containing many allegories of great spiritual realities which came to light in the new covenant. Another example is that of Sarah and Hagar in Galatians.

"Ministration of death . . ." The old covenant was thus titled because 3,000 souls perished the day the law was given; it was called the law of "sin and death" (Rom. 8:2). However, Paul here laid stress on the diminishing radiance of Moses' face, interpreting the veil as being used to prevent Israel's *seeing the glory fade away.* Thus the veil symbolized the blindness of Israel, not only in the old covenant, but also in the rejection of Christ the head of the new covenant; and the disappearing glory of Moses' face symbolized the abrogation of the old covenant. Commenting on that allegorical prophecy of the Mosaic covenant's being abrogated, Farrar noted that the term

[20]*Ibid.*

"abrogated" or its equivalent occurs 22 times in Paul's epistles.[21]

"Which glory was passing away . . ." Paul seized upon the fact of the vanishing radiance of Moses' countenance as an allegorical promise that the entire OT covenant would, in time, be discontinued, or taken out of the way.

The complaint of Foy E. Wallace, Jr., regarding the RSV's rendition of this paragraph is fully justified. He said:

> They have omitted "done away" (v. 7), "abolished" (v. 13), and "is done away in Christ" (v. 14) . . . This chapter clearly affirms the abolition of the *ministration of death* (the Old Covenant). They have clobbered the entire chapter of 2 Corinthians 3.[22]

Verse 9, *For if the ministration of condemnation hath glory, much rather doth the ministration of righteousness exceed in glory.*

The whole relationship between the two covenants was dealt with by Paul in Hebrews (See CH, pp. 176-179); and, despite the fact that the total abrogation of the old covenant is stated here, it is incidental to the truth being stressed, that is, that the new covenant is more glorious.

Verses 10, 11, *For verily that which hath been made glorious hath not been made glorious in this respect, by reason of the glory that surpasseth. For if that which passeth away was with glory, much more that which remaineth is in glory.*

"That which hath been made glorious . . ." refers to the old covenant.

"Not been made glorious in this respect . . ." that is, not as glorious as the new covenant.

"By reason of the glory that surpasseth . . ." means "because of the glory of the new covenant."

"That which passeth away . . ." is needlessly softened in this version. As the RV margin gives it, the better rendition is "is being done away."

---

[21]F. W. Farrar, *op. cit.*, p. 59.
[22]Foy E. Wallace, Jr., *op. cit.*, p. 438.

Paul's stress in these verses of the fading glory and ultimate abrogation of the law of Moses was directly related to the problems at Corinth. Macknight was almost certainly correct in his view that:

> These observations (of Paul) concerning the glory or excellence of the gospel above the law, were made by the apostle to convince the Corinthians how ill-founded was the boasting of the false teacher, who assumed to himself great honor on account of his knowledge of the law of Moses, and who erroneously enjoined obedience to the law, as necessary to salvation.[23]

Verses 12, 13, *Having therefore such a hope, we use boldness of speech, and are not as Moses who put a veil upon his face, that the children of Israel should not look stedfastly on the end of that which was passing away.*

Paul's argument in these verses might be paraphrased rather bluntly as, "Well, anyway, we do not have to put a veil over our face like Moses did. Our gospel is clear and plain." Dummelow's paraphrase is: "Since our hopes for the future of the gospel are so great, we speak frankly and boldly. We do not seek to conceal anything as Moses concealed his face with a veil."[24]

"Was passing away . . ." is better rendered "was being done away" (RV margin), because in this marginal rendition there is implied the conscious purpose of God in "doing away" with the old covenant. That old covenant was not something passed away with time; Almighty God consciously abrogated it, on the basis that Israel had broken it (Heb. 8:9).

Clines observed that "Concealment was not necessarily Moses' motive for the veil; Paul is probably thinking that it was God's providence that the Israelites never saw that the glory was fading."[25]

Verses 14, 15, *But their minds were hardened: for until this very day at the reading of the old covenant, the same veil*

---

[23]James Macknight, *Apostolical Epistles and Commentary* (Grand Rapids: Baker Book House, 1969), p. 342.

[24]J. R. Dummelow, *Commentary on the Holy Bible* (New York: The Macmillan Company, 1937), p. 931.

[25]David J. A. Clines, *op. cit.*, p. 423.

remaineth, it not being revealed to them that it is done away in Christ. But unto this day, whensoever Moses is read, a veil lieth upon their heart.

Paul got a lot out of every metaphor he used. As Cline suggested: "Paul rang all the changes on *veil* here."[26] In these verses, it stands for the hardening of Israel; but the most significant thing is the fact of the veil's being done away in Christ! An immense body of truth is related to *Christ and the Veil,* as the word is used in scripture. The rending of the veil of the temple during our Lord's crucifixion, for example, compels the linking of many of the most significant truths in the Bible under the subject of Christ and the Veil. See CM, pp. 486-489. Without Christ, the OT is an impenetrable mystery. Paul pointed out here that the Jews who did not believe in Jesus were blinded to many of the most significant things in the OT. "Few passages in the NT emphasize more strongly that the Old Testament scriptures are fully intelligible only when Christ is seen to be their fulfillment."[27]

Verse 16, *But whensoever it shall turn to the Lord, the veil is taken away.*

"It shall turn to the Lord . . ." The marginal reading is, "any man shall turn"; this being true of course, but the "it" would seem to be a reference to Israel.

Verse 17, *Now the Lord is the Spirit: and where the Spirit of the Lord is, there is liberty.*

Paul does not here fuse the persons of the Lord and the Holy Spirit; for it is Christ who sends the Spirit.

"There is liberty . . ." When a Christian is converted, receiving the Holy Spirit as an earnest of redemption, there is bestowed at the same time freedom: (1) from the law (Gal. 4:18), (2) from fear (Rom. 8:13), (3) from the law of sin and death (Rom. 8:2), (4) from sin (Rom. 6:18), and (5) from corruption (Rom. 8:21).

Filson's understanding of what Paul meant here is:

---

[26]*Ibid.*
[27]R. V. G. Tasker, *op. cit.*, p. 67.

> Christ and the Spirit are one in nature and share in the guidance of the church . . . Here, in saying that the Lord is the Spirit, he means especially that as Spirit the Lord can be with his people everywhere.[28]

As Kelcy said, "Christ and the Spirit are separate personalities; but, because of the closeness of their work, there is a practical identity; and to turn to either is to turn to the other"[29]

> The *thou shalt* and *thou shalt not* of the OT disappear in the presence of the Spirit of adoption (Gal. 4:7) through which we become imitators of God as beloved children (Eph. 5:1), walking in love.[30]

The above comment from Russell is typical of many false deductions based upon Paul's teaching in this chapter. Jesus our Lord gave many negative commandments which may not be ignored by any Christian who hopes to be received in heaven. See Matthew 5:19. There are seven negative commandments in the first twenty verses of Matthew 6. It is simply not true that "in Christ" we are freed from any "thou shalt" or "thou shalt not" commands. Liberty in Christ does not grant license.

Verse 18, *But we all with unveiled face beholding as in a mirror the glory of the Lord, are transformed into the same image from glory to glory, even as from the Lord the Spirit.*

On the identification of Lord and Spirit, see under preceding verse.

"Unveiled face . . ." All Christians, not just one man, as in the case of Moses, behold the glory of the Lord; and no veil is required. This has a transforming effect on all who do it. It is in the looking of the Christian upon the Lord, as invariably entailed in the worship of him, that a miracle of transformation is wrought in his life. Here Paul revealed the secret of how to "be . . . transformed" (Rom. 12:2).

---

[28]Floyd V. Filson, *Interpreter's Bible* (Nashville: Abingdon Press, 1953), Vol. X, p. 312.

[29]Raymond C. Kelcy, *Second Corinthians* (Austin: R. B. Sweet Co., 1967), p. 24.

[30]John William Russell, *Compact Commentary on the NT* (Grand Rapids: Baker Book House, 1964), p. 443.

"Beholding as in a mirror . . ." The word "beholding" in classical Greek means "looking at one's self in a mirror"; "But that requires steady looking when mirrors are metal, and so the word came to mean simply, *to gaze steadily.*"[31]

"From the Lord the Spirit . . ." McGarvey gave the import of this to be, "Now Jesus is that Spirit, or new covenant of which I have been speaking (vv. 3, 6 & 8); and where that new covenant is, there is liberty, especially the liberty of seeing (without a veil)."[32] In this view, spirit would not be capitalized. Tasker also favored this understanding of it. He said, "(What the Christian beholds) is the manifestation of Christ's glory which is made in his word and by his Spirit, whose office it is to glorify Christ by revealing him to us."[33]

"We all . . ." The notion has persisted in history that only certain special persons could be transformed in Christ; but as John Calvin (as quoted by Hughes) said, "It is evident that Paul is speaking of an experience that is common to all believers."[34] Under the old covenant, only the face of Moses shone; only the high priest went into the Holy of holies; only the priests might serve at the altar, etc., etc. But in the glorious new covenant, "All who are Christ's, whether great or small, whether known or unknown, have this blessed privilege of beholding and being transformed."[35]

---

[31]David J. A. Clines, *op.cit.*, p. 423.
[32]J. W. McGarvey, *op. cit.*, p. 186.
[33]R. V. G. Tasker, *op. cit.*, p. 67.
[34]Philip E. Hughes, *op. cit.*, p. 117.
[35]*Ibid.*

CHAPTER 4

Broomall has an interesting outline of this chapter, as follows:

The hidden and the open (1,2).
The blinded and the enlightened (3).
Slaves and Master (5).
Darkness and Light (6).
The frail and the mighty (7).
Trials and triumph (8-10).
Death and life (11,12).
The written and the spoken (13).
The past and the future (14).
Grace and thanksgiving (15).
The outer and inner man (16).
Affliction and glory (17).
The seen and the eternal (18b).[1]

Verse 1, *Therefore seeing we have this ministry, even as we obtained mercy, we faint not.*

"We . . ." in this chapter refers to Paul, at least mainly, and secondarily to his fellow workers."[2] However, it is especially the apostles who are in view here.

"This ministry . . ." is a reference to "the new covenant."[3]

"Even as we obtained mercy . . ." This clause is very significant as showing that the new covenant brought to mankind through the gospel of Christ "is not an achievement of human ability but a consequence of divine mercy."[4] This is in fact an acknowledgment on Paul's part of his own utter unworthiness, "because mercy is shown only to the guilty, the condemned, and the hopeless."[5]

---

[1]Wick Broomall, *Wycliffe Bible Commentary* (Chicago: Moody Press, 1971), p. 664.
[2]Floyd V. Filson, *Interpreter's Bible* (Nashville: Abingdon Press, 1953), Vol. X, p. 314.
[3]David Lipscomb, *Second Corinthians* (Nashville: The Gospel Advocate Co., 1937), p. 57.
[4]Philip E. Hughes, *Paul's Second Epistle to the Corinthians* (Grand Rapids: Wm. B. Eerdmans Publishing Co., 1962), p. 122.
[5]*Ibid.*

Verse 2, *But we have renounced the hidden things of shame, not walking in craftiness, nor handling the word of God deceitfully; but by the manifestation of the truth commending ourselves to every man's conscience in the sight of God.*

"We have renounced . . ." This does not refer to any recent renunciation on Paul's part, but to the fundamental renunciation of all the works of the devil at the time of his conversion to Christ. As Farrar put it: "We renounced them once and forever at our baptism."[6]

"Hidden things . . . craftiness . . . deceitfully . . ." Rather than viewing this as Paul's defense of himself from criticism imputing such devices to him by his enemies, it is preferable, as Kelcy did, to see this as Paul's allusion "to such underhanded methods of certain false teachers at Corinth."[7] This, therefore, is not Paul's defense of himself, as widely supposed, but his charges against them! Allo supported this view thus:

> Plainly Paul has someone in view — and in such a manner that he will not fail later on to disclose who it is. It is in chapters 10 to 13 that this will be done. These rumblings of polemic, still vague and muffled, certainly have the air of preparing the way for a decisive explanation rather than of recalling one which has already been given.[8]

The fashionable explanation of much of the Corinthian letters as Paul's attempts to defend himself against slanders is lacking in both discernment and logic. Paul simply was not the kind of a man who was always on the defensive. Before he has finished this letter, he will take the offensive in such a manner as to demonstrate the fundamentally offensive and aggressive nature of his life and preaching.

"Craftiness . . ." refers to tricky and deceitful devices which no faithful preacher of the word of God may use.

"Handling deceitfully . . ." No greater sin exists than that of perverting and polluting the word of God, whether by toning

---

[6]F. W. Farrar, *Pulpit Commentary* (Grand Rapids: Wm. B. Eerdmans Publishing Company, 1950), Vol. 19, 2 Cor., p. 89.

[7]Raymond C. Kelcy, *Second Corinthians* (Austin: R. B. Sweet Co., 1967), p. 28.

[8]Philip E. Hughes, *op. cit.*, p. 122.

down its requirements, or adulterating it with purely secular teachings. Such a corruption of the word of God, according to Lenski, is "the most dastardly of all the dastardly deeds done in the world."[9]

"Manifestation of the truth . . ." This does not mean merely that Paul spoke the truth, which of course he did; but the reference is to that whole system of truth brought in Christianity. As Hillyer said, "*Truth* is almost a technical term for *Christ* or *gospel.*"[10]

"To every man's conscience . . ." Paul did not mean by this that everybody believed him, but that his life and teachings were of such a character that every man *should have* believed him. The next verse is somewhat of an implied diatribe, replying to the unstated question, "Then why have not all believed?"

Before leaving this verse, the comment of Tasker should be noted:

> Although the intellects of men and women may be attracted by the sophistries and subtleties of "the essayist in the pulpit" it is the plain unadulterated gospel that alone strikes home to man's conscience. "Repent and believe the gospel" must ever be the burden of one who is preaching *in the sight of God.*[11]

Verse 3, *And even if our gospel is veiled, it is veiled in them that perish.*

This verse replies, as in a diatribe, to the objection that Paul's gospel was veiled to some. One of the great marvels of the glorious truth in Christ Jesus is that to many people it is absolutely hidden. However, not for a moment does Paul allow any man to be blameless in the inability to see the truth. If one does not see it, it is his fault. "The veil (that prevents their seeing) is woven by their own prejudices and corrupt affec-

---

[9]R. C. H. Lenski, *The Interpretation of St. Paul's First and Second Epistles to the Corinthians* (Columbus: Wartburg Press, 1937), p. 955.

[10]Norman Hillyer, *The New Bible Commentary, Revised* (Grand Rapids: Wm. B. Eerdmans Publishing Co., 1970), p. 1079.

[11]R V. G. Tasker, *The Second Epistle of Paul to the Corinthians* (Grand Rapids: Wm. B. Eerdmans Publishing Co., 1958), p. 70.

tions."[12] As Jesus said it, "Men love darkness rather than the light because their deeds are evil" (John 3:19). Man's moral condition determines whether or not he will see the truth.

"Them that perish . . ." The scholars insist that this is a mistranslation and should read, "in them that are perishing." Plumptre said, "The force of the present participle, as not excluding the thought of future change, should be noted."[13] Even hardened sinners who will not see the truth still have the option of changing if they will.

Verse 4. *In whom the god of this world hath blinded the minds of the unbelieving, that the light of the gospel of the glory of Christ, who is the image of God, should not dawn upon them.*

"In whom . . ." Macknight translated this "by whom" and referred it to intellectual sinners in high places whom the devil uses as instruments in blinding yet others.[14]

Satan, God of This World

"The god of this world . . ." "Satan is not here called the god of the *cosmos*, but god of *this age*."[15] Nevertheless, as Filson said, "Christ has broken the grip of Satan on mankind, but his remaining power is so great that Paul can call him the god of this present evil age."[16] McGarvey was right in declaring that this passage does not impute deity to Satan. "Satan is not a god properly, but is merely one in reference to those who have sinfully made him such."[17] Many believe, as did Lipscomb, that the sin of Adam "transferred the allegiance and rule of the world from God to the devil";[18] but the conviction here is that all of Satan's authority is usurped, that only what God permits is he able to do; and as for the notion that Satan in any meaningful sense rules the world, Nebuchadnezzar had to eat

---

[12]James Macknight, *Apostolical Epistles and Commentary* (Grand Rapids: Baker Book House, 1969), Vol. II, p. 350.

[13]E. H. Plumptre, *Ellicott's Commentary* (Grand Rapids: Zondervan Publishing House, 1959), Vol. VIII, p. 375.

[14]James Macknight, *op. cit.*, p. 350.

[15]F. W. Farrar, *op. cit.*, p. 89.

[16]Floyd V. Filson, *op. cit.*, p. 316.

[17]J. W. McGarvey, *Second Epistle to the Corinthians* (Cincinnati: Standard Publishing Company, 1916), p. 188.

[18]David Lipscomb, *op. cit.*, p. 59.

grass for seven years in order to learn that "The most High ruleth in the kingdom of men, and giveth it to whomsoever he will" (Dan. 4:25). This means that Satan's promise to give Christ the rulership of the world in return for falling down and worshiping the devil (Matt. 4:4ff) was an unqualified falsehood.

Other NT passages that refer to Satan in a similar manner to that of Paul here are:

> "the prince of the powers of the air" (Eph. 2:2).
> "the prince of this world" (John 12:31; 14:30; 16:11).

"Blinded the minds . . ." This refers to "hardening" as it is called in other places in the NT (Rom. 1:21; 11:7,25, etc.). An extensive study of this phenomenon was undertaken in the Commentary on Romans, and reference is here made to pages 39-51, 392-419. Blinding, darkening and hardening all refer to the same thing. The condition that results is sinful, and at the same time punishment for sin. Hardening occurs when the individual rebels against God, who then allows Satan to have his way, with a result of further hardening; and thus, in a sense God hardens men, as in the case of Pharaoh (Rom. 9:17,18). Satan was never able to blind any person who had not already rebelled against God.

"That the light . . ." refers to the illumination of the minds of all who accept Christ.

"Of the gospel of the glory of Christ . . ." The gospel of Christ is the source of all spiritual light. It is a gospel of glory, and that glory is of Christ.

"That the light . . . should not dawn upon them . . ." The great purpose of Satan is to prohibit any true knowledge of the Lord Jesus Christ. Tertullian pointed out that Satan used superstition to blind men. He said: "The whole superstition of this world has gotten into his hands, so that he blinds effectively the hearts of unbelievers."[19]

"Who is the image of God . . ." Other NT passages in which Christ is referred to as God's image are:

> "Who is the image of the invisible God" (Col. 1:15).
> "The very image of his substance" (Heb. 1:3).

---

[19]As quoted by Philip E. Hughes, *op. cit.*, p. 128.

"He that beholdeth me beholdeth him that sent me" (John 12:45).

"He that hath seen me hath seen the Father" (John 14:9).

Christ is the image of God in two ways. (1) As a perfect man, he, like Adam, was "in the image of God" (Gen. 1:26). (2) As God in human form, Jesus accurately mirrored the Father's will for mankind.

Verse 5, *For we preach not ourselves, but Christ Jesus as Lord, and ourselves as your servants for Jesus' sake.*

"We preach not ourselves . . ." As Lipscomb declared, "This cannot mean that Paul excluded all reference to himself or his faith and maintained altogether an impersonal tone in his preaching."[20] The meaning is that Paul rejected all personal claims to any human authority on his part, preaching only what Christ commanded him to preach. "All is of God; nothing is of self."[21]

"But Jesus as Lord . . ." The supreme Lordship of Christ was central in all apostolic preaching. This is recognized by every Christian whose very confession, at the time of his conversion, begins with "confessing Jesus as Lord" (Rom. 10:9).

"And ourselves your servants for Jesus' sake . . ." The Greek word here rendered "servants" is *doulos*; and it means *slaves*. "Paul is not suggesting, however, that he is a slave of the Corinthians."[22] There is but one Master, who is Christ the Lord; and it is purely "for his sake" that the apostle assumed the role of a slave of the Christians at Corinth.

Verse 6, *Seeing it is God that said, Light shall shine out of darkness, who shined in our hearts, to give the light of the knowledge of the glory of God in the face of Jesus Christ.*

"Light shall shine out of darkness . . ." This verse carries strong overtones of Paul's conversion after the blinding light he witnessed on the Damascus road. Furthermore, the reference to Genesis 1:3, where it is written, "Let there be light,"

---

[20]David Lipscomb, *op. cit.*, p. 60.
[21]Philip E. Hughes, *op. cit.*, p. 132.
[22]*Ibid.*

links the original creation with the new spiritual creation in Christ (5:17). Tasker gives a quotation from Chrysostom as follows:

> Then indeed he said, Let it be; and it was. But now he said nothing, but himself became Light for us. For the apostle does not say, "has also now commanded," but "he himself shined."[23]

"The glory of God in the face of Jesus Christ . . ." The only true knowledge of God which is available to men is comprehended in the life and teachings of the Son of God. As Wesley put it: "It is more useful for us to behold God as he appears in his only-begotten Son, than to investigate his secret essence."[24] Paul's allusion seems to be the fact that he had seen the blessed face of the Son of God in the blinding light that overwhelmed him on the road to Damascus, and that he unhesitatingly identified the face of Christ with the glory of God.

Verse 7, *But we have this treasure in earthen vessels, that the exceeding greatness of the power may be of God, and not from ourselves.*

The thought of this verse is that God entrusted the gospel to men who had none of the trappings of earthly power and honor, in order that the great success of the gospel would not be accredited to its messengers as men, but unto the eternal God who inspired them. And, although it is true, as Lipscomb said, that any earthly body "is an unworthy receptacle for so glorious a message,"[25] yet there seems to be in view here the lowly earthly estate of the apostles.

Earthen Vessels

"In earthen vessels . . ." The figure is possibly drawn from the "small pottery lamps, cheap and fragile, that could be bought in the shops of Corinth";[26] or from the custom observed in Roman triumphs, in which the silver or other precious

---

[23]R. V. G. Tasker, *op. cit.*, p. 72.

[24]John Wesley, *One Volume NT Commentary* (Grand Rapids: Baker Book House, 1972), *in loco.*

[25]David Lipscomb, *op. cit.*, p. 62.

[26]Philip E. Hughes, *op. cit.*, p. 135.

metals looted from conquered peoples was melted down and poured into clay pots to be carried in the procession. "Herodotus tells us that Darius melted his gold into earthen pots, which could be broken when it was wanted."[27] Tiffany's in New York City once displayed a fantastically large and beautiful diamond on a small piece of driftwood. As Reid said, "A frail vessel of earth, a little clay lamp, was often used to hold the light."[28]

A great many commentators stress the ephemeral nature of frail and transitory mortal life in connection with this; but the preferable view is that of seeing the apostles who had been fishermen and tax collectors, and who were the most remarkably ordinary men; and Paul, as the most gifted of them, yet drastically handicapped by the thorn in the flesh, which may have been the bitter hatred of his whole race and nation, as well as by his unimpressive personal appearance — seeing *such men* literally take the whole world for Jesus Christ!

"That the power may be of God, and not from ourselves . . ." Let any man consider the facts: (1) of the difficulty encountered in turning pagan worshipers away from their idols, or the power required to woo men away from the fleshly lusts in which they lived, or the strength of fleshly ties that had to be severed, of the animosity and hatred that invariably came from priests, magistrates and others whose vested interests were jeopardized by the acceptance of a new religion, and the combined opposition to Christianity of every evil and shameful institution in the entire social order of that period; and (2) the fact that none of the apostles had any standing as worldly authorities, or even as respected teachers, and having no other background except that of laborers, etc. Let any man consider all of that, and then let him declare that God's purpose was indeed served by placing the inestimable riches of the treasures of the gospel in *earthen vessels*, in order that the power of the new faith would be recognized as coming from God himself, and not from any abilities of its human advocate.

---

[27]J. R. Dummelow, *One Volume Commentary on the Holy Bible* (New York: The Macmillan Company, 1937), p.932.

[28]James Reid, *Interpreter's Bible* (Nashville: Abingdon Press, 1953), Vol. X, p. 318.

Verses 8-10, *We are pressed on every side, yet not straitened; perplexed, yet not unto despair; pursued, yet not forsaken; smitten down, yet not destroyed; always bearing about in the body the dying of Jesus, that the life also of Jesus may be manifested in our body.*

As Macknight said, "This is supposed to refer to the Grecian games";[29] but the figure of a race (the third analogy) would not be true in such a comparison, because Paul's enemies were not in a Christian race with Paul. Plumptre believed that "The imagery here belongs to the soldier on active service."[30] It is perhaps best to forget about any special analogy that Paul might have had in mind and to consider these clauses merely as "the great paradoxes of the Christian life."[31] His own experiences during his apostolical ministry were the true background of all that is said here.

"Pressed . . . but not straitened . . ." Moffatt translated this "harried, but not hemmed in." On Paul's first missionary tour, his enemies had chased him everywhere, but were never able to hem him in.

"Perplexed, yet not unto despair . . ." The disorders at Corinth were certainly perplexing to Paul, but there is no evidence that he ever despaired.

"Pursued, yet not forsaken . . ." Forty men pursued Paul with a view to killing him, but he was not forsaken of the Lord (Acts 23:12ff). Both Lenski and Carver state that "The metaphor here is that of a mortal chase and flight."[32]

"Smitten down, yet not destroyed . . ." As Bruce paraphrased this, "Knocked down, but not out!"[33] Paul was literally stoned and left for dead (Acts 14:19); and that is surely an example of his being knocked down but not knocked out!

"Always bearing about in the body the dying of Jesus . . ." The thought here is that the same vicious hatred of every evil

---

[29]James Macknight, *op. cit.*, p. 355.
[30]E. H. Plumptre, *op. cit.*, p. 376.
[31]William Barclay, *The Letters to the Corinthians* (Philadelphia: The Westminster Press, 1954), p. 223.
[32]Frank G. Carver, *Beacon Bible Commentary* (Kansas City. Beacon Hill Press, 1968), Vol. 8, p. 534.
[33]William Barclay, *op. cit.*, p. 223.

element on earth which finally succeeded (with God's permission) in nailing Jesus to the cross was now focused upon the Lord's apostles. This was the fulfillment of exactly what Jesus had promised. "A servant is not greater than his Lord. If they persecuted me, they will persecute you . . . all these things will they do unto you for my name's sake" (John 15:20, 21).

"That the life of Jesus may be manifested in our body . . ." The apostles were partakers both of the sufferings of Jesus and of the life of Jesus, a life which they were able to impart to others by preaching of the gospel. Paul correctly read the two, the sufferings and the spiritual life imparted to others, as directly related to Jesus. Also, it should be noted here that Paul viewed both the death of Jesus and the life of Jesus as historical facts. For him there was no such distinction as that alleged by unbelieving critics who speak of "the historical Jesus" and the "risen Jesus." They were both historical!

Verse 11, *For we who live are always delivered unto death for Jesus' sake, that the life also of Jesus may be manifested in our mortal flesh.*

"This verse repeats, and so emphasizes the thought of verse 10."[34] See under preceding verse for comment.

Verse 12, *So then death worketh in us, but life in you.*

Paul is not here complaining to the effect that he suffers all of the hardships, and the Corinthians receive all of the benefits. He has reference to the causal effect of his persecutions with their result in many conversions. Paul's many escapes from death and all of the other providences which had preserved his life miraculously through so many dangers were a part of the irrefutable evidence that God was with him. There was no denying the fact, as pointed out by Trasker, that:

> The power of the risen Jesus was being revealed here and now in his own body. The apostles were thus witnesses in deed as well as in word to the truth of their Lord's resurrection.[35]

---

[34]Floyd V. Filson, *op. cit.*, p. 321.
[35]R. V. G. Tasker, *op. cit.*, p. 74.

Verse 13, *But having the same spirit of faith, according to that which is written, I believed, and therefore did I speak; we also believe, and therefore also we speak.*

"According to that which is written . . ." This was Paul's formal designation of what he was about to quote as a passage from the word of God; and again the carelessness of the RSV in murdering this clause should be noted but not excused. Of all the places to find a correction of their error . . . it is in the Interpreter's Bible! "Paul cites the Psalm passage as scripture, according as it is written; the RSV rendering does not make this clear."[36]

"I believed, and therefore did I speak . . ." This is from Psalm 116:10, a psalm which is titled, "Thanksgiving for Deliverance from Death" in the RV. It was indeed appropriate that Paul, who had so frequently been delivered from death, should use the same words here. It is possible that Paul had read this Psalm frequently during his tribulations. G. Campbell Morgan identified this verse as revealing the secret of effective preaching. Because Paul believed, his testimony had the ring of truth. Morgan concluded with the imperative: "If you do not believe, shut your mouth!"[37] This writer would add that if men do not believe the word of God, let them refrain from wasting our time with their books on the subject.

In this verse Paul disclosed the first of four reasons which explained his endurance of so many trials. No. 1, he truly believed God's word.

Verse 14, *Knowing that he that raised up the Lord Jesus shall raise up us also with Jesus, and shall present us with you.*

Here Paul calmly faced the ultimate prospect of his own death, giving the lie to all of the fancy allegations that he thought the Second Coming would occur in his lifetime. Here he affirmed that the Lord would raise him from the dead!

"With Jesus . . ." cannot mean at the same time with Jesus, for Jesus had already been raised from the dead and had ascended to the right hand of the Majesty on High.

---

[36]Floyd V. Filson, *op. cit*, p. 322.
[37]G. Campbell Morgan, *The Corinthian Letters of Paul* (Old Tappan, N. J.: Fleming H. Revell Co., 1946), p. 239.

"With you . . ." This has to mean that Paul also expected that all of the Corinthians would die before the Second Coming, because here he envisioned their being presented (see Col. 1:28) with himself. This verse is reason No. 2. Paul knew that death itself would not rob him of the crown of life, nor would it rob his Corinthian converts, despite the fact that both he and his converts would pass through it.

Verse 15, *For all things are for your sakes, that the grace, being multiplied through the many, may cause the thanksgiving to abound unto the glory of God.*

"For all things are for your sakes . . ." This is reason No. 3. Paul's hardships were actually contributing to the conversion of many souls, and also to their being grounded and established in the faith. This occurred because it would not have been possible for any man to suppose that such trials, dangers and persecutions as those endured by Paul would have marked the efforts of any insincere charlatan.

"Through the many . . . unto the glory of God . . ." Here is reason No. 4. Paul endured because his sufferings glorified God by the bringing of many souls unto salvation.

Verse 16, *Wherefore we faint not; but though our outward man is decaying, yet our inward man is renewed day by day.*

"Wherefore we faint not . . ." has the meaning of "For the four reasons just cited, he was able to endure."

"Our outward man is decaying . . ." This is not a reference to the "old man" (Rom. 6:6; Eph. 4:22; Col. 3:9), having the simple meaning that his physical body, with all of its powers, was moving inexorably to its dissolution. All of the powers and glory of mortal life are like a flower that blooms and then crumbles into dust; and how sad it would be for man if there was nothing to anticipate except the grave.

"Inward man is renewed day by day . . ." The true believer in Christ is not overly disturbed by the erosion and decay of all physical life, because his soul is feasting upon that Bread which came down from heaven, even our Lord Jesus Christ. The inner spiritual life, which is the glory of the "new creature" in Christ, does not diminish or fade. "Brighter the way groweth each day," in the words of an old hymn. Happy indeed are they who rejoice in the growing strength of the inner man as the swift seasons roll. For those who are without this treasure, the decay of the outward is the decay of everything.

Verse 17, *For our light affliction, which is for the moment, worketh for us more and more exceedingly an eternal weight of glory.*

The surprise of this verse is that the epic sufferings of Paul should be termed "our light affliction"; This cannot mean, literally, that they were in any sense "light"; but that *in comparison* with the ultimate glory of Christians, they are light. James Macknight has an inspiring paragraph on this verse, as follows:

> It is hardly possible to express the force of this passage as it stands in the original. Nothing greater can be said or imagined. The apostle, about to describe the happiness of the righteous in heaven takes fire. He calls it not glory, merely, but a weight of glory, in opposition to the light thing of our affliction, and an eternal weight of glory, in opposition to the momentary duration of our affliction, and a most exceeding eternal weight of glory, as beyond comparison greater than all the dazzling glories of riches, fame, power, pleasure, or than anything that can be possessed in the present life![38]

Both Macknight and Plumptre stressed the repetition of "exceedingly" by Paul in the Greek, which is literally, "worketh for us exceedingly, exceedingly, etc."[39] This is an idiom meaning "exceeding the superlative."

Verse 18, *While we look not at the things which are seen, but at the things which are not seen: for the things which are seen are temporal; but the things which are not seen are eternal.*

The entire genius of the Christian life, indeed the entirety of faith in both the old and new covenants, is here distilled and isolated as to its pure essence. Trusting God, believing and obeying him, are finally nothing more than what is revealed here.

---

[38]James Macknight, *op. cit.*, p. 359.
[39]E. H. Plumptre, *op. cit.*, p. 378.

Seeing the Invisible

If one can see it, it cannot last. All visible things are temporal, whether flowers, suns or galaxies; and it also applies to that which one sees when he looks at himself in a mirror. The author of the book of Hebrews (just who could this have been, if not Paul?) devoted almost all of chapter 11 to an exposition of this verse, leaving the impression that the writer of this passage, after thinking about it for more than a decade, took up the OT and applied the principle stated here to all of the salient features in it. Note the following:

Introduction: Faith itself is "a conviction of things not seen" (v. 1). This does not mean things which are merely overlooked, but things which, by their very nature, cannot be seen at all. "Things not seen" include everything in the whole theater where faith operates. Such things as the understanding of how the universe was created, the incarnation of Christ, the judgment of the world by the deluge, the Second Advent, the final judgment, and the assignment of his final destiny to every man — in fact, everything of ultimate importance relates to the things invisible. It has been a failure to discern this quite obvious and simple truth in Hebrews 11:1 which has contributed so heavily to scholarly disagreements about what is meant by that passage.

I. God framed the universe itself out of things unseen (stated invertedly). "Hath not been made out of things which appear" (11:3). Modern science has proved that atoms, the building blocks of all creation, are not merely invisible, but are also practically nothing at all, being electrically charged particles in orbit around other particles and in the aggregate composed almost entirely of space. It is literally true that the whole universe is made of "things unseen," even regarding the tiniest particles of it; and, in addition to that, the great fundamental laws controlling all things in space, such as gravity, centrifugal and centripital forces, inertia, radiation, etc., are, all of them, invisible.

II. Noah, acting upon God's instructions, preserved through the flood a new beginning for the human family. "Being warned of God concerning things not seen as yet" (11:7). Such a flood as God promised had never occurred before; and it was a sheer act of faith for Noah to believe in "thing not seen as yet."

III. Abraham likewise trusted in the invisible; and although the word "unseen" is not used in connection with his obedience, the thought is surely in this, "For he looked for the city that hath the foundations, whose builder and maker is God" (11:10). That city, to be sure, was invisible in any ordinary sense.

IV. Jacob, when near death, blessed his sons and "made mention of the departure of the children of Israel" (11:22). This was trust in "things unseen" by virtue of their being future.

V. Moses forsook Egypt and cast his lot with Israel; "For he endured as seeing him who is invisible," i.e., the invisible God (11:27). No greater test of trusting the "unseen" was ever successfully met. The wealth, glory, power and splendor of Egypt were very visible. Moses could see the armies, orchards, palaces and pyramids which belonged to Pharaoh and might also have belonged to him; but he trusted the promises of the invisible God.

VI. This is exactly the challenge of faith in every generation, to believe in the things which no one can see. Heaven, hell, the final judgment of all men, the Second Coming, the resurrection of the dead practically everything of importance in Christian faith, regards the "things that are unseen," and which things are designated here by Paul as eternal.

VII. "He that believeth and is baptized shall be saved" (Mark 16:16) regards the same confidence in "things not seen." The new birth is invisible; and, although the outward act of baptism may be seen, such things as the pollution of a soul by sin, the surrender of the heart to God, the forgiveness of the sinner which takes place not on earth but in the heart of God, and the resultant change of directions deriving from the new birth — none of these things can be seen literally. They belong in that category of "things not seen as yet." However, since the universe itself is made of "things unseen," no one need ever fear to step out firmly and confidently upon the promise of God. "The things which are unseen are eternal."

VIII. Just as God is invisible (11:27), the Holy Spirit is also invisible. The fruits of the Spirit (Gal. 5:22) are not visible, but are like the blessed Spirit himself whom no man has ever seen.

IX. The same principle is operative in the public worship of Christians. The Lord said, "For where two or three are gathered together in my name, there am I in the midst of them" (Matt. 18:20). One may look around him at church, but he will not see the Lord, except by the eyes of faith. Nevertheless, that presence of Christ in the worship is the eternal blessing of the church. Being "unseen," his influence is the eternal essence of every true worship service in his name.

(Note: Further discussion of this intriguing subject is found in CH, chapter 11.)

CHAPTER 5

In the first paragraph of this chapter, Paul spoke of the spiritual body which is to replace the present earthly body of Christians at the time of the Second Advent and judgment of the last day (1:10), and then delivered some of the profoundest teachings in holy scripture regarding the ministry of reconciliation, of which Paul, along with the other apostles, was an ambassador (11-21).

Verse 1, *For we know that if the earthly house of our tabernacle be dissolved, we have a building from God, a house not made with hands, eternal, in the heavens.*

This is Paul's declaration of his certainty (not mere belief) of the existence of the soul after death, when clothed with a glorious new body, it shall live in eternal felicity with God. Of course, this should be understood as the distinctive hope of Christians.

"We know . . ." "This accent of certainty is found only in the Christian writers."[1] Such confidence did not derive from any human conclusions; but, as Hillyer said, "This was not by human reasoning, but by divine revelation."[2]

"Earthly house . . . tabernacle . . ." The word here is actually "tent," which is as good a symbol of that which is transient and temporary as could be imagined. Paul was a tentmaker, and this is exactly the type of metaphor that should have been expected from him; and, added to that was the fact of Israel's having dwelt in tents during the forty years of the wilderness wanderings. No tent could last permanently when exposed to the elements; and the same is true of men's mortal bodies when exposed to the inevitable erosion of time.

"A building from God . . ." This does not deny that men's mortal bodies are also, in a sense, "from God"; but it has

---

[1]F. W. Farrar, *Pulpit Commentary* (Grand Rapids: Wm. B. Eerdmans Publishing Co., 1950), Vol. 19, 2 Cor., p. 119.

[2]Norman Hillyer, *The New Bible Commentary, Revised* (Grand Rapids: Wm. B. Eerdmans Publishing Co., 1970), p. 1079.

special reference to that God-created spiritual body which shall replace the decaying bodies of mortal flesh.

"A house not made with hands . . ." Paul made tents with his hands; but the glorious resurrection body is far above and beyond anything that human hands might contrive.

"Eternal in the heavens . . ." When the soul of a Christian is clothed with that wonderful and glorious spiritual body, decay and death shall be no more; and the soul of the redeemed shall enjoy eternal life.

Regarding the hope of eternal life, it is a fact that the deepest instincts of men's hearts perpetually turn to it. "Man is, by terms of his existence, a being of eternity; and he cannot unmake himself."[3] "There is a deep and wide testimony in man's nature to the existence of God, and of a future life. It may be pronounced either true or false, but it must be admitted to exist."[4] The great affirmation of Christianity is that all of the subliminal longings for immortality in human hearts shall be gloriously realized in Christ Jesus.

Verse 2, *For verily in this we groan, longing to be clothed upon with our habitation which is from heaven.*

"In this we groan . . . has reference to mortal infirmity and the increasing burden of years which press more and more upon every earthly life. Paul's own extraordinary hardships and sufferings might have been in view primarily in this place; but, as Kelcy said, "In this body we groan from pains to which flesh is heir."[5] Or, as Filson stated it: "This reflects Paul's desire to be free from the afflictions and imperfections of this life."[6]

"Longing to be clothed upon . . ." The notion that Paul was here expressing a dread of being a disembodied spirit during the interval between death and the judgment is obviously incorrect. "Clothed upon" does not refer to something Paul

---

[3]Liddon, as quoted by John Wesley, *One Volume NT Commentary* (Grand Rapids: Baker Book House, 1972), *in loco.*

[4]*Ibid.*

[5]Raymond C. Kelcy, *Second Corinthians* (Austin: R. B. Sweet Co., 1967), p. 32.

[6]Floyd V. Filson, *Interpreter's Bible* (Nashville: Abingdon Press, 1953), Vol. X, p. 327.

hoped for at death but to the ultimate replacement of the old body with a new one in the final day. The idea is that of "putting on a new garment to replace the old one."[7] Some commentators, arguing from the peculiar expression "clothed upon," have interpreted this as something that would be done to the physical body, and not to something that would replace it.

Verse 3, *If so be that being clothed we shall not be found naked.*

"Not be found naked . . ." It is a gross error to suppose that this has any reference to the notion of the ancient Greeks, to the effect that "disembodied spirits were under the earth and capable of taking part in life anywhere in the universe."[8] Paul had in mind here the sad truth that some who might expect to be clad with the glorious resurrection body in the final judgment will have no such thing, but be found naked instead. True Christians will be gloriously clothed in eternity; but for those lukewarm and self-satisfied Christians who think their "faith alone" is all they need, eternal nakedness shall be their disappointment. That is why the apostle John instructed that class of Christians to "Buy of me (the Lord) white garments that thou mayest clothe thyself, and that the shame of thy nakedness be not made manifest" (Rev. 3:18). Although salvation is of grace and of the free gift of God, there is a certain "clothing of oneself" that is required of all who would not be naked in eternity. However men may deny this, it is true, as Paul will state dogmatically a little later in verse 10.

Wesley's comment on "We shall not be found naked" is most perceptive, saying that it referred to one whose appearance in the presence of the King was without "the wedding garment."[9] The application of the man without the wedding garment to the "nakedness" in view here is perfect (Matt. 22:11). In the Saviour's parable, the naked one was indeed a guest; he had been invited, had answered the call, and had accepted the King's invitation, even sitting down at his table; but not having the wedding garment, he was "naked" in the eyes of

---

[7]*Ibid.*
[8]Norman Hillyer, *op. cit.*, p. 1079.
[9]John Wesley, *op. cit., in loco.*

the King and was cast into "the outer darkness." In exactly the same way, Christians who neglect or refuse to do the things Christians are commanded to do will appear "naked" in judgment. "Faith only" is nakedness in the eyes of God.

Verse 4, *For indeed we that are in this tabernacle do groan, being burdened; not for that we would be unclothed, but that we would be clothed upon, that what is mortal may be swallowed up of life.*

"Being burdened . . ." This is by further explanation of what Paul meant by "groan." The physical body is an increasing burden with advancing years; and this is perhaps the saddest thing about life on earth. However powerful and glorious the physical body may be for a season, the burden grows heavier and heavier till at last the weary burden bearer stumbles into a grave. This thought was touched upon by Paul in this:

> The Lord Jesus Christ; who shall fashion anew the body of our humiliation, that it may be conformed to the body of his glory, according to the working whereby he is able even to subject all things unto himself (Phil. 3:21).

"The body of our humiliation . . ." This is inspired comment upon the body which is a burden and in which Paul said "we groan." The body of any mortal, at last, is the body of his humiliation. Many years or even decades may pass with little evidence of the humiliation in view here; but inevitably the blow falls.

Illustration: This writer's father was a man of extraordinary strength, and at the age of 80 years still led singing for the village congregation. Then, one day when he was 90 years old, he took this son into a private room where they played a phonograph record, made many years earlier, when the father's voice was young and vigorous and beautiful. As we listened, both of us burst into tears; and Dad said "Ah son now we know what Paul meant by "the body of our humiliation."

"Not that we would be unclothed . . ." This has the meaning, "Not that we want to die."

"But that we would be clothed upon . . ." means, "Nevertheless, we still long to possess that eternal body."

"That what is mortal may be swallowed up of life . . ." This has the same weight as 1 Corinthians 15:53, 54, being an obvious reference to what is written there; and here also, in all probability, lies the explanation of the peculiar form "clothed upon."

Verse 5, *Now he that wrought us for this very thing is God, who gave us the earnest of the Spirit.*

Other references of the apostle to the "earnest" of the Holy Spirit are in 1:22 and Ephesians 1:13. The meaning of "earnest" is exactly that of the word as used by realtors in sealing the purchase of a piece of property. It is a token, or pledge, that the whole contractual price will be paid. The application is that through God's impartation of the Holy Spirit (in token measure) to all who are baptized into Christ, there is a pledge of the total redemption God promised to them that believe and obey his word. Some have taken this "gift of the Holy Spirit" (Acts 2:38), or "Holy Spirit of promise" (Eph. 1:13), as it is called, for a promise of direct guidance of his children on the part of God, without regard to the sacred scriptures; but, of course, this is the grossest error. In any language, a "token" may not be misconstrued as the full possession of God's gracious gift of the Spirit. Evidence of possession of this gift is found in the manifestation of the fruits mentioned in Galatians 5:22.

Verse 6, *Being therefore always of good courage, and knowing that, whilst we are at home in the body, we are absent from the Lord.*

Russell's explanation of this is: "Christ is indeed here and with us always; but, in the clearer vision of the life to come, our realization of his presence will make this present existence to have been absence by comparison."[10]

"Always of good courage . . ." Confidence in the fundamental Christian truth that "No matter what may happen to my body, absolutely nothing can happen to *me*!" is the basis of true Christian courage. The thought is like that expressed poetically:

> Like the bird be thou
> That for a moment rests

---

[10]John William Russell, *Compact Commentary on the NT* (Grand Rapids: Baker Book House, 1964), p. 445.

Upon the topmost bough.
  He feels the branch to bend
And yet as sweetly sings,
Knowing he hath wings!

Verse 7, *For we walk by faith, not by sight.*

This is only a parenthesis, and yet one of the epic statements of scripture. In the previous chapter, Paul had just enunciated the principle that it is regard for the "things unseen" which motivates all Christian behavior, and that only those "things invisible" are eternal; and, since faith regards primarily eternal things, it is impossible to walk by sight. Furthermore, in the cosmic dimensions of that superastronomical theater where is played out the colossal drama of human redemption from sin, faith in God is a far better aid of the understanding than mere knowledge (or sight) could ever be. The simplest facts of eternity, everlasting life, salvation and knowing God are totally beyond the powers of finite exploration. Therefore the word is, "Trust God; for you cannot *know*!" This does not disparage revelation, but it is intended to stress the truth that the finite cannot fully know the infinite.

Verse 8, *We are of good courage, I say, and are willing rather to be absent from the body, and to be at home with the Lord.*

Wesley made this verse the basis of declaring that "The happiness of saints (upon their death) is not deferred till the resurrection";[11] because, as he said, "Paul evidently thinks of no alternative except to be either at home in the body or at home in the Lord."[12] Much as men desire to know about that interval between death and the resurrection, very little may be dogmatically affirmed. None of the dead whom Jesus raised to life ever spoke one word about their experience in death; and such statements as "they rest from their labors" (Rev. 14:13), "Our friend Lazarus has fallen asleep" (John 11:11), etc. — such words forbid the building of any "explanations" on such a passage as this.

Verse 9, *Wherefore also we make it our aim, whether at home or absent, to be well-pleasing unto him.*

---

[11]John Wesley, *op. cit., in loco.*
[12]*Ibid.*

This was merely Paul's way of saying, "Whether we live or die, it is our total purpose to please the Lord."

Verse 10, *For we must all be made manifest before the judgment-seat of Christ; that each one may receive the things done in the body, according to what he hath done, whether it be good or bad.*

Judgment, Only One

"For we must all . . ." This means everybody who ever lived, or ever yet shall live, upon this earth. It is absolutely astounding that brilliant men would try to limit this to "All Christians." Hillyer declared this to mean "all Christians, i.e., no unbelievers."[13] The same opinion was voiced by Clines, "All Christians, not all men."[14] Inasmuch as the NT knows and mentions only one judgment, there can be no reconciliation of that truth with any opinion limiting the judgment scene in this verse to Christians only. The problem does not lie in what Paul taught here, but in the theory of justification by "faith only"; of which, as Tasker said, "Some commentators stress the seeming inconsistency between the doctrine of justification by faith alone and the doctrine of verse 10 that Christians no less than non-Christians will be finally judged by their actions."[15] The blunt truth is that verse 10 is not merely "inconsistent" with the theory of justification by "faith alone"; it is a dogmatic contradiction of it.

As Plumptre said:

> It would have seemed almost impossible, but for the perverse ingenuity of the system-builders of theology, to evade the force of this unqualified assertion of the working of the universal law of retribution. No formula of justification by faith, or imputed righteousness, or pardon sealed in the blood of Christ, or priestly absolution, is permitted by St. Paul to mingle with his expectations of

---

[13]Norman Hillyer, *op. cit.*, p. 1080.

[14]David J. A. Clines, *A New Testament Commentary* (Grand Rapids: Zondervan Publishing House, 1969), p. 426.

[15]R. V. G. Tasker, *The Second Epistle of Paul to the Corinthians* (Grand Rapids: Wm. B. Eerdmans Publishing Co., 1958), p. 83.

> that great day, as revealing the secrets of men's hearts, awarding to each man according to his works![16]

Thus, it was for the clever and ingenious purpose of supporting the "faith only" theory of justification, that scholars have tried to make the judgment scene in verse 10 something different from the general judgment. However, attention is called to the following:

JUDGMENT DAY

"The judgment seat of Christ . . ." In this phrase, the apostle followed the invariable pattern of the NT in refering to the judgment day in the singular. Not even once in the NT is there any reference to more than one judgment. Note:

> Jesus said, "They shall give an account in the day of judgment" (Matt. 12:36).
> The men of Nineveh shall stand up in the judgment with this generation (Matt. 12:41).
> The queen of the south shall rise up in judgment with this generation (Matt. 12:42).
> Whosoever shall say, "Thou fool" shall be in danger of the judgment (Matt. 5:22).
> It shall be more tolerable for Tyre and Sidon in the judgment than for you (Luke 10:14).
> More tolerable for the land of Sodom and Gomorrah in the day of judgment, etc. (Matt. 10:15).
> God hath appointed a day in which he will judge the world by that man whom he hath appointed (Acts 17:31).
> We shall all stand before the judgment seat of God (Rom. 14:10).
> It is appointed unto men once to die, and after this, judgment (Heb. 9:27).

From this it is crystal clear that the foolish notion of a succession of judgment days is nowhere to be found in the word of God, despite the fact of its being advocated in the notes to the Scofield Bible! There is no reason whatever to believe that "the judgment seat of Christ" which Paul mentioned in this verse is

---

[16]E. H. Plumptre, *Ellicott's Commentary* (Grand Rapids: Zondervan Publishing House, 1959), Vol. VII, p. 380.

any different from the one he mentioned in Romans 14:10. The Gospel of John likewise supports the concept of one judgment day (see CJ, pp. 149-50; also CM, pp. 408-411).

Thus, we may be absolutely certain that every man, including every Christian, shall in the last analysis be judged according to his deeds, whether good or bad. There will be no such thing in the judgment as a man of vile deeds being entered into heaven on the basis that "Well, after all, he was a believer!" This cornerstone of Protestant heresy is effectively blasted by Paul's stern words in this passage.

In this connection, however, it is appropriate to add that "the blood of Jesus Christ cleanseth us from all sin" (1 John 1:7); but this promise is for them that "walk in the light." Even the most deplorable sins can be forgiven, and will be forgiven them that continue "in Christ," as believing, baptized Christians, striving to do the will of the Lord, and visibly associated with his kingdom in the present world; nor is it alleged that they could ever achieve or merit redemption as being due to their success in living as God directed; but the whole premise of eternal salvation includes the conscious, serious *effort* of the twice-born to live the new life which was bestowed upon them. "Faith" is no magic device for avoiding this eternal truth.

The whole thrust of this verse is that people who do not live right shall perish eternally. It is not expected that this truth could ever be popular.

Verse 11, *Knowing therefore the fear of the Lord, we persuade men, but we are made manifest unto God; and I hope that we are made manifest also in your consciences.*

"The fear of the Lord . . ." One of the genuine errors of the AV was the rendition of this as "the terror" of the Lord. Paul used the same word in Ephesians 5:21, and Luke used it in Acts 9:1; but as Lipscomb said, " 'Fear' in all of these passages means reverence and devotion."[17]

"We persuade men . . ." It is not God but men who should be persuaded, God having already done everything that even God could do to bring redemption to fallen humanity.

---

[17]David Lipscomb, *Second Corinthians* (Nashville: The Gospel Advocate Company, 1937), p. 74.

"Made manifest unto God . . ." Paul was saying in this that God already knew the sincerity and integrity of his soul and that he hoped the Corinthians also had been able to discern the same thing. "If Paul had not walked continually in the fear of God (Acts 9:31), he might have yielded to the temptation to curry favor with his hearers by whittling down his message to suit their tastes."[18]

Verse 12, *We are not again commending ourselves unto you, but speak as giving you occasion of glorying on our behalf, that ye may have wherewith to answer them that glory in appearance, and not in heart.*

Throughout this part of this noble epistle, Paul was laying the groundwork for a decisive attack upon his enemies that would be unleashed in chapter 10. There is a hint of what is to come here; but for the moment Paul was establishing a few facts with reference to himself, these being (1) his integrity (v. 11), (2) the acute need to commend himself (v. 12), (3) his motivation of doing it all for the sake of the Corinthians (v. 13), (4) that the love of Christ compelled such action on his part (v. 14), and (5) that as an ambassador of Christ commissioned to deliver the word of reconciliation to men, the utmost necessity lay upon him to the effect that he should not merely affirm his own credentials but that he should also press an unrelenting attack against the enemies of the truth (v. 18ff).

"Commending ourselves . . ." "What Paul says is not self-praise; he is only giving his friends in Corinth some facts which they may use in his defense."[19] "Paul had dangerous detractors at Corinth, about whom he will have more to say in chapters x and xi."[20] Hughes also was impressed with the overtones of this verse which are a clear indication of "the unity and coherence of this epistle."[21] We join him in the following quotation from Allo:

> It is plain as Windisch has well observed, that this as yet vague allusion to a subject which will be treated with

---

[18]R. V. G. Tasker. *op. cit.*, p. 83.
[19]Raymond C. Kelcy, *op. cit.*, p. 34.
[20]R. V. G. Tasker, *op. cit.* p. 84.
[21]Philip E. Hughes, *Paul's Second Epistle to the Corinthians* (Grand Rapids: Wm. B. Eerdmans Publishing Co., 1962), p. 189.

> such precision and emphasis in the concluding chapters shows that those chapters were not yet written. When they read or hear them, the Corinthians will no longer need that "something by way of rejoinder" should modestly be suggested to them. The eagle is beginning to cast its gaze from on high on the martens and foxes; but the moment has not yet come to swoop down in vertical descent.[22]

Paul could never have written the mild words of this verse if the Corinthians had already received such a forthright and devastating exposure of Paul's enemies as that contained in chapters 10, 11. Thus the notion (and it is only that) of those chapters being a fragment of a lost "severe letter" Paul had delivered to Corinth in the interval between the two canonical epistles cannot be logically supported. As this mighty epistle moved to its climax, the holy passions of the matchless apostle gradually reached a plateau of inspiration, from which, with a vigor unsurpassed in scripture, he unleashed the full powers of his righteous anger against those emissaries of the devil who were opposing his work in Corinth.

"Them that glory in appearance . . ." The false teachers were boasting of certain external advantages, probably their wealth or social standing; but "in heart" they were wolves in sheep's clothing.

Verse 13, *For whether we are beside ourselves, it is unto God; or whether we are of sober mind, it is unto you.*

It is difficult to know exactly what Paul was saying in this.

"Whether we are beside ourselves . . ." This could be a hint of criticism directed against Paul by the false teachers. A governor called Paul "mad" (Acts 26:24); and even the Saviour was accused of being "beside himself" (Mark 3:21). In any case, all that Paul did was "unto God" and "unto" the Corinthians, i.e., for their sake.

Verse 14, *For the love of Christ constraineth us; because we thus judge, that one died for all, therefore all died.*

"Love of Christ constraineth us . . ." Did Paul here refer to his own love of Christ, or to Christ's love of him? "It matters

---

[22]*Ibid.*

little whether this be interpreted as a subjective genitive, 'Christ's love to men,' or as an objective genitive, 'our love to Christ'; the two suppose and interfuse each other."[23]

"One died for all . . ." Here is the same "all" encountered in verse 10, and it includes all who ever lived. "He is the propitiation for our sins; and not for ours only, but also for the whole world" (1 John 2:2). The atonement established in Christ's death was no piecemeal affair, but was big enough to cover all the men and all the sins of all times and places.

"Therefore all died . . ." Carver's discerning comment is:

> In view of Christ's death, *all men are dead* in respect to any spiritual self-sufficiency. The simplest interpretation is that the fact that Christ died for all proves that all were dead.[24]

From this it appears that those who are not converted, and by means of the new birth "raised with Christ," shall inevitably continue in a state of death throughout eternity. The death of Christ proved that every man deserves death; and, in the spiritual sense, all died and continue in death, till they shall be "raised to walk in newness of life" *in Christ.*

Verse 15, *And he died for all, that they that live should no longer live unto themselves, but unto him who for their sakes died and rose again.*

The argument is that men who have been redeemed from death by Christ who died (and rose again) in their stead should live in conscious appreciation of their eternal debt of love and gratitude to Christ.

"And rose again . . ." This is the climax of the verse. Without the resurrection of Christ, his death was nothing; for a dead Saviour could not save. The grand theme of the NT is "the death, burial, and resurrection of the Son of God, according to the scriptures." "Death without resurrection would evacuate Calvary of all meaning."[25]

---

[23]F. W. Farrar, *op. cit.*, p. 121.
[24]Frank G. Carver, *Beacon Bible Commentary* (Kansas City: Beacon Hill Press, 1968), Vol. 8, p. 551.
[25]Norman Hillyer, *op. cit.*, p. 1080.

Verse 16, *Wherefore we henceforth know no man after the flesh: even though we have known Christ after the flesh, yet now we know him so no more.*

"Know no man after the flesh . . ." The new manner of life for Christians follows the principle laid down here. "They no longer measure men by human standards of race, natural gifts, social standing, or possessions."[26] No sooner had Paul written this than he remembered how, before his conversion, he had measured the Christ himself by those very standards. This he at once confessed and repudiated.

"Even though we have known Christ after the flesh . . ." There are some things this does not mean. It does not mean that Paul associated with Christ during the Lord's ministry. It does not mean that Paul was drawing any distinction between the historical Christ and the risen Christ. It does not mean that Paul's apostleship was here taking some radical turn away from truth which he had believed and taught up to this time. This latter interpretation, of course, has been advocated by men like Baur and Stanley;[27] but such theories overlook the fact that this whole epistle was written by Paul to prove just the opposite of their speculation, namely that the totality of Paul's life and teaching since his acceptance of Christ was absolutely true and consistent.

Regarding the alleged meaning that Paul, as a disciple of Gamaliel, might have had some association with Jesus during his ministry; although this was by no means impossible, it is clear that Paul's meaning here is that:

> Prior to his conversion, his knowledge of Christ had been after the flesh, formed in accordance with external and mistaken standards; but his conversion had meant the transformation of his knowledge of Christ.[28]

"Yet now we know him so no more . . ." Paul no longer judged Christ after the false and artificial standards of the Pharisaical class to which he had once belonged.

---

[26]Raymond C. Kelcy, *op. cit.*, p. 35.
[27]Philip E. Hughes, *op. cit.*, p. 199.
[28]*Ibid.*

Verse 17, *Wherefore if any man is in Christ, he is a new creature: the old things are passed away; behold they are become new.*

In Christ

"In Christ . . ." A phenomenal blindness is the only thing that could account for the total absence from the writings of so many scholars of any reference whatever to this little prepositional phrase which is nothing if not *the very eye of Christianity*. Paul used this expression, or its equivalent, 169 times![29] Failure to appreciate what Paul means by this is to misunderstand everything. Paul had just written that all men are dead spiritually, a deadness that shall never abate unless they are risen again *in Christ*. In Christ, a new spiritual life is given to the convert; in Christ all of his previous sins are cancelled; in Christ he is endowed with the Holy Spirit; in Christ a new and glorious life begins; in Christ old values are rejected, old standards repudiated, and old lusts are crucified; in Christ are "all spiritual blessings" (Eph. 1:3); out of Christ, there is nothing but death, remorse, hopelessness and condemnation; in Christ there is the life eternal!

In the light of the above, how is it that one can read 57 commentaries and find not one single reference to the all-important question of "How does one find the status of being 'in Christ' "? The answer to this question is the concern of every man ever born, or at least it should be. Here is the answer:

> Or are ye ignorant that all we who were baptized into Christ Jesus were baptized into his death? (Rom. 6:3).
>
> As many of you as were baptized into Christ did put on Christ (Gal. 3:27).
>
> For in one Spirit were we all baptized into one body (1 Cor. 12:13).

The baptism "into one body" in the third reference above is exactly the same as being baptized into Christ, because the one body is the spiritual body of Christ. The entire NT gives no

---

[29]John McKay, *God's Order* (New York: Macmillan Company, 1953), p. 67.

other means, provides no other device, and suggests no other ceremony or action that can bring the believer *into Christ.* Why? Because there is none.

But, it is alleged that "faith in Christ" saves; and so it does, but notice the meaning of this oft-repeated and frequently misunderstood expression. "Faith in Christ" means faith exercised by a believer who is "in Christ," having been baptized into him. For any believer who has not been baptized, his faith is not "in Christ" (because *he* is not in Christ); and thus the believer's faith prior to his baptism is not "in Christ" at all, but "out of Christ." The preposterous assumption that one who is not "in Christ" at all may have, in fact, "faith in Christ" is an utter impossibility. These are among the significant reasons why the dominating expression in this marvelous verse is in the words "if any man is in Christ," which appear at the head of the verse. Not a word subsequently appearing in the verse applies to any person in heaven or upon earth who is *not* "in Christ."

Verse 18, *But all things are of God, who reconciled us to himself through Christ, and gave unto us the ministry of reconciliation.*

"All things are of God . . ." The marvelous blessings "in Christ" are of God, as Paul would explain a moment later, because God was in Christ, Christ being called *God* no less than ten times in the Greek NT. It was the Second Person of the Godhead, however, who entered earth life as a man, bore the sins of the whole world and offered himself upon Calvary as a propitiation for the sins of the whole world.

"Who reconciled us . . ." Men are the ones who need to be reconciled; and this thought is again implied here.

"And gave unto us . . ." This is a reference to the apostles of Christ, to whom was committed the ministry of reconciliation, meaning the glad news of the redemption available to every man "in Christ." In a far lesser sense, every Christian is also a custodian of the good news; but in the original and plenary sense, this applies only to the apostles of Christ.

Verse 19, *To wit, that God was in Christ reconciling the world unto himself, not reckoning unto them their trespasses, and having committed unto us the word of reconciliation.*

God in Christ

"God was in Christ . . ." The RV, RSV and others revised the punctuation of this verse, omitting the comma after Christ, doing so for the sole purpose of avoiding the dogmatic affirmation that "God was in Christ"; but, even as the verse is allowed to stand without the comma, the meaning shines through in spite of all efforts to soften it. If God was not in Christ, it would have been impossible for him through Christ to have reconciled the world unto himself! It was precisely this perfect identity with Christ that gave meaning and efficacy to all that Christ did.

> It is the presence of God in Christ which gives to the sacrifice of the cross its infinite value; the doctrine of redemption depends on that of the hypostatic union, a doctrine with which these verses are impregnated.[30]

The many translators and commentators who leave out the comma make up a rather noisy chorus to the effect that the old rendition is not correct; but noise is not argument; and, as Wesley said, "Either translation is grammatically and theologically admissible";[31] and this writer prefers the AV rendition for its stress upon the divinity of Christ. Furthermore, some of those who prefer the RSV, etc., do so not upon textual grounds, but upon prior theological positions. Thus Clines said, "The phrase sounds Johanine rather than Pauline, so the latter translation is preferred."[32] The fundamental error in such a view is the failure to see that Paul and John are one in their views of salvation in Christ. Young scholars, especially, ought not to be intimidated by the nonsense that would try to cover up the agreement between John and Paul. And, as for the impression prevailing in some, to the effect that recent scholars know anything about translating scripture that was unknown to older translators (with the one exception of new manuscript evidence and certain archeological discoveries), this may be confidently denied. This verse as it stands in the AV was so translated by many of the greatest scholars who ever lived, including: Origen, Erasmus, Luther, Calvin, Bach-

---

[30]Philip E. Hughes, *op. cit.*, p. 208.
[31]John Wesley, *op. cit.*, in loco.
[32]David J. A. Clines, *op. cit.*, p. 427.

mann, Allo, Chrysostom, Meyer, Alford, Olhausen, Hodge, Denney, Plummer, Strachan, Filson, and the RSV margin. "God was in Christ."

"Not reckoning unto them their trespasses . . ." The heavenly strategy by which God could, in righteousness. leave off reckoning unto sinners their sins is simply that of the "spiritual body" of Jesus Christ. Men who renounce self, obey the gospel, and are added to the body of Christ, are no longer (legally) themselves, but *Christ.* They are then reckoned to be "in Christ," truly identified with Christ, participants in his death, sharers of Christ's righteousness, and thus wholly justified, not in their original personal identity, but "in Christ and as Christ." Extensive studies of the whole problem of justification are given in the *Commentary on Romans.* See CR, chapter 3, etc.

"Unto us the word of reconciliation . . ." This is parallel to the last clause of the preceding verse; and this double reference led quite naturally to Paul's exposition of his status as God's ambassador, in the next verse.

Verse 20, *We are ambassadors therefore on behalf of Christ, as though God were entreating by us: we beseech you on behalf of Christ, be ye reconciled to God.*

"Ambassadors . . ." Throughout history, the office of an ambassador has been one endowed with plenary authority; and it is this aspect of Paul's ministry which is stressed here. David Lipscomb laid heavy stress upon this most important office of Christ's apostles. He said:

> The apostles were and are the ambassadors of Christ. They sustained a relation to the gospel that no other preachers in their day or since ever sustained or could sustain. They were the *revealers* of the gospel. All others are only proclaimers of what the apostles revealed. No preacher today has any revelation, nor can he claim to be a witness of the resurrection. He has no authority to declare remission of sins; but he can only point to the apostles' declaration on the subject. He may preach the gospel, but he cannot reveal it. He has no message that is not already made known. He does not have the credentials of an ambassador; he cannot work miracles; and God will not work with him in signs and wonders confirming

> the word that he preaches ... We may not expect any more ambassadors until the Lord has a new message for mankind.[33]

"Be ye reconciled to God ..." Men can be reconciled to God in only one way, and that is by complying with the conditions God has laid down in the gospel, which conditions are antecedent and prerequisite to salvation. "There are conditions on the part of man. Christ died for all, but not all will be saved."[34] The ambassadors of Christ, in the NT, have made it clear what men should do to be reconciled to God. There is no other way.

"Christ ... God ..." "The apostle makes no difference between Christ and God, Christ himself being the Second Person of the eternal Godhead."[35] As Christ's ambassador, Paul could declare the conditions of reconciliation with God.

Verse 21, *Him who knew no sin he made to be sin on our behalf; that we might become the righteousness of God in him.*

The great substitutionary passages of Isaiah 53 are behind such a declaration as this. Christ bore the sins of all men; his stripes were the healing of all men. his chastisement was the peace of all men; his suffering was the salvation of all men. "God laid upon him the iniquity of us all."

"The righteousness of God ..." All of the righteousness of God ever achieved upon earth was wrought by Jesus our Lord. Those who would participate in the righteousness of God must do so "in him," that is, "in Christ." It has been admitted by all who ever studied the question that only "the righteousness of God" can save men; and that righteousness is "in Christ"; thus no man can be saved out of Christ. In this context, it should also be observed that the righteousness of God was the achievement of God himself in Christ; and, in answer to the question of what constituted that righteousness, it was the perfect faith and obedience of Christ. The faith that saves, in any absolute sense, is therefore the *faith of Christ*, a fact dogmatically affirmed no less than seven times in the Greek

---

[33]David Lipscomb, *op. cit.*, p. 83.
[34]Raymond C. Kelcy, *op. cit.*, p. 36.
[35]Philip E. Hughes, *op. cit.*, p. 210.

NT (see CR, pp. 118-140). Furthermore, even in the case of the faith of Christ, it was not "faith only," but the perfect faith and obedience of the Son of God which wrought the true righteousness which is the foundation of all human salvation *in him!*

CHAPTER 6

Paul here discussed the trials of ambassadors for Christ (1-10), made a strong emotional appeal to the Corinthians (11-13), and gave instructions against Christians mixing with the pagans (14-18).

Verse 1, *And working together with him we entreat also that ye receive not the grace of God in vain.*

The words *with him* are italicized in the RV, indicating that they are not a part of the Greek text; and, as often in such additions, the meaning is obscured rather than clarified. The thought is that Paul himself was working together with both God and the Corinthians, which work was necessary even for an apostle, that he might not have received the grace of God in vain. He entreated them also to observe the same diligent activity on behalf of the gospel that he was demonstrating in his own life.

Grace of God in Vain

"Grace of God in vain . . ." No apostle could have warned against such a possibility if it never existed; and the words of Olshausen (quoted by Hughes) on this passage are true. He said:

> Paul unquestionably considers the possibility of grace received by the individual being again lost . . . the dangerous error of predestination, which asserts that grace cannot be lost, is unknown to Scripture.[1]

In fairness to Hughes, it should be noted that he rejected this, declaring that Olshausen's opinion "can only have been dictated by prejudice . . . the doctrine of predestination is certainly not unknown in Scripture."[2] Such a rebuttal to obvious truth, however, is typical; but it is not prejudice to read the holy scriptures exactly as they are written; and, while it is

---

[1]Philip E. Hughes, *Paul's Second Epistle to the Corinthians* (Grand Rapids: Wm. B. Eerdmans Publishing Co., 1962), p. 217.
[2]*Ibid.*

true enough that predestination is taught in the scriptures (as regards the body of Christ, and not as it regards individuals), it is not predestination which is denied, but the *error of it* (as Olshausen said) which interprets the doctrine as teaching that a true Christian *cannot* fall from grace and be eternally lost. The *possibility* is plainly inferred in the strongest possible manner by Paul in this very verse.

Receiving God's grace in vain was a fate with which the Corinthians were flirting in a most dangerous manner through their close association with the pagan society around them; and McGarvey accurately viewed this verse as "an introduction" to the stern admonitions beginning in verse 14; but "Before giving the warning (vv. 14ff), he paused to establish his character, influence and authority among them."[3]

As Plumptre said:

> The Corinthians had believed and been baptized, and so they "had received the grace"; but the freedom to choose good or evil still remained, and if they chose evil they would frustrate the end for which the grace was given.[4]

There is nothing unbiblical in the concept of a Christian's "working" to avoid receiving the grace of God in vain. Did not this same apostle command the Philippians to "work out your own salvation with fear and trembling" (Phil. 2:12)? Was Paul not himself "working together" with God, with the Corinthians, or with his fellow apostles (as variously interpreted) as stated in this very verse. And in such work is there the slightest hint of the grace of God being denied as the true source of salvation? How preposterous, therefore, is the remark of Tasker to the effect that these Corinthians were already working and even depending on their works for salvation! He said: "Perhaps they still clung to the belief that they could achieve their own salvation; and to harbor any such delusion is to receive the grace of God *in vain*!"[5] It is much more likely

---

[3]J. W. McGarvey, *Second Epistle to the Corinthians* (Cincinnati: The Standard Publishing Co., 1916), p. 199.

[4]E. H. Plumptre, *Ellicott's Commentary* (Grand Rapids: Zondervan Publishing House, 1959), Vol. 8, p. 383.

[5]R. V. G. Tasker, *The Second Epistle of Paul to the Corinthians* (Grand Rapids: Wm. B. Eerdmans Publishing Co., 1958), p. 92.

that the Corinthians were suffering from the delusion that they would be saved "by faith alone" even while linking up in the most shameful manner with pagan associates.

Verse 2 (*For he saith, At an acceptable time I hearkened unto thee, and in a day of salvation did I succor thee: behold, now is the acceptable time; behold, now is the day of salvation*).

The passage in Isaiah from which this comes is:

> Thus saith the Lord, In an acceptable time have I heard thee, and in a day of salvation have I helped thee: I will preserve thee and give thee for a covenant of the people, to establish the earth (49:8).

This passage was addressed "To the Servant of Jehovah, the type primarily of Christ, and then of all who are 'in Christ.' "[6] Thus it is clear that in his appeal to this scripture, Paul was referring to the gospel age as "the day of salvation" and the "acceptable time." However, Paul at once added some inspired comment of his own making the application personal and immediate.

"Now is the acceptable time . . . now is the day of salvation . . ." The urgency of immediate acceptance of the gospel was also stressed by the author of Hebrews (3:7,8,13), and for discussion of this subject, see CH, pp. 74-75.

"Now . . ." It should be noted that this tightens the urgency even beyond the passage of Hebrews. There, the message is "*Today* . . . harden not your hearts"; here it is "*Now* is the day of salvation."

Verse 3, *Giving no occasion of stumbling in anything, that our ministration be not blamed.*

Hillyer has a quotation which catches the background of Paul's thought in this place. "There are people who will be glad of an excuse not to listen to the gospel or to take it seriously, and they will look for such an excuse in the conduct of its ministers."[7] It was precisely to avoid giving anyone such an excuse that Paul so strenuously defended his own reputa-

---

[6]F. W. Farrar, *Pulpit Commentary* (Grand Rapids: Wm. B. Eerdmans Publishing Co., 1950), Vol. 19, 2 Cor., p. 144.

[7]Norman Hillyer, *The New Bible Commentary, Revised* (Grand Rapids: Wm. B. Eerdmans Publishing Co., 1970), p. 1081.

tion. No minister can be careless of the opinion that others may hold concerning his life and conduct.

Verse 4, *But in everything commending ourselves as ministers of God, in much patience, in afflictions, in necessities, in distresses.*

"Commending ourselves . . ." refers to the exhibition and demonstration in Paul's life of the utmost integrity of character which was daily exemplified in all of the patterns of his total behavior.

"Ministers of God . . ." Paul included other apostles with himself in this, as "ministers of God"; but he also called himself the "servant of Christ" (Rom. 1:1). In this, of course, he could not have meant that he was the servant of two masters, because Jesus had flatly declared that "No man can serve two masters" (Matt. 6:24). The meaning is plain. Paul considered God and Christ as one.

"In much patience . . ." Regarding the word thus rendered, Barclay said:

> It is an untranslatable word . . . It describes the ability to bear things in such a triumphant way that it transfigures them and transmutes them. Chrysostom has a great panegyric on this *hupomone*, this triumphant Christian endurance. He calls it the root of all goods, the mother of piety, the fruit that never withers, a fortress that is never taken, a harbor that knows no storms.[8]

This great word flies like a banner over the whole succeeding list.

All of the following difficult circumstances, called by Chrysostom "a blizzard of troubles,"[9] and by Broomall "a multicolored rainbow glowing with the graces of Paul's ministry"[10] are listed by Paul without regard to any strict outline. It should be remembered that Paul was writing a letter by dictation and that he was not formulating some classical essay.

---

[8]William Barclay, *The Letters to the Corinthians* (Philadelphia: The Westminster Press, 1954), p. 237.

[9]*Ibid.*

[10]Wick Broomall, *Wycliffe Bible Commentary* (Chicago: Moody Press, 1971), p. 670.

A failure to do this very thing is responsible for most of the wild speculation by scholars regarding this epistle.

"In afflictions . . ." Paul was beset by countless hazards and difficulties, all of which, in a sense, were afflictions.

"In necessities . . ." could refer to practically anything that Paul was compelled, by necessity, to do in order to further the gospel.

"In distresses . . ." These were of every kind: (1) personal rejection by former friends, (2) disease, (3) shipwrecks, (4) plots to murder him, (5) charges laid against him before governors, (6) anxieties for the churches, (7) travel delays, etc., etc.

Verse 5, *In stripes, in imprisonments, in tumults, in labors, in watchings, in fastings.*

"In stripes . . ." "These were of two kinds, from Jewish whips, and Roman rods; but of the five scourgings (by the Jews), not one is mentioned in Acts, and only one of the Roman scourgings."[11] In this connection, it is mandatory to understand the NT as a very fractional record of all that either Jesus Christ or his apostles did. Any total record would have required more than a library (John 20:30; 21:25). The sacred narrative of all historical and personal data pertaining to that sacred company who brought mankind the gospel is piecemeal, only the tip of the iceberg. Therefore, arguments from the silence of the word of God on any subject are not merely unreliable, but are extremely foolish.

"In imprisonments . . ." By this, Paul did not refer to either his imprisonment in Caesarea, or that in Rome, for they were subsequent to this letter. The imprisonment in Philippi had already occurred. "Clement of Rome states that Paul was in prison no fewer than seven times."[12] "In tumults . . ." All of the early preachers, especially the apostles, often found their services broken up with riots. "Paul was assaulted in Iconium, Lystra, Philippi, Thessalonica, Corinth, Ephesus and Jerusa-

---

[11]F. W. Farrar, *op. cit.*,p. 45.
[12]William Barclay, *op. cit.*, p. 238.

lem."[13] The NT records all of those instances, but no one knows how many were left unrecorded.

"In labors . . ." This would include many and diverse activities; but the thought is that Paul pressed the work of preaching the gospel with the utmost vigor and perseverance. He constantly *worked at it.*

"In watchings . . ." The Greek word here, according to Hughes, shows that we should understand this as "times of sleeplessness";[14] but certainly not as insomnia. Paul watched all night on the occasion of the shipwreck (Acts 27:29); and this may be taken as an example of things that often occurred in which Paul would have had no opportunity to sleep. His arduous physical labors would have made it certain that he *could sleep* when he had the chance!

"In fastings . . ." has no reference to formal or religious fasts of any kind, but to periods of hunger brought on by times when he had insufficient money, or when incessant labor delayed the opportunity to eat.

Verse 6, *In pureness, in knowledge, in longsuffering, in kindness, in the Holy Spirit, in love unfeigned.*

Paul's total lack of any classical classification of the things he was mentioning is revealed here by his inclusion of the Holy Spirit in a list of the Spirit's gifts. This has so frustrated some commentators that they have rendered it "a spirit that is holy."[15]

"In pureness . . ." The primary meaning of this would be "chastity," especially in a place like Corinth; but the sincerity and integrity of the total life are also included by it.

In this verse Paul has moved from a catalogue of difficulties to a record of the inward qualities of his own life which had enabled him to attain the victory through so many hardships.

"In knowledge . . ." This is a tribute to the word of God, in Paul's case largely the OT scriptures, which had provided the

---

[13]James Macknight, *Apostolical Epistles and Commentary* (Grand Rapids: Baker Book House, 1969), Vol. II, p. 376.

[14]Philip E. Hughes, *op. cit.*, p. 225.

[15]Norman Hillyer, *op. cit.*, p. 1081.

power to understand and overcome all hardships. Many of the greatest problems of the OT would probably never have been explained without the matchless learning and perceptive powers of this great apostle. Justification by faith, the spiritual body of Christ, the significance of "in Christ," the mystery of the hardening of Israel—and many other subjects are singularly illuminated by the mind of Paul.

"In longsuffering . . ." Even yet, after so many centuries, the amazing forbearance and tenderness of Paul's dealings with "babes in Christ" like those in Corinth are evident for all to see. No matter what was wrong, or how often difficulties came, Paul always had time to try to put it all back together again.

"In kindness . . . in the Holy Spirit . . . in love unfeigned . . ." Both kindness and love are among the fruits of the Spirit (Gal. 5:22); but Paul was merely mentioning everything that had helped him through the storms.

Verse 7, *In the word of truth, in the power of God; by the armor of righteousness on the right hand and on the left.*

"The word of truth . . ." Although some have seen this as a mere affirmation of Paul that he always spoke the truth, it is more likely that it means "the gospel" (Col. 1:5), the divine body of truth which Paul customarily preached.

"In the power of God . . ." God had worked with Paul, as in the case of all the other apostles, enabling him to perform signs and wonders and mighty deeds, thus "confirming the word" (Mark 16:20). This, of course. was one of the secret springs of his power and endurance.

"By the armor of righteousness . . ." Paul loved this figure and developed it fully in Ephesians 6:13-17. Every item in the whole panoply answers finally for identification as "the word of God." This mention of the right hand and left hand refers to offensive weapons (like the sword in the right hand), and defensive weapons (like the shield borne by the left hand), as more fully evident in Ephesians.

Verse 8, *By glory and dishonor, by evil report and good report; as deceivers, and yet true.*

The uninhibited nature of Paul's letter shines here. In the case of "glory and dishonor," it is the good which is mentioned first; but in the next pairing, it is the evil which is first mentioned. All of these expressions have the weight of declaring Paul's fidelity to the faith and constant prosecution of his labors as an apostle *regardless of all circumstances.*

Verse 9, *As unknown, and yet well known; as dying, and behold we live; as chastened, and not killed.*

To Paul's enemies, especially among the hierarchy in Jerusalem, he had become a "nobody"; he was dead, the custom of having a funeral for defectors from Judaism having in all probability been observed in regard to Paul; and no less than five times they had beaten him unmercifully. But, actually, far from being a nobody, Paul became the most famous man of all ages, other than the Christ himself. And as for his being dead, the funeral for Paul (if they had one) was premature. At Lystra they stoned him and dragged him out of the city; but he rose up to claim Timothy from that environment and to make his letters to him a part of the word of God for twenty centuries!

Verse 10, *As sorrowful, yet always rejoicing; as poor, yet making many rich; as having nothing, and yet possessing all things.*

"Sorrowful ... rejoicing ..." This dual quality of the Christian life pertains to all believers, and not merely to Paul. In a world of sin, mortality, and many frustrations, "sorrow" is inevitable; but the distinguishing characteristic of faith in Christ is joy. Paul exemplified this as did no other. In his Philippian letter, for example, written from a dungeon in Rome, the words, "Rejoice, and again I say, Rejoice" are almost a litany throughout it. How marvelous are the joys in Christ! The knowledge of the Savior's love, the consciousness of sins forgiven, the confident hope of everlasting life, and the present possession of the blessed Holy Spirit within—such things surcharge the soul with joy unspeakable. "Solid joys and lasting pleasures only Zion's children know."

"Poor ... many rich ..." Clarke commented on this thus:

> The gospel faithfully preached betters the condition of the poor. It makes them sober, frugal, dependable and diligent. They therefore both have and gain by religion, and this must lead to increase of property. They are thus

made rich in comparison with their state of drunkenness, wastefulness and laziness before they became Christians.[16] (Condensed and paraphrased.)

This must be reckoned among the most astounding comments ever made on a passage of scripture; and, despite the fact that it focuses on a secular meaning that Paul never intended, it is nothing but blunt, unequivocal truth; and the lives of countless thousands of people have dramatically demonstrated it.

It must be admitted, however, that Paul was not speaking of material riches at all, but of the unsearchable riches in Christ Jesus.

Verses 11-13, *Our mouth is opened unto you, O Corinthians, our heart is enlarged. Ye are not straitened in us, but ye are straitened in your own affections. Now for a recompense in like kind (I speak as unto my own children), be ye also enlarged.*

"Our mouth is opened unto you . . ." means "I have spoken fully and frankly to you."

"Our heart is enlarged . . ." means "We have great affection for you."

"Ye are not straitened in us . . . means "My affection for you is not diminished."

"Ye are straitened in your affections . . ." means "You do not love us fully as you should."

"Now for a recompense in like kind . . ." means "I ask you to love me fully, as I love you."

"Be ye enlarged . . ." means "Let your affections for me abound."

This shows how a literal translation sometimes fails to carry the true meaning to people whose manner of speech is so different from that which prevailed in the first century. Therefore, despite our deep mistrust of all paraphrases, we shall attempt one for these three verses:

---

[16]Adam Clarke, *Commentary on the Whole Bible* (New York: Carlton and Porter, 1829), Vol. VI, p. 340.

> Paraphrase: We have spoken fully and frankly to you, O Corinthians, and our. heart goes out to you and takes you in. Our love for you is not diminished, but rather increased; but you do not love me as you should (otherwise, you would do a better job of defending me against my enemies). Now, why do you not repay me with the kind of love I have lavished upon you? I am speaking to you as my own children. Let your love for me, therefore, be multiplied, even as mine is for you.

It is the plaintive note in the meaning here which probably colored to some extent what Paul was about to say; and the realization, as he spoke these words, that the false teachers at Corinth had succeeded in stealing the affections of the Corinthians away from Paul (at least to some extent)—that sudden realization triggered the devastating attack he now delivered against those sons of the devil in Corinth.

Verse 14, *Be not unequally yoked with unbelievers: for what fellowship have righteousness and iniquity? Or what communion hath light with darkness?*

This apostolical order has at least two anchors in what Paul had just written. (1) He had just warned them against receiving the grace of God "in vain" (6:1); and (2) he had just touched upon a truth which undoubtedly had superlative impact upon his emotions, that being the loss of love for Paul on the part of the Corinthians. It was the encroachment of paganism against the holy faith which was the ground of the warning in verse 1 and the cause of the defection mentioned in verses 11-13; and it was directly in response to both of these that the scathing attack on paganism was delivered. Scholars who see some unreasonable break here and start prattling about "interpolations" have just failed to read the sacred text.

Unequally Yoked

"Unequally yoked with unbelievers . . ." This meant that no Christian had any business making alliances of any kind with pagans; and yes, that certainly includes marriage. Why should any Christian wife accept a pagan for a husband? This writer has known many who did it to their sorrow; but it was never anything but a sin. Paul was not here discussing the situation where one of a pagan couple had obeyed the gospel and the other had not; he had already dealt with that. Here he was laying down a rule that forbade such alliances in the first place. Furthermore, there is nothing here that limits the application to marriage. Any close alliance with a pagan partner in business, recreation, marriage, or any other kind of union can mean nothing but disaster for the Christian.

Illustration: Two men went in business together; one had the money, and the other had the experience. After about a year, the one who had the experience had the money, and the one who had had the money had the experience!

With a little distortion, the above is a good example of every partnership with a pagan. And, as for the question of whether or not there are any pagans today, the answer must be that there are many whose morals and ideals are as pagan as those of the days of Aphrodite Pandemos.

"What fellowship . . . what communion . . . ?" Christianity and paganism are antithetical, as diverse as righteousness and wickedness, or light and darkness.

Verse 15, *And what concord hath Christ with Belial? or what portion hath a believer with an unbeliever?*

The two questions here and the other two in the preceding verse are so stated as to require the negative answer. They are all four, in fact, intended as affirmations that Christ has no concord with Belial . . . etc.

"Belial . . ." This is a synonym for "Satan."

Verse 16, *And what agreement hath a temple of God with idols? for we are a temple of the living God; even as God said, I will dwell in them, and walk in them; and I will be their God, and they shall be my people.*

As Plumptre said: "We see clearly the drift of the apostle's thought. His mind travels back to the controversy about things sacrificed to idols."[17] Paul no doubt remembered those broad-minded "Christians" who could sit down in an idol's temple; but the bitter fruit of it was the rejection of himself by those who should have loved him. He had never intended any license

[17]E. H. Plumptre, *op. cit.*, p. 386.

whatever in regard to idols; but he had done his best in that first letter to keep from saying anything that might be construed as a denial of Christian liberty; but no such necessity is upon him now. Their liberty had become license, their love hatred, or at best lukewarmness; and their Christianity had degenerated till they stood in danger of having received the grace of God in vain.

"We are a temple of the living God . . ." This is the basis of Paul's demand that no compromise whatever be made with paganism. He had developed that metaphor extensively in the first letter; but he reinforced it here with the quotation from Exodus 29:45, deriving from it the principle that "wherever God dwells is the true temple of God." As Tasker expressed it, "There is still a temple of God, but it consists of the whole company of Christian believers."[18] For further discussion of the church as God's true temple, see CA, pp. 142-144. Not only did Paul view the church as God's true temple as contrasted with the idol temples of Corinth, but it was also God's true temple with respect to the great temple of the Jews in Jerusalem.

Verses 17-18, *Come ye out from among them, and be ye separate, saith the Lord,*

> *And touch no unclean thing;*
> *And I will receive you.*
> *And will be to you a Father,*
> *And ye shall be to me sons and daughters, saith the Almighty.*

Many have spoken of the fact that Paul here combined the thought of several OT passages, even adding some words of his own (re: daughters); but it seems best to view this passage not as a blundering effort of the apostle to quote the OT, but as his own inspired words, which quite naturally, of course, used some of the terminology of previous holy writings.

"Come ye out . . . touch no unclean thing . . ." Isaiah 52:11 has this:

> Depart ye, depart ye, go ye out from thence, touch no unclean thing; go ye out of the midst of her; be ye clean, that bear the vessels of the Lord.

---

[18]R. V. G. Tasker, *op. cit.*, p. 99.

However, as cited above, Paul was not "quoting scripture" here; he was *writing scripture*. The difference is apparent in the formula by which he introduced this paragraph. He did not say, "Thus it is written,' but "Thus saith the Lord" the magnificent formula used a thousand times by the holy prophets of the OT, and here used by the blessed Paul, and for exactly the same purpose! It is from this evident truth that we feel compelled to reject as irreverent and inaccurate such a comment as the following:

> Paul quoted from memory, and so long as he got the substance right he did not worry about the actual wording. It was not the letter of the scripture but the message of the scripture which mattered to Paul.[19]

The denial of any validity to such a view is implicit in the fact that nobody ever got the message of the scripture without getting it from the words of scripture. As further proof that Paul was writing, and not merely quoting God's word, the mention of "daughters" must be considered conclusive. That did not come out of any of the passages suggested by Paul's words here, but it was a brand new revelation by the Spirit of God through the apostle Paul. Concerning this inclusion of the word "daughters," David Lipscomb said:

> It is characteristic of Christianity that it was the first system that ever recognized the dignity of women and raised them generally to the same moral and spiritual level with men. This was very suitable at Corinth, where above all other places in the world, women were lured to their ruin by organized immoralities under the cloak of religion.[20]

Regarding the application of this paragraph, which is actually concluded in verse 1 of the following chapter, it must be said that the same principles are binding today. It is true that paganism has lost its old forms; but no person in his right mind can be unaware of the neo-paganism which today threatens to engulf the world. All of the old essentials of paganism are still operative. The deification of humanity, the

---

[19]William Barclay, *op. cit.*, p. 249.

[20]David Lipscomb, *Second Corinthians* (Nashville: The Gospel Advocate Company), p. 97.

gross emphasis upon the secular, the material, the sensual and devilish are still struggling to dominate the minds of mankind. The so-called sex liberation, the abandonment of ancient moral values, and the encroaching dishonesty, selfishness and libertinism even in the highest echelons of government—all of these and many other things proclaim in tones of thunder that paganism is still around.

CHAPTER 7

The first verse of this chapter concludes the paragraph which began at 6:14. Verses 2-4 are a concluding thought connected with Paul's appeal in 6:11-13. Paul's stern warning to the Corinthians to come out from among the pagans and "be ye separate" (6:14-7:1) came right in the middle of his touching plea for their reciprocation of his love; and despite the widespread scholarly prejudice that views this as something incongruous, it appears exactly where such a blast should have been expected. Coupled with his yearning for a full renewal of their love to him, the demand for their separation from paganism was Paul's revelation to them of the one thing and the only thing that could have made possible such a renewal. Therefore, such opinions as the following should be rejected:

> There is no doubt that this passage comes in very awkwardly. When we omit it and when we read straight on from 6:13 to 7:2 we get perfect sense. This stern section seems out of place with the glad and joyous love of the verses on each side of it.[1]

Barclay's objections are similar to the views of many scholars who evidently consider it fashionable to assault the unity of this epistle for such flimsy reasons. Just what, really, is their argument? There are just two arguments in view, and there is nothing important in either one of them. Argument No. 1 is that a person can omit these fifteen verses and get perfect sense out of what is left. Is that an argument? No! Through the NT, there are numerous parentheses, paragraphs, verses, or chapters that could be painted out without destroying the sense and continuity. As a matter of fact, the middle chapter of the Sermon on the Mount, if removed, would not destroy the sense and continuity of Matthew's gospel; but that certainly does not prove that it does not belong. Certain pages of Barclay's book could be pasted together without any interruption of sense or continuity. This so-called argument is

---

[1]William Barclay, *The Letters to the Corinthians* (Philadelphia: The Westminster Press, 1954), p. 245.

absolutely worthless and unbecoming to the scholars that stoop to use it.

Then, there is Argument No. 2. What is it? "It seems out of place!" However, when the purpose of Paul's stern section here (the 15 verses) is understood as related to the larger paragraph in which it lies embedded, one has an argument which contradicts the notion that the passage is misplaced. Paul's order to separate from paganism is as much a part of his plea for the love of the Corinthians, as would be a husband's plea to an estranged wife to forsake her illicit lover in the very middle of his plea for her affection; and there has never been a critic who could deny it. Argument No. 2, therefore, is also illogical, contrived, forced and unreasonable.

It is not the purpose of this work to explore all of the criticisms directed against the NT; because a hundred libraries would be insufficient for such a task. This criticism of 6:14-7:1 has been explored because it is absolutely typical of all criticism of sacred scripture. When you have seen one criticism, you have seen them all! In a lifetime of devoted study in the Holy Bible, this writer has never seen a worthy criticism against the word of God.

Chapter Outline

The conclusion of Paul's plea for the love of the Corinthians is given in verses 1-4; and the rest of the chapter is a resumption of the line of thought that Paul had interrupted at 2:14. In verses 5-16, he takes up the story of his meeting with Titus in Macedonia, speaking of the comfort and joy derived from that meeting, of his new hope and joy for the Corinthians, and of his appreciation of the corrections they had made in keeping with his instructions.

Verse 1, *Having therefore these promises, beloved, let us cleanse ourselves from all defilement of the flesh and spirit, perfecting holiness in the fear of God.*

This is a reiteration of the command to "be ye separate" (6:17), only here it is reinforced by Paul's appeal to the promises certified to the Corinthians because of their status as God's true temple.

"Holiness in the fear of God . . ." Only those who are holy shall see God (Heb. 12:10, 14). Absolute perfection is required of all who would enter heaven (Matt. 5:48). How then can any man be saved? It is admitted by all that perfection in any absolute sense is impossible for mortal man. The answer lies in the perfection of Jesus Christ; and those who accept his gospel, believing, repenting and being baptized "into Christ" are in that manner made a part of Christ, his spiritual body the church, being in a true sense *actually* Christ. In that state of being "in Christ" and fully identified with him, all of the perfection of Christ himself is credited to all of the members of the Lord's body. That is why Paul could say, "That we may present every man perfect in Christ" (Col. 1:28).

However, Paul did not say that "we *will* present every man" (that is, every Christian), but that "we *may* present," indicating that Christ's perfection, while truly available for every Christian, does not pertain to him automatically. That the manner of a person's life is in some manner determinative appears from what is said here. The practical answer lies in the truth that God will in no case require of a man a perfection which is beyond his power, promising to forgive every sin that a Christian commits; but a Christian must work at it, sincerely and truly, and never stop trying. In all the Bible there is no indication that God will forgive any man for not doing the things which he easily could do, but will not do, or forgive those who continue in presumptuous sin. Paul here commanded the Corinthians to "cleanse themselves" from all defilements of the flesh and to perfect "holiness in the fear of God." This was not something which would be accomplished apart from themselves, but something they themselves were to do.

Verses 2-4, *Open your hearts to us: we wronged no man, we corrupted no man, we took advantage of no man. I say it not to condemn you: for I have said it before, that ye are in our hearts to die together and to live together. Great is my boldness of speech toward you, great is my glorying on your behalf: I am filled with comfort, I overflow with great joy in all our affliction.*

"Open your hearts to us . . ." "This means literally, 'make room for us.' "[2] Paul's immediate mention of wronging, corrupting and taking advantage of "no man" is best understood not as a defense of himself against such charges, but as a contrast between himself and those false teachers at Corinth who were doing those very things. There is an infinite pathos here. Paul was saying, "You find a place in your affections for those who do such things, can you not find also a place for me,"[3] who preached the gospel to you and by whose preaching you were saved?

"In our hearts to die together and to live together . . ." This was an affirmation of Paul's love in the idiom known to all times and peoples. Ruth the Moabitess spoke her love to her mother-in-law, "Where thou lodgest, I will lodge. . . . Where thou diest, will I die, and there will I be buried" (Ruth 1:16, 17). In the Odes iii, 9, of Horace (65-9 B.C.), strong and loving affection was expressed thus:

With thee I fain would live;
With thee I fain would die.[4]

But there is a very significant variation in Paul's use of that ancient idiom, for in Paul's words here, death is mentioned first and life later. Broomall was probably correct in his explanation that for the Christian "death must precede eternal life in glory."[5]

"Glorying, comfort and joy . . ." In verse 4, these words indicate that "There rushed upon Paul's memory the recollection of the good news that Titus had brought";[6] therefore, he poured out these moving words of appreciation, personal thanksgiving and joy.

Verse 5, *For even when we were come into Macedonia our flesh had no relief, but we were afflicted on every side; without were fightings, within were fears.*

---

[2]Frank G. Carver, *Beacon Bible Commentary* (Kansas City: Beacon Hill Press, 1968), p. 567.

[3]E. H. Plumptre, *Ellicott's Commentary* (Grand Rapids: Zondervan Publishing House, 1959), Vol. VII, p. 389.

[4]E. H. Plumptre, *op. cit.*, p. 388.

[5]Wick Broomall, *Wycliffe Bible Commentary* (Chicago: Moody Press, 1972), p. 673.

[6]E. H. Plumptre, *op. cit.*, p. 388.

Having been unable to link up with Titus at Troas, as he had hoped, Paul had journeyed on into Macedonia; and this is a glimpse of the strong uncertainties and anxieties which assailed him before his meeting with Titus. The genuine reality, pathos and appeal of Paul's words here are timeless. No wonder they have been incorporated into the hymnology of the church:

> Just as I am! Though tossed about
> With many a conflict, many a doubt,
> With fears within, and foes without,
> O Lamb of God, I come! I come![7]

Verse 6, *Nevertheless he that comforteth the lowly, even God, comforted us by the coming of Titus.*

No joy, however wonderful, could induce Paul to forget the God who had provided it; and this mention of his comfort was accompanied by his acknowledgment of the Father who "comforteth the lowly." How precious is such an attitude!

"By the coming of Titus . . ." The importance of this man, to whom one of the sacred books of the NT is addressed, suggests additional attention to what is revealed of him.

Titus

Titus was a Greek Christian who had been converted by Paul (Titus 1:4), a true friend of the apostle, an able and diligent helper, and his companion on the missionary field. It is not improbable that he was a brother of Luke who wrote the gospel. Both F. F. Bruce and Sir William M. Ramsay receive the speculation that Titus was Luke's brother, giving that as the reason why Luke in Acts nowhere mentioned Titus by name, especially in view of the fact that Luke apparently avoided doing so in relating a circumstance (Acts 20:4) where Titus' name would have been very appropriate.[8]

Furthermore, the very first notice of Titus is in Acts 15:2, where Luke referred to him, but not by name; the certainty

---

[7]Clarlottie Elliott, Hymn: *Just as I Am* (Woodworth) (Cincinnati: Standard Publishing Company), Hymn No. 131.

[8]Sir William M. Ramsay, *St. Paul the Traveler*, pp. xxxviii, 390. Also, F. F. Bruce, *The Book of Acts* (Grand Rapids: Wm. B. Eerdmans, Publishers, 1954), p. 406.

that Titus was the one mentioned derives from Galatians 2:3. Other NT references to Titus are found in 2 Timothy and Titus; but his name occurs most frequently (eight times) in 2 Corinthians.

Titus' importance in the development of Christianity is seen in the fact that "he was a representative test case"[9] on whether or not Gentiles had to be circumcised to be Christians (Acts 15:13-29).

As will appear later in this epistle, Titus was entrusted with very important missions by Paul. He had apparently acted as Paul's deputy in the business discussed in this chapter; and, at a later time, he was in charge of the work in Crete, where he was living when Paul addressed to him the epistle to Titus.

He was loved and respected by Paul, evidently having a character of the most noble aspects, and continuing with the apostle throughout his ministry. Hughes said that "2 Timothy 4:10 indicates that Titus was with Paul for a while during his last imprisonment in Rome."[10]

Verse 7, *And not by his coming only, but also by the comfort wherewith he was comforted in you, while he told us your longing, your mourning, your zeal for me; so that I rejoiced yet more.*

"Not by his coming only . . ." It was not the mere presence of Titus, wonderful as that was to Paul, which brought him so much joy, but the good news that Titus revealed regarding the situation in Corinth.

"Your longing . . . mourning . . . zeal for me . . ." Despite the presence of false teachers and bitter enemies of the truth in Corinth, there were those who truly loved Paul, mourned for the shameful sins which had brought disgrace upon them all, and kept up their loving affection for the holy apostle who had broken unto them the bread of life.

Verse 8, *For though I made you sorry with my epistle, I do not regret it: though I did regret it (for I see that that epistle made you sorry, though but for a season).*

---

[9]*ISBE*, p. 2,988.

[10]Philip E. Hughes, *Paul's Second Epistle to the Corinthians* (Grand Rapids: Wm. B. Eerdmans Publishing Co., 1962), p. 76.

"I did regret it . . ." Some critics cite this as proof that Paul could not possibly have made such a remark about 1 Corinthians; but the alleged proof is not here. It was most natural that Paul should have had many tearful regrets about sending a letter which laid bare the immorality and lovelessness of a whole church. It is a safe assumption that none of the scholars who are so dogmatic about this place, denying that it could refer to 1 Corinthians—that not one of them ever engaged in such a spiritual effort as that which burdened Paul's heart when he undertook the discipline of the Corinthians. As any man who ever did such a thing must testify, it is a burden of great anguish and sorrow; it is a time of flowing tears and sorrow and heartbreak; it is a time of deep soul-searching and of bewildering wonderment whether this or that should have been said, should have been written, or should have been done. Any man who has been through it knows exactly what Paul meant by this; and that 1 Corinthians is just such a letter as to have provided the grounds of deep misgivings on the part of the apostle who wrote it is a stark fact that cannot be denied.

Verse 9, *I now rejoice, not that ye were made sorry, but that ye were made sorry unto repentance; for ye were made sorry after a godly sort, that ye might suffer loss by us in nothing.*

"Rejoice . . . that ye were made sorry . . ." It was not their sorrow which brought Paul's joy, but the fruit of that sorrow. It had led them to obey his instructions, having produced repentance in their hearts.

Verse 10, *For godly sorrow worketh repentance unto salvation, a repentance which bringeth no regret: but the sorrow of the world worketh death.*

Repentance

"Repentance unto salvation . . ." It is strange, and at the same time significant, that the apostles always indicated repentance as being "toward," i.e., in the direction of, or "unto" salvation, as here. Peter said that God had granted the Gentiles repentance "unto life"; Mark noted that repentance was "unto the remission of sins" (1:4); and in Acts 20:21, it is declared that "Both to Jews and to Greeks repentance *toward* God and faith *toward* our Lord Jesus Christ" constituted a part of the Pauline testimony to all men. The direction impact of these references cannot be overlooked. Of all the primary steps of obeying the gospel, i.e., faith, repentance, confession and baptism, all are said to be "unto" or "toward" salvation, God, Christ and the remission of sins; whereas of baptism alone is it declared that it is "into Christ."

Further comment on the subject of repentance will be found in CH, pp. 17, 18, CL, pp. 287-290, CR, 367-370, etc.

Several important teachings with regard to repentance appear in this verse: (1) Christians who commit sin are commanded to repent, the same being an invariable duty of all men, aliens and Christians alike. In the case of sin, repentance is never waived. (2) Christians who commit sin, until they do repent are not in a saved condition, else the repentance of the Corinthians could not have been said to be "unto" salvation. (3) Repentance is not sorrow for sin, which in many cases is mere "sorrow of the world" due to the inconvenience caused by sin or its discovery. (4) Even godly sorrow is not repentance, but a condition that produces repentance. What then is repentance? It is a change of the will, with regard to sin, preceded by godly sorrow and followed by "fruits worthy of repentance" (Matt. 3:9; also see CM, p. 28).

"Sorrow of the world worketh death . . ." Through remorseful sorrow for sin, Judas committed suicide; and there have been countless other examples of the sorrow of the world working death; but what is mentioned here goes beyond physical consequences and speaks of "eternal death, which is the opposite of salvation" (Rom. 5:21).[11]

Verse 11, *For behold this selfsame thing, that ye were made sorry after a godly sort, what earnest care it wrought in you, and what clearing of yourselves, yea what indignation, yea what fear, yea what longing, yea what zeal, yea what avenging! In everything ye approved yourselves to be pure in the matter.*

"We cannot be certain of the precise significance in the given circumstances of each of the different aspects of the

---

[11]F. W. Farrar, *Pulpit Commentary* (Grand Rapids: Wm. B. Eerdmans Publishing Co., 1950), Vol. 19, p. 171.

Corinthians' response to Paul's letter."[12] Rather than a speculative attempt to explain all of those wonderful results of their repentance in response to apostolical instruction, this writer favors the consideration of this exultant and triumphant exclamation of Paul as an exuberant description of the victory that always appears when men accept the word of God and obey it.

"Clearing of yourselves . . ." suggests that their wholehearted repentance and prayers had resulted in their complete forgiveness.

"What indignation . . ." is the indignation against sin which every sincere Christian manifests.

"What fear . . ." refers to the holy fear of God and reverence for his sacred word.

"Yea what longing . . ." is a reference to that hungering and thirsting after righteousness, mentioned by the Saviour in the Sermon on the Mount (Matt. 5:6).

"Yea what zeal . . ." True repentance always results in the multiplication of Christian works; and the conversion of the Corinthians had inspired all of them to redoubled participation in the work of the Lord.

"Yea what avenging . . ." There is a hint in this that the Corinthians had turned upon their false teachers with the full anger and determination of men aroused to do God's will and to remove the influence of all persons standing in the way of it. It could be also that Paul felt that their righteous "about face" had in a certain sense avenged him of his own personal enemies and detractors in their city. Certainly, it is wrong to import any vindictiveness into this remark.

"Ye approved yourselves to be pure in the matter . . ." This has reference to some special event, perfectly known to both Paul and the Corinthians, but hidden as far as the men of all subsequent generations are concerned. We should beware of the gross speculative comments which tell all about what lay behind these words. Hughes' pertinent comment is:

---

[12]Philip E. Hughes, *op. cit.*, p. 274.

> Having taken action, the past was put right and they were in a state of purity so far as the affair (all of that immorality mentioned in the first epistle) was concerned. There is no need for Paul to specify any details, since it is all too familiar to them. Hence he just refers to it as "the matter," or "the affair."[13]

All speculation on this should be rejected, because Paul who knew all of the details covered them here; and those commentators who tell all about it are guilty, not merely of going beyond what is written, but of dishonoring the apostolical reticence as well. Why should they who *do not know* tell us what Paul who *did know* refused to tell?

Verse 12, *So although I wrote unto you, I wrote not for his cause, that did the wrong, nor for his cause that suffered the wrong, but that your earnest care for us might be manifest unto you in the sight of God.*

Paul's avoidance of specifics in this verse was for the very purpose of not focusing attention upon any individual, either wronged or wrong-doer; and this left the way open for destructive critics, intent on destroying the credibility of the entire epistle, to move in and supply the specifics Paul purposely avoided. Such conduct is not merely reprehensible, but devilish. They assert, for example, that by the words "his cause that suffered the wrong" Paul was referring to himself! The following comment is an example of this type of presumption:

> When Paul had visited Corinth there had been a ring-leader to the opposition. The short, unhappy visit had been poisoned by the activity of one man. This man had clearly personally insulted Paul![14]

While true enough that there was a second, and probably "painful" visit, little is known of it. It is extremely doubtful that there was any single ring-leader in Corinth, for there were many factions. The ring-leader is merely a postulation by speculative critics and never really existed. "This man's" insulting Paul is nonsense. Two verses later in this very

---

[13]*Ibid.*, p. 275.
[14]William Barclay, *op. cit.*, p. 201.

paragraph, Paul declared, "I was not put to shame!" (7:14). That, of course, gives the lie to the speculations; so they went to work on that, telling us how broadminded Paul was, how he never held anything against anybody, and that "he did not take the matter personally at all!"[15] Such interpretations of the word of God are sheer foolishness; and we have invented a word for all such speculations. They are pure *fembu*!

"Wronged . . . wrong-doer . . ." These words actually applied to many at Corinth, not just a few persons, and absolutely not just one person. There were many who had gone to law against brethren before pagan judges, to mention only one thing; and Paul here purposely resorted to impersonal terms for reasons of tact, his great purpose being, not to open old wounds, but to arouse them to compliance with their duty, which compliance would manifest their "earnest care for Paul in the sight of God."

Verse 13, *Therefore we have been comforted: and in our comfort we joyed the more exceedingly for the joy of Titus, because his spirit hath been refreshed by you all.*

Paul's words here signal a total victory in Corinth. As Filson said:

> "By you all" (in this verse 13), combined with "everything" (v. 14), "all" (v. 15) and "in all things" (v. 16), indicates that the entire church responded to Titus' appeal and is now loyal to Paul.[16]

These expressions by Paul, however, are hyperbole. As will be seen in chapter 10, there were still pockets of resistance and much wrong-doing still remaining at Corinth. All the sacred writers used this figure of speech, exaggerating for the sake of emphasis.

The first thing that any commentator must learn if he would have any hope of true interpretation is that the sacred writings abound in figures of speech. One cannot progress any further than the third chapter of Matthew (3:6) without confronting hyperbole. There it was stated that "Jerusalem, all Judaea,

---

[15] *Ibid.*, p. 202.
[16] Floyd V. Filson, *Interpreter's Bible* (Nashville: Abingdon Press, 1953), Vol. X, p. 362.

and all the region around Jordan; and they were baptized in Jordan." This, despite the repeated "all," is hyperbole; because Luke categorically stated, "Howbeit the Pharisees and lawyers rejected the counsel of God against themselves, being not baptized"! (Luke 7:30). We are making a point of this, because Filson, and other challengers of the unity of 2 Corinthians, blindly ignore the obvious hyperbole in these verses, construing "all" as inclusive of absolutely everyone in the Corinthian church. And why do they do this? The answer is in Filson's comment, as follows:

> This fact argues that chapters 10-13 do not belong to this letter, but were more likely part of the earlier "stern letter"; the rebuke of those chapters could hardly be addressed to a church whose entire membership is now as loyal as 7:14-16 says it is![17]

What Filson here called "this fact" is not a fact at all but a misinterpretation of Paul's hyperbole; and one may only be amazed at the lengths to which scholars will go in their efforts to deny the unity and integrity of this and other sacred writings. There is utterly no reason for a crass literal construction of Paul's words here. Such commentators decry the "literalists" and "fundamentalists" for their interpretations of NT truth; but, in this case, they themselves are the "literalists" and "fundamentalists," incapable of recognizing a simple figure of speech. If one gave a party, and "everybody" came, could it then be intelligently stated that nobody went to the football game the same night, because "everybody" went to the party? This is the exact parallel of Filson's so-called argument in the above quotation. It is this type of *fembu* which discredits much of the exegesis encountered today.

Verse 14, *For if in anything I have gloried to him on your behalf, I was not put to shame; but as we spake all things to you in truth, so our glorying also which I made before Titus was found to be truth.*

Before Titus had gone to Corinth to assist the Corinthians in their reception and obedience with reference to 1 Corinthians, Paul had spoken glowingly to Titus, "glorying on behalf" of

---

[17]*Ibid.*

the Corinthians. All of the complimentary things he had said of them had turned out to be true. That Paul could have gloried on their behalf even before he learned of the correction of their immoralities shows that his glowing compliments, however deserved by some, were not deserved by all of them. This is further reason for understanding Titus' comforting report as applicable to many, but not to all.

"I was not put to shame . . ." has the meaning of Paul's complimentary remarks to Titus about them had proved to be fully justified. Who then is capable of believing that there ever occurred some mysterious fiasco in which "the ring-leader insulted the apostle Paul personally"? More *fembu!*

Verse 15, *And his affection is more abundantly toward you while he remembereth the obedience of you all, how with fear and trembling ye received him.*

Paul, in this, spoke of the obedience which had marked the conduct of the Corinthians toward the preaching of Titus, and also a tactful word of Titus' appreciation of their receiving and obeying him.

"Obedience of you all . . ." Far from meaning "everybody in the church with no exceptions," the expression "you all" is merely the grammatical plural of "ye" as it stands in the last clause. It has the meaning of "you" (plural). Incidentally, the only possible plural of "you" in the English language is "you all," if the number intended is greater than "you two," "you both," "you three," etc. In light of this fact, there are only two possible meanings of "you all" as used here. It is either a simple plural for the Corinthian church; or, if anything more is intended, it would have to be hyperbole.

Verse 16, *I rejoice that in everything I am of good courage concerning you.*

The victory had been won; Titus' mission had succeeded; but the problems that remained could be dealt with in confidence. The many were back on the right road; and, with this fundamental achievement, Paul was fully confident of the future of his precious converts at Corinth. Filson spoke of this as "unqualified assurance"; but encouraging words to weak and sinful Christians like those in Corinth could never have been intended to mean that they were perfect and had no further need of Paul. The very epistle we are studying, which was about to be dispatched to Corinth by the hands of Titus, *proves* that the apostle knew many instances in which they still needed correction, teaching, and disciplining. It is not Paul's assurance here that proves he could not also have written chapters 10-13; but it is chapters 10-13 which prove the nature of the assurance here expressed. It regarded hope, more than it regarded fulfillment.

CHAPTER 8

In this and the following chapters are found "the most complete instructions about church giving which the NT contains."[1] The principles to be respected in the discharge of this duty were outlined by Halley, as follows:

> Though it is offering for charity, we presume the principles here stated should be the guide for churches in the taking of all of their offerings. The gifts should be voluntary, proportionate, systematic, and above reproach in the manner of their business administration.[2]

The outline of chapter 8 has respect to three reasons presented by Paul as motivation for the liberal giving which he suggested for the Corinthians: "The example of the Macedonians (1-8), the example of Christ (9), and the requirements of honor (8:10-9:5)."[3]

Verses 1, 2, *Moreover, brethren, we make known to you the grace of God which hath been given in the churches of Macedonia; how that in much proof of affliction the abundance of their deep joy and their deep poverty abounded unto the riches of their liberality.*

Christian paradoxes abound in these verses. What an astounding thing it is that "two of the loveliest flowers of Christian character, *joy* and *liberality*,"[4] should bloom in the Macedonian poverty fields. Their poverty was extreme and unusual in an age when poverty was almost universal. McGarvey pointed out that:

> Macedonia had suffered in three civil wars, and had been reduced to such poverty that Tiberius Caesar, hearkening to their petitions, had lightened their taxes.

---

[1]Henry H. Halley, *Bible Handbook* (Grand Rapids: Zondervan Publishing House, 1927), p. 555.

[2]*Ibid.*

[3]Wick Broomall, *Wycliffe Bible Commentary* (Chicago: Moody Press, 1971), p. 675.

[4]R. V. G. Tasker, *The Second Epistle of Paul to the Corinthians* (Grand Rapids: Wm. B. Eerdmans Publishing Co., 1958), p. 111.

> But in addition to this general poverty, the churches had been made poor by persecution (2 Thess. 1:4).[5]

Macknight saw in Paul's mention of other people's poverty in this letter to Corinth, "A delicate insinuation that the more opulent Corinthians should equal or exceed what had been given by the Macedonians."[6] The afflictions of the Macedonians had been aggravated from the very first declaration of the gospel among them by those unreconciled elements in Judaism who had sent their emissaries throughout Macedonia in order to harass and hinder Paul's preaching; and, as Farrar said, "This had excited the hatred of the Gentiles toward Christianity."[7] In this connection, see Acts 16:20; 17:5,13.

The collection that Paul had in mind here was for the poor Christians in Jerusalem, although the destination of the funds is not stressed.

The joy and liberality demonstrated by the Macedonians sprang from their consciousness of the forgiveness of their sins and the pure happiness of restored fellowship with God. Their liberality was a spontaneous expression of that joy.

"Liberality . . ." The RV margin gives this word as "singleness." Tasker explained this thus:

> The word translated *liberality, haplotes*, means simplicity or single-mindedness; and, as in Romans 12:8, it refers to giving which was uncalculating and free from ulterior motives.[8]

Verses 3-5, *For according to their power, I bear witness, yea and beyond their power, they gave of their own accord, beseeching us with much entreaty in regard of this grace and the fellowship in the ministering to the saints: and this, not as we had hoped, but first they gave their own selves to the Lord, and to us through the will of God.*

---

[5]J. W. McGarvey, *Second Epistle to the Corinthians* (Cincinnati: The Standard Publishing Company, 1916), p. 210.

[6]James Macknight, *Apostolical Epistles and Commentary* (Grand Rapids: Baker Book House, 1969), Vol. II, p. 396.

[7]J. W. Farrar, *Pulpit Commentary* (Grand Rapids: Wm. B. Eerdmans Publishing Co., 1950), Vol. 19, 2 Cor., p. 195.

[8]R. V. G. Tasker, *op. cit.*, p. 112.

"These three verses constitute one continuous sentence in the original ... a long and characteristically Pauline sentence."[9] The verb "gave" governs the whole statement.

"Beyond their power ... not as we had hoped ..." Their giving was above what Paul had expected, and even beyond what their extreme poverty indicated as possible.

"Beseeching us with much entreaty ..." It is clear from this that Paul "had urged some restraint in their giving, in view of their dire poverty."[10]

"Fellowship ... ministering ..." The fellowship refers to their participation in the collection, and the ministering to the service which the money would render to the poor Christians in Jerusalem. Filson pointed out that "for no other church, or churches, was a collection ever taken, as far as we learn."[11] It is wrong, however, to make this mean that only "the mother church" had a right to be so helped. In fact, "mother church" is not a NT concept at all, such remarks as the following from Barclay, having no support from the scriptures. He said:

> The Church of Jerusalem was the Mother Church of all Churches; and it was Paul's desire that all the Gentile Churches should remember and help that Church which was their mother in the faith.[12]

As a matter of fact, Antioch, a Gentile congregation, was "the mother church" of all the churches founded by Paul. It was Antioch, not Jerusalem, which sent him forth with the gospel; and it was the "so-called" mother church in Jerusalem which opposed receiving any Gentiles at all, except upon the basis of their prior circumcision; and, added to all this, Paul himself flatly contradicted the notion that the Jerusalem of earth was in any sense a mother church, saying, "The Jerusalem that now is in bondage. . . . The Jerusalem which is above is free, which is our mother" (Gal. 4:25, 26).

---

[9]Philip E. Hughes, *Paul's Second Epistle to the Corinthians* (Grand Rapids: Wm. B. Eerdmans Publishing Co., 1962), p. 289.

[10]Raymond C. Kelcy, *Second Corinthians* (Austin: R. B. Sweet Co., 1967), p. 49.

[11]Floyd V. Filson, *Interpreter's Bible* (Nashville: Abingdon Press, 1953), Vol. X, p. 365.

[12]William Barclay, *The Letters to the Corinthians* (Philadelphia: The Westminster Press, 1954), p. 254.

"They first gave themselves to God . . ." If understood as a reference to their "first" becoming Christians, this would have the meaning of "in order of time"; but, as Wesley said, "It is better to understand it of 'the order of importance,' i.e., 'above all.' "[13] Of course, in point of time, all Christian graces are derived from the first decision to give oneself to the Lord.

Verse 6, *Insomuch that we exhorted Titus, that as he had made a beginning before, so he would also complete in you this grace also.*

We are heartily in agreement with Tasker who said:

> This visit would seem to have taken place about a year before (9:2); and it may be a legitimate inference that Titus himself was the bearer of 1 Corinthians in which Paul's instructions on this subject were given (1 Cor. 16:1ff).[14]

"The grace also . . ." That Paul's words here may be touched with a bit of friendly irony may not be ruled out. Certainly, some of the first epistle is loaded with outright sarcasm; and, in a church of so many pretensions to "knowledge," and with Paul's immediate reference to their abounding in "knowledge," there would seem to be here a very delicate suggestion that perhaps the deeds of the Corinthians ought to catch up with their "knowledge."

Verse 7, *But as ye abound in everything, in faith, and utterance, and knowledge, and in all earnestness, and in your love to us, see that ye abound in this grace also.*

"In everything . . ." Again, Paul's use of hyperbole is in evidence. Not only does this mean a great deal less than "everything, absolutely," but there might even be implied some deficiency in the qualified areas of Paul's explanation of it. See under verse 6. But Paul here magnanimously extended to them this accolade regarding their excellence in certain graces with the admonition that the grace of giving should also be exemplified in them in a degree proportionate to their excellence in other graces.

---

[13]John Wesley, *One Volume NT Commentary* (Grand Rapids: Baker Book House, 1972), *in loco.*

[14]R. V. G. Tasker, *op. cit.*, p. 113.

Verse 8, *I speak not by way of commandment, but as proving through the earnestness of others the sincerity also of your love.*

"The sincerity also of your love . . ." A glance at verse 7 reveals that Paul had just said that they abounded "in their love." How can this be anything else except a gentle reminder that their "abounding love" needed proving by their deeds? It is thus evident that scholarly objections to chapter 10, founded on the premise that Paul was already perfectly satisfied with everything at Corinth, are founded upon a false premise.

"Not by way of commandment . . ." It is not giving, as demanded and extorted by inexorable demands of divine law, that can bless the giver, but giving spontaneously and freely done, and springing from motives of love, appreciation, gratitude and thanksgiving. It is that kind of giving, and only that kind, that ever did the giver any good.

Verse 9, *For ye know the grace of our Lord Jesus Christ, that, though he was rich, yet for your sakes he became poor, that ye through his poverty might become rich.*

"Though he was rich . . ." Adam Clarke's perceptive comment on this should be remembered. He said:

> If Jesus Christ was only a man, in what sense could he be rich? Joseph and Mary were poor in Jerusalem, and poor in Nazareth; and, from the stable to the cross, Jesus never possessed any property among men, nor did he have anything at his death to bequeath, except his peace! The question of the riches of Christ, on the Socinian scheme, can never be satisfactorily answered.[15]

The riches of Christ are those riches which pertained to his status with God and equality to God before the world was (John 17:5), the riches of his eternal power and godhead, the riches of his everlasting divinity and glory. Only such an explanation as this can pertain to Paul's words here.

"He became poor . . ." Christ's becoming poor has a double meaning, (1) referring to the contrast between his eternal state and his incarnation, and (2) also to the extraordinary poverty

---

[15]Adam Clarke, *Commentary on the Whole Bible* (New York: Carlton & Porter, 1829), Vol. VI, p. 349.

of his earthly state as compared with the affluence of some of his contemporaries.

"For your sakes . . ." It should ever be remembered that Christ forsook heaven with its glory to live upon earth with its shame in order to redeem men from the curse of sin. It was not merely for the sake of the Corinthians, but for the sake of every man, that he thus "humbled himself" and took upon him the form of a servant, and was found obedient, even to the death on the cross!

As Hughes said,

> Paul felt none of the embarrassment which is displayed by some modern scholars who, because of a preconceived antipathy to "supernaturalism," would prefer to dismiss this doctrine of Christ's pre-existence.[16]

The simple, objective truth of Christianity is founded upon the conviction of the supernatural. In the final analysis, if there is no supernatural, there is no Christianity. So-called Christians who do not believe in the supernatural are unbelievers; and there can be no reconciliation of the supernaturalness of Christianity with the existential and speculative denials of it. What is affirmed in the NT is either true or false; and this student of the NT believes it to be true. Paul here assumed as fact, nor did he even pause to defend it, that Christ existed with God before the earth was created. No one can know the mind of Paul without seeing this fundamental truth.

Verse 10, *And herein I give my judgment: for this is expedient for you, who were the first to make a beginning a year ago, not only to do, but also to will.*

"Expedient for you . . ." Paul ever had in mind the best interests of his converts; and, regardless of what they may have thought about it, it was to their advantage to acquire and improve the grace of giving.

"A year ago . . ." As Hughes supposed, "It would seem that their original zeal in this matter had flagged."[17] He further suggested that this slackening zeal might have been due to

---

[16]Philip E. Hughes, *op. cit.*, p. 301.
[17]Philip E. Hughes, *op. cit.*, p. 303.

natural apathy, or to mistrust of Paul induced by false teachers; but the simple fact of Corinth having been a troubled, factious and sinful congregation was more than enough to have diminished their interest in any kind of giving to further the work of the Lord. When trouble strikes a church, the collection is the first thing to suffer.

"It was about a year before this that Paul in his first epistle had suggested the contribution; . . . and they had begun to obey."[18] This obvious reference to 1 Corinthians shows how little need there is to suppose that there was a "severe letter" in the interim. The blame which Paul tactfully imputed to the Corinthians here is inherent in the fact of their having been the first to act, apparently with enthusiasm; but they had suddenly grown cold. Paul's mention of his not "commanding" them carried the implication that it was then merely a matter of their doing what they had already promised and committed themselves to do.

Verse 11, *But now complete the doing also; that as there was the readiness to will, so there may be the completion also out of your ability.*

Given its bluntest interpretation, this means, "Get with it, and do what you have already promised to do. It is not enough to promise!"

Verse 12, *For if the readiness is there, it is acceptable according as a man hath, not according as he hath not.*

This was written to relieve the Corinthians of any thought that a certain amount of money was required of them. It was not some given amount that Paul was insisting upon, but the doing of whatever they could do. The intention and willingness to give were far more important than any merely quantitative consideration. The case of the widow's two mites (Mark 12:43,44) was used by the Saviour himself to prove that one with very small means could actually give even more than those with abundance. See CMK, pp. 264-267.

Christians must give, there being no such thing as a penurious, ungenerous, stingy Christian. Regarding the

---

[18]Adam Clarke, *op. cit.*, p. 349.

amount that should be given, David Lipscomb wrote: "It is clearly a self-deception for an individual to think he pleases God under the perfect dispensation of Christ while doing less than the Israelites did under the typical dispensation."[19] For further discussion of this, see CH, pp. 144-146.

Many who profess to be giving "the widow's mite" are doing no such thing. That *amount* they indeed give; but it is not "all their living" as was the case with her. Lipscomb said, "Her sacrificial example has been profaned many times"[20] in order to hide the meanest selfishness.

Verses 13, 14, *For I say not this that others may be eased and ye distressed; but by equality: your abundance being a supply at this present time for their want, that their abundance also may become a supply for your want; that there may be equality.*

The thought here is not that the gifts of the Corinthians would ease the burden of the Macedonians in raising the collection, but that those now able to give might, in time, be themselves the ones in need, and that giving should be done as a recognition of the uncertainties and vicissitudes of life. The fact that certain people *now* are not in need is no guarantee that their lack of need will be permanent.

Another thought in this was pointed out by Tasker:

> In verse 13, Paul points out the absurdity of almsgiving if giving to others means plunging the donors into "distress." Charity must not be used for the encouragement either of laziness or luxury.[21]

"That there may be equality . . ." Deplorable indeed are the remarks of some who would make Paul by these words a champion of the savage "leveling" of all men, as advocated in the political philosophy which would enable some to live by the sweat of other men's faces. Paul's object here was the relief of want, not an artificial equalization of property. In Paul's philosophy, a man who would not work was to be denied the privilege of eating (2 Thess. 3:10). As Hughes said:

---

[19]David Lipscomb, *Second Corinthians* (Nashville: The Gospel Advocate Company), p. 113.
[20]*Ibid*. p. 114.
[21]R. V. G. Tasker, *op. cit.*, p. 117.

> There is no justification for the presumption that a wealthier Christian, simply because he is a brother in Christ, should support an idle member of the church. Religious parasitism has no place in the New Testament. . . . The poor are commanded "with quietness to work, and to eat their own bread," inculcating on the poor the duty of self-support to the extent of their ability.[22]

At the same time, possessions may not be held by any Christian without regard to legitimate claims of those in want or distress. The great principles of Christ recognized the rights of property, but at the same time imposed upon its possessors the obligations of genuine liberality and sincere regards for the needs of others.

Verse 15, *As it is written, He that gathered much had nothing over; and he that gathered little had no lack.*

This is a quotation from Exodus 16:18, where is described the gathering of the manna; and, in the typical things which happened in that miraculous situation, one may read the prophecy of all subsequent history of mankind. Those who tried to hoard the manna found that "it bred worms and stank" (Ex. 16:20); and this is precisely what is true of hoarded wealth in all ages.

"He that gathered much had nothing over . . ." The richest men who ever lived "have nothing over" when death comes. In the final analysis, all that any man has is what he truly needs and uses.

"He that gathered little had no lack . . ." Even men with the most meager incomes may often diminish their requirements and find a little to be sufficient. The great lesson is that the man with much should ever hold his stewardship of abundance as subject to the just claims of the man whose necessities are impossible for himself unaided to meet. This is especially true of "the household of faith."

Verse 16, *But thanks be to God, who putteth the same earnest care for you into the heart of Titus.*

Paul here emphasized the fact that Titus, who probably delivered the 1 Corinthian letter, and who would shortly

---

[22]Philip E. Hughes, *op. cit.*, p. 307.

deliver the epistle then being written, was of one mind and heart with Paul, not merely in regard to the collection, but also in regard to the earnest care and love of the Corinthians themselves. Considerations of tact are surely in view here.

Verse 17, *For he accepted indeed our exhortation; but being himself very earnest, he went forth unto you of his own accord.*

"He accepted . . . went forth . . ." These words do not express past tense at all; but, as Kelcy said, "Paul here used what grammarians call an *epistolary aorist*, speaking of the event as already completed, because it would be completed when the Corinthians read this epistle."[23] The deduction that Titus bore this second epistle to Corinth is also derived from this verse.

Verse 18, *And we have sent together with him the brother whose praise in the gospel is spread through all the churches.*

Adam Clarke capitalized the word "Gospel" in this verse, making it bear the meaning that the brother Paul sent with Titus was the author of one of the canonical gospels. Scholars, of course, generally dispute such a meaning; but it positively must be allowed as possible. If this brother was Luke (as some of the oldest traditions affirm), it would mean that Luke had been concerned with compiling a gospel long before the date usually assigned to the third Gospel (which is by no means an impossibility). However, whether or not this was Luke (and no one really knows), one thing is positively evident: there was a written gospel even at this early date, a fact confirmed by Luke's introduction (1:1-5).

"Through all the churches . . ." The brother mentioned was known "through all" the churches. It is amazing that the same scholars who pin so much faith in the absolute superlatives of 7:13-15 are here very quick to affirm that "Here, *all* may refer only to the churches sharing in the collection"![24] This, however, is arbitrary. Certainly, some "gospel" was read by every church on earth at that time; and it must be allowed that the author of whatever gospel that was is the man Paul referred to here. The personal view of this writer is that this is a reference to the evangelist Luke and to the gospel that bears his name.

---

[23]Raymond C. Kelcy, *op. cit.*, p. 51.
[24]Floyd V. Filson, *op. cit.*, p. 372.

None of the objections to this view is convincing. For full discussion of the subject, see the Commentary of Philip E. Hughes on this epistle, pp. 312-316.

Verse 19, *And not only so, but who was also appointed by the churches to travel with us in the matter of this grace, which is ministered by us to the glory of the Lord, and to show our readiness.*

These are further remarks about the "brother" whose fame through all the churches was in the gospel. Luke was Paul's constant traveling companion; and in the word here that the churches had appointed someone to travel with Paul, there is strong inferential support for the view that he was none other than Luke. The good sense of the churches in appointing a physician to this task is evident, and this would also explain who paid Luke's charges for those long years of his abandonment of his medical practice for the purpose of traveling with Paul. The real objections that some scholars have to this view is that it blows their late dating of the Gospel of Luke right out of the water. If one is not married to the theory of a late date for Luke, the supposition that Luke is probably the one Paul mentioned here is quite reasonable.

Verse 20, *Avoiding this, that any man should blame us in the matter of this bounty which is administered by us.*

"Avoiding this . . ." This word "avoiding" is a nautical term. "It means *furling sail,* i.e., taking precautions in anticipation of danger."[25]

There is no area of human behavior more likely to give occasion of slander than that of handling public funds; and Paul's precautions were not merely wise; they are also an apostolical precedent that should be observed by the churches of all times and places. The wise, prudent and business-like handling of a congregation's financial affairs is without exception prerequisite to any general confidence of a congregation in its leadership.

Verse 21, *For we take thought for things honorable, not only in the sight of the Lord, but also in the sight of men.*

---

[25]F. W. Farrar, *op. cit.*, p. 197.

The thought of this verse is surely contained in Proverbs 3:4, which reads: "So shalt thou find favor and good understanding in the sight of God and man." It is not enough for God to know that a man's conscience is clear; he should order his affairs in such a manner that men will also be aware of it. Paul surely did this; and therefore the notion is rejected that Paul was always trying to respond to slanders of his enemies. He did not wait till slander was alleged but took steps to refute lies before they were spoken. Plumptre thought it remarkable that Paul evidently found help for his daily guidance from the book of Proverbs, showing that even one who was taught by the Spirit "could find daily guidance in a book which seems to many almost below the level of the spiritual life."[26]

Verse 22, *And we have sent with them our brother, whom we have many times proved earnest in many things, but now much more earnest, by reason of the great confidence which he hath in you.*

This was the third member of the group Paul sent to Corinth with 2 Corinthians. Nothing is known of who this brother was, other than what is written here.

Verse 23, *Whether any inquire about Titus, he is my partner and my fellow-worker to you-ward; or our brethren, they are the messengers of the churches, they are the glory of Christ.*

From this it is clear that there were three in the group, Titus and the other brethren being mentioned separately.

"Messengers of the churches . . ." This is the same word translated "apostles" in a number of NT passages, but these were apostles only in a secondary sense. Hillyer declared, "This does not put them into the same category as Paul and Peter who are 'apostles by the will of God.'"[27] Furthermore, these were in no sense plenary delegates, commissioned by the churches to decide either doctrine or policy. They were messengers of information only, not messengers of plenary power.

---

[26]E H. Plumptre, *Ellicott's Commentary* (Grand Rapids: Zondervan Publishing House, 1959), Vol. VII, p. 393.
[27]Norman Hillyer, *The New Bible Commentary, Revised* (Grand Rapids: Wm. B. Eerdmans Publishing Co., 1970), p. 1082.

Lipscomb has some weighty words in this connection. He said:

> Those messengers could not change or modify any decision, nor legislate for God, nor determine what was best for the churches, nor meet other messengers and organize a body, nor confer with one another on how the Lord should act, nor sit in judgment, nor otherwise change or direct the work of the churches.[28]

Thus it is clear that some modern "church messengers" are in no sense justified by what these men did.

Verse 24, *Show ye therefore unto them in the face of the churches the proof of your love, and of our glorying on your behalf.*

This line is as stern as anything in chapters 10ff. When a person has professed love, and the object of such alleged love hurls the challenge to "prove it" in the face of a competent witness just cited, and "before the face of all the churches," there is absolutely nothing "mild" in such a response. It is absolutely incredible that the scholarly efforts to disturb the unity of this epistle should be grounded in such a colossal misunderstanding of plain words as must be their view that "a change of tone" comes in chapter 10. It simply is not so. The same tone of stern apostolical reprimand pervades every line of this remarkable letter.

The chapter division which ends here comes right in the middle of Paul's argument which was continued in what is labeled the next chapter. He will continue his instructions on Christian giving in Chapter 9.

---

[28]David Lipscomb, *op. cit.*, p. 118.

CHAPTER 9

"Some consider chapter 9 a separate note written by Paul earlier than chapter 8,"[1] but such a notion is merely the knee-jerk reflex of critical minds seeking to destroy the unity of this epistle; and no solid logic of any kind supports it. "These verses are not a misplaced fragment, for the connection in thought is close with the preceding verses."[2] These verses are an intensification of Paul's appeal to the Corinthians to make good on their promises of a year ago and to make up a bountiful contribution for the poor saints in Jerusalem. As the careful student of the NT soon learns, this type of objection is groundless, contrived and absolutely unreliable. As Hughes said, "We are confronted with a hypothesis which is entirely without support of external evidence or of any tradition."[3] Besides that, "There is a very close connection between chapter 8 and the opening verses of chapter 9."[4]

An outline of this chapter has two divisions: (1) Paul's reasons for sending the brethren instead of coming himself (1-5), and (2) the blessings of Christian giving (6-15).

Verse 1, *For as touching the ministering to the saints, it is superfluous for me to write to you.*

"For . . ." "This word indicates a logical link with the immediately preceding matter."[5] Also, in this same connection, Tasker pointed out that "to write" as used here indicates the same thing. "The present tense of the infinitive 'to write' signifies 'to go on writing.' "[6]

"Ministering to the saints . . ." Wesley's quaint comment on this was, "Anything that conveyed God's good gifts from one

---

[1]Norman Hillyer, *The New Bible Commentary, Revised* (Grand Rapids: Wm. B. Eerdmans Publishing Co., 1970), p. 1083.

[2]Frank G. Carver, *Beacon Bible Commentary* (Kansas City. Beacon Hill Press, 1968), Vol. 8, p. 584.

[3]Philip E. Hughes, *Paul's Second Epistle to the Corinthians* (Grand Rapids: Wm. B. Eerdmans Publishing Co., p. 321.

[4]*Ibid.*

[5]*Ibid.*

[6]R. V. G. Tasker, *The Second Epistle of Paul to the Corinthians* (Grand Rapids: Wm. B. Eerdmans Publishing Co., 1959), p. 123.

member of the church to another was, in the apostle's eye, 'a ministry.' "[7]

Verse 2, *For I know your readiness, of which I glory on your behalf to them of Macedonia, that Achaia hath been prepared for a year past; and your zeal hath stirred up very many of them.*

"Your readiness . . ." does not mean that the promised contribution had actually been prepared, but that they had been prompt to promise their full cooperation. Furthermore, as Plumptre observed:

> The urgency of Pauls' present appeal indicates a latent misgiving whether he had unconsciously overstated the fact, and had mistaken the "will" that had showed itself for an actual readiness to send the money when it was called for.[8]

It would have been a permanent disgrace to the Corinthians if, after being held up as an example to others, they themselves should have fallen short.

Verse 3, *But I have sent the brethren, that our glorying on your behalf may not be made void in this respect; that, even as I said, ye may be prepared.*

"I have sent . . ." in this place "has the meaning of 'I am sending.'"[9] This is another example of the "epistolary aorist," as used in 8:17 above.

"Glorying . . ." "Paul's glorying here is neither in men nor in human achievements as such."[10] His glorying is in the grace of God as manifested in the beauty of lives which had been touched with the knowledge of Jesus the Lord.

Verse 4, *Lest by any means, if there come with me any of Macedonia and find you unprepared, we (that we say not ye) should be put to shame in this confidence.*

---

[7]John Wesley, *One Volume NT Commentary* (Grand Rapids: Baker Book House, 1972), *in loco.*
[8]E. H. Plumptre, *Ellicott's Commentary* (Grand Rapids: Zondervan Publishing House, 1959), p. 394.
[9]R. V. G. Tasker, *op. cit.*, p. 124.
[10]Philip E. Hughes, *op. cit.*, p. 323.

"Lest by any means . . ." does not have any meaning of uncertainty. "It is not hypothetical, but = 'when,' as in 13:2."[11]

"We should be put to shame . . ." This is a marvelous example of Paul's use of "we" in order more fully to identify himself with his readers for the purpose of making a more delicate and forceful appeal. All commentators are compelled to recognize the device here, where Paul spelled it out; and it is a shame that so many have failed to recognize exactly the same use of it in Hebrews 2:3. In this place, there could have been no shame whatever upon Paul through any default of the Corinthians. It was not his own face which Paul sought to save by this admonition, but the reputation of the Corinthians.

Verse 5, *I thought necessary therefore to entreat the brethren, that they would go before unto you, and make up beforehand your aforepromised bounty, that the same might be ready as a matter of bounty, and not of extortion.*

"Before . . . beforehand . . . aforepromised . . ." This repeated emphasis on the fact that they had already promised this collection more than a year ago had an element of sternness in it that should not be overlooked. The allegation that Paul was, in these first nine chapters, expressing his absolute and unreserved satisfaction with everyone at Corinth is founded upon a gross misinterpretation of a great many things contained in them, including the sharp dissatisfaction inherent in such a sentence as this.

"Bounty . . . not of extortion . . ." It is remarkable to read the comments designed to soften the force of the word "extortion." which by implication is here applied to all radical and high-pressure methods of fund raising. Such methods are here called by their true name. Paul was saying that, more than anything else, and certainly more than the money, he wanted the Corinthians to *desire* the fulfillment of their promise.

Filson correctly read the implied criticism of Paul's words here, as indicating that "There had already been too much

---

[11]David J. A. Clines, *A New Testament Commentary* (Grand Rapids: Zondervan Publishing House, 1969), p. 433.

delay."[12] Macknight's paraphrase of this verse is:

> For that reason I thought it necessary to entreat the brethren, that they would go before me to you, and excite you to complete, before my arrival, your formerly announced gift, that the same might be thus prepared at my coming to Corinth, as a gift willingly bestowed, and not as a thing extorted from you by my importunity, as from persons of a covetous disposition.[13]

Having thus disposed of the explanation of why he was sending messengers on ahead for the purpose of raising the collection, Paul devoted the balance of this chapter to extolling the joys and benefits of Christian giving.

Verse 6, *But this I say, He that soweth sparingly shall reap also sparingly; and he that soweth bountifully shall reap also bountifully.*

Other scriptures which carry this same implication are found in Proverbs 11:24, 19:17 and Luke 6:38; and strong disagreement is felt with regard to downgrading the motivation appealed to here. Clines' view that "This is not a very exalted motive for giving"[14] should not be accepted. Giving as an exhibition of trust in God's promise to bless the giver is as exalted as any other motive taught in the word of God.

Verse 7, *Let each man do according as he hath purposed in his heart: not grudgingly, or of necessity: for God loveth a cheerful giver.*

The importance of consecrated Christian giving is so great, that the following studies with reference to it are included.

Why Give

God owns the world and everything in it. Underlying the entire structure of the word of God is a ledge-rock principle of divine ownership. God owns the earth, by right of creation; and when man was introduced, he appeared, not as an owner, but

---

[12]Floyd V. Filson, *Interpreter's Bible* (Nashville: Abingdon Press, 1953), Vol. X, p. 375.

[13]James Macknight, *Apostolical Epistles with Commentary* (Grand Rapids: Baker Book House, 1969), Vol. II, p. 411.

[14]David J. A. Clines, *op. cit.*, p. 433.

as a gardener in Eden. Every beast of the forest, every bird of the mountains, and every beast of the field, even "the world and its fullness" belong to God (Ps. 50:10-12). Society's permission to certain people to occupy God's earth, or to hold its estates, does not contravene the divine ownership. Title deeds and legal grants always have regard to social custom, not divine authority. No man "owns" any of the earth; it belongs to God by the dual right of creation and constant maintenance.

All men, especially Christians, are themselves the property of God. Paul had warned these Corinthians already that they were not their own, having been bought with a price (1 Cor. 6:20). Men are called God's "own servants . . . his goods" (Matt. 25:14; Luke 19:13). Paul loved to speak of himself as the "bondslave" of Christ (Rom. 1:1); and, in light of the life he lived, it was no pious pretense. Even in the dim light of the OT, there is profound recognition of this great truth so frequently overlooked by the professed followers of Christ today. David said:

> But who am I, and what is my people, that we should be able to offer so willingly after this sort, for all things come of thee; and of thine own have we given thee (1 Chron. 29:14)?

All men are accountable to God as stewards of his wealth. In very much the same sense that Joseph was the slave of Potiphar yet had control of all of Potiphar's possessions, the Christian is the slave of Christ and answerable to the Master for his handling of the Lord's goods, a day of reckoning being clearly revealed in the NT. "And after a long time, the Lord of those servants cometh and reckoned with them" (Matt. 25:19). The parables both of the talents and of the pounds likewise teach the same thing; and, when men's possessions are treated as Jesus' property, it will be the end of the problem of how much to give. The solution will be not in the decision of what to give to the work of the Lord, but in the decision of how much of the Lord's own possessions should be diverted to the selfish ends of the steward.

The proper motivation in giving is determinative. The great gift of Ananias and Sapphira was rejected because it was motivated by selfishness; and the gift of the widow's mites, though exceedingly small, was praised by Jesus because of her true devotion. Some pretend to be giving "all I can," whereas everyone knows that their "all" is merely the leftovers from a gluttonous feast of selfishness. God will judge the hearts of men.

It is obvious that impure and unworthy motives in giving cause the loss to the giver of any divine approval. Any motive that is based upon pride, vain glory or selfishness is wrong and should be put far away from every Christian. The incentives that should impel men to give are revealed in God's word; and among those which are high and holy are the following:

God himself is a motive. The Father in heaven is the first and greatest of motives. He so loved the world that "he gave" (John 3:16), and for one to be like the great King of heaven and earth, he should give. Let men teach their hearts to give; and, if they do this, their hands will not need teaching. God has proposed to win back to himself a big, lost and sinful world, putting all of the resources of heaven itself into the effort. He has called up his reserves and is doing all that even God could do to save humanity. Yet, despite all that has been done through many thousands of years, entire nations lie in rebellion and darkness; millions know not his mercy; the blessed Father needs our help; and what a privilege it is to help God himself by giving toward the realization of the Creator's plans.

Christ is a motive. It was to this that Paul appealed in verse 15, below, "Thanks be to God for his unspeakable gift." Christ redeemed men; and it is a strangely perverse and hardened heart that cannot find in this unspeakable truth the key that will unlock the springs of liberality.

Illustration: At a slave-auction long ago, the tears of a slave-girl arrested the attention of a traveler, her obvious agony being so unlike the indifference of the rest who were being sold. He paid a great price for her redemption, yet no joy came to her face when told that she was free. She had been born a slave and did not know what it meant; but at last, when the traveler was ready to depart, and as he told her what she must do after he was gone, it finally dawned in her heart what had happened; and, with her first breath, she said, "I will follow him! I will serve him all the days of my life!" Despite every reason against it, that is exactly what she did. Ever afterward, when her unselfish service drew the remarks of people who noticed it, she had only one word of response: "He redeemed me; he redeemed me!" Should it be any different for us who have been redeemed with the precious blood of Christ? May that attitude perish which views participation in the body of Christ as merely a kind of insurance against all of the hereafter, for which a premium, the lowest possible, is paid. May we serve Jesus Christ as sinners bought with blood should serve him; and, when men notice the joy of our service, our pure happiness, and our free and liberal giving, let the answer ring out, "He redeemed me!"

The church of Christ is a motive. The church is truly the bride of Christ (Rev. 21:9), the spiritual body of the Redeemer himself (Eph. 1:22,23); and what is done to the church is done to Christ. For further discussion of this, see CA, pp. 180-181. Any man who would spend his money more lavishly upon himself alone, neglecting to provide the barest necessities for his wife, boasting all the while of how he loved her, would deserve the reputation of a criminal hypocrite. So also does the man who spends all that he can get his hands upon for his own selfish indulgements and then casts some trifling gift into the treasury of the Lord. How beautiful was Jesus' entrusting the care of his beloved mother to the apostle John; but the care of his bride the church has been entrusted to us! The needs of the church the body of Christ are a basic motivation for giving that is truly Christian.

The world is another motive. There are four thousand millions of reasons why men should give liberally to God's work. All of the sin, pain and sorrow; all of the defeat, doubt and despair; and all of the sad groanings of miserable humanity are reasons why men should give. Let men give so that broken hearts can be healed by the love of Jesus and quickened with the gospel of salvation. Unloose the strings, therefore, not of the purse, but of the heart. When Jesus saw the multitudes, "He had compassion on them." That same compassion inspires the Christian giver.

I myself am a motive. Back in 8:14, Paul warned the Corinthians that there could come a time when their "want" might require the generous help of others; and every Christian should take this possibility seriously. At some future time, the Christian may find himself in the agony of doubt, or of some blinding sorrow; and, if such should come to pass, it will be the church that helps him to ride out the period of distress. Then, may those who are able to do so build the sacred walls of the church a little higher by their faithfulness and liberality.

Illustration: This writer held the funeral for a ragged old man who sought refuge from bitter weather in an old wagon yard one dark night and died of neglect before day dawned. It turned out that he had once been prosperous and a nominal Christian who gave nothing to the church *in that very city.* In his hour of need, a false pride refused to utter the plea that would have saved his life; and his neglect of the church became at last the neglect of himself.

Contrast that with the case of David, who in the hour of his extremity, was handed the sword of Goliath, which long previously his own hands had deposited in the temple. It is no wonder, then, that a son of David said, "Cast thy bread upon the waters, for thou shalt find it after many days!" A legitimate application of this is found in the life of a person who gives and gives to God's church, and one day finds the church to be his own exceedingly great reward.

Gifts to Christ are saved; all else is lost. Earth has no safe deposit boxes; "Moth . . . rust . . . thieves, etc." corrupt and corrode all human treasures, as the Saviour warned (Matt. 6:19, 20). Joaquin Miller's poetic eulogy of Peter Cooper stressed the impressive truth that "All you can hold in your cold, dead hand is what you have given away!" This is particularly true of what is given to Christ, that is, to his church. Men need to be reminded that giving to the church is giving to Christ. The glory and praise of men can be received by giving to other things, but the NT commands men to "give glory to God in the church" (Eph. 3:21). Some who give vast sums to civic and social organizations and to political and fraternal orders, while neglecting the church, should lay this to heart.

Partnership with God, a motive. "Enter thou into the joy of thy Lord" (Matt. 25:21) was the accolade given by Jesus to the faithful steward; or, as Goodspeed translated it, "Come, share your Master's enjoyment."[15] Is not this a partnership with the Lord? Christ is not in business for himself alone, but for the benefit of his slaves; and no man can afford to hinder what Christ would do for him by a rebellious refusal to handle as Christ commanded those few goods (or many) that were entrusted to his care and stewardship by the Lord.

God gave many marvelous opportunities to angels, who kept watch over the cradle of the infant Jesus, who helped the Lord in the wilderness of temptation, who supported him in Gethsemane, who rolled the stone from his grave, who escorted him to glory to receive the kingdom from the Father; but to mortal men, like ourselves, God reserved the priceless opportunity of becoming his partners!

Men love cheerful givers. In this very verse, Paul made the fact of God's loving a cheerful giver a means of motivating the Corinthians. Well, that is no mystery. Men do too! There is no more certain way into the hearts of men than by the practice of a sincere and honest liberality. Stinginess is universally despised; and it was no accident that the ancient drawings of the fabled King Midas always decorated him with ass's ears! He was justly hated for his selfish greed.

A generous man or woman, on the other hand, is given a welcome in the heart of mankind. This is a worthy motive for giving, because it is certainly a mark of the highest character when one desires the love of men. However, it is the love of men, not their praises, which is the true motive.

"*God loves a cheerful giver.*" Has there ever been a human being who could decide that he does not wish to be loved of God? For any thoughtful person, this must be the greatest motive of all. That the eternal and omnipotent God should love a mortal man is a concept so wonderful that it surpasses the powers of human imagination to understand it; but here Paul bluntly stated it. No human liberality, therefore, could be too great; for the love of God to men is beyond any comparison with the feeble and insufficient means of any man, or of all men, to

---

[15]Edgar J. Goodspeed, *The New Testament, an American Translation* (Chicago: The University of Chicago Press, 1923), *in loco.*

merit it. But this glorious promise! Who is there who can fail to find a mighty inspiration in it?

If God loves a man, it is better than his being loved by the richest and most powerful man on earth. If God loves a man, no matter how much he gives, God will not let him suffer for doing so. When God loves a person, the special providence of the Almighty will follow him all the days of his earthly pilgrimage. May God help every Christian to take these things into account.

Verse 8, *And God is able to make grace abound unto you; that ye, having always all sufficiency in everything, may abound unto every good work.*

Generous giving, as Tasker said, "seems very hazardous";[16] but Paul here stated the truth that where the generous spirit is, God will provide the means of expressing it. The amount of any man's giving is inevitably influenced by his trust, or mistrust, of the promise here.

Verse 9, *As it is written,*

> *He hath scattered abroad, he hath given to the poor;*
> *His righteousness abideth forever.*

"As it is written . . ." "This exact construction occurs twelve times in Romans, twice in 1 Corinthians, and twice in this epistle (8:15 and here). Nowhere else does Paul use it."[17]

The Psalm Paul here quoted is 112:9, a passage which describes the blessedness of the man who fears God. As Hughes said, "The words read like the epitaph of a philanthropist."[18] Paul appealed to the passage here as additional motivation for giving.

Verse 10, *And he that supplieth seed to the sower and bread for food, shall supply and multiply your seed for sowing, and increase the fruits of your righteousness.*

Here is further inducement for giving liberally. Paul had already said in verse 6 that the man who sowed sparingly

---

[16]R. V. G. Tasker, *op. cit.*, p. 126.
[17]Wick Broomall, *Wycliffe Bible Commentary* (Chicago: Moody Press, 1971), p. 679.
[18]Philip E. Hughes, *op. cit.*, p. 332.

should reap sparingly, and that the bountiful sower should also reap bountifully. The whole thrust of this chapter concerns how men should give. A collation of NT teaching on how men should give is as follows:

How to Give

God is deeply concerned about how men give, for it is not enough that one merely turn a part of his wealth or income to holy uses. It is of primary importance that such be done in a manner approved of God. Note the following on how not to give:

Not for vain-glory. In the Sermon on the Mount, Jesus warned that giving should not be done "to be seen of men" (Matt. 6:1-4).

Not grudgingly (2 Cor. 9:7). It is a positive violation of God's law for any man to permit himself to be high-pressured into giving to the church, or anything else. Giving should mark a Christian's character, because of what he is, not because of a good sales talk. As Paul suggested to Philemon, "Without thy mind, I would do nothing; that thy benefit should not be as it were, of necessity, but willingly" (v. 14).

Not deceitfully. Ananias and Sapphira (Acts 5:1ff) are the NT examples of this error; but it may well be feared that even now there are many who pretend a liberality they do not have.

Not without love. The gift of all one's earthly goods "without love" profits the giver "nothing" at all (1 Cor. 13:3). Nothing big, or good, or beautiful can come out of a loveless gift. True giving cannot be practiced without feeling, as for example, when a man might throw food to a stray dog.

Not while estranged from a brother. "First be reconciled to thy brother, and then come and offer thy gift" (Matt. 5:23, 24) — that is Christ's command; and it may not be violated with impunity.

What then are the guidelines for proper giving?

It should be done with simplicity. See Romans 12:8. Simplicity oils the rough usages of charity in such a manner that the recipient is not wounded. On the contrary, an ostentatious giver is an offense: (1) to the observer because of his vulgarity,

(2) to the recipient of alms because of his pride and lovelessness, and (3) to the heavenly Father because of his vanity and conceit.

In the name of Christ. "For whosoever shall give you a cup of cold water in my name, because ye belong to Christ, verily I say unto you, He shall in no wise lose his reward" (Mark 9:41). All that a Christian does should be done in the name of the Lord (Col. 3:17). In a practical sense, this generally means doing it through the church, which is the spiritual body of Christ.

Systematically. "Upon the first day of the week" (1 Cor. 16:2). The meaning of the NT is that giving should be done regularly on the first day of every week. Systematic and continual giving is far better than great gifts poured out after long neglect of this duty. Systematic giving creates and sustains the habit of giving, keeping the springs of the Christian heart open.

Liberally. Liberal giving means just that. Christ described it in this command: "Give, and it shall be given you; good measure, pressed down, and shaken together, etc." (Luke 6:38).

Sacrificially. A Christian's body is "a living sacrifice" (Rom. 12:1). It is not enough that men give merely crumbs that fall from the table where self is feasted. The writer of Hebrews, in speaking of giving, said, "For with such sacrifices, God is well pleased" (13:16). This means that men should give enough to God that it requires sacrifice to do it.

Cheerfully. This noble chapter requires this quality (9:7). A man said he could give a dollar much more cheerfully than he could give a hundred dollars; but that is not what Paul meant. The cheerful giver is the one who derives joy from obeying the Lord and imitating the Giver of all things by his own obedience. Under every divine commandment is the great principle of benefit to the one who obeys it. Only the givers are happy people. The *miser* is so-called because he is *miser*able.

Purposefully. This is another quality stressed in this chapter (9:7). This shows that giving should be in accordance with the inward purpose and intention of the giver; and it does no justice to this principle when a man merely thrusts a hand into his pocket and casts whatever might be handy into the collection.

Secretly. "That thine alms may be in secret" (Matt. 6:3, 4). This principle applies especially to person-to-person giving, a grace in which every Christian must share; but it does not mean that every man's giving is his business alone. On the contrary, Paul commanded the church to withdraw from the covetous man (1 Cor. 5:11); and thus the elders of the church surely have the right to know of one's giving, yes, the amount of it, and to discipline the covetous.

Upon a basis of equality. Again, from this chapter (8:13, 14), there is apostolical instruction on how to give. It was never God's plan that 20% of the church should give 90% of the church budget, allowing all of the religious hitch-hikers to take a free ride. God's way is a way of equality. This cannot mean equal amounts, for that would be manifestly unfair. If the total amount needed is divided by the membership total, and each man "gives his part," it would be only a trifle for some and utterly impossible for others. The only method of finding an equality is for all to give a certain percentage of their income; and the ancient principle of giving a tithe to God (which is 10%) is a good place to start. The tithe was recognized as the duty of all men to Almighty God, long before there was any such thing as Judaism upon this earth. Abraham paid tithes to Melchizedek (Heb. 7:7), a priest of God Most High, at a time when the Jewish dispensation was merely an unfulfilled prophecy. For full discussion of this see CH, pp. 143-146.

One's self to be given first (2 Cor. S:5). When one gives his heart to the Lord, in his conversion to Christ, the problem of giving is already solved. For the person who finds difficulty in becoming a liberal giver, it would be well for him to ask himself, "Have I really given myself to the Lord?"

Verse 11, *Ye being enriched in everything unto all liberality, which worketh through us thanksgiving to God.*

"Being enriched in everything . . ." This is a promise that Christians who give as they should will "in everything" be enriched, meaning, not merely in their financial ability, but in countless other ways also. This heavenly promise is the pledge of God himself that giving pays rich dividends to the giver. We have seen how some decry the motive of this promise in men's hearts (v. 6); but the inspired apostle did not hesitate to place it in his appeal here; and this is far more than enough authority for respecting it. As Plumptre said, "The context points primarily to temporal abundance";[19] but it is quite evident that many other blessings are likewise included.

Dividends Received From Giving

Underlying every sacred commandment is the purpose of God to achieve the utmost happiness and benefit for the obedient child of God; and obedience to the commandment to give, in the normal progress of human life on earth, is inevitably rewarded with the richest possible dividends.

The classical example of the rich young ruler (Matt. 19:16ff) is a startling demonstration of this principle. When he knelt at the feet of Jesus and asked how to inherit eternal life, the Lord commanded him to sell all that he had and give it to the poor and to come and "follow" the Lord Jesus (Mark 10:21). The Lord's command to this rich young ruler was for the man's own benefit, not the benefit of Jesus. The Lord did not need his money; Judas was already stealing what little the Lord had; and, in a short time, the Lord intended to die upon the cross. Furthermore, there was no special crisis among the poor, and the distribution of one man's estate could hardly have benefited any of them permanently. Would this rich young ruler have benefited from full and complete compliance with Jesus' command? The answer is affirmative.

Forty years after this young man knelt at Jesus' feet, God poured out the accumulated wrath of centuries upon Jerusalem. The young man was old when that happened, and there is no reason to doubt that he stood with his countrymen against Rome. All of his wealth and posterity were swept away in an hour by the soldiers of Vespasian and Titus. If he perished, along with over a million others, or if through some chance his life was spared to see the Holy City forever humbled under the feet of the Gentile, there was for him, in either case, no joy, no consolation, no hope. Did he remember what Jesus said about

---

[19]E. H. Plumptre, *op. cit.*, p. 396.

selling it all and giving it away? What if he had obeyed? If he had been a member of the Christian community, he would have believed Jesus' prophecy, and with all believers would have fled to Pella till the storm was passed. It is clear enough that this young man's best earthly interests would have been served by doing exactly what Jesus commanded. But so would every man's! There were special circumstances involved in Jesus' words to "sell all" in his case; and this is not a requirement of being a true Christian; but the command for liberal giving is applicable to all who obey the gospel; and, for ourselves, no less than for him, Jesus commanded that which will benefit his followers, not only in the eternal world, but *now* and *here*. (See full discussion of the rich young ruler in CM, pp. 295-296.)

Satisfaction. Giving as the holy scriptures command pays a one thousand per cent dividend in satisfaction. This is precisely the thing that all men are seeking; and, in their efforts to procure it, they leave home and friends, travel over continents and oceans, climb mountains and cross deserts, build skyscrapers, torture their bodies, sear their consciences, and deaden their souls — all they want is satisfaction! However, the deepest needs of the soul can never be satisfied by any such activity. The true satisfaction is available only in Christ. He said, "He that loseth his life for my sake shall find it" (Matt. 10:39).

It is in giving that the great satisfaction is discovered. The smile of an orphan child given to a benefactor over a glass of milk is worth more than the fickle praise of a multitude. The joy of seeing one soul turn to the holy Christ is sweeter than all the pleasures of earth. Giving provides benefits to the needy, glory to God and satisfaction for the giver. Souls having not the courage to give are missing the most wholesome satisfaction life affords.

A higher standard of living. What is the mystery of two families from the same neighborhood with approximately the same income, same number of children, same health, same obligations, etc., but one of which has a standard of living dramatically higher than the other? The mystery is even more perplexing when it is discovered that the family with the higher standard gives liberally to the church, whereas the other never gives anything.

What is the explanation of this family which gives and gives and yet has more? It is found in the influence of Christianity in their lifes. The other family pays a heavy liquor bill, indulges in gambling, wastes time and money on all kinds of questionable entertainment, involves itself with immoral and unprincipled associates. A son takes up with bad company, incurs a heavy fine, gets drunk and wrecks the family car, etc., etc. The wisest investment any man can make is a regular and faithful contribution to the church. In actual money it will save him many times over what he gives, closing sources of waste, extravagance and sin that would otherwise be open. He will actually find a higher standard of living by faithful giving to the work of the Lord.

The terrible cost of not giving. A man grew very rich and had no time for the church. "All the church wants is my money," was his reply to every invitation. His only son grew up in a Christless home, became a libertine and a squanderer. One day, he quarreled bitterly with his father, while drinking heavily, and in an angry fit shot and killed his father. Something like this, or worse, will happen to every home where the teaching of Christ is refused. It probably never occurred to that unfortunate man that what the church really wanted was not his money at all, but the true salvation of himself and his family. Sure, faithfulness would have cost him part of his money; but Satan took all of it, and his life and soul along with it! One makes his choice and pays the penalty if he chooses wrong.

But there are some who are determined to beat God's system. They will go to church and bring up a Christian family without giving, or at least without giving very much. If such is attempted, the children will see through the sham and hypocrisy of it. One cannot love the Lord and the church without giving to it; and, if one is not a giver, his religion is worthless; and all men will know instinctively that he does not love the Lord or his church and that his pretensions are false. The unchristian life is far more expensive than the Christian life.

Increased prosperity. In this chapter, Paul declared that the bountiful sower will reap a bountiful harvest; and that is a pledge of increased prosperity. Some people are almost afraid to hope for prosperity, fearing that it might be wrong to do so; but one of the apostles prayed for a friend, "that thou mayest prosper and be in health, even as thy soul prospereth" (12 John 2). It is not the apostle's intention, however, that prosperity should exceed spiritual growth, but keep pace with it.

The principle of increased prosperity for true Christians is not a mere inference from some ambiguous text, but an imperial decree from on high. The Son of God said:

> Verily, I say unto you, there is no man that hath left house, or brethren, or sisters, or father or mother, or wife or children or land, for my sake and the gospel's, but he shall receive an hundred fold now in this time, houses and brethren and sisters, and mothers, and children, and lands, with persecutions, and in the world to come eternal life (Mark 10:29).

Some profess not to believe this; but no one who ever tried it disbelieves it. God's hand is still visible in the affairs of men. "He that soweth bountifully shall reap also bountifully." Here is the explanation of the mystery as old as Solomon, that "There is that scattereth and yet increaseth; and there is that withholdeth more than is meet, but it tendeth to poverty" (Prov. 11:24, 25).

A better personality. All the world is divided into two classes, the givers and the hoarders. One class is continually becoming more and more selfish and unlovable; and the other class is forever increasing in the grace and knowledge of the Lord and are "changed from glory to glory" by his gracious Spirit (2 Cor. 3:18). The ancient allegory of the two seas, Galilee and the Dead Sea, is true. For the Galilee people, life's blessings flow in, but also outward to bless and benefit others; and for the Dead Sea people, life's blessings flow in but never out. The giver becomes a Galilee person, full of sweetness and love; but the Dead Sea person becomes an old salt, crusted over with selfishness and cynicism, full of hatred and apprehension. A Christian who gives as the Lord commanded invariably becomes a Galilee person. This is exactly the type of personality that commands the highest honor and respect in any community on earth.

Friends out of the Mammon. Jesus was speaking of the use of wealth when he commanded his follows to:

> Use mammon, dishonest as it is, to make friends for yourselves, so that when you die, they may welcome you to the eternal abodes (Luke 16:9).[20]

See exegesis of this passage in CL, pp. 349-351. The friends to be made by the wise use of money are the Father, the Son, the Holy Spirit, the angels of God. The eternal abodes are the mansions of the blessed, the "many mansions" of the Fathers' house (John 14:1ff). This is the eternal dividend for those who honor the Saviour's command to give; and, in this passage, Jesus did not fail to connect the stewardship of money with the welcome of the redeemed eternally. Christians who are lame in the giving department have simply overlooked the fact that an unbelievable percentage of the whole NT is devoted to this subject.

A memorial before God. It was written of Cornelius that an angel of heaven stood in his house and said, "Cornelius, thy prayers and thy alms have come up as a memorial before God" (Acts 10:4). The deep, eternal longing of human souls to be remembered after death is realized only by faithful Christian givers. Not only will they be remembered on earth, but in heaven. God will take account of the gifts tendered by his children; and this is the most glorious thought of all. Also, there is the lavish gift of Mary of Bethany who poured out the priceless nard upon the feet of Jesus. The Master said, "Wheresoever this gospel shall be preached in the whole world, there shall also this which this woman hath done be told for a memorial of her" (Matt. 26:13). Faithful giving creates a memorial of the giver before God in heaven.

The return of the principal. Bob Hope once said that he was more interested in the return of his money than the return on it! The super-colossal climax of dividends received from Christian giving is the ultimate return to the giver of all that he

---

[20]James Moffatt, *The Bible, A New Translation* (New York: Harpers), *in loco.*

gave. Jesus said, "Lay up for yourselves treasures in heaven, etc." (Matt. 6:19-21). This is proof that the Master will repay at the last day the full account with all accrued dividends. When Christ gave this teaching, he also called attention to the doubtful and insecure investments that men make on earth, where moth, rust, thieves, and all kinds of dangers threaten not merely the dividends, but the principal also. "Riches make themselves wings and fly away as an eagle toward heaven" (Prov. 23:5). If any man doubts this, let him ask the man who has seen his life's savings swept away in a fire, a robbery, a revolution, an epidemic, a flood, a drouth, an earthquake, a tornado, a broken trust, a wreck, an accident, an unjust law, or by means of any one of a thousand unpredictable disasters which may strike like lightning at any time and at any place.

Nobody ever gave Jesus anything, whether a grave, as did Joseph; or a basket lunch, as did the lad; or anything else, without receiving more than he gave. Joseph received his grave again; and the little lad was the lawful owner of the twelve basketfuls taken up after the feast! Let men try giving it to Jesus. No investment can compare with that.

These studies on the subject of giving have been included in this commentary because of the near-universal need for Christians to be taught and to understand the truth about the central duty of the Christian life.

Verse 12, *For the ministration of this service not only filleth up the measure of the wants of the saints, but aboundeth also through many thanksgivings unto God.*

"The wants of the saints . . ." refers to the necessities which they lacked, and not to things which they merely wanted. Desirable as the relief of the saints was, this was by no means the whole benefit of the collection. As Wesley said, "Its chief value consisted in the spiritual results."[21]

"Many thanksgivings unto God . . ." The Lord's name would be glorified, souls convinced of the truth of the gospel, and converts won for Christ; but, beyond all these objective achievements of their liberality, there would be the multiplication of grace within the hearts of the givers themselves.

---

[21]John Wesley, *op. cit., in loco.*

Verse 13, *Seeing that by the proving of you by this ministration they glorify God for the obedience of your confession unto the gospel of Christ, and for the liberality of your contribution unto them and unto all.*

"By the proving of you . . ." Giving is the divine test of Christianity. Non-givers are non-Christian.

"The obedience of your confession . . ." By virtue of one's conversion, he is already pledged as a giver to support God's work. That he shall, in fact, do so is inherently demanded by his confession.

Verse 14, *While they themselves also, with supplication on your behalf, long after you by reason of the exceeding grace of God in you.*

Paul here continued to elaborate the spiritual benefits that would come from the contribution at Corinth. The recipients would remember them with thanksgiving in their prayers, "supplications on your behalf."

"Long after you . . ." The reputation and honor of the Corinthians would be enhanced and magnified.

"The exceeding grace of God in you . . ." shows that Paul was projecting a very liberal and bountiful contribution and that he was not looking for a merely token response to his appeal. In regard to the question of how much money they might have given, Carver has this:

> The apostle's appeal proved successful, for a few months later he wrote from Corinth to the Romans that "Macedonia and Achaia have been pleased to make a contribution for the poor among the saints in Jerusalem" (15:26 NASB).[22]

Verse 15, *Thanks be to God for this unspeakable gift.*

Scholarly opinion of what the gift is in this verse is sharply divided; but the view which appears most reasonable is that which understands the gift to be the Lord Jesus Christ himself, who is THE gift of God.

---

[22]Frank G. Carver, *op. cit.*, p. 584.

"Unspeakable . . ." is hardly the word that Paul would have chosen for any lesser gift than the Saviour; and, while it is true that the working of the grace of God through Christ in the hearts of the Corinthians is in view here, it is not such a work of Christ but Christ himself who is meant. Plumptre spoke of some who believe the gift here to be the Holy Spirit, on the basis of Acts 2:38f; but it is that word "unspeakable" which, more than anything else, compels one to see in the gift "none other than Jesus Christ himself."

CHAPTER 10

There is a break in thought with the beginning of this chapter, but it is nothing which can reasonably reflect on the unity of the epistle. Any man writing on a number of subjects in a single letter, and having something rather sensitive to communicate, would quite naturally reserve it till the concluding part of the letter. All of the scholarly guesses about a "severe" letter having been penned at a time between the two canonical letters, such letter having first been lost, then a part of it discovered, and then inserted by some unknown "editor" at this particular place in 2 Corinthians is too preposterous a surmise to have any weight at all. Why would any "editor" have placed such a recovered lost letter in a place like this? All such speculations perish in the total absence of any manuscript authority, and of any tradition whatever that any such thing ever happened. Even Filson admitted that it is only upon internal evidence that the "severe letter" hypothesis can be advocated.[1]

The so-called internal evidence evaporates under scholarly analysis; and, as Philip E. Hughes declared:

> Paul's sternest remarks refer not to the Corinthians in general, but to the false teachers (designated "some" in verse 2). Besides, it is not difficult to show that passages in this concluding section are plainly very much of a piece with themes and matters introduced in earlier chapters.[2]

The proposition that there is nothing severe in the first nine chapters is likewise false, and can be advocated only by misreading the hyperbole in 7:13ff (see notes above). Also, the notion of some "ring leader" is contrary to the picture of several factions as given in the first epistle. It is amazing that critical scholarship should be so insistent about something so valueless as their "severe letter" fantasy. Even if it existed,

---

[1]Floyd V. Filson, *Interpreter's Bible* (Nashville: Abingdon Press, 1950), pp. 270-271.

[2]Philip E. Hughes, *Paul's Second Epistle to the Corinthians* (Grand Rapids: Wm. B. Eerdmans Publishing Co., 1962), p. 343.

and even if chapter 10ff is part of it, it is admitted by all that Paul wrote it, that it is inspired, canonical and absolutely trustworthy. So what is to be gained by all this imaginative, intellectual tap-dancing about the "severe letter"? It is more than extraordinarily worthless.

Verse 1, *Now I Paul myself entreat you by the meekness and gentleness of Christ, I who in your presence am lowly among you, but being absent am of good courage toward you.*

Paul was about to deal with "some" who were still incorrigible sinners at Corinth (v. 2); but his attitude toward his beloved converts has not changed. He "entreats," as always, being filled with the meekness and gentleness of Christ.

"In your presence . . . lowly . . ." From the days of Chrysostom, this has been thought to echo some of the slanders of Paul's enemies who had been saying that "when present he was mild and timid, but when absent full of boldness."[3]

Verse 2, *Yea, I beseech you that I may not when present show courage with the confidence wherewith I count to be bold against some, who count of us as if we walked after the flesh.*

The thought in this is that Paul was purposely mild and timid when present with the whole congregation, and that he was beseeching the majority of them, even here, that they would not be offended by that confident courage he was prepared to demonstrate against the "some," not only in what he was about to write, but also when he would soon appear among them personally. There is no admission on Paul's part here that there was anything "weak" about his personal appearance. The whole theory of these later chapters "blasting the whole congregation" is nullified by the distinction between the "you" which included the whole congregation and the"some" which referred to the false teachers.

Verse 3, *For though we walk in the flesh; we do not war according to the flesh.*

"Flesh . . ." is used in two senses here, a distinguishing Pauline trademark. Although still in the body (the flesh), his warfare is not according to the nature of unregenerated and

---

[3]*Ibid.*, p. 346.

sinful men, whose works are governed by material and secular considerations (according to the flesh).

Verse 4, (*For the weapons of our warfare are not of the flesh, but mighty before God to the casting down of strongholds*).

What were Paul's weapons? "We learn from 1 Thessalonians 5:8, Ephesians 6:11-16, that they were the energies of spiritual powers given by the Eternal Spirit."[4]

"Casting down of strongholds . . ." "This phrase is essentially military";[5] and the imagery is that of a bitter and relentless warfare. The strongholds were those entrenched and fortified positions of institutionalized sin which dominated the Corinthian culture, and indeed the whole social fabric of the ancient Roman Empire. Satan had organized evil on a worldwide scale; and the teachings of Jesus Christ were leveled against every form of wickedness, no matter how securely it was embedded in the gross culture of that era.

"Mighty before God . . ." Paul's meaning here is that he had the proper ammunition to blow up and destroy the entrenched positions of the devil. History demonstrated that Paul's evaluation of the weapons at his disposal was correct.

Verse 5, *Casting down imaginations, and every evil thing that is exalted against the knowledge of God, and bringing every thought into captivity to the obedience of Christ.*

"Imaginations . . ." appear here in company with other evils; and despite the fact of man's imagination being a glorious distinction between himself and the lower creations, the misuse of it is superlatively sinful. It was true then, and it is true now. It is the "imagination" of scholars which seeks to challenge the unity of this epistle; and there is hardly any attack ever launched against Christianity that has not been grounded in the evil imagination of its enemies.

"High things . . . and every thought . . ." The imagery is still that of evil men, under the power of Satan, who have exalted themselves against the gospel truth, and who are

---

[4]E. H. Plumptre, *Ellicott's Commentary* (Grand Rapids: Zondervan Publishing House, 1959), Vol. III, p. 397.
[5]*Ibid.*

entrenched, as in a castle with "battlements and high towers which Paul must attack,"[6] in order to vanquish them. The word "thought" shows that the conflict is not physical, but it is in the realm of ideas and imaginations against the truth. Men have always had trouble with their imagination, the deluge itself having been the God-imposed penalty for man's imagination, which was "only evil continually" (Gen. 6:5).

Verse 6, *And being in readiness to avenge all disobedience, when your obedience shall be made full.*

"Your obedience shall be made full . . ." This does not mean, as Filson asserted, that "the church's obedience is here yet to come";[7] but that it was to be made *complete* when Paul had disposed of "some" who were enemies of the truth. There is in this passage an implied admission that their obedience, even at that time, was approaching fullness. The thing that would complete it was Paul's determination, or "readiness," to destroy the influence of the "some" who were still holding out against the truth.

Verse 7, *Ye look at the things which are before your face. If any man trusteth in himself that he is Christ's, let him consider this again with himself, that, even as he is Christ's, so also are we.*

"Ye look at what is before your eyes . . ." should be understood as imperative, as in RSV, "Look at what is before your eyes," giving the meaning of "Take a look at what is obvious."[8]

"If any man . . ." "This probably refers to an outstanding example of the false apostles who had gone to Corinth to try to supplant Paul."[9] Whoever he was, he was pretending to be Christ's; but his pretensions were refuted by the certainty of Paul's being actually "of Christ."

Verse 8, *For though I should glory somewhat abundantly concerning our authority (which the Lord gave for building you up, and not for casting you down), I shall not be put to shame.*

---

[6]J. R. Dummelow, *Commentary on the Holy Bible* (New York: The Macmillan Company, 1937), p. 939.

[7]Floyd V. Filson, *op. cit.*, p. 385.

[8]Frank G. Carver, *Beacon Bible Commentary* (Kansas City: Beacon Hill Press, 1968), Vol. 8, p. 593.

[9]Floyd V. Filson, *op. cit.*, p. 385.

The parenthesis here is very significant, showing that the strong exercise of his authority, both in this part of the letter and in the impending visit, was not in any manner directed against the great faithful majority. It was solely for the purpose of checkmating the evil, false apostles who intended to put Paul to shame. Notice the distinction between Paul's "casting down" envisioned of the false apostles, and his "not for casting you down" when addressing the whole congregation. Those who read these chapters as a tirade against the whole church have simply failed to read it.

Verse 9, *That I may not seem as if I would terrify you by my letters.*

This too is addressed directly to the great faithful majority, the thought being that "Paul could with justification elaborate upon the nature and extent of his apostolic authority, but refrained."[10] He did not wish to terrify the young converts whom he dearly loved, and the vast majority of whom were faithful and obedient. He had no such restraint as regarded the false apostles; and he seems to be saying here that "it is not you but *them* whom I wish to terrify."

Verse 10, *For, His letters, they say, are weighty and strong; but his bodily presence is weak, and his speech of no account.*

"They say . . ." proves that Paul had in mind a number of false teachers, not merely "the ring leader" postulated by the critics. And as for their slander, it is precarious indeed to put any confidence in it. No man who knows the biography can suppose for an instant that his bodily presence was "weak" in any sense, or that he lacked power as a public speaker. Their lies to the contrary should be rejected.

Verse 11, *Let such a one reckon this, that, what we are in word by letters when we are absent, such are we also in deed when we are present.*

By this sharp retort, Paul denied the slander; but despite this, one may still read all kinds of comments about the weakness of Paul's personal presence. The achievements of his

---

[10]R. V. G. Tasker, *The Second Epistle of Paul to the Corinthians* (Grand Rapids: Wm. B. Eerdmans Publishing Co., 1956), p. 136.

matchless life, as well as Paul's blunt rejoinder here, prove his amazing power and strength.

"Paul here is rebutting with calmness and dignity the false charge that he was in any way different from what he was when present."[11]

Verse 12, *For we are not bold to number or compare ourselves with certain of them that commend themselves: but they themselves, measuring themselves by themselves, and comparing themselves with themselves, are without understanding.*

The dramatically repeated plurals in this verse compel the understanding of several false apostles, rather than some special "ringleader." As Farrar pointed out, this verse ties in with what Paul had already written "in 3:1 and 4:12."[12]

"The value of a comparison depends on the standard";[13] and, as for the standard itself, in this case, and for them that used it, Paul had a single estimate. They were "without understanding"!

Verse 13, *But we will not glory beyond our measure, but according to the measure of the province which God apportioned to us as a measure, to reach even unto you.*

"The measure of the province . . ." One can only marvel at a translation like this. According to the Greek, as cited in the RV margin, the word is *measuring-rod*, which certainly makes a lot more sense than the word our translators substituted for it. Paul's plain meaning is that in the "glorying" or "boasting" he is about to do, he shall stay within the limits which God authorized in order to authenticate the message he is addressing to the Corinthians, "to reach even unto you." The noble words of McGarvey on this place are:

> Though the whole world was Paul's bishopric (Gal. 2:7-9), yet he contents himself with saying that it included Corinth. In the eyes of his opponents, Corinth was the

---

[11]F. W. Farrar, *Pulpit Commentary* (Grand Rapids: Wm. B. Eerdmans Publishing Co., 1950), Vol. 19, 2 Cor., p. 240.

[12]*Ibid.*

[13]John William Russell, *Compact Commentary on the NT* (Grand Rapids: Baker Book Rouse, 1964), p. 452.

> sum and center of all things, but in the larger life of Paul, it was a mere dot in a limitless field of operations.[14]

Verse 14, *For we stretch not ourselves overmuch, as though we reached not unto you: for we came even as far as unto you in the gospel of Christ.*

Paul here stated that his authority was fully ample to reach Corinth without, in any sense, "stretching" it! The perspective of the false teachers was local; Paul's was universal. Paul had come to Corinth in the first place, not as a final destination, but as a stop en route on a preaching tour of vast dimensions.

Filson very properly applied this passage to the false teachers as follows:

> The self-important intruders, when they came to Corinth, were going where they had not been sent by God. But not so with Paul. He went to Corinth under the guidance and direction of God. Corinth was included ("you also") in his assigned field of work.[15]

Verse 15, *But not glorying beyond our measure, that is, in other men's labors; but having hope that, as your faith groweth, we shall be magnified in you according to our province unto further abundance.*

In this verse, again, "province" is substituted for *measuring-rod*, because it is clear that he is speaking of a "field of labor" allotted to himself.

"In other men's labors . . ." God had sent the apostle to Corinth; the field was therefore his; and the false apostles, not Paul, were the intruders and usurpers.

"Having hope . . . as your faith groweth . . . we shall be magnified . . ." In all of this, Paul's love and appreciation for the Corinthians (in the great majority) shines conspicuously. He had the highest hopes of them. They had faith which Paul believed would grow; and his personal hopes of their magnifying him as their true and lawful leader were strong. Note that Paul used the present tense. His confidence in them was of the present, not something which belonged to the past.

---

[14]J. W. McGarvey, *Second Epistle to the Corinthians* (Cincinnati: Standard Publishing Co., 1916), p. 224.

[15]Floyd V. Filson, *op. cit.*, p. 389.

Verse 16, *So as to preach the gospel even unto the parts beyond you, and not to glory in another's province in regard of things ready to our hand.*

Macknight's paraphrase of this makes the correct application to the false teachers as follows:

> So as to preach the gospel in the regions beyond you, where no person hath yet preached, and not in another man's bounds, to take praise to myself on account of things already prepared, that is, of churches already planted, as the false teacher hath done.[16]

This was Paul's affirmation that even after correcting the disorders that still existed among them, he had no intention whatever of settling down there to exploit them, as the false apostles were doing. His mission was still pointed to all the world.

Verse 17, *But he that glorieth, let him glory in the Lord.*

The false teachers were glorying in many things, but in nothing that God had done through them. They were preening themselves like peacocks, boasting of their credentials, which were doubtless as phony as they were, bragging of their "liberty" to attend idol feasts, and flaunting the sophisticated rhetoric in vogue among the Greeks. There was nothing of the Lord in any of that; and Paul here nailed them down as wicked imposters. Whatever they had done, God had not authorized any of it.

Verse 18, *For not he that commendeth himself is approved, but whom the Lord commendeth.*

Paul's work among the Corinthians had been marked by the authority and blessing of God, they themselves having accepted the gospel through his preaching; and, in the light of those facts, the honor that some of them were willing to give the false prophets was as scandalous as it was unjust and wicked.

---

[16]James Macknight, *Apostolical Epistles and Commentary* (Grand Rapids: Baker Book House, 1969), p. 429.

"The only true ground of approval is to do the work of Christ."[17] Reluctant as Paul was to mention his own personal qualifications, he would nevertheless do so, in order to show by whatever standards chosen, that the false teachers were infinitely below him whom God had commissioned as the apostle to the Gentiles. Even in the boasting which he was reluctant to do, Paul selected his sufferings, hardships, and tribulations, as there could be no charge of human vanity in the recounting of them. He poured out his heart in the succeeding chapter.

---

[17]John Wesley, *One Volume NT Commentary* (Grand Rapids: Baker Book House, 1972), *in loco.*

CHAPTER 11

This chapter, along with the first 10 verses of the next chapter, is printed in the RV in but two paragraphs, the general theme of which is Paul's Apostolic Labors and Sufferings. This is sometimes called Paul's Boasting Chapter. A large number of different subjects are touched upon, and it ranks as one of the most interesting passages in the NT.

Verse 1, *Would that ye could bear with me in a little foolishness.*

Paul was about to speak of his own labors, sufferings and qualifications; and, to him, it was distasteful and somewhat embarrassing to do so; however, the false apostles who had intruded themselves into the Corinthian scene had spoken of the apostle so adversely, and the rather naive Corinthians had shown such vulnerability to their seductions, that Paul destroyed them in the withering attack recorded here, reluctantly meeting them upon their own grounds, and, in a sense, stooping to their level of personal boasting in order to do it.

His enemies were only a minority of the Corinthian church; and even these "are divided into two classes, the leaders and the led; and Paul does not always keep these separate in his mind."[1] Yet in this chapter, "He clearly appealed to those who were led and denounced those who led them."[2] The great majority at Corinth had Paul's confidence. He believed they would bear with him and not misunderstand his motives. Carver said, "Again he is giving voice to his underlying confidence in the church at Corinth, as expressed in 7:4, 14, 16, 8:24, and 9:2."[3] Some would understand this verse as imperative, i.e., a plea that the Corinthians would bear with Paul (as in RV margin); but the preferred meaning is, "Yet my prayer is

---

[1]J. W. McGarvey, *Second Epistle to the Corinthians* (Cincinnati: The Standard Publishing Company, 1916), p. 225.

[2]*Ibid.*

[3]Frank C. Carver, *Beacon Bible Commentary* (Kansas City: Beacon Hill Press, 1969), Vol. 8, p. 601.

not necessary, for you do, in fact, bear with me."[4] Thus the unity of this epistle is evident in the fact that "His confidence in the Corinthians, his 'boldness' on their behalf, shines clearly through."[5]

"A little foolishness . . ." God's word commands that a fool should be answered according to his folly (Prov. 26:5), and this was exactly the thing Paul proposed to do here.

Verses 1, 2, *Would that ye could bear with me in a little foolishness: but indeed ye do bear with me. For I am jealous over you with a godly jealousy: for I espoused you to one husband, that I might present you as a pure virgin to Christ.*

"Godly jealousy . . ." "This means a jealousy like that of God, not a mean, blind or unworthy passion, but a justified concern for the honor and purity of the church at Corinth."[6]

"Espoused you to one husband . . ." "The word 'espoused' is used of the act of a father who gives his daughter in marriage."[7] Broomall noted that "The espousal took place at conversion; the 'presentation' will be consummated at the Second Coming";[8] however, Kelcy was correct in not limiting the "presentation" to the Second Coming. "It includes the thought of himself as presenting them to Christ as a 'pure virgin' all along during his ministry."[9] Romans 12:1f confirms Kelcy's view of this.

"Paul was very far from despising marriage, since he made it a symbol"[10] of the final union of the church with her Lord.

"As a pure virgin to Christ . . ." This whole verse means that Paul was just as jealously concerned for the purity of the

---

[4]R. V. G. Tasker, *The Second Epistle of Paul to the Corinthians* (Grand Rapids: Wm. B. Eerdmans Publishing Co., 1958), p. 144.

[5]Philip E. Hughes, *Paul's Second Epistle to the Corinthians* (Grand Rapids: Wm. B. Eerdmans Publishing Co., 1962), p. 373.

[6]Floyd V. Filson, *Interpreter's Bible* (Nashville: Abingdon Press, 1953), Vol. X, p. 392.

[7]E. H. Plumptre, *Ellicott's Commentary* (Grand Rapids: Zondervan Publishing House, 1959), Vol. VII, p. 401.

[8]Wick Broomall, *Wycliffe Bible Commentary* (Chicago: Moody Press, 1971), p. 682.

[9]Raymond C. Kelcy, *Second Corinthians* (Austin: R. B. Sweet Co., 1967), p. 62.

[10]E. H. Plumptre, *op. cit.*, p. 401.

church as a father would be for the purity of a daughter betrothed to a kingly bridegroom.

Verse 3, *But I fear, lest by any means, as the serpent beguiled Eve in his craftiness, your minds should be corrupted from the simplicity and the purity that is toward Christ.*

For a list of other NT passages bearing upon the great apostasy, see CA, pp. 395, 396, and CM, p. 96.

At the time of Paul's writing, only a few of the Corinthians were under the domination of the false apostles, "But there was a risk that they might distract the church as a whole from its loyalty to Christ."[11] Historically, and as regards the entire church on earth, Paul's fears were more than justified.

The great analogy between Eve as the wife of Adam I and the church as the wife of Adam II is in bold relief here. The seduction of Eve was therefore viewed by Paul as a prophecy of the seduction of the church. Paul dealt with this at length in 2 Thessalonians 2. Just as Satan through subtlety deceived Eve, Paul feared that the false apostles, doing the work of Satan, would deceive the church.

Several things of great importance appear in these lines. (1) The account of the temptation and fall as recorded in Genesis "was regarded by the inspired writers of the NT not as myth, allegory or fiction, but as a true record of what happened."[12] (2) Human egotism has ever been the point of vulnerability of men. As Tasker said:

> From Eve onwards the human heart has been prone to be deceived by those who, appearing to have wisdom, insinuate the most destructive of all lies, i.e., that men are not under an imperative duty to recognize and obey God.[13]

"Craftiness . . ." This is even a stronger word than "subtlety," the corresponding word in Genesis; and it means "an extreme malignity which is capable of anything."[14]

---

[11]R. V. G. Tasker, *op. cit.*, p. 145.
[12]David Lipscomb, *Second Corinthians* (Nashville: The Gospel Advocate Company), p. 136.
[13]R. V. G. Tasker, *op. cit.*, p. 146.
[14]Frank G. Carver, *op. cit.*, p. 603.

"The serpent beguiled Eve . . ." True and historical as the Genesis account is, there are mysteries in it which remain unknown. Macknight spoke of one of these thus:

> Some think that the devil in that history is called a serpent figuratively, because in tempting Eve he used the qualities natural to serpents; and that the punishment inflicted on him, namely, his being confined to our atmosphere, is figuratively expressed by his going on his belly and eating dust. But others think that in the history of the fall the devil is called a serpent because he assumed the appearance of a serpent: and that after the fall a change was actually made in the form and state of that animal as a memorial of the devil's having abused its primitive form.[15]

Verse 4, *For if he that cometh preacheth another Jesus, whom we did not preach, or if ye receive a different spirit, which ye did not receive, or a different gospel, which ye did not accept, ye do well to bear with him.*

The translation of the last clause cannot be correct; for the very thing Paul wanted to correct was their "bearing with" any false apostle. The true meaning must be similar to the following renditions:

> You manage to put up with that well enough (NEB).
> Ye bear with him (the false apostle) nobly.[16]
> You put up with that finely.[17]

"He that cometh . . ." "This either designates the outstanding leader among the false apostles, or is a generic reference to all of this group."[18] Since it is not known that there was any "outstanding leader," it is better understood as "any man that cometh" to proclaim so false a doctrine. All of the true apostles were "sent" of God; but the false apostles were mere "comers" who commissioned themselves and were in no sense messengers from God.

---

[15]James Macknight, *Apostolical Epistles and Commentary* (Grand Rapids: Baker Book House, 1969), p. 433.
[16]J. R. Dummelow, *Commentary on the Holy Bible* (New York: The Macmillan Company, 1937), p. 940.
[17]R. V. G. Tasker, *op. cit.*, p. 148.
[18]Floyd V. Filson, *op. cit.*, p. 393.

"Preacheth another Jesus . . . etc." It is not revealed in the NT exactly what the false teaching was. "Every opinion concerning the character and identity of these false apostles is ventured only in the realm of conjecture."[19] It is enough for us to know that their teachings were unsound, tended to immorality, denied essential truth and were utterly destroyed by Paul's inspired epistles.

As McGarvey said, "These first four verses are an introduction"[20] to the main theme of the chapter; and this verse fits in, according to Dummelow's paraphrase, thus:

> My fear is not without reason, for you are certainly very favorably inclined to those who bring a different gospel; but if you can tolerate them, you can surely tolerate me.[21]

Verse 5, *For I reckon that I am not a whit behind the very chiefest apostles.*

For ages, this has been construed as a reference to the Twelve, especially to Peter, James and John, the inner circle of that sacred group; but the true meaning, as advocated by McGarvey, Kelcy and many others, appears to be that "chiefest apostles" is Paul's designation of the false apostles who were troubling Corinth. The reasons underlying what is now the generally accepted interpretation are these:

(1) The Greek words for "chiefest apostles" occur only twice in the NT; and, "As fresh light is thrown on the language of the NT, it is increasingly probable that Paul coined the word thus rendered."[22] Tasker especially favored this view.[23] Only here and in 12:11 is it found.

(2) The pronouns in verses 13-15 logically refer to "chiefest apostles"; and there they are designated as "false apostles" and servants of Satan.

(3) In speaking of the true apostles, Paul called them "the Twelve" (1 Cor. 15:5); and it is hard to believe that he would

---

[19]Philip E. Hughes, *op. cit.*, p. 358.
[20]J. W. McGarvey, *op. cit.*, p. 226.
[21]J. R. Dummelow, *op. cit.*, p. 940.
[22]Philip E. Hughes, *op. cit.*, p. 379.
[23]R. V. G. Tasker, *op. cit.*, p. 149.

have used the words here of them, words which are quite properly rendered "super-apostles."

(4) The context favors understanding this as a reference to the false apostles; and, as Plumptre said:

> The whole tone of the passage ought to have made it impossible for any commentator to imagine that these words referred to Peter and James and John as the pillars of the church of Jerusalem (Gal. 2:9). Of them Paul spoke, even in his boldest moment, with respect, even where respect is mingled with reproof.[24]

For these reasons, then, we shall construe "chiefest apostles" as a term of derogation applied sarcastically by Paul to the false teachers. However, the obvious truth must also be stated that, even if it did refer to Peter, James and John, it is also true of them, no less than it was true of the false apostles! Which of the Twelve themselves had any such record as is here revealed of the blessed Paul? It must be received as fact, then, that such a comment as the following from Macknight cannot be denied; for the basis of it, i.e., that Paul was not a whit behind Peter, James and John, etc., is solid truth, no matter how these words are understood. He said: "Let the Papists reconcile this account which Paul gives of himself as an apostle, with their pretended supremacy of Peter over all the apostles."[25]

Verse 6, *But though I be rude in speech, yet am I not in knowledge; nay, in every way have we made this manifest unto you in all things.*

"Rude in speech . . ." In no single area of Christian literature is there a more widespread and generally accepted error than the notion that the apostle Paul was deficient as a public speaker. Filson spoke of Paul's lack as a speaker, saying, "He admits it," and citing this verse along with 10:10, 1 Corinthians 1:17 and 2:4.[26] First, we shall glance at these verses which are supposed to be Paul's admission that he was a poor speaker.

---

[24]E. H. Plumptre, *op. cit.* p. 401.
[25]James Macknight, *op. cit.*, p. 434.
[26]Floyd V. Filson, *op. cit.*, p. 394.

The verse here: "Rude in speech" does not mean lacking agility as a speaker. "One definition of 'rude' is 'forceful or abrupt'; and our translators could have more worthily supplied such terms, if substitute they must; but there is no end to their tampering with the text."[27] Wallace was referring to the perversion of this verse in the RSV, which has "unskilled in speaking," which is of course a gross falsehood. See treatise below on Paul a Skilled Speaker. The principal point, however, is that Paul here made a sarcastic reference to the slander of the false apostles; and the true meaning is, "They say I am rude in speech; but it has to be admitted that my speech makes sense, whereas theirs does not!" There is no thought whatever of Paul's making a confession here that, after all, he is not a very good speaker.

"His speech is contemptible . . ." Paul did not say this of himself. The text says, "*They say* . . . his speech is contemptible" (10:10); and just why should such an allegation from servants of Satan be allowed as gospel truth? Commentators who take this as a fact are poor friends of Paul; with friends like them, he does not need any enemies!

"Christ sent me . . . to preach the gospel, not in wisdom of words . . ." (1 Cor. 1:17). This has no reference whatever to Paul's ability as a speaker, but reveals his rejection of the stylish but worthless oratorical style of the Greeks. See treatise below on Greek Oratory.

"I came unto you . . . not with excellence of speech or of wisdom . . . not in persuasive words of wisdom . . . not in the wisdom of men . . ." (1 Cor. 2:1-5). All that is said in the above paragraph applies equally here. There is not a hint in either place of Paul's ability. He was an eloquent and powerful speaker. All of these expressions he was applying to the Greek oratory which he rejected as worthless, not because he *could not have used it*, but because he knew a better way.

Greek Oratory

---

[27]Foy E. Wallace, Jr., *A Review of the New Versions* (Fort Worth: Foy E. Wallace, Jr., Publications, 1973), p. 440.

Volumes could be written about the oratorical conceit of the Greeks. Their speakers assumed an emphatic distance, constructed their speeches with all kinds of decorative phraseology, gloried in balanced phrases and clauses, sought stunning effects by the use of alliteration, used words which sounded good, no matter what their meaning, modulated their voices in undulating cycles of dynamic contrast, adopted an "oratorical tone" much like the "holy voice" affected by some preachers, skillfully employed a hundred different gestures, each having its hidden significance and known only to the profession, timed their gesticulations so that the ictus always occurred exactly with the intonation of the proper syllable, strutted like peacocks before their audiences, exposing their good Grecian profiles in moments of dramatic pause (Paul was a Jew and had no such profile), arranged their speeches in classical outlines, cut, altered or perverted all material to suit the outline, paused at predetermined intervals to receive the applause of their hearers, and produced by such devices what they called an oration! This ornate, artificial and worthless kind of speaking resulted at last in the destruction of Greece; but in Paul's day it was still very stylish and popular among the self-imagined intelligentsia of a place like Corinth. The various references in these epistles to "wisdom of words," "wisdom of men," "excellency of speech," etc., are precise and exact designations of the bombastic, worthless oratory of the Greeks, described above. That is what *they* meant by such terms; and Paul used the terms in exactly the same sense. Now, as regards Paul's ability as a speaker, see article below.

Paul a Skilled Speaker

It may well be doubted if a more effective speaker ever lived. The great apostle to the Gentiles who preached before governors and kings delivered messages which, even in the abbreviated form of their preservation, have fired the imagination of men in all ages. Among his achievements are the following:

He interrupted and calmed a vicious and unprincipled mob in the Jerusalem temple, a mob which stood transfixed, hypnotized and breathless for the great oration recorded in Acts 22. It is impossible to suppose that any weak speaker could have done a thing like that.

While speaking in the streets of Athens, the center of Greek culture, Paul was invited by responsible members of the Areopagus to speak before the highest tribunal in the Greek world. Would they have invited an "unskilled" speaker? A thousand times, NO! Invitations before that tribunal were not casually passed out to mere street-preachers. The oration that he delivered there resulted in the baptism of one of the mighty judges and an undetermined number of other converts; and the content of it has challenged the thinking of nineteen centuries!

Paul's eloquence before Festus was of such persuasive and glowing quality, that when the governor entertained royalty (Agrippa II and Bernice), he presented the apostle for the entertainment of his royal guests! Does that sound like he was a timid, embarrassed, weak and incompetent speaker? Commentators who affirm such nonsense should be ashamed. Paul's address on that occasion was so impressive, that even when Festus tried to break up the meeting, the king and his royal consort refused to leave till Paul had finished! Weak preaching? Absolutely NO!

Paul converted rulers of synagogues, the governor at Paphos, the chamberlain of the City of Corinth and enjoyed the friendship of the politarchs of Ephesus. He was bilingual, possibly trilingual, and one of the best educated men of his generation. As a high sheriff of the Sanhedrin, he enjoyed a post of honor and trust which was its own inherent testimony to the man's unusual and outstanding ability, which would of necessity have included mastery of the art of speaking. No man ever communicated his ideas to humanity any better than Paul did.

Another incident confirming the views expressed here happened at Lystra, where the pagan citizens of that Lycaonian city hailed the apostle as "Hermes" (Acts 14:12). And who, pray tell, was Hermes? He was the chief speaker for the gods of Grecian civilization! Weak speaker? The Lycaonians thought he was the chief speaker of the gods!

"Though I speak with the tongues of men and of angels . . ." (1 Cor. 13:1). This probably is as good an estimate of Paul's speaking ability as any that was ever written; and the lines could reflect unconsciously his own subjective awareness of his superlative ability as a mover of mankind with the spoken word.

It is our humble prayer that students of the sacred scriptures will recover themselves from the stupid error of thinking that Paul was an "unskilled" speaker. It is quite evident that much of the gratuitous downgrading of Paul as a gifted speaker derives from the thought that it is stylish, in a literary sense, to do so.

Verse 7, *Or did I commit a sin in abasing myself that ye might be exalted, because I preached to you the gospel of God for naught?*

The bitter sarcasm of this is evident. "Professional Greek rhetoricians (alluded to in v. 6) would be suspect if they failed to demand fees."[28] Paul's sarcastic question is, "Have you been so completely taken in by these false apostles that you could believe I am a sinner because I did not demand your money when I preached to you the gospel?" As Lipscomb said, "This is bitter irony . . . he was deeply hurt by the ungenerous construction of his generosity."[29]

It really is not certain that all of the alleged slanders against Paul which he answered in these lines were really spoken against him, although most commentators seem to assume this. However, Clines pointed out that,

> It can be argued that these extremely perverse criticisms were not actually made, but are ironically imagined by Paul in order to contrast his own and the false apostles' attitude to financial support.[30]

Verse 8, *I robbed other churches, taking wages of them that I might minister unto you.*

During Paul's eighteen months ministry at Corinth when the Corinthians had been converted, he had received no money from them. He had decided that, in Corinth, the gospel would in some manner be compromised by his asking and receiving support of his many converts.

---

[28]Norman Hillyer, *The New Bible Commentary, Revised* (Grand Rapids: Wm. B. Eerdmans Publishing Co., 1970), p. 1085.

[29]David Lipscomb, *op. cit.*, p. 141.

[30]David J. A. Clines, *A New Testament Commentary* (Grand Rapids: Zondervan Publishing House, 1969), p. 436.

It was in Corinth that Paul had labored as a tent maker, working with Aquila, in order to be free to preach without charge. It was from Corinth that he had written the letters to the Thessalonians, among whom also he had preached without imposing any financial burden upon them (I Thess. 2:9). "It was Paul's custom when preaching in a place to accept no gifts from the local people, despite the fact that it imposed a severe hardship upon himself."[31]

"I robbed other churches . . ." This is a reference to the churches of Macedonia (mentioned a moment later); and thus, "It is once again that the 'earnestness of others' (8:8) is set before the Corinthians; and in this we may discern another internal strand uniting these last four chapters to those which precede them."[32]

Verse 9, *And when I was present with you and was in want, I was not a burden on any man; for the brethren, when they came from Macedonia, supplied the measure of my want; and in everything I kept myself from being burdensome unto you, and so will I keep myself.*

See comment under preceding verse.

"When they came from Macedonia . . ." These were in all probability Silas and Timothy. Based upon the record in Acts 15:40 and 16:1ff, and upon inferences from 1 Thessalonians 3:1, those were the two men referred to here, but not by name, as the Corinthians already knew who had come from Macedonia. Even this bounty only supplemented Paul's earnings as a tent maker.

"I was not a burden on any man . . ." The word here translated "burden" is a medical term derived from the name of a certain kind of fish listed by Aristotle, a creature which benumbed people who came in contact with it. Its being in the vocabulary of physicians has led to the supposition that "Paul may have derived it from Luke."[33]

Verse 10, *As the truth of Christ is in me, no man shall stop me of this glorying in the regions of Achaia.*

---

[31]Philip E. Hughes, *op. cit.*, p. 385.
[32]*Ibid.*, p. 386.
[33]E. H. Plumptre, *op. cit.*, p. 402.

Paul did not here rule out the acceptance of funds from Christians in other places, but vehemently declared that nothing would induce him to get on the payroll of the Corinthians. All of Paul's considerations in such a decision may not be clear to us; but it is safe to believe that there were very good reasons for this; and, especially at this time, "Paul knew the spot he had them (the false apostles) in, and he meant to keep them there."[34] Even the most naive persons in Corinth could not have failed to be impressed by the fact of Paul's obvious sincerity, a fact demonstrated and made certain by his attitude toward money.

Verse 11, *Wherefore? because I love you not? God knoweth.*

The false apostles hoped to induce Paul to accept money from the Corinthians; but this Paul adamantly refused to do. However, this was not a sign of lack of love for them, but just the opposite. He would do nothing that would give the false apostles an excuse for claiming to be on the same level with Paul. This was due to Paul's loving determination to destroy the hold of those parasites upon his beloved Corinthian converts. The false apostles were already feeling the pinch of the situation in which they found themselves. One of the things they gloried in was that of taking money from the Corinthians; and so, "They desire an occasion for inducing Paul to accept payment as they do, so that the disadvantage forced upon them by the contrast might be removed."[35] This will be made clear in the next verse.

Verse 12, *But what I do, that I will do, that I may cut off occasion from them that desire an occasion; that wherein they glory, they may be found even as we.*

This is a somewhat tricky and involved sentence; but the meaning is apparently that suggested by Tasker:

> Those superlative apostles receive pay for their work, and would like for this difference between them and Paul to be eliminated by Paul's behaving as they do, so that they may be on an equality with him.[36]

---

[34]Frank G. Carver, *op. cit.*, op. 608.
[35]Philip E. Hughes, *op. cit.*, p. 392.
[36]R. V. G. Tasker, *op. cit.*, p. 153.

"But what I do, that will I do . . ." Paul meant by this, "I will go right on doing as I have done all along." Why should he have taken the heat off of them?

Verse 13, *For such men are false apostles, deceitful workers, fashioning themselves into apostles of Christ.*

These men at Corinth were in no sense genuine, being phony selfseekers playing the religious game for money. Lies and deception were their stock in trade; they were evil hypocrites pretending to be apostles of Christ. It is a marvel that they had managed to put together a following at Corinth; but such is the mystery of iniquity that they were fully able to do so; and the marvel of our own times is that wicked and lying deceivers are still doing the same thing. Hughes described such a marvel thus:

> It is no less so in our own day when an individual has only to make the most preposterous claims for himself in order to gain for himself an enthusiastic and undiscerning following. In every age, the church is under the necessity of holding fast to the doctrine of those who are Christ's true apostles. That doctrine, in a word, is that which we possess in the writings of the New Testament.[37]

Verse 14, *And no marvel; for even Satan fashioneth himself into an angel of light.*

The explanation reveals that such developments as that of false teachers stealing the church away from the Lord are no "marvel" at all, in one sense, but merely what should have been expected in view of the nature and tactics of the evil one. The tactics of such deceivers follow closely the pattern of Satan in Eden. (1) As Satan flatly denied God's word, evil teachers do the same today, stridently declaring their soul-destroying doctrine of salvation "by faith alone," contradicting the word of God which says men "are not justified by faith alone" (James 2:24). (2) As Satan promised Eve that she and Adam would "be as gods," the sophisticated false teachers of this generation are doing everything in their power to deify humanity. (3) The same triple allurements of fleshly delight, pride of life, and lust of the eye which overthrew Eve are today

---

[37]Philip E. Hughes, *op. cit.*, p. 393.

carrying the thoughtless into every kind of sin. (4) As Satan pretended to be wise, so do the false teachers of all generations masquerade as wise ones, people in the "know" who make light of God's commands and rush into rebellion against the Creator. These are the people who make fun of Christian ordinances, deny the claims of God's church upon men's loyalty, and represent Almighty God as a doting, loving Father who will never punish anybody, and who will never notice the crimes of blood, lust and savagery raging under his very nose. And as for worshiping God, "Let that be every man doing exactly what he pleases, when he pleases, if he pleases; and God will at last save everybody." See under v. 15, below.

Verse 15, *It is no great thing therefore if his ministers also fashion themselves as ministers of righteousness; whose end shall be according to their works.*

In connection with this and the preceding verse, it has been suggested by some that "Paul may be alluding to a Jewish legend that Satan appeared to Eve in the form of an angel and sang hymns like the angels";[38] but such a tale could hardly be anything except human imagination. There does not seem to be in view here any actual event of Satan's transforming himself into an angel of light; but, in all probability, this is a metaphorical statement of the exceedingly great power of Satan to deceive men. He even appeared before the Lord during our Master's temptation, advocating a sinful act and backing up the temptation with a misquotation from the Holy Bible (Matt. 4:4ff).

"Ministers of righteousness . . ." This the false teachers do literally; and, from this basic truth, there derives the necessity for every soul who would be true to God to "search the scriptures daily, whether these things are so" (Acts 17:11). Not one teaching of the NT is free from the corrupting devices of men; there are none of its doctrines that have not been denied; and there is no commandment in it which is not rejected out of hand, if not by one false teacher, then by another. To borrow a line from Jesus (out of context), "What is written . . . how readest thou?" (Luke 10:26).

---

[38]David J. A. Clines, *op. cit.*, p. 437.

Verse 16, *I say again, Let no man think me foolish; but if ye do, yet as foolish receive me, that I also may glory a little.*

Paul here stated that his boastings were in no sense foolish. They were the only way to open the eyes of those being deceived by the false boasters. Nevertheless, Paul said, "Even if you think I am foolish, let me boast a little in order for you to see how silly, by comparison, are the claims of those "superlative apostles" who are leading some of you around by the nose!" As Paul had already explained, "Any boasting he did was not for his own sake but theirs, and for the sake of the purity of the gospel in their midst."[39]

Verse 17, *That which I speak, I speak not after the Lord, but as in foolishness, in this confidence of glorying.*

"Not after the Lord . . ." It is astounding that commentators will render this as did Dummelow, "I am not speaking now under the inspiration of Christ."[40] The New International Version renders it, "I am not speaking now as the Lord would";[41] but the RSV perverted it completely, giving this: "What I am saying, I say not with the Lord's authority, but as a fool!" This despite Paul's having just said, "Let no man think me foolish!" (v. 16). Paul was familiar with both "authority" and "inspiration"; and, if he had meant anything like the words attributed to him in RSV, he would have used those words. The fact that he did not use them shows that something else was meant.

It means that his words *if spoken in conceited boasting* would not be "after the Lord"; but Paul was not speaking in that manner at all, but *as in* foolishness. In that latter usage of such boasting, there can be no question. Of course they were spoken. "after the Lord," i.e., according to the will of the Lord.

"Not after the Lord . . ." was interpreted thus by Kelcy:

> It was not the Lord's usual method; but Paul speaking by inspiration, certainly had the Lord's approval. The

---

[39]Philip E. Hughes, *op. cit.*, p. 396.
[40]J. R. Dummelow, *op. cit.*, p. 941.
[41]*New International Version* (Grand Rapids: Zondervan Publishing House, 1973), *in loco.*

> Lord granted this use of boasting because it was the best weapon to use in the situation Paul faced.[42]

The view advocated by Kelcy goes all the way back to Chrysostom and has been known for ages as the correct view of what is said here. Many of the so-called translations have committed grievous sin in the perversion of Paul's words here. It should be noted that Paul did not say that he was speaking "in foolishness" but "as in foolishness." In that distinction lies the understanding of verse 17.

Two things are in view here: (1) boasting for reasons of personal pride, and (2) boasting for the purpose of saving a church, when no better method was available. The first of these is indeed "not after the Lord"; but the second, in the circumstances, most assuredly was. Chrysostoni phrased it like this: "By itself (boasting) is indeed not of the Lord, but by Paul's intention it becomes so."[43]

This is not any more complicated than a score of other difficult passages in Paul's writings.

Verse 18, *Seeing that many glory in the flesh, I will glory also.*

Having laid the groundwork for it, being careful to reveal his natural loathing at being forced, in a sense, to resort to such a thing, and also his pure intention of redeeming his beloved converts from the control of their enemies, Paul announced in this verse his purpose of proving the utter worthlessness of the false apostles' vaunted credentials, not one of whom could even approach the matchless authentication manifested in a true apostle like Paul. When the hay and stubble of their false claims were viewed alongside the pure gold of God's work in the life of Paul, only a fool could have failed to see the difference.

Verse 19, *For ye bear with the foolish gladly, being wise yourselves.*

This is sarcastic irony at its withering best. The sting in it comes from the obvious meaning, "Such smart people are

---

[42]Raymond C. Kelcy, *op. cit.*, p. 66.
[43]Philip E. Hughes, *op. cit.*, p. 397.

bigger fools than the fools they indulge!"[44]

Verse 20, *For ye bear with a man, if he bringeth you into bondage, if he devoureth you, if he taketh you captive, if he exalteth himself, if he smiteth you on the face.*

Titus had no doubt given Paul a first-hand account of such scandalous conduct on the part of the false teachers; and the majority of the Corinthians must have blushed to hear this factual record of their cowardice and servility in submitting to it.

The failure of some of the Corinthians had been in their putting up with the arrogance and aggressiveness of the false apostles and in submitting to it as if they were actually true apostles, incredibly failing to notice how antiChristian and contrary to the Holy Spirit their outrageous behavior surely was. Note what these false apostles were doing:

Bringing into bondage. This could have meant that they were being enslaved to keep the ceremonial laws of the Jews (see Gal. 2:4; 5:1).

Devouring them. This, like most of what is said here, has overtones of the Pharisaical methods in Jerusalem. Jesus, for example, said that they "devoured widows' houses" (Matt. 23:14). They took as much money and substance as they could lay hold of.

Taking them captive. This suggests 2 Timothy 2:26, where Paul spoke of Satan's taking people "captive" to do his will. The false apostles were leading the people into gross sin.

Exalting themselves. "Light is thrown on Paul's meaning here by what he had already said about 'every high thing that is exalted against the knowledge of God' (10:5)."[45] Those evil men were placing their own words above the word of God.

Smiting in the face. Whether this was literal or not has been disputed; but representatives of that class who had smitten the Son of God himself in the face would have been perfectly in character by perpetrating such actions against the Lord's

---

[44]R. C. H. Lenski, *The Interpretation of St. Paul's First and Second Epistles to the Corinthians* (Columbus, Ohio: Wartburg Press, 1937), p. 1261.
[45]Philip E. Hughes, *op. cit.*, p. 400.

followers. The view here is that there is no reason to suppose it was anything but physical.

Verse 21, *I speak by way of disparagement, as though we had been weak. Yet whereinsoever any is bold (I speak in foolishness), I am bold also.*

Hughes' paraphrase of the first sentence here is: "I confess to my shame, that as compared to those super-apostles, I have been weak!"[46] If arrogance, greed, deceit, tyranny, oppression and the robbery of Christians of their wealth are marks of true Christian oversight, Paul was willing to admit that in those categories he had indeed fallen somewhat behind the super-apostles who were plundering the church of God at Corinth. This is sarcastic irony.

Verse 22, *Are they Hebrews? so am I. Are they Israelites? so am I. Are they the seed of Abraham? so am I.*

This is the best hint of all regarding the identity of the false apostles. They evidently belonged to the fierce Judaizers who almost succeeded in stealing the church of God itself. Although speaking here of fleshly descent from Abraham, Paul had a much higher view of who were really Israelites and the true seed of Abraham. The Christians are the true Israelites, as well as the genuine seed of Abraham. Paul developed this extensively in Romans, and also in Galatians 3:29.

Verse 23, *Are they ministers of Christ? (I speak as one beside himself) I more; in labors more abundantly, in prisons more abundantly, in stripes above measure, in deaths oft.*

"Ministers of Christ . . ." This is not, as suggested by some, a reference to a sinful "Christ party" at Corinth (1 Cor. 1:12); for, if it had been, Paul would not have said, "I more."

"As one beside himself . . ." The RSV descends to the level of a ridiculous paraphrase in rendering this "I am talking like a madman." As Wallace said, "That certainly is not a translation of anything Paul said." [47] This has the same meaning of "as in foolishness" in verse 17.

---

[46]*Ibid.*
[47]Foy E. Wallace, Jr., *op. cit.*, p. 440.

"Labors . . . prisons . . . stripes . . . deaths . . ." Although somewhat of a loose summary of what he was about to relate, it is obviously extemporaneous. The amazing sufferings and tribulations suffered by Paul were so numerous that they tumbled over each other in his mind as he dictated these words. Aside from the Christ himself, whoever suffered as did Paul for the propagation of Christianity?

"All that follows from here to verse 28, inclusive, is proof of Paul's right to call himself a minister of Christ.[48] All of the things mentioned here at the outset would be elaborated further on.

Verse 24, *Of the Jews five times received I forty stripes save one.*

If those false apostles, as appears likely, were part of the old hierarchal crowd in Jerusalem, it must have required divine power for Paul to speak of them as mildly as he does. A Jewish beating with stripes was a cruel, brutal and inhuman punishment. It was founded on Deuteronomy 25:3 which fixed forty stripes as the number inflicted. The barbarous instrument was a three-ply scourge of knotted leather thongs, with the knots so arranged as to give the maximum pain and injury to the victim. The thirty-nine blows were delivered thirteen on the chest, thirteen on the right shoulder, and thirteen on the left shoulder. Neither the NT nor any other history mentions any of these five cruelties inflicted upon Paul, showing how little is actually known of all that he suffered for the cause of Christ.

Verse 25, *Thrice was I beaten with rods, once was I stoned, thrice I suffered shipwreck, a night and a day have I been in the deep.*

"Beaten with rods . . ." In Acts is the record of Paul's being thus beaten at Philippi; but nothing is known of the other two punishments (Acts 16:22, 23).

"Once was I stoned . . ." Acts 14:19 describes this event, in which Paul was apparently thought to be dead by his enemies. It occurred at Lystra.

---

[48]E. H. Plumptre, *op. cit.*, p. 405.

"Thrice I suffered shipwreck . . ." As this was written before the shipwreck on Malta, it has to refer to events nowhere else recorded. Paul made no less than nine voyages before these lines were written and another nine afterward.[49] Travel by ship in those times was hazardous indeed.

"A night and a day . . . in the deep . . ." "After one of the shipwrecks, Paul spent a night and a day clinging to wreckage while adrift at sea."[50] At least four times, the blessed apostle heard the dreadful cry, "Abandon ship"; and anyone who ever heard it once knows the soul-chilling terror of such an experience. Paul's sufferings are a glorious odyssey surpassing that of Homer, or any other; and, when it is remembered that this brief record is practically all that men know of it, the surpassing modesty and humility of the matchless Paul are almost unbelievable.

Verse 26, *In journeyings often, in peril of rivers, in perils of robbers, in perils from my countrymen, in perils from the Gentiles, in perils in the city, in perils in the wilderness, in perils in the sea, in perils among false brethren.*

A thousand pages could not tell the whole story if God had given it to us; but the vast majority of the events which stormed Paul's memory in this recital are forever shrouded in the modesty of Paul and in the mists of nineteen centuries. Yet these mountain peaks which here are momentarily lifted for a fleeting glance of them are of the highest interest. Nevertheless, we shall leave them just as they are. The scattered bits of information by which we might piece out a little more of the odyssey here and there fade into the background of this brief, stark catalogue of apostolical sufferings and tribulations. How dearly were purchased the glorious rights of all subsequent generations in the gospel of Christ by such advocates as Paul the apostle!

Verse 27, *In labor and travail, in watchings often, in hunger and thirst, in fastings often, in cold and nakedness.*

Paul's hardships were genuine and included physical hunger, cold, nakedness, thirst, unending toil and a host of other hardships which these things suggest but do not elaborate.

---

[49]Philip E. Hughes, *op. cit.*, p. 411.
[50]Floyd V. Filson, *op. cit.*, p. 401.

"Watchings . . ." His day and a night in the ocean following a shipwreck was one of these; but what were the others? Did he think of that dark night before the wreck on Malta when his watching saved the ship from being abandoned by its crew? What is suggested by this list is just as interesting as what is related.

"In fastings . . ." Were these devotional, or were they of those times of hunger and thirst mentioned in the same breath? Some say one thing, some another; but we do not know. Paul's boasting was taking a turn that no one but himself could have anticipated; and the fact that shines in all of this is that Paul was boasting of his sufferings, his hardships, his persecutions for the name of Christ, his providential survivals of many deaths, and his merciless tortures from rods and stripes. It should be evident to all that no man ever boasted like this, except one under the direct inspiration of God.

Verse 28, *Besides those things that are without, there is that which presseth upon me daily, anxiety for all the churches.*

"Those things that are without . . ." NEB renders this, "These external things just enumerated"; but RSV has "Apart from other things," indicating that even this astounding list is but the tip of the iceberg. Nevertheless, it was not any of those things that happened to Paul, but his deep and faithful concern for his Christian converts that he reserved as the climax of his credentials as a true apostle. The loving concern and care for all the churches God had blessed him to establish; that was the heart of Paul. Everything else was peripheral. One wonders if the Corinthians did not weep when they read this. Could any human being be so unresponsive to pure and holy love as not to be touched by what was written here? The only answer we have is history. The false apostles disappeared, their names unknown, their doctrines not identified, even their number merely a conjecture; but the church of Corinth continued through centuries; and these priceless letters are living treasures nineteen centuries afterward! Oh Lord, blessed be thy holy name!

Verse 29, *Who is weak, and I am not weak? who is caused to stumble, and I burn not?*

This elaborates Paul's perfect identification of himself with those whom he converted.

"Burn . . ." as used here is probably "to burn with indignation."[51]

Verse 30, *If I must needs glory, I will glory of the things which concern my weakness.*

This verse should be understood retrospectively as well as prospectively. It flies like a banner over all that Paul mentioned in this entire section through 12:10. The great spiritual power of Paul was inherent in the strength through weakness which marked his whole life. As Hillyer wisely observed: "In this verse, Paul looks back to the experiences he has just catalogued. A 'boastful' person, in the ordinary sense, would never have mentioned such things."[52]

Circumstances had required Paul to boast; but he turned the occasion into one that stressed his own mortal weakness and dependence upon God. No man without the direction of God's Spirit would have boasted in any such manner.

Verse 31, *The God and Father of our Lord Jesus, he who is blessed for evermore knows that I lie not.*

Recalling what he had just written, the list seemed almost unbelievable, even to Paul; and the sheer size and significance of it led him to affirm in these most solemn words the absolute truth of every syllable of it. This verse, like the one before it, "must be understood as applicable to all that Paul had said or was about to say."[53]

Verses 32, 33, *In Damascus the governor under Aretas the king guarded the city of the Damascenes in order to take me: and through a window was I let down in a basket by the wall, and escaped his hands.*

Some scholars have objected to what they call the intrusion of this compact little narrative into Paul's letter at this point, insinuating that it is misplaced, or an interpolation, and that it apparently does not belong here. Such opinions are due to a lack of discerning Paul's evident purpose in the exceedingly significant placement of these verses exactly where they are found.

---

[51]*Ibid.*, p. 403.
[52]Norman Hillyer, *op. cit.*, p. 1076.
[53]J. W. McGarvey, *op. cit.*, p. 234.

Before relating the glorious experience of being caught up into the third heaven, Paul would again emphasize his humility, doing so by placing the narrative of his undignified and inglorious flight from Damascus in the dead of night squarely alongside the account of his rapture into heaven, making the incident here a foil of the glorious experience next related. The same purpose is evident in the account of the thorn in the flesh, which account hems in the rapture narrative at the end of it. Hughes commented on this as follows:

> Paul's rapture into the third heaven is hemmed in, as it were, on one side by the escape from Damascus, and on the other by the humiliating record of the "thorn in the flesh" (12:7ff) . . . Paul was determined to keep himself in true perspective, that of a weak, unworthy mortal who owes everything to the grace of Almighty God.[54]

In this connection, it should be remembered that the chapter division here is awkward, tending to obscure the logical connection in the three episodes, the glorious one in the center, and the two inglorious ones on either side of it.

"In Damascus . . ." The account of what occurred here harmonizes perfectly with Luke's record of the same event (Acts 9:23-25) "There is no discrepancy between Luke's assertion that the Jews watched the gates and Paul's that the ethnarch did so."[55] The word here rendered "governor" is actually "ethnarch" (RV margin). The ethnarch was appointed by the central authority to look after the interests of some particular race, in this case, the Jews. He was most certainly a Jew himself, as were those whom he appointed to guard the city.

"Under Aretas the king . . ." It is this little phrase that gives one of the few solid clues to the chronology of Acts and the Pauline letters. Aretas reigned over Nabatea from 9 B.C. to 40 A.D.[56] The only time during his long reign, however, when he had authority over Damascus was during the reign of

---

[54]Philip E. Hughes, *op. cit.*, p. 422.
[55]*Ibid.*
[56]*The New Bible Dictionary* (Grand Rapids: Wm. B. Eerdmans Publishing Company, 1962), p. 80.

Caligula (37-41 A.D.).[57] Both Augustus and Tiberius who preceded Caligula, and Nero and his successors after him were the recognized rulers in Damascus; but the absence of any coins with Caligula's image in the collection of many coins from Damascus bearing images of the other Roman emperors confirms the fact mentioned here by Paul, not that anything Paul said *needed* confirmation, but as another demonstration of his total accuracy. Paul's escape from Damascus sometime during Caligula's short reign together with the fact of the escape's being three years after his conversion fixes the date of the apostle's baptism between the years 35-40 AD.

"Through a window . . ." The comment of Tasker is appreciated. He said: "RSV translates this, 'through a window in the wall'; and though the window was *in the wall*, this is not an accurate translation of the original."[58] One might ask what is wrong with giving the true meaning in different words? What is wrong? The translator's integrity is at stake. If the translator is not going to give what the original *says*, he is not translating at all, but paraphrasing; and heaven knows that in this generation some place is needed where *what God said* may be read, and not merely what some men think he meant.

"Was I let down . . . and escaped . . ." It is impossible to read the words "was I let down" apart from the sequel "he was caught up" (2:4). It is the abasement of his undignified escape that Paul deliberately placed as a foil of his being caught up into heaven.

There also seems to be in Paul's narrative of this event a feeling on his part that it was symbolical, typical and prophetic of all the hardships and sufferings that he was destined to undergo as a Christian, and at the same time a pledge of God's perfect providence and blessing which would inevitably protect and preserve him for the fulfillment of the task to which God had called him. The victory of Christ over the proud persecutor also shines in this event; because nothing could have shown any more dramatically the contrast between Saul of Tarsus and Paul the apostle, than the two situations of his approach to

---

[57]*The Encyclopaedia Britannica* (Chicago: William Benton, Publisher, 1961), p. 599.
[58]R. V. G. Tasker, *op. cit.*, p. 169.

Damascus and his exit from it. He approached breathing out threatenings and slaughter, but he fled as a hunted animal in the dead of night. There at Damascus he sheathed forever the sword of the persecutor and unsheathed the eternal sword of the Spirit, the gospel of Christ. Strangely enough, even in the ignomy of this humiliating withdrawal from Damascus, Paul joined the company of the immortal heroes of Israel. Over the wall of Jericho, Rahab delivered the faithful spies; and David, the shepherd king himself, was delivered from death through a window (Josh. 2:15; 1 Sam. 19:12).

CHAPTER 12

Subjects treated by Paul in this chapter are: the revelations he received from the Lord (1-6), the counteracting thorn in the flesh (7-10), another regret at the necessity of glorying (11-12), his independence (13-15), a reply to false charges (16-18), and certain cautions and warnings (19-21).

Verse 1, *I must needs glory, though it is not expedient, but I will come to visions and revelations of the Lord.*

"Though it is not expedient . . ." is rendered, "there is nothing to be gained by it"; but, as Filson said:

> Paul does not mean literally that there is nothing to be gained by it, for he hopes by the boasting, forced upon him, to make the Corinthians see that they have been wronging him and following the false leaders at Corinth . . . he feels driven by a necessity which he cannot evade.[1]

Kelcy has a similar view, "The boasting is not expedient as far as making a real contribution to the spiritual state of the Corinthians is concerned."[2]

"Visions and revelations . . ." As John Wesley put it, "Visions are seen; revelations are heard."[3] The plural here, as regards both visions and revelations, supports the possibility that the "third heaven" and "Paradise" could have been the subjects of different visions.

"Of the Lord . . ." identifies the Lord as the source of the visions and revelations, not as the object of them. "The genitive *of the Lord* is subjective, not objective."[4]

Verse 2, *I know a man in Christ, fourteen years ago (whether in the body, I know not; or whether out of the body, I know not; God knoweth), such a one caught up, even to the third heaven.*

---

[1]Floyd V. Filson, *Interpreter's Bible* (Nashville: Abingdon Press, 1953), Vol. X, p. 405

[2]Raymond C. Kelcy, *Second Corinthians* (Austin: R. B. Sweet Co., 1967), p. 70.

[3]John Wesley, *One Volume NT Commentary* (Grand Rapids: Baker Book House, 1972), *in loco.*

[4]R. V. G. Tasker, *The Second Epistle of Paul to the Corinthians* (Grand Rapids: Wm. B. Eerdmans Publishing Co., 1958), p. 169.

"A man in Christ . . ." The center and circumference of Pauline theology are summed up in the phrase "in Christ." The thought behind the use of the third person here is that it was not as himself that these experiences came to him, but that "as Christ" and "in Christ" he was granted those things. On this account, his glorying is "glorying in the Lord," not in himself.

"Whether in the body . . . out of the body . . ." Paul simply did not know what state he was in; and modesty should restrain all commentators from elaborating on what it was.

"Such a one caught up to the third heaven . . ." Since the apostle Paul here quite obviously resorted to the third person when narrating these events, the critics who deny the authorship of the book of Jonah on the ground that it was written in the third person are refuted. The words "caught up" are the same that Luke used of Philip (Acts 8:39) and that Paul used of the resurrection (1 Thess. 4:17).

"Fourteen years ago . . ." "This was in 41-42 A.D., some years after his escape from Damascus."[5] There is nothing known of any vision Paul had at that time, except what is related here; although he had numerous visions. It is futile to attempt to identify this with any of the known visions recorded elsewhere.

"The third heaven . . ." This is mentioned only here in the NT; and there is no certainty about what is meant. Lipscomb outlined the three heavens as understood by the Jews thus:

> (1) The air or atmosphere where the clouds gather (Gen. 2:1, 19), (2) the firmament containing the sun, moon and stars (Deut. 18:3; Matt. 24:29), and (3) God's dwelling place (Matt. 5:12 16 45 48).[6]

There are no geographical connotations whatever in these words, for the third heaven where God dwells is not a thing of space and physical location at all. It is a state of being beyond, above and higher even than the second heaven. Robinson's

---

[5]Norman Hillyer, *The New Bible Commentary, Revised* (Grand Rapids: Wm. B. Eerdmans Publishing Co., 1970), p. 1086.

[6]David Lipscomb, *Second Corinthians* (Nashville: The Gospel Advocate Co.), p. 157.

remarkable blindness to this fact enabled him to write: "Now it seems there is no room for God, not merely in the inn, but in the entire universe; for there are no vacant places left."[7] The eternal Spirit is ubiquitous; and as Paul said, "in him we live, and move and have our being" (Acts 17:26). Finite man cannot understand infinity. The great value of this astounding revelation of Paul the apostle does not lie in what is explained (as a matter of fact, he did not *explain* anything); but its value lies in the revelation that no explanation of such things is possible.

There has never been anything written that carries any greater internal evidence of being the truth, than what Paul wrote here. The visions and revelations referred to occurred more than fourteen years previously; and it may be assumed that Paul would never have mentioned them at all, except for their connection with the "thorn in the flesh." Furthermore, when he finally recorded them, he did so with the most tantalizing brevity, requiring only ten words in Greek to describe both the visions of the third heaven and of Paradise. Plainly, Paul did not intend to convey any information at all beyond the fact that he had experienced such marvelous events. He explained his brevity (v. 4) by declaring it to be (1) an outright impossibility to elaborate, and (2) contrary to God's will, even if he could have done so. Finite, limited, mortal and sinful men simply do not possess the intellectual tools to comprehend, either the God and Father of mankind, or the nature of his dwelling place. Of God, men may know only what is revealed; and, even with regard to that, only a fool could believe that man fully understands all of that, in any complete sense. Therefore, as far as "the third heaven" is concerned, this writer does not profess to know anything beyond the truth that an apostle was "caught up" into it.

Verses 3-4, *And I know such a man (whether in the body, or apart from the body, I know not; God knoweth), how that he was caught up into Paradise, and heard unspeakable words, which it is not lawful for a man to utter.*

The repetition of the same thought in verses 2 and 3 ("whether in the body . . .") is difficult to interpret. "Opinion is

---

[7]John A. T. Robinson, *Honest to God* (Philadelphia: The Westminster Press, 1963), p. 13.

divided as to whether the apostle is merely repeating what he had just said, or is describing"[8] a second event. There are many scholars on both sides of the question. The conviction here is that Paul described two experiences taking place on one occasion. The time of "fourteen years ago" thus applies to both. Paul's repetition here is for the purpose of applying his ignorance of what state he was in to both events. The plural "visions" (12:1) is thus fulfilled by the two here given; and, as Hughes said, "The word 'and' at the beginning of this sentence at least seems to indicate that he is narrating something additional."[9]

Paradise

There is another important consideration which supports the understanding of two events, rather than merely one,; and that is Paul's use of the word "Paradise." There is no authority whatever for making this mean the same thing as "the third heaven," despite the fact of endless arguments that they are the same.

"Paradise . . ." This word in the NT is found only here and in Luke 23:43 and in Revelation 2:7. If it is true, as has been assumed, that the third heaven is the place of God's dwelling (see under verse 2), Jesus had not yet ascended to it on the day he rose from the dead; for he said to Mary Magdalene, "Touch me not, for I have not yet ascended to my Father" (John 10:17). Yet the Lord had promised the thief on the cross, "Today shalt thou be with me in Paradise" (Luke 23:43). In the light of these scriptures we must set aside the learned opinions to the effect that Paradise and the third heaven are the same place. Jesus had been with the thief in Paradise already, but he had not yet ascended to the third heaven. However, we call attention to the "if" that stands at the head of this paragraph. As Farrar said:

> Such questions are clearly insoluble, and I leave them where I find them. We shall never understand this

---

[8]Philip E. Hughes, *Paul's Second Epistle to the Corinthians* (Grand Rapids: Wm. B. Eerdmans Publishing Co., 1962), p. 435.
[9]*Ibid.*

> passage otherwise than in the dim and vague outline in which St. Paul purposely left it.[10]

"Unspeakable . . . unlawful . . ." In these words are Paul's reasons for not satisfying human curiosity about the things he mentioned (see under verse 2, above). "Paul here revealed nothing, either of what he saw or what he heard. The NT deliberately veils the next life, though it makes plain what is needful for our salvation."[11]

Verse 5, *On behalf of such a one will I glory: but on mine own behalf I will not glory, save in my weakness.*

"Such a one . . . such a man . . . such a one . . ." (vs. 2, 3 and 5). Each is the equivalent of "a man in Christ" (v. 2) and should be understood as Paul's repeated affirmation of the truth of his experiences being, in a sense, not his own but Christ's. It was in unity with Christ that the events occurred. In that exalted sense, therefore, Paul could not glory on his own behalf. "All spiritual blessing in the heavenly places is in Christ" (Eph. 1:3). The theology of our age needs to do a lot of work on the concept of being "in Christ," a concept mentioned by Paul 169 times, not counting the three at the head of this paragraph. If one is ever saved, he shall not be saved as himself, but as Christ, in Christ, and fully identified with Christ.

Verse 6, *For if I should desire to glory, I shall not be foolish; for I shall speak the truth: but I forbear, lest any man should account of me above that which he seeth me to be, or heareth from me.*

The first half of this was paraphrased by Wesley thus, "It could not justly be accounted folly to relate the naked truth."[12] There is also an insinuation here that the wicked "apostles" in Corinth were not telling the truth. Regarding the second half of this verse, Carver said that one of the great reasons for Paul's refusal to go any further with his narration of visions was that "he did not want anyone to form an estimate of him

---

[10]F. W. Farrar, *Pulpit Commentary* (Grand Rapids: Wm. B. Eerdmans Publishing Co., 1950), Vol. 19, 2 Cor., p. 291.
[11]Norman Hillyer, *op. cit.*, p. 1086.
[12]John Wesley, *op. cit., in loco.*

that goes beyond what he sees in Paul or hears from him."[13] Macknight interpreted these lines as follows:

> He showed them the absurdity of fancying that the whole of a teacher's merit lies in the gracefulness of his person, in the nice arrangement of his words, and in the melodious tones with which he pronounces his discourses.[14]

Those things, of course, were the principal commendations of the false teachers at Corinth. It would appear, however, that Filson really got to the heart of Paul's message here, saying:

> To recount further instances (of his visions) would be speaking the truth; but he refrains so they may judge him, not by his secret visions, which could be challenged by hostile men, but by what he had done.[15]

Verse 7, *And by reason of the exceeding greatness of the revelations, that I should not be exalted overmuch, there was given to me a thorn in the flesh, a messenger of Satan to buffet me, that I should not be exalted overmuch.*

Thorn in the Flesh

Like the visions themselves, the thorn in the flesh is little more than a hint, revealed in terms of tantalizing brevity, and described by enigmatical allusions which have puzzled men for centuries. The thorn has been speculatively identified as follows:

> Tertullian thought it was a headache.[16]
> Klausner believed it was epilepsy.[17]
> Ramsay identified it as recurrent malarial fever.[18]
> Chrysostom said it was "all the adversaries of the Word.[19]

---

[13]Frank G. Carver, *Beacon Bible Commentary* (Kansas City: Beacon Hill Press, 1968), p. 624.
[14]James Macknight, *Apostolical Epistles and Commentary* (Grand Rapids: Baker Book House, 1969), p. 455.
[15]Floyd V. Filsen, *op. cit.*, p. 406.
[16]Tertullian, *De Pudis*, xiii, 16.
[17]Joseph Klausner, *From Jesus to Paul* (New York: The Macmillan Co., 1943), pp. 325-330.
[18]Sir William M. Ramsay, *St. Paul the Traveller and Roman Citizen* (London: Hodder and Stoughton, 1903), p. 97.
[19]R. V. G. Tasker, *op. cit.*, p. 176.

Calvin made it "fleshly temptation."[20]
Luther considered it "spiritual temptation."[21]
Knox decided it was "infirmities of the mind."[22]
Catholic commentators, generally, "lustful thoughts."[23]
McGarvey: "acute, disfiguring ophthalmia."[24]
Macknight spoke of some who believed it was "the false teachers."[25]
Lightfoot suggested "blasphemous thoughts of the devil."[26]
Alexander was sure it was "Malta fever."[27] Etc., etc.

It would seem rash to some to venture an opinion in the face of such a mountain of scholarly disagreement; but this writer would like to get in his two cents worth also. The thorn in the flesh is believed to be the malignant opposition of secular Israel, a view contained but not specified in Chrysostom's identification. The reasons for this opinion are as follows:

(1) Any crippling or disabling bodily ailment simply does not conform to the amazing strength and endurance of the matchless apostle. "He is revealed in the NT as a man of exceptionally strong constitution and remarkable powers of physical endurance."[28]

(2)"In the flesh" as used in this verse would almost surely indicate a bodily infirmity; but Hughes declares the word to be "for the flesh,"[29] thus leaving the question open. Paul thus avoided words which would have implied bodily sickness. The meaning appears to be "a thorn in the flesh for the duration of Paul's fleshly life."

(3) Paul described the thorn as "a messenger of Satan," which can be nothing but personal in its import; and because the Canaanites were called "thorns in the sides" of the

---

[20]*Ibid.*
[21]*Ibid.*
[22]R. A. Knox, *The Epistles and Gospels*, p. 79.
[23]Philip E. Hughes, *op. cit.*, p. 444.
[24]J. W. McGarvey, *Second Corinthians* (Cincinnati: The Standard Publishing Company, 1916): p. 236.
[25]James Macknight, *op. cit.*, p. 455.
[26]J. B. Lightfoot, *The Epistle to the Galatians*, p. 189.
[27]W. M. Alexander, *St. Paul's Infirmity* (London: The Expository Times, 1904), Vol. X.
[28]R. V. G. Tasker, *op. cit.*, p. 175.
[29]Philip E. Hughes, *op. cit.*, p. 447.

Israelites (Num. 33:55), there is strong evidence here that Paul referred to bitter and relentless enemies of the gospel, doing the work of Satan; and that is a perfect description of the hardened secular Israelites who engaged in every device that hell could suggest in their godless and persistent opposition to Paul throughout every moment of his apostleship.

(4) In Thessalonians there is a probable reference to the thorn in the flesh, wherein Paul said, "Satan hindered me" (2:18); and a reference to the occasion of that remark (Acts 17:9) indicates that the Jewish opposition had contrived (through Paul's friends) an agreement that prevented his return. Again, the thorn had impaled him; and what was it? The hardened countrymen of the apostle himself. See CA, pp. 332, 333.

(5) Understanding the thorn in the flesh as the savage animosity of hardened Israel explains a number of things which otherwise would have no explanation: (a) the humiliating effect of this upon Paul himself. He had even dared dispute with the Lord in his protestations that the Jews would believe him (Acts 22:19); but their stubborn refusal was a continual humiliation to Paul throughout his life. (b) No bodily infirmity could have had the counteractive effect upon Paul's pride that was implicit in the rejection by Israel of the gospel he preached. Every town he ever entered, he went to them first, only to be despised, rejected, hated, persecuted, stoned and prosecuted by every means at Satan's disposal. Furthermore, this was directed against him who loved Israel so much that he would have given his life if they could have been saved, declaring:

> I could wish that I myself were anathema from Christ for my brethren's sake, my kinsmen according to the flesh: who are Israelites: whose is the adoption, and the glory, and the covenants, and the giving of the law, and the service of God, and the promises (Rom. 9:3,4).

Yes, the thorn in the flesh was the rejection of Christ on the part of the chosen people; and therein lies the explanation of (c) why the Lord did not remove it. It was simply not within the purpose of God to overrule the freedom of the will of those who elected to hate the Saviour. It was with Paul, as it was with Samuel when the Lord asked, "How long wilt thou mourn for Saul, seeing I have rejected him?" (1 Sam. 16:1). At the end of

Paul's third prayerful entreaty for the Lord to remove the thorn, the Saviour assured him that it was enough that he had personally received the grace of Jesus. The old and persistent dream of winning glorious Israel to Christ was most reluctantly, and yet obediently, forsaken by the apostle, as indicated by the magnificent eleventh chapter of Romans, written subsequently to this epistle.

Verses 8-9, *Concerning this thing I besought the Lord thrice, that it might depart from me, And he hath said unto me, My grace is sufficient for thee: for my power is made perfect in weakness. Most gladly therefore will I rather glory in my weakness, that the power of Christ may rest upon me.*

"Might depart from me . . ." If the thorn is understood as advocated above, what is meant by Paul's prayer that it might depart from him? The thorn in Paul was the humiliation, the shame and ignomy, from every earthly viewpoint, of his total and irreconcilable separation from the people he loved better than life itself; and that could have departed only by the conversion of Israel which Paul so eagerly and faithfully tried to bring about. Paul continually viewed his lack of success in winning Israel as weakness; and from the earthly viewpoint it was weakness.

"My grace is sufficient . . ." Christ only, and not Christ as an accepted and honored hero of redeemed secular Israel, was enough, not merely for Paul, but for all who ever lived on earth. Paul here accepted this, determined even to glory in his weakness.

Verse 10, *Wherefore I take pleasure in weakness, in juries, in necessities, in persecutions, in distresses, for Christ's sake: for when I am weak, then am I strong.*

"Wherefore . . ." This verse describes Paul's living with the thorn unremoved; and there is not a word of sickness, disease, or near-sightedness, or anything of the kind. It is "injuries, persecutions, etc." of which he speaks; and what were these but the multiplied efforts of the hardened Israel against the gospel of Christ? Nevertheless, Paul will continue, thorn and all; even with the humiliation of his noblest personal aspirations in their rejection; even in that weakness he is strong. Furthermore the testimony of nineteen centuries proves that he was correct in this.

Verse 11, *I am become foolish: ye compelled me; for I ought to have been commended by you: for in nothing was I behind the very chiefest apostles, though I am nothing.*

"I am become foolish . . ." Paul says, "You have compelled me to boast of myself, whereas in truth you should have been recommending me yourselves, especially since I certainly rank as high as those super-super apostles of yours!"

"Chiefest apostles . . ." For exegesis on this, see under 11:5.

Hughes has a wonderful paragraph on this passage in which the unity of the epistle is demonstrated to be proved and strengthened by what is said here. For those interested in pursuing this further, see *op. cit.*, p. 455. The allegations of critics on this subject are actually worthy of very little consideration.

"I am nothing . . ." Paul's meaning is that "as a mere man" he is nothing; but as "an apostle of Christ," he possessed the mighty weapons necessary to the overthrow of every evil and the establishment of the Lord Jesus as the singular hope of all men, in all times and places.

Verse 12, *Truly the signs of an apostle were wrought among you in all patience, by signs and wonders and mighty works.*

Jesus Christ had promised his holy apostles that they would be able to perform miracles and that God would work with them, "confirming the word" (Mark 16:20); and Paul enjoyed that prerogative along with the other apostles. Paul laid hands on the sick, and they recovered (Acts 28:8); he was bitten by a poisonous viper without harm (Acts 28:5); he raised the dead (Acts 20:9ff); he spoke with other tongues (1 Cor. 14:18); and there were countless other miracles not recorded (Rom. 15:19); furthermore, the first three cited above were attested and certified by a competent physician in the person of Luke. Scholars who talk about being "reasonable" should be reasonable about these apostolical miracles. Paul was writing to a congregation that contained bitter and unscrupulous enemies of the truth; yet Paul dared to call attention to his miracles in this letter. Could he possibly have done such a thing unless they were indeed legitimate, accepted and proved miracles? Every logic on earth answers, NO.

"Signs, wonders and mighty deeds . . ." are not three classes of miracles, but three characteristics of all genuine miracles, the same having been given for "signs," that is, confirmatory signs of the truth of what the apostles taught. In fact, miracles never had any other purpose.

"Signs of an apostle . . ." Filson's comment on this is precious:

> Writing to churches that would have challenged him if he had falsified facts, Paul unhesitatingly refers to such miracles; he knows that even his enemies cannot deny their occurrence. The study of miracles must begin by accepting the fact that many such remarkable events happened. Moreover this verse implies clearly that other true apostles were doing similar mighty works.[30]

"Were wrought . . ." By this Paul disclaimed personal credit for his mighty miracles, regarding himself "only as the instrument of the power of God."[31]

Verse 13, *For what is there wherein ye were made inferior to the rest of the churches, except it be that I myself was not a burden to you? forgive me this wrong.*

"Forgive me this wrong . . ." "The statement is ironical."[32]

Verse 14, *Behold, this is the third time I am ready to come to you; and I will not be a burden to you: for I seek not yours, but you: for the children ought not to lay up for the parents, but the parents for the children.*

"The third time . . ." Although these words may properly be construed as a reference to planning a third visit, McGarvey said, "Evidently it was to be his third visit."[33] This leads to the conclusion that a second visit, in between the two canonical epistles, was made, the one usually referred to as "the painful visit." While this appears to be true enough, a warning should be sounded against all of the nonsense that has been written about what occurred on that visit, if it really happened. There

---

[30]Frank V. Filson, *op. cit.*, p. 411.
[31]Frank G. Carver, *op. cit.*, p. 631.
[32]J. R. Dummelow, *Commentary on the Holy Bible* (New York: The Macmillan Company, 1937), p. 942.
[33]J. W. McGarvey, *op. cit.*, p. 237.

is not one word of authentic record nor a single hint in any tradition as to what took place. None may deny that a third visit automatically means there had been two others; but not even the approximate time of when it took place may be affirmed from the basis of the scanty references to it here, in 2:1, 13:1, and 12:21. See notes on those references.

"I will not be a burden to you . . ." Paul will not alter his purpose of preaching in Corinth without their financial support.

"Not yours, but you . . ." Paul wanted more than money from them; he wanted them.

"Children ought not to lay up for parents . . ." This teaching should not be misunderstood. As Carver said:

> The apostle made use of this analogy only as an illustration of why he did not take advantage of his right as a minister in the gospel. He does not mean by this that grown children have no obligation to their elderly parents when they are in need.[34]

Verses 15-16, *And I will most gladly spend and be spent for your souls. If I love you more abundantly, am I loved the less? But be it so, I do not myself burden you; but, being crafty, I caught you with guile.*

"If I love you more abundantly, am I loved the less . . ." Paul's sacrifices in not receiving their money were actually founded in his abundant love for them; and surely that should not have caused them to love the apostle less.

"But be it so . . ." Far from changing his mind about it, Paul here revealed that at that very moment the allegations against him were being circulated to the effect that he was taking them "by guile." The slander was that, whereas Paul did not take money personally, he was getting the big collection being raised for the poor saints. This, of course, meant that if he took money, it would be playing into the hands of the false teachers.

Verse 17, *Did I take advantage of you by any of them whom I have sent unto you?*

---

[34]Frank G. Carver, *op cit.* p. 634.

Paul's reply here indicates the nature of the "guile" in verse 16.

As David Lipscomb interpreted this:

> His contemptible enemies not only stated that Paul did not dare accept support, but insinuated that there was something suspicious about the collection he was taking, and that perhaps he had a secret personal interest in it.[35]

Also in this same vein, many commentators have remembered the words of John Calvin: "It is customary for the wicked impudently to impute to the servants of God whatever they themselves would do, if they had it in their power."[36]

Verse 18, *I exhorted Titus, and I sent the brother with him. Did Titus take any advantage of you? walked we not in the same spirit? walked we not in the same steps?*

Tasker convincingly affirms that "I sent" as used here should not be translated in the past tense, but as "epistolary," and translated in English as the present tense; because these men "had not arrived in Corinth when 2 Corinthians was written, but they will have done so by the time the Corinthians receive the letter."[37] This is an important distinction, having the impact of proof that "chapter 12 was not written before chapter 8."[38] This, of course, refutes any notion of these last chapters being part of a previously written "severe letter." The argument is simple enough. Titus is standing by, here in chapter 12, just as he was in chapter 8, to bear this epistle to the Corinthians.

"Did Titus take advantage of you . . ." is a reference to Titus' having begun the business of the collection at the time of the delivery of the first epistle. It does not refer to an interim visit of Titus between the canonical epistles. The understanding of the epistolary tense in this verse is crucial in the interpretation of it. Filson also testified that "The visit meant here is perhaps the first one."[39] Paul's question affirms in the

---

[35]David Lipscomb, *op. cit.*, p. 165.
[36]Philip E. Hughes, *op. cit.*, p. 465.
[37]R. V. G. Tasker, *op. cit.*, p. 183.
[38]*Ibid.*
[39]Floyd V. Filson, *op. cit.*, p. 414.

accepted idiom of that day the absolute integrity, honesty and sincerity of Titus and the unnamed Christian brother.

Verse 19, *Ye think all this time that we are excusing ourselves unto you. In the sight of God speak we in Christ. But all things, beloved, are for your edifying.*

The first sentence here carries the thought that the Corinthians ought not to consider Paul's words as a mere defense of himself; on the contrary, he was speaking "in Christ," that is, by the direct inspiration of the Holy Spirit; and every word he has written is for the purpose of their edification.

"Beloved . . ." This word is the grave of every opinion to the effect that these chapters are a thundering condemnation of the whole Corinthian church. Despite Filson's affirmation that "these chapters cannot be taken as directed only to a rebellious minority,"[40] it is absolutely impossible to take them any other way. The precious word "beloved" is here directed to the great faithful majority, by whose loyalty Paul displaced and expurgated the church of its false teachers.

Verse 20, *For I fear, lest by any means, when I came, I should find you not such as I would, and should myself be found of you such as ye would not; lest by any means there should be strife, jealousy, wraths, factions, backbitings whisperings, swellings, tumults.*

Carver, with many other eminent commentators, properly saw this verse as "No doubt applicable only to a minority of the church."[41] It should also be noted that the four pairs of disorders are exactly those which existed at the time of the writing of 1 Corinthians, making this letter a logical sequel to that, and not to some supposed "severe letter" written later. The problem was that, despite the good news brought by Titus, "there was still a minority of Christians in the city who were still carnally minded and undisciplined in the school of Christ."[42] It was that faction still impressed with the false apostles against whom these warnings were directed.

---

[40]*Ibid.*, p. 412.
[41]Frank G. Carver, *op. cit.*, p. 637.
[42]R. V. G. Tasker, *op. cit.*, p. 185.

Verse 21, *Lest again when I come my God should humble me before you, and I should mourn for many of them that have sinned heretofore, and repented not of the uncleanness and lasciviousness which they have committed.*

Paul was determined that nothing would prevent his cleaning up the mess in Corinth. Neither the displeasure of the sinners to be rebuked, nor his own pathetic grief over the fallen, nor any humiliation before God that would come of dealing with such wickedness would deter the effective steps contemplated. There was no way then, nor is there now, for the holy teachings of Christ to be accommodated to the lustful sins mentioned here. The magnificent Paul would meet the challenge frontally; there would be no compromise; and either the sinners would renounce their sins or the church of God would renounce them.

Filson identified these last two verses (20-21) as "one of the strongest arguments"[43] for repudiating these last four chapters as part of this epistle. If these verses are the "strongest" arguments in favor of such a hypothesis, the hypothesis has practically no support at all; because, as we have seen, there is nothing here which is required to be interpreted in any such manner.

"Uncleanness, fornication, lasciviousness . . ." These are not mere synonyms for one sin, but are a general description of all kinds of profligate living. "Uncleanness" means luxurious impurity and profligacy; "fornication" refers to promiscuous sex indulgence and prostitution; "lasciviousness" describes all kinds of misconduct and defiance of public decency.

"Lest again when I come my God should humble me . . ." Clines insisted that "again" modifies "humble" instead of "when I come."[44] Likewise Hughes commented that "What Paul fears here is a second humiliation."[45] If that is so, why does the word "again" in the Greek text stand at the head of the sentence, prior to and adjacent to the verb (a participle) "coming," and further removed by the pronoun "me" from that

---

[43]Floyd V. Filson, *op. cit.*, p. 416.
[44]David J. A. Clines, *A New Testament Commentary* (Grand Rapids: Zondervan Publishing House, 1969), p. 440.
[45]Philip E. Hughes, *op. cit.*, footnote, p. 472.

which it is alleged to modify?"[46] This is clearly another case of scholars bolstering their subjective opinions by tampering with the text. The AV and the RV both have properly placed "again" as a modifier of Paul's coming, and not of any anticipated humiliation. Even the RSV refused to go along by changing it, leaving it as it is here. Of course, what is intended by the change is to make this a comment of Paul on that "painful visit." We do not deny that there was another visit; but this verse may not be pressed into service to prove it.

---

[46] *The Interlinear Greek-English Testament,* The Nestle Greek Text (Grand Rapids: Zondervan Publishing House, 1958), p. 739.

CHAPTER 13

Having already exercised marvelous patience with the Corinthian congregation, the apostle in this chapter stated his intention of coming to them as soon as he could with a view to having a genuine showdown regarding the minority of the congregation, including the false apostles, who had been causing the trouble (1-10); he concluded with an affectionate greeting to them all, a thumbnail summary of the epistle, and the world-famed trinitrian doxology, perhaps the most widely used on earth (11-14).

Verse 1, *This is the third time I am coming to you. And by the mouth of two witnesses or three shall every word be established.*

"The third time . . ." Paul's establishing the church in Corinth was his first visit; and afterward there had been a second, probably between the times of the two canonical epistles; and the one Paul proposed here was the third. Nothing is known of that second visit except what may be inferred from the scanty allusions to it in this epistle. There is no basis for giving any credibility to the imaginative descriptions of that second meeting, in which it is alleged that Paul was insulted, etc., etc. If anything like that had happened, and we cannot believe that it did, would he at this time have convened a court with himself in charge, summoned the witnesses, named the occasion, declared the rules of procedure and ordered the Corinthians to get ready for it?

"Two witnesses or three . . ." The principle of justice requiring that no accused person be convicted upon the testimony of a single witness was established in the law of Moses (Num. 35:30; Deut. 19:15); and Jesus had indicated the continuing validity of the principle in Matthew 18:16. Paul's introduction of this OT injunction without the usual "it is written" indicates that even at this early date it was universally accepted in the church. Hughes observed that "The minimum number of witnesses was two; and three were preferable to two."[1] Barclay's description of what Paul announced in these verses is:

> To put it in our modern idiom, Paul insists there must be a showdown. The ill situation must drag on no longer. Paul knew that there comes a time when trouble must be faced. If the healing medicines fail, there is nothing for it but the surgeon's knife.[2]

"Every word shall be established . . ." Incredibly, some scholars have so far missed the meaning of this that they actually suppose that by this Paul meant, "Any charge still being made against Paul when he arrives will need substantiation by witnesses."[3] It is impossible to imagine, however, that Paul was going to Corinth to clear himself. On the contrary, he would go to discipline and correct *them* and to cast out of God's church all incorrigible offenders. Clines was therefore correct in referring this to charges "of Corinthian against Corinthians,"[4] and not to Paul. A full reading of the OT passage appealed to by Paul in this verse makes it absolutely clear what he intended to do:

> This is almost verbatim the rendition from LXX, meaning: I will judge, not without examination, nor will I abstain from punishing upon due evidence; I shall now assuredly fulfill my threats.[5]

Some scholars, apparently convinced by their own imaginations of what happened on the second visit, are in gross error by viewing the forthcoming confrontation as a church trying the apostle Paul. Such a notion is incompatible with everything in the NT.

Verse 2, *I have said beforehand, and I do say beforehand, as when I was present the second time, so now, being absent, to*

---

[1]Philip E. Hughes, *Paul's Second Epistle to the Corinthians* (Grand Rapids: Wm. B. Eerdmans Publishing Co., 1962), p. 474.

[2]William Barclay, *The Letters to the Corinthians* (Philadelphia: The Westminster Press, 1954), p. 297.

[3]Norman Hillyer, *The New Bible Commentary, Revised* (Grand Rapids: Wm. B. Eerdmans Publishing Co., 1970), p. 1087.

[4]David J. A. Clines, *A New Testament Commentary* (Grand Rapids: Zondervan Publishing House, 1969), p. 441.

[5]W. J. Conybeare, *Life and Epistles of St. Paul* (Grand Rapids: Wm. B. Eerdmans Publishing Co., 1966), p. 463.

them that have sinned heretofore, and to all the rest, that, if I come again, I will not spare.

The RV version in this place is inferior to the RSV, which gives the proper sense and should be read instead of this, the same being one of the exceptions to the general superiority of the RV. The labored and unnatural rendition in RV was contrived as a conformity to the generally held opinions of scholars (until recent times) that there was no "second visit." The literal translation from the Greek makes it certain that there was a second visit.

The RSV rendition of verse 2 is as follows:

> I warned those who sinned before and all the others, and I warn them now while absent, as I did when present on my second visit, and that if I come again I will not spare them.

This significant rendition makes it absolutely clear that Paul was just as much in charge of that "painful visit" as he proposed to be in charge of the proposed third visit, having given all of those sinners there a firm and vigorous warning.

"If I come again . . ." does not imply any doubt as to Paul's return. As Clines said, " 'If I come again' is not hypothetical but = 'when I come again.' "[6] This idiom was used by Christ himself in John 14:3, where "if I go" means "when I go."

Regarding the long-established interpretation of the three visits spoken of here, Schoettgen and Clarke insisted that the three visits were (1) Paul's establishing the Corinthian church, (2) the first epistle to the Corinthians, and (3) the present epistle, understood in the epistolary sense as already sent, and yet also identified as a visit Paul yet intended to make.[7] In close connection with that interpretation, Farrar and others understood the "three witnesses" of verse 1 to be the two canonical Corinthians plus the apostle himself.[8] As MaGarvey

---

[6]David J. A. Clines, *op. cit.*, p. 441.

[7]Adam Clarke, *Commentary on the Whole Bible* (New York: Carlton & Porter, 1829), Vol. VI, p. 372.

[8]F. W. Farrar, *Pulpit Commentary* (Grand Rapids: Wm. B. Eerdmans Publishing Co., 1950), Vol. 19, 2 Cor., p. 313.

said, "Such interpretations are fanciful."[9] Nevertheless, it was for the purpose of accommodating some of these fanciful views that the RV thus rendered the passage.

"I will not spare . . ." This shows that "The apostolical churches were not independent democratic communities, vested with supreme authority over their own members. Paul could cast out of them whom he would."[10] Of course, apostolical authority was eventually succeeded by a government of independent congregations by scripturally appointed and qualified elders functioning under the authority of the scriptures.

Verse 3, *Seeing that ye seek a proof of Christ that speaketh in me; who to you-ward is not weak, but is powerful in you.*

Broomall was correct in seeing this verse "as a definite affirmation of the apostle's inspiration and authority. Rejection of him meant rejection of Christ."[11] Denney also pointed out that:

> In challenging Paul to come and exert his authority, in defying him to come with a rod, in presuming on what they called his weakness, they were really challenging Christ.[12]

Some of the false apostles had been saying: "No matter how boldly he writes, when he comes he will be weak and unimpressive"; but Paul here promised to come and discipline them in the sternest manner.

Verse 4, *For he was crucified through weakness, yet he liveth through the power of God. For we also are weak in him, but we shall live in him through the power of God toward you.*

Macknight's paraphrase of verse 4 is thus:

> For, though indeed Christ was crucified by reason of the weakness of his human nature, which was liable to death, yet he now liveth by the power of God. And though

---

[9]J. W. McGarvey, *Second Epistle to the Corinthians* (Cincinnati: Standard Publishing Company, 1916), p. 240.

[10]Hodge as quoted by R. V. G. Tasker, *The Second Epistle of Paul to the Corinthians* (Grand Rapids: Wm. B. Eerdmans Publishing Co., 1958), p. 187.

[11]Wick Broomall, *Wycliffe Bible Commentary* (Chicago: Moody Press, 1971), p. 688.

[12]James Denney, *Expositor's Bible* (Grand Rapids: Wm. B. Eerdmans Publishing Co., 1947), Vol. V, 2 Cor., p. 806.

> I also, his apostle, am weak, as he was, being subject to persecution, infamy, death; I shall nevertheless show myself alive in him, by exercising the power of God among you, punishing you severely if you do not repent.[13]

The weakness of Christ mentioned here applies only to those weaknesses inherent in the fact of incarnation. Being a man, Christ was subject to death. "The Lord assumed our nature with all its infirmities, death included, bore them all for our sake, and then shook them all off forever when he rose from the dead."[14]

"We shall live in him through the power of God in you . . ." By this, Paul meant that severe punishment would be visited upon gross and impenitent sinners at Corinth. Just as Christ the humble sufferer has now ascended to the throne of God, Paul will put aside the weakness of his patience and forbearance and exercise the full power of his apostolic office against the wicked deceivers. Some believe that Paul referred to supernatural judgments like that which afflicted Elymas.

Verse 5, *Try your own selves, whether ye are in the faith; prove your own selves. Or know ye not as to your own selves, that Christ is in you? unless indeed ye be reprobate.*

Someone at Corinth had suggested that Paul "prove" himself by exercising the authority he claimed, perhaps suggesting that they would like to examine him; but here Paul thundered the message that he would conduct a trial, not of himself, but of them, they, not himself, being the persons who needed to prove that they were in the faith.

"Christ is in you . . ." is a complimentary remark. Despite the sins of some, Christ was yet in the Corinthian church, unless, of course, the whole church had become "reprobate," a possibility that Paul rejected in the last clause. Again, there is witness here to the fact that the major part of the Corinthian congregation was entitled to all the wonderful things Paul said about them in chapters 1-9, a further attestation of the unity of the epistle.

---

[13]James Macknight, *Apostolical Epistles with Commentary* (Grand Rapids: Baker Book House, 1969), p. 469.

[14]John Wesley, *One Volume NT Commentary* (Grand Rapids: Baker Book House, 1972), *in loco.*

"In the faith . . ." is a significant word, as used here, being a synonym for the Christian religion. In many references where Paul speaks of "faith," it has exactly the same meaning as here. Usually, when Paul says "saved by faith," it is not the subjective faith of the believer, but an objective reference to Christianity, which is meant.

Verse 6, *But I hope that ye shall know that we are not reprobate.*

Paul's logic here is to this effect: "You know only too well that Christ is in you; and by that very fact you already have proof of Christ speaking in me, through whom the message of Christ was brought to you."[15] If any should consider Paul reprobate, then they themselves would inevitably be reprobate also, as Paul was, in a sense, their father in the gospel.

Verse 7, *Now we pray to God that ye do no evil; not that we may appear approved, but that ye may do that which is honorable, though we be reprobate.*

The meaning of this is: "We pray to God that you may lead a pure and holy life, not to do us credit, but because it is right, even though we should be like false apostles."[16] A shade of meaning is also present as in Clines' comment: "I would rather you did what is right, even if that means that I should not look like a true apostle, because of no need to take strong disciplinary measures."[17] Of course, Paul would have been more completely demonstrated as a true apostle if, in response to gross evil, he should have invoked such a penalty as fell on Elymas; on the other hand, if the Corinthians repented, as he hoped they would, he would appear among them as his usual kindly and tolerant self; and, in that latter case, Paul's honor would not have been so dramatically demonstrated.

Verse 8, *For we can do nothing against the truth, but for the truth.*

---

[15]Philip E. Hughes, *op. cit.*, p. 481.

[16]J. R. Dummelow, *Commentary on the Holy Bible* (New York: The Macmillan Co., 19.

[17]David J. A. Clines, *op. cit.*, p. 441.

"The word 'truth' here refers to the gospel message which Paul preached";[18] "we . . ." is a reference to Paul himself along with all the other holy apostles, having this meaning: "We apostles cannot exercise our miraculous power in opposition to the truth, but always in support thereof."[19] It was a moral impossibility for Paul to use the great powers God had given him, merely for the sake of impressing the false apostles at Corinth. The reason for bringing that up here was that if the Corinthians should set things in order before Paul's arrival, there would be no startling powers displayed when Paul came. Of course, that is exactly the way Paul wanted it to be.

Verse 9, *For we rejoice when we are weak, and ye are strong: this we also pray for, even your perfecting.*

"When we are weak . . ." means "when we appear weak" because of no need to exhibit divine power. "He is perfectly willing to be deprived of the opportunity to manifest apostolic power at Corinth, and thus be thought weak by some."[20]

"Even your perfection . . ." It is not the conversion of a whole congregation which is suggested by this, but the conversion of the rebellious minority, thus perfecting the whole congregation. The word thus rendered in the Greek is "restoration"; as Hughes said, "The word means a correct articulating of limbs and joints in a body."[21] Thus is made clear the necessity of seeing these last four chapters, not as a blanket indictment of the whole church. The body had not at this point been destroyed, although some of its members needed "restoration," or "perfecting" as in RV.

Verse 10, *For this cause, I write these things while absent, that I may not when present deal sharply, according to the authority which the Lord gave me for building up, and not for casting down.*

This is a more concise statement of what Paul has been saying in the previous verses. "Paul's ardent desire to forestall

---

[18]Floyd V. Filson, *Interpreter's Bible* (Nashville: Abingdon Press, 1953), Vol. X, p. 421.
[19]James Macknight, *op. cit.*, p. 471.
[20]Raymond C. Kelcy, *Second Corinthians* (Austin: R. B. Sweet Co., 1967), p. 78.
[21]Philip E. Hughes, *op. cit.*, p. 484.

any need for rebuke shows his great wisdom in developing the church along lines of love, with no display of authority"[22]

Verse 11, *Finally, brethren, farewell. Be perfected; be comforted; be of the same mind; live in peace: and the God of love and peace shall be with you.*

"Farewell . . ." is actually "rejoice";[23] for Paul is not saying "good-bye" until a little later. Lipscomb was impressed with the fact that "no names are mentioned here"[24] despite the fact of Paul's knowing so many of them. This is quite natural. Any minister writing to a great congregation where his acquaintance was extensive would never single out just a handful for personal reference. It is a failure to understand this evident fact which led to Brunner's repudiation of the 16th chapter of Romans because of the many personal references in a letter to a church where he had never labored.[25] However, it was precisely because Paul had *not* lived in Rome that he could send greetings to all of his friends in a general letter to the church. To have done so here at Corinth would have offended every person whose name he might have omitted. See discussion of this in CR, p. xiv. Such a criticism proves that some scholars are totally ignorant of the personal relations problems invariably associated with a congregation of Christians.

"Be perfected; be comforted; be of the same mind; live in peace . . ." "This closing fourfold appeal aptly summarizes Paul's letter."[26] A similar summary of 1 Corinthians is 16:13. As this passage stands, it fails to give the vigorous impact Paul probably intended. Filson admitted that these words "may be in the middle voice,"[27] thus giving the meaning exactly as it is rendered in the Nestle Greek text: "restore yourselves" and "admonish yourselves." This is the true meaning, because as regards both restoration and admonition, it is the will of the

---

[22]John William Russell, *Compact Commentary on the NT* (Grand Rapids: Baker Book House, 1964), p. 457.

[23]*Interlinear Greek-English Testament*, Nestle Greek Text (Grand Rapids: Zondervan Publishing House, 1958), p. 740.

[24]David Lipscomb, *Second Corinthians* (Nashville: The Gospel Advocate Co.), p. 173.

[25]Emil Brunner, *The Letter to the Romans* (Philadelphia: The Westminster Press, 1956), p. 11.

[26]Norman Hillyer, *op. cit.*, p. 1088.

[27]Floyd V. Filson, *op. cit.*, p. 423.

person which is prerequisite to either one of them being accomplished. Thus the thought is similar to "work out your own salvation" (Phil. 2:12).

Verse 12, *Salute one another with a holy kiss.*

The Holy Kiss

Dummelow called this "the token of brotherhood in the early church."[28] Other references to it in the NT are Romans 15:16, 1 Corinthians 16:20, 1 Thessalonians 5:26, and 1 Peter 5:14. Peter called it the "kiss of love"; but it is called the "holy kiss" elsewhere. This form of brotherly greeting, however, existed long before Christianity. Jesus rebuked the Pharisee for withholding the customary kiss of greeting (Luke 7:45), and Judas used it treacherously in the betrayal (Mark 14:44f). Carver said the practice came from "the Jewish synagogues, where the sexes were segregated in worship."[29] It is plain that Paul was not here commanding a form of greeting, but regulating a custom that already existed. Kelcy understood this verse to mean, "The kiss of greeting, a social custom of the times, was not to be a meaningless formality; it was to be holy."[30] Lipscomb also took the same view of this, saying, "The object of the Holy Spirit in referring to the kiss was to regulate a social custom, and not to institute an ordinance."[31] "Like our handclasp today, the kiss was a symbol of mutual confidence; and, where the Corinthians were concerned, a sign of the healing of old divisions."[32]

Paul's reference to the "holy" kiss thus contained an embryonic warning of things to come. The Christian congregations continued to use it as Christianity spread over the world; and the historical churches soon developed the custom into a liturgy. Plumptre tells how the custom was observed about the third century, as described in Apostolic Constitutions. Instructions were sent to the churches with this:

---

[28]J. R. Dummelow, *op. cit.*, p. 944.
[29]Frank G. Carver, *op. cit.*, p 644.
[30]Raymond C. Kelcy *op. cit.* p 78.
[31]D. L. Lipscomb, *op. cit.*, p. 174.
[32]Philip E. Hughes, *op. cit.*, p. 488.

> Let the deacons say to all, "Salute ye one another with a holy kiss"; and let the clergy salute the bishop, the men of the laity salute the men, and the women were to salute the women. Deacons were to watch that there was no disorder during the act.[33]

Another very early testimony regarding this kiss, and the abuses that had crept into the observance of it, was given by Clement of Alexandria, thus:

> Love is not proved by a kiss. . . There are those that make the church resound with a kiss, not having love itself within. The shameless use of a kiss occasions foul suspicions and evil reports. . . Gentle manners require that a kiss be chaste and with a closed mouth. There is an unholy kiss, full of poison, counterfeiting sanctity. "This is the love of God," says John, "That we keep his commandments," not that we stroke each other on the mouth.[34]

Despite abuses, the custom prevailed till the thirteenth century, when the Western Church abolished it, and substituted "the act of kissing a marble or ivory tablet, upon which some sacred object, such as the crucifixion, had been carved."[35] The device was passed from one person to another during the observance of what by that time had become a "rite"; and the device itself was called "the Osculatorium."[36]

Verse 13, *All the saints salute you.*

This included not merely Paul and his companions but included all Christians throughout the world. Although the Corinthians were not personally known by very many Christians throughout the ancient world, nevertheless the community of interest, mutual affection, and highest brotherly respect were properly considered to be the right of every Christian on earth. This word indicated clearly that Paul still considered the church at Corinth as a valid part of the larger body of Christ on earth, and that in spite of the disorders which threatened them. See 1:1, and also 1 Corinthians 1:4.

---

[33]E. H. Plumptre, *Ellicott's Commentary* (Grand Rapids: Zondervan Publishing House, 1959), Vol. VIII, p. 416.

[34]Clement of Alexandria, *The Instructor in Ante-Nicene Father* (Grand Rapids: Wm. B. Eerdmans Publishing Co., 1956), Vol. II, p. 291.

[35]*Ibid.*, p. 417.

[36]*Ibid.*

Verse 14, *The grace of the Lord Jesus Christ, and the love of God, and the communion of the Holy Spirit, be with you all.*

This great trinitarian doxology is one of the most widely used on earth, the beauty and effectiveness of it being known to millions in all nations. The NT nowhere mentions by name the doctrine of the Trinity; and there are doubtless aspects of that doctrine which are not fully scriptural; but the fact of there being three persons in the godhead unmistakably shines in passages like this and Matthew 28:18-20. For further thoughts on this subject, see CM, pp. 33, 34, 525.

Commentators are agreed that there is nothing formal or stylized about this doxology; otherwise, the Father would have been mentioned first. As Clines said, "What makes it so impressive is the spontaneous, unconscious formulation of it."[37]

The fact that, only a short generation after the crucifixion of Christ, his name should have been adoringly linked with that of Almighty God and the blessed Holy Spirit in a prayer is an allegation of his deity. Thus, as Broomall said, "This epistle opens (1:2) and ends with an affirmation of the deity of Christ."[38]

"Grace of Christ . . . love of God . . . communion of the Holy Spirit . . ." As Tasker said, "As the first of the three genitives here is subjective, it is probable that the other two should be construed in the same way."[39] It is therefore the grace Christ showed to men, dying for their salvation (not the grace of men toward Christ), and the love of God toward men in the sending of his only begotten Son, and the communion with mankind on the part of the Holy Spirit. in the sacred writings of holy scripture, and not personal indwelling in Christian hearts as the earnest of human redemption. Just as the grace of Christ and God's love are *their* actions, the communion of the Holy Spirit is the Spirit's action (a thing not true of the earnest at all, for the earnest is sent by the Father, as in Galatians 4:6); and the epic achievement of the Holy Spirit for all men is seen in the inspired messages of holy writ.

---

[37]David J. A. Clines, *op. cit.*, op. 443.
[38]Wick Broomall, *op. cit.*, p. 689.
[39]R. V. G. Tasker, *op. cit.*, p. 191.

This priceless doxology prayerfully closes the Second Epistle to the Corinthians; and, after all that has been said, of censure and warning, the lowest sinner in the congregation is made a beneficiary of this apostolical benediction, no less than all the rest. "It is upon all, the slanderers, the gainsayers, the seekers after worldly wisdom, the hearkeners to false doctrine, as well as upon the faithful and obedient."[40] Surely here is the overflowing of a heart full of true love for the tried and tempted, for weak and sinful Christians. Nothing ever written before or since this Spirit-breathed epistle to Corinth ever succeeded in reaching and sustaining such a high level of personal impact, not only upon a troubled church of nineteen hundred years ago, but upon every soul that has the grace to receive it.

---

[40]John Wesley, *op. cit., in loco.*

BIBLIOGRAPHY

Authors and Sources Quoted in this Commentary

Alexander, W. M., *St. Paul's Infirmity* (London: The Expository Times, Vol. X).

Allo, E. B., *Saint Paul: Seconde Epitre Aux Corinthiens* (Paris, 1956).

Barclay, William, *The Letters to the Corinthians* (Philadelphia: The Westminster Press, 1954).

Broomall, Wick, *Wycliffe Bible Commentary* (Chicago: Moody Press, 1971).

Bruce, F. F., *Answers to Questions* (Grand Rapids: Zondervan Publishing House, 1972).

Bruce, F. F., *The Book of Acts* (Grand Rapids: Wm. B. Eerdmans Publishing Company, 1954).

Calvin, John, *Commentary on 1 Corinthians* (Grand Rapids: Wm. B. Eerdmans Publishing Company, 1954).

Carver, Frank G., *Beacon Bible Commentary* (Kansas City: Beacon Hill Press, 1968), Vol. 8.

Clarke, Adam, *Commentary on the Whole Bible* (New York: Carlton & Porter, 1829), Vol. VI.

Clement of Alexandria, *Ante-Nicene Fathers* (Grand Rapids: Wm. B. Eerdmans Publishing Company, 1956), Vol. II.

Clines, David J. A., *A New Testament Commentary* (Grand Rapids: Zondervan Publishing House 1969)

Conybeare, W. J., *Life and Letters of St. Paul* (Grand Rapids: Wm. B. Eerdmans Publishing Company, 1966).

Denney, James, *Expositor's Bible* (Grand Rapids: Wm. B. Eerdmans Publishing Company, 1947), Vol. V.

Diaglott, The Emphatic (Brooklyn: Watch Tower Bible and Tract Society).

Dummelow, J. R., *One Volume Commentary on the Holy Bible* (New York: The Macmillan Company, 1937).

Elliott, Charlotte, *Hymn: Just As I Am* (Woodworth) (Cincinnati: The Standard Publishing Company).

Encyclopaedia Britannica (Chicago: William Benton, Publisher, 1961).

Farrar, F. W., *The Pulpit Commentary* (Grand Rapids: Wm. B. Eerdmans Publishing Company, 1950), *2 Cor.*, Vol. 19.

Filson, Floyd V., *Interpreter's Bible* (Nashville: Abingdon Press, 1953), Vol. X.

Goodspeed, Edgar J., *The New Testament, An American Translation* (Chicago: The University of Chicago Press, 1923).

Halley, Henry H., *Bible Handbook* (Grand Rapids: Zondervan Publishing House, 1927).

Hillyer, Norman. *The New Bible Commentary: Revised* (Grand Rapids: Wm. B. Eerdmans Publishing Company, 1970).

Hughes, Philip E., *Paul's Second Epistle to the Corinthians* (Grand Rapids: Wm. B. Eerdmans Publishing Company, 1962).

Interlinear Greek-English Testament, Nestle Greek Text (Grand Rapids: Zondervan Publishing House, 1958).

International Standard Bible Encyclopaedia (Chicago: The Howard-Severance Company, 1915).

Kelcy, Raymond C., *Second Corinthians* (Austin: R. B. Sweet Co., 1967).

Klausner, Joseph, *From Jesus to Paul* (New York: The Macmillan Company, 1943).

Knox, R. A., *The Epistles and Gospels.*

Lenski, R. C. H., *The Interpretation of St. Paul's First and Second Epistles to the Corinthians* (Columbus, Ohio: Wartburg Press, 1937).

Lewis, Jack P., *Historical Backgrounds of Bible History* (Grand Rapids: Baker Book House, 1971).

Lightfoot, J. B., *Commentary on the Epistle to the Galatians.*

Lipscomb, David, *Second Corinthians* (Nashville: The Gospel Advocate Company).

McGarvey, J. W., *Second Epistle to the Corinthians* (Cincinnati: The Standard Publishing Company, 1916).

MacKay, John, *God's Order* (New York: The Macmillan Company, 1953).

Macknight, James, *Apostolical Epistles and Commentary* (Grand Rapids: Baker Book House, 1969).

Moffatt, James, *The Bible, A New Translation* (New York: Harpers).

Morgan, G. Campbell, *The Corinthian Letters of Paul* (Old Tappan, N. J.: Fleming H. Revell Company, 1946).

Munck, Johannes, *Paul and the Salvation of Mankind* (London, 1958).

New Bible Dictionary (Grand Rapids: Wm. B. Eerdmans Publishing Company, 1962).

New International Version of the NT (Grand Rapids: Zondervan Publishing House, 1973).

Plumptre, S. H., *Ellicott's Commentary* (Grand Rapids: Zondervan Publishing House, 1959), Vol. VII.

Ramsay, Sir William M., *St. Paul the Traveller and Roman Citizen* (London: Hodder & Stoughton, 1903).

Robinson, John A. T., *Honest to God* (Philadelphia: Westminster Press, 1963).

Russell, John William, *Compact Commentary on the NT* (Grand Rapids: Baker Book House, 1964).

Tasker, R. V. G., *The Second Epistle of Paul to the Corinthians* (Grand Rapids: Wm. B. Eerdmans Publishing Company, 1958).

Tertullian, *Ante-Nicene Fathers* (Grand Rapids: Wm. B. Eerdmans Publishing Company, 1957).

Wallace, Foy E., Jr., *A Review of the New Versions* (Fort Worth: The Foy E. Wallace, Jr., Publications, 1973).

Wesley, John, *One Volume Commentary* (Grand Rapids: Baker Book House, 1972).

INDEX

*Indicates special article.